The Demolinguistic Situation in Canada

Past Trends and Future Prospects

Réjean Lachapelle
and
Jacques Henripin

Translated by
Deirdre A. Mark

The Institute for Research on Public Policy
L'Institut de recherches politiques

Montreal

Printed in Canada
ISBN 0 920380 42 5

Legal Deposit First Quarter
Bibliothèque nationale du Québec

Cette publication existe également en version française.

Canadian Cataloguing in Publication Data
Lachapelle, Réjean, 1944-
    The demolinguistic situation in Canada

Prefatory material and summary in English and French.
Issued also in French under title: La situation
démolinguistique au Canada.
Bibliography: p.
ISBN 0-920380-42-5

1. Canada—Population—Ethnic groups.* 2. Canada—
Population—Statistics. 3. Migration, Internal—
Canada. 4. Population forecasting—Canada.
I. Henripin, Jacques, 1926-   II. Institute for
Research on Public Policy. III. Title.

HB3529.L3313   305.8'00971   C81-090120-X

The Institute for Research on Public Policy/L'Institut de recherches politiques
2149 Mackay Street
Montreal, Quebec
H3G 2J2

Founded in 1972, THE INSTITUTE FOR RESEARCH ON PUBLIC POLICY is a national organization whose independence and autonomy are ensured by the revenues of an endowment fund, which is supported by the federal and provincial governments and by the private sector. In addition, the Institute receives grants and contracts from governments, corporations, and foundations to carry out specific research projects.

The *raison d'être* of the Institute is threefold:

— To act as a catalyst within the national community by helping to facilitate informed public debate on issues of major public interest

— To stimulate participation by all segments of the national community in the process that leads to public policy making

— To find practical solutions to important public policy problems, thus aiding in the development of sound public policies

The Institute is governed by a Board of Directors, which is the decision-making body, and a Council of Trustees, which advises the board on matters related to the research direction of the Institute. Day-to-day administration of the Institute's policies, programmes, and staff is the responsibility of the president.

The Institute operates in a decentralized way, employing researchers located across Canada. This ensures that research undertaken will include contributions from all regions of the country.

Wherever possible, the Institute will try to promote public understanding of, and discussion on, issues of national importance, whether they be controversial or not. It will publish its research findings with clarity and impartiality. Conclusions or recommendations in the Institute's publications are solely those of the author, and should not be attributed to the Board of Directors, Council of Trustees, or contributors to the Institute.

The president bears final responsibility for the decision to publish a manuscript under the Institute's imprint. In reaching this decision, he is advised on the accuracy and objectivity of a manuscript by both Institute staff and outside reviewers. Publication of a manuscript signifies that it is deemed to be a competent treatment of a subject worthy of public consideration.

Publications of the Institute are published in the language of the author, along with an executive summary in both of Canada's official languages.

Dr. Roger Blais, P.Eng.
  Director, Centre québécois d'innovation
    industrielle, Montreal
Robert W. Bonner, Q.C.
  Chairman, British Columbia Hydro &
    Power Authority, Vancouver
Professor John L. Brown
  Faculty of Business Administration &
    Commerce, University of Alberta,
    Edmonton
George Cooper
  McInnes, Cooper & Robertson, Halifax
James S. Cowan
  Stewart, MacKeen & Covert, Halifax
Dr. Marc Eliesen
  Director of Research, New Democratic
    Party, Ottawa
W.A. Friley
  President, Skyland Oil, Calgary
Dr. Donald Glendenning
  President, Holland College, Charlottetown
Chief Judge Nathan Green
  Provincial Court of Nova Scotia, Halifax
Dr. Leon Katz, O.C.
  Department of Physics, University of
    Saskatchewan, Saskatoon
Tom Kierans
  President, McLeod, Young, Weir Ltd.,
    Toronto
Dr. Leo Kristjanson
  President, University of Saskatchewan,
    Saskatoon
Allen T. Lambert, O.C.
  Director and Former Chairman,
    Toronto-Dominion Bank, Toronto
Terrence Mactaggart
  President, Niagara Institute,
    Niagara-on-the-Lake
Dr. John McCallum
  Faculty of Administrative Studies,
    University of Manitoba, Winnipeg
Professor William A.W. Neilson
  Faculty of Law, University of Victoria
R.D. Nolan, P. Eng.
  Vice-President & General Manager, Neill
    & Gunter Ltd., Fredericton
Robert Olivero
  President, Management House Ltd.,
    St. John's
Professor Marilyn L. Pilkington
  Osgoode Hall Law School, Toronto
Eldon D. Thompson
  President, Telesat Canada, Vanier
Dr. Israel Unger
  Department of Chemistry, University of
    New Brunswick, Fredericton

Philip Vineberg, O.C., Q.C.
  Phillips, Vineberg, and Associates,
    Montreal
Dr. Norman Wagner
  President, University of Calgary
Ida Wasacase
  Director, Saskatchewan Indian Federated
    College, University of Regina
Professor Paul Weiler
  Mackenzie King Professor,
    Harvard University, Cambridge
Dr. John Tuzo Wilson, C.C., O.B.E.
  Director General, Ontario Science Centre,
    Toronto
Right Rev. Dr. Lois Wilson
  Moderator, United Church of Canada,
    Kingston
Ray Wolfe, C.M.
  Chairman and President, The Oshawa
    Group, Toronto

Ex Officio Members
Dr. Kell Antoft
  President, Institute of Public
    Administration of Canada
Dr. Lloyd Barber
  President, Association of Universities &
    Colleges of Canada
Dr. Pierre Bois
  President, Medical Research Council
Dr. Owen Carrigan
  Representing the Canada Council
Dr. Larkin Kerwin, C.C.
  President, National Research Council
Dr. Gilles Paquet
  President, Social Science Federation of
    Canada
Dr. David Slater
  Chairman, Economic Council of Canada
Dr. Stuart Smith
  Chairman, Science Council of Canada
Dr. Marc-Adélard Tremblay
  President, Royal Society of Canada

Table of Contents

List of Tables, Figures, and Map

Figures

Foreword

The demographic situation of language groups has always been a topic of great concern to public opinion in Canada and has occasionally given rise to bitter controversy. We therefore felt it was essential to undertake a research project on this question. The project was funded by the Federal-Provincial Relations Office of the Canadian government and was headed by Réjean Lachapelle, project director at the Institute.

This book is the key work of our research project. It presents the greater part of the results obtained, with the exception of the study dealing with the school population of Quebec. All studies generated by the project will, in any case, be published by the Institute in the coming months.

It will be noted that Lachapelle and Henripin have limited themselves to the description, analysis and, where possible, the explanation of facts. They have deemed it wise to offer suggestions and recommendations sparingly. I do not believe this can be termed evading the issue. They simply felt it preferable, in dealing with such a sensitive subject, to distinguish clearly between the contribution of the demographer and that of the citizen. The reader who seeks "concrete proposals" is free to consult the reports of the many commissions that have held inquiries into this subject.

As is the case for all its publications, the Institute disclaims any responsibility for the statements of fact or opinions expressed by the authors of this report.

Gordon Robertson
President
April 1980

Avant-propos

La situation démographique des groupes linguistiques a toujours été, au Canada, un objet de préoccupations dans l'opinion publique, et elle a même parfois suscité de vives controverses. Il nous a donc paru important d'engager un programme de recherche sur cette question. Ce programme a été financé par le Bureau des relations fédérales-provinciales du gouvernement du Canada, et il a été dirigé par Réjean Lachapelle, directeur de projet à l'Institut.

Le présent ouvrage constitue la pièce maîtresse du programme de recherche. Il réunit l'essentiel des résultats qui ont été obtenus, sauf pour ce qui concerne l'étude qui a été faite sur la population scolaire du Québec. Quoi qu'il en soit, tous les travaux émanant de ce programme de recherche seront publiés par l'Institut au cours des prochains mois.

On pourra constater que MM. Lachapelle et Henripin s'en sont tenus à la description, à l'analyse et, quand c'était possible, à l'explication des faits. Ils ont cru bon d'être avares de suggestions et de recommandations. Mais il ne s'agit pas là, je crois, d'une dérobade. Il leur a paru préférable, en cette matière délicate, de bien distinguer l'apport du démographe de celui du citoyen. Au reste, le lecteur friand de « propositions concrètes » n'aura qu'à se reporter aux nombreuses commissions d'enquête qui ont abordé cette question.

Comme pour toutes les publications de l'Institut, les déclarations et les opinions que contient le présent rapport sont la responsabilité entière des auteurs.

Gordon Robertson
Président
Avril 1980

Preface

When a study manages to present correct analyses and enlightening viewpoints, this is often because the authors were posed on the shoulders of giants. We can always credit them with having been able to profit from the teaching of leading figures in their own and related fields. This, however, is the only credit we can lay claim to. In demography, we have drawn immensely upon the works of Jean Bourgeois-Pichat, Louis Henry, Nathan Keyfitz, and Norman B. Ryder—the last two being originally from Canada and having attained celebrity in the United States—and, in mathematical sociology, on those of Raymond Boudon and James S. Coleman. We also acknowledge our debt to the rich and subtle thought of Alfred Sauvy, who has succeeded in placing demography on a plane with other great syntheses.

More specifically, we have, throughout this study, drawn with great profit on the remarkable works of Stanley Lieberson (an American sociologist of Canadian origin) and especially his far-reaching study on the socio-linguistic situation of francophones in Canada. We have also benefited from the precise and rigorous studies of John De Vries and Robert Maheu. The often innovative work of Charles Castonguay and Richard J. Joy was also highly stimulating. Although the social sciences are not the focal point of their professional careers, these authors have, in devoting their leisure time to the study of language groups, contributed new and often daring perspectives, while seeking to ally respect of the facts with service to the public as a whole.

It should be emphasized that this book is only one of the products of a vast research programme undertaken by The Institute for Research on Public Policy, with the help of a grant from the Federal-Provincial Relations Office of the Canadian government. Many researchers participated in this programme. Diane Vanasse has carried out a solid, well-structured study on the school population of Quebec; this study which, like others, will be published separately, was edited by Michèle Gervais who also prepared a synthesis. Michèle Gervais also participated in the studies dealing with migration. Donald G. Cartwright has completed a most interesting historical and geographical essay on the situation of language groups, and some of his conclusions are referred to in the first two chapters. Susan Fletcher and Leroy O. Stone carried out numerous estimates and prepared the documents on which, to a certain extent, Chapter Six dealing with migration was based. We should also stress the great contribution made by Leroy O. Stone in the development of hypotheses regarding internal migration. For many of us, and especially for the project director, he was a wise and experienced guide, who freely gave both criticism and advice. Lastly, we should mention the contribution made by Jean Dumas to the study on mortality.

A scientific study is always a collective undertaking, not only because it attempts to add a solid block to the ever-growing edifice of science, but also because it presupposes the participation of countless people whose exact contribution is difficult to circumscribe. We therefore organized a seminar and repeatedly sought advice. We were thus able to profit from the experience and competence of a great many researchers and specialists. In this connection, we would especially like to thank Roderic Beaujot, Charles Castonguay, John De Vries, Claude Dionne, Richard J. Joy, Marc Laplante, Yolande Lavoie, Jacques Légaré, Claude Lemelin, André Lux, Marc Termote, and Russell Wilkins. We examined all the comments we received very attentively. Given the limited time frame within which we worked, we were unfortunately unable to take advantage of all the relevant suggestions we received. Consequently, none of these commentators should be held responsible for any weaknesses or deficiencies that may be found in our study.

A research project such as ours cannot be successfully carried out without the co-operation of competent technical help and the daily support of a diligent secretarial staff. Yves Rieux, of I.P. Sharp Ltd., did a remarkable job on the computer-related work, in particular on writing and implementing the simulation programme. The many other technical aspects were handled precisely, capably, and imaginatively by Madeleine Bourdouxhe, Linda Demers, Nguyen thi Hac, Gilbert Lachapelle, and Camille Tardieu. Typing and other secretarial work was competently and professionally carried out, in often difficult conditions, by Josée Ouellette-Simard, Lise Jutras, Marjolaine Boudreault, and Céline Campbell.

Finally, throughout the study, we benefited from the support and advice of Raymond Breton, programme director of The Institute for Research on Public Policy. He was a subtle and highly imaginative counsellor, and we are indebted to him for many suggestions that were to improve the quality of the text. In this connection, we should also like to mention the contribution of Ann McCoomb and Mado Reid, who prepared, edited, and checked the manuscript.

Réjean Lachapelle
Jacques Henripin

Préface

Quand une étude présente à l'occasion des analyses justes et des aperçus éclairants, c'est souvent que les auteurs étaient juchés sur les épaules de géants. On peut certes leur reconnaître le mérite d'avoir su tirer profit des enseignements des maîtres de leur discipline et des disciplines voisines. Et c'est au reste le seul mérite que nous nous accordons volontiers. Nous avons inlassablement puisé, pour la démographie, chez Jean Bourgeois-Pichat, Louis Henry, Nathan Keyfitz et Norman B. Ryder—les deux derniers étant des Canadiens d'origine qui ont acquis la notoriété aux États-Unis—, et, pour la sociologie mathématique, chez Raymond Boudon et James S. Coleman. Nous devons beaucoup aussi à la pensée riche et nuancée d'Alfred Sauvy, qui a su élever la démographie à la hauteur des grandes synthèses.

Plus immédiatement, nous avons toujours côtoyé avec profit, tout au long de cette étude, les travaux remarquables de Stanley Lieberson (sociologue américain d'origine canadienne), et spécialement son ouvrage pénétrant sur la situation sociolinguistique des francophones du Canada. Nous avons également profité des études précises et rigoureuses de John De Vries et de Robert Maheu. Fort stimulants furent aussi les travaux souvent novateurs de Charles Castonguay et Richard J. Joy. Bien que les sciences sociales ne soient pas au centre de leur vie professionnelle, ces auteurs ont, en y consacrant leurs loisirs, apporté à l'étude des groupes linguistiques des perspectives nouvelles et parfois audacieuses, tout en cherchant à allier le respect des faits au souci du service à la collectivité.

Le présent ouvrage ne constitue, soulignons-le, que l'un des produits d'un vaste programme de recherche qu'a entrepris l'Institut de recherches politiques grâce à une subvention du Bureau des relations fédérales-provinciales du gouvernement du Canada. De nombreux chercheurs ont participé à ce programme de recherche. Diane Vanasse a effectué une étude solide et bien structurée sur la population scolaire du Québec; cette étude, qui, comme d'autres, sera publiée à part, a été revue par Michèle Gervais, et elle en a, de plus, réalisé une synthèse. Michèle Gervais a également participé aux travaux qui ont porté sur la migration. Donald G. Cartwright a réalisé un intéressant essai historique et géographique sur la situation des groupes linguistiques; certains des résultats de cette étude sont évoqués dans les deux premiers chapitres. Susan Fletcher et Leroy O. Stone ont effectué de nombreuses estimations et préparé des documents qui ont constitué en quelque sorte les fondements à partir desquels le chapitre six, portant sur la migration, a pu être élaboré. Soulignons aussi l'importante contribution qu'a apportée Leroy O. Stone lors de la confection des hypothèses relatives à la migration interne. Il fut aussi pour plusieurs, et spécialement pour le directeur du projet, un conseiller sage et expérimenté, ne ménageant ni ses critiques ni ses suggestions. Mentionnons enfin l'apport de Jean Dumas à l'étude sur la mortalité.

Une étude scientifique est toujours une oeuvre collective. Et cela non seulement parce qu'elle s'efforce d'apporter une pièce solide à l'édifice perpétuellement inachevé de la science, mais encore parce qu'elle suppose le concours de nombreuses personnes dont il est difficile de décrire précisément les apports. Ainsi, nous avons organisé un séminaire et sollicité à plusieurs reprises des commentaires. Nous avons pu par là profiter de l'expérience et de la compétence d'un grand nombre de chercheurs et de spécialistes. Nous aimerions à ce propos remercier tout spécialement Roderic Beaujot, Charles Castonguay, John De Vries, Claude Dionne, Richard J. Joy, Marc Laplante, Yolande Lavoie, Jacques Légaré, Claude Lemelin, André Lux, Marc Termote et Russell Wilkins. Nous avons examiné attentivement toutes les remarques qui ont été faites. Faute de temps, nous n'avons pu, malheureusement, mettre à profit toutes les suggestions pertinentes que nous avons reçues. C'est dire que les commentateurs ne sauraient être tenus responsables des faiblesses et des lacunes qu'on pourrait déceler dans notre étude.

Un projet de recherche comme le nôtre ne saurait être mené à bien sans la collaboration d'un personnnel technique compétent et l'appui quotidien d'un secrétariat diligent. Yves Rieux, de la société I.P. Sharp, s'est acquitté d'une manière remarquable des tâches reliées à l'informatique, en particulier de la rédaction et de l'implantation du programme de simulation. Les nombreux autres travaux techniques ont été effectués avec précision, sûreté et imagination par Madeleine Bourdouxhe, Linda Demers, Nguyen thi Hac, Gilbert Lachapelle et Camille Tardieu. Quant à la frappe des textes et au secrétariat, ils furent assurés avec compétence et rigueur, dans des conditions parfois difficiles, par Josée Ouellette-Simard, Lise Jutras, Marjolaine Boudreault et Céline Campbell.

Enfin, tout au long de l'étude, nous avons bénéficié de l'appui et des conseils de Raymond Breton, directeur de programme à l'Institut de recherches politiques. Il fut un commentateur nuancé et fort imaginatif. Nous lui sommes redevables de plusieurs suggestions qui devraient améliorer la lisibilité du texte. À ce propos, signalons les travaux d'appoint de Ann McCoomb et de Mado Reid, qui ont préparé, revu et vérifié le manuscrit.

Réjean Lachapelle
Jacques Henripin

The Authors

Réjean Lachapelle studied anthropology and demography at the University of Montreal, and epidemiology and the genetics of populations in Paris. His first appointment was professor of behavioural sciences in the Faculty of Medicine at the University of Sherbrooke. As project director at The Institute for Research on Public Policy from 1975 to 1979, he co-ordinated the research programme on the situation of linguistic groups in Canada. He is now director of research at the Ministry of Cultural Communities and Immigration of Quebec.

Other than his research on the demography of linguistic groups, he is particularly interested in the methodological aspects of demography, the problems raised by the use of population forecasts, as well as the analysis of fertility. He is the author of numerous articles on these subjects.

Jacques Henripin studied economics at the University of Montreal and later at the University of Paris where he obtained a doctorate in 1953. While in Paris, he became interested in demography under the direction of researchers at the Institut national d'études démographiques. Since 1954, he has been a professor at the University of Montreal, and in 1965 he set up the Department of Demography.

His research has concentrated on fertility, infant mortality, the evolution of ethnic and linguistic groups, relations between the economy and the population, demographic forecasts, and population policies. He has written several books and over fifty scientific articles.

Deirdre Mark is a free-lance translator. She studied at Mount St. Vincent University in Halifax. She holds a Diploma in Translation from McGill University, as well as a Diplôme de traducteur from the École supérieure d'interprètes et de traducteurs (Paris) and a Diplôme d'études supérieures spécialisées in translation from the Sorbonne-Nouvelle (Paris III).

Summary

Originally inhabited by the Indians, colonized by the French from the beginning of the seventeenth century, conquered by the British in 1759–1760, Canada has since been the scene of demographic competition between anglophones and francophones. As early as the first decades of the nineteenth century, anglophones outnumbered francophones, at least in what would correspond to present-day Canada. The proportion of anglophones increased to the detriment of francophones up until the mid-nineteenth century; thereafter, from 1851 to 1951, the proportion of francophones—or more specifically persons of French origin—remained at around 30%. This century-long equilibrium was the result of the compensating action of factors working in opposite directions. Because of their high fertility rate, francophones were able, in the long run, to counterbalance the detrimental effects of international migration. Subsequently, following the Second World War, the "excess fertility" of francophones diminished rapidly and almost disappeared during the 1960s. This unforeseen development, which surprised many observers at least by its abruptness, led to fears that the proportion of francophones would be severely decreased, not only in Canada as a whole, but also in Quebec and particularly in the Montreal area. Did this mean that francophones were endangered even in their Quebec stronghold, where they represent 80% of the population? This and other related questions are examined in this work.

Our main conclusions are set out below.

TRENDS IN LINGUISTIC COMPOSITION

1. There is a strong probability that, in Canada as a whole, the proportion of francophones will decrease during the next few decades, while that of anglophones will increase. This trend is the continuation of the evolution observed over the past twenty-five years. The proportion constituted by the French group (here taken as persons whose mother tongue, i.e., the language first spoken and still understood, is French) dropped from 29.0% in 1951 to 26.9% in 1971 and to 26.0% in 1976, while the English mother-tongue group grew from 59.1% in 1951 to 61.5% in 1976. Anglophones (those persons whose home language, i.e., the language most often spoken within the family, is English) already made up 67.0% of the Canadian population in 1971, against 25.7% for francophones. By the year 2000, the proportion of anglophones could reach between 68.0% and 72.0%, and that of francophones, between 21.0% and 24.0%.

2. It is highly probable that the anglophone and francophone populations will become more and more concentrated, the latter in Quebec and the former in the rest of Canada. From 1951 to 1976, the proportion of Canadians of French mother tongue residing in Quebec grew from 82.3% to 84.8%, while the English mother-tongue group declined constantly: 5.6% in 1976 compared to 6.7% in 1951. If we use home language rather than the mother tongue, the concentration is even more clearly marked, at least for francophones. In 1971, the percentage of francophones residing in Quebec was 87.8%; by the year 2000, this proportion should be between 89.0% and 92.0%. The anglophone population of Quebec could decrease from 6.1% in 1971 to between 3.2% and 5.6% thirty years from now.

3. In Quebec itself, it is probable that the weight of the francophone group will increase in the coming decades, while that of the anglophone group will shrink. The English mother-tongue fraction decreased constantly between 1931 and 1976, from 14.9% to 12.8%. The size of the French group has grown in inverse proportion to that of the third-language group (neither French nor English). From 1931 to 1951, the French group grew from 79.8% to 82.5%, while the third-language group went from 5.3% down to 3.7%. In the following years, the French group shrank to 80.7% in 1971, then increased to 81.1% in 1976, while the third-language group grew rapidly up until 1971 (6.2%), then decreased slightly in 1976 (6.1%). By the year 2000, the proportion of francophones could be somewhere between 81.0% and 85.0%, while anglophones would represent 10.0% to 13.0%; in 1971, these two groups represented 80.8% and 14.7% of the Quebec population respectively. The percentage ranges given above correspond to what we consider to be the most likely developments. If the scope is extended to include other plausible, but less likely, developments, we would have to increase these ranges considerably. For instance, if the socio-economic situation in Quebec were to remain mediocre for the next thirty years—although this would be most surprising—while francophones attained greatly improved social and linguistic status, the proportion of anglophones could then decrease to 9.1%, while the francophone group would grow to 86.5%. If, on the other hand, the socio-economic situation were to remain good over thirty years—although this would be unprecedented—while the social and linguistic status of francophones improved only slightly, the proportion of anglophones could swell to 15.8%, and that of francophones could shrink as low as 79.3%.

4. In the contact regions of Quebec (the Eastern Townships, Montreal, the Outaouais), it is probable that the proportion of francophones will increase over the next few decades and that of anglophones will decrease. From 1951 to 1976, the size of the English group in the Montreal region decreased from 23.3% to 20.0%. The French mother-tongue group saw its relative strength decrease from 1951 (69.5%) to

1961 (68.4%), while the third-language group grew from 7.2% to 10.2%; subsequently, the proportion of francophones increased to 69.4% in 1976 (68.9% in 1971). By the beginning of the next century, the proportion of francophones could stand at between 70.0% and 79.0%, while that of anglophones would be between 14.0% and 23.0%; it should be recalled here that francophones and anglophones represented respectively 68.8% and 23.3% of the Montreal-area population in 1971. With respect to the Eastern Townships, steady growth in the proportion of francophones has been observed over the past hundred years, and there seems to be no reason why this trend should not continue over the coming decades. In 1871, people of British origin represented 56.0% of the population of that region, while those of French origin represented 39.0%; a hundred years later, in 1971, the proportions were 14.0% and 83.0% respectively. If mother tongue rather than ethnic origin is considered, the same trend can be observed. From 1941 to 1976, the English group went from 24.0% to 14.2%, while the proportion of the French group increased from 75.0% to 84.5%. In the Outaouais, however, recent developments in linguistic composition have broken with the trend of the past hundred years. Between 1871 and 1971, the proportion of persons of British origin fell from 50.0% to 16.0%, while that of the French-origin group increased from 46.0% to 79.0%. Between 1971 and 1976, however, a decrease was observed in the proportion of French mother-tongue persons, from 79.3% to 78.5%, while the English group increased slightly, from 18.8% to 18.9%. This is the result of a number of factors, all of which are no doubt linked to the national capital development policy implemented by the federal government during this period. As to what the future holds, it is more difficult to predict the evolution of linguistic distribution in the Outaouais than that of the Eastern Townships or Montreal. We nevertheless feel that the proportion of francophones ought to increase at least slightly in the long term, unless this region should continue to show a sizeable positive migratory balance for some time to come.

5. In Canada less Quebec, it is highly probable that the proportion of anglophones will increase during the next few decades, while that of francophones will decrease. Outside Quebec, the relative size of the French mother-tongue population decreased from 7.2% in 1951 to 5.4% in 1976. The English group decreased in strength from 1951 (77.6%) to 1961 (76.8%), then increased to 79.7% in 1976. These changes are but the reverse image of those observed for the third-language group: the proportion of those whose mother tongue was neither French nor English increased from 15.2% to 16.7% between 1951 and 1961, then decreased to 15.6% in 1971 and 14.9% in 1976. Composition based on home language no doubt gives a better picture of the respective size of the various linguistic communities. This information is only available for the 1971 census. In that year, anglophones accounted for 87.2% of the population of Canada minus Quebec. Francophones represented only 4.4%. By the year 2000, the latter could represent

2.2% to 3.5%, while the proportion of anglophones should be between 87.3% and 91.7%.

6. In Southeast as well as Northeast Ontario, it is highly probable that the proportion of francophones will decrease over the coming decades, while that of anglophones will grow. These two regions bordering on Quebec count large francophone minorities; these are, however, on the decline, particularly in the Southeast (which includes the city of Ottawa). Between 1951 and 1976, the proportion of French mother-tongue persons decreased from 37.6% to 34.5% in the Northeast and from 35.7% to 25.7% in the Southeast. At the same time, the relative size of the English group increased from 49.5% to 57.1% in the Northeast and from 61.3% to 66.2% in the Southeast. We fail to see what could cause a lasting reversal of these trends in the coming decades.

7. In North-and-East New Brunswick, it is unlikely that there will be any sizeable variation in linguistic composition over the next few decades. This other region bordering on Quebec was home to over 95.0% of New Brunswick francophones in 1971. It should be noted that the population of this region in 1871 was mainly of British origin (57.0%). Subsequently, the group of British origin decreased to 34.0% in 1961, while the proportion of those of French origin grew from 41.0% in 1871 to 62.0% in 1961. If we consider the composition by mother tongue rather than ethnic origin, however, we see that the French group reached its peak in 1951 (59.6%), following which it decreased until 1971 (58.0%), then stabilized (also at 58.0% in 1976). The English group, on the other hand, grew from 39.4% to 40.8% between 1951 and 1971, reaching 41.0% in 1976. Changes in linguistic composition in recent years have been quite slow, and this will probably be the case in the future as well.

VARIATIONS IN DEMOLINGUISTIC FACTORS

Four factors have a direct influence on the evolution of linguistic composition: mortality, fertility, linguistic mobility, and migration. Variations in these factors account for the trends described above.

Mortality

8. Francophones have a higher death rate than anglophones. Following a period of reduction, the over-mortality of francophones rose over the past decade or so. Henceforth, however, differences in mortality play a negligible part in the evolution of linguistic composition.

Fertility

9. The excess fertility of francophones has practically disappeared in all regions; for Canada as a whole, an under-fertility can even be observed. Women born between 1906 and 1911 whose home language was

French (they would be in the 60−64 age group in 1971) had an average number of children about 50% greater than their anglophone counterparts. Among those born between 1921 and 1926, francophones were 25% more fertile, but members of the French group born after 1935 tended to be under-fertile. Over the last two five-year periods (1966−1971 and 1971−1976), it has been estimated that the total fertility rate of the French group, again for Canada as a whole, was 5% less than that of the English group. Although at first glance this may seem surprising, under-fertility of the French group is not observed either in Quebec or in the rest of Canada. In both regions, there is even a slight excess fertility of about 10%. The relatively low fertility of the French group in Canada as a whole is basically the result of the concentration of this group in one region, that is, Quebec, which since the mid-1960s has been characterized by a fertility rate lower than the Canadian average.

Linguistic Mobility

10. In Canada as a whole, linguistic mobility clearly favours the English group; it is slightly disadvantageous to the French group, moderately disadvantageous to the endogenous-language (Amerindian) group, and highly disadvantageous to the exogenous-language group. More than 80% of those born in Canada whose mother tongue is not English, French, or Amerindian generally adopt English as their usual language when they become adults. This group thus has no specifically Canadian linguistic existence and is maintained by the inflow of immigrants from other countries. This is why we have designated it by the name "exogenous-language group." In addition, more than 90% of young adult exophones (those who claim to speak these languages at home) were born outside Canada.

11. The French group always shows appreciable losses in its linguistic exchanges with the English group, except in regions of Quebec where anglophones are only a small minority. Considering the demographic effects of linguistic mobility, we can distinguish five categories of regions. The first category includes those regions where linguistic transfers are almost balanced between the French and English groups; these are mainly regions in the interior and border areas of Quebec where persons of English mother tongue form less than 5% of the population. The Eastern Townships could also be included in this category, although the mobility of the French group is a little higher than in the other regions mentioned. The Montreal region constitutes the second category, because of the size of the third-language group. Although the English group constitutes a minority in this region (accounting for about 20% of the population), it is not only at an advantage in its linguistic exchanges with the French group, it also receives more than 70% of the language transfers from the third-language group. If francophones are to counterbalance gains made by the English group through language transfers, they must maintain a 15% to 20% advantage in fertility over the anglophones. The same holds true for the Outaouais and North-and-East New Brunswick regions, which form the third category. In these two regions, however, the only way francophones can compensate for gains by the English group is through fertility, since the third-language group is practically non-existent. In the Montreal region, fertility would also compensate for gains made by the English group to the detriment of the third-language group, since the French group's losses are lower. In all the foregoing regions, francophones constitute the majority of the population. The fourth category includes the Southeast and Northeast regions of Ontario, where francophones represent respectively 25% and 30% of the population. The French group has suffered considerable losses in these regions, to the point where they would need a fertility advantage of about 50% to counterbalance them. The final category is formed by all the other regions of Canada. These regions are very strongly anglophone. Language transfers from the French group are so massive that it is almost impossible to counterbalance the effects without considerable migration from francophone regions.

12. **Outside Quebec, the linguistic mobility of the French group has increased over the years, with the possible exception of New Brunswick, where it appears to have decreased slightly from 1971 to 1976.**

13. **Within Quebec, the linguistic mobility of the English group has increased, that of the French group has stabilized, and language transfers from the third-language group to the English group have increased, at least until 1976. In so far as the demographic effects of language transfers are concerned, however, the changes have been slight: the English group has always benefited greatly from language transfers, although it appears that the gap between the English and French groups now has a tendency to decrease slightly.**

14. **Proportionately to the other official language group in a given region, the bilingualism rate of the French group is much higher than that of the English group.** This is due not only to the importance of English in international communication, but above all, it seems, to the preponderance of anglophones in the upper categories of the socio-professional hierarchy. This is what we call inequality bilingualism.

Migration

15. **Our analysis shows that at least between 1966 and 1976, international migration has clearly favoured the third-language group and, relatively speaking, most often penalized the English and French groups, both in Quebec and in the rest of Canada.** We should make it clear that for Canada as a whole, international migration is less to the advantage of the French group than to that of the English group. Although it is highly

possible that in the past the demolinguistic effects of international migration were quite variable, we may nevertheless safely suggest that for most of the periods characterized by high net immigration, these effects must have been quite similar to those estimated for the last two five-year periods.

16. In almost all regions, internal migration has, relatively speaking, favoured the French group over the English group during the last two five-year periods. This situation is no doubt related to the fact that the French mother-tongue population represents a much higher proportion of the population than the English mother-tongue group in those regions where the migratory balance is negative. This regional imbalance probably slows down to some extent the internal migration of members of the French group, since they mainly circulate between regions with francophone majorities.

17. The propensity to leave Quebec for other regions of Canada is much stronger for persons whose mother tongue is English than for those whose mother tongue is French; by the same token, members of the French group are much more likely to migrate into Quebec from other parts of Canada than are those who belong to the English group. For the periods 1966−1971 and 1971−1976, the migrating propensity of the minority group (English in Quebec, French elsewhere in Canada) was ten to fifteen times higher than that of the majority group in the same region.

18. It would seem that those persons who adopt English as their home language have a higher propensity to leave Quebec for other parts of Canada than do those who choose French.

19. Whatever their point of departure in Canada or in other countries, emigrants whose mother tongue is French have a higher tendency than those of other groups to move to regions having a francophone majority; conversely, emigrants whose mother tongue is English are more likely than those of the French group to head for regions having an anglophone majority. There would thus appear to be two distinct migratory systems in Canada, one towards regions that are mainly francophone, the other towards regions that are mainly anglophone. These are obviously not perfect replicas one of the other. In some regions, the relation to one system or the other could be described as second-degree. Thus, out-migrants from Northeast Ontario whose mother tongue is French have a slightly greater tendency to move to Southeast Ontario than to Quebec; however, French mother-tongue out-migrants from Southeast Ontario have a very high tendency to move into Quebec. There is also the case of English mother-tongue out-migrants from three regions of Quebec (the Eastern Townships, the Interior, and the Periphery) who for the most part settle in the Montreal region; English-group out-migrants who leave Montreal move, almost without exception, to regions having an anglophone majority. Southeast Ontario and Montreal may thus be said to act as relay points.

Abrégé

Peuplé d'abord par les Amérindiens, puis colonisé par les Français à partir du début du dix-septième siècle, ensuite conquis par les Britanniques en 1759–1760, le Canada est depuis lors le théâtre d'une concurrence démographique entre les anglophones et les francophones. Dès les premières décennies du dix-neuvième siècle, les anglophones surpassent en nombre les francophones, du moins dans le territoire qui correspond au Canada actuel. Et, jusqu'au milieu de ce siècle, la proportion des anglophones s'accroît aux dépens de celle des francophones. Après quoi, de 1851 à 1951, la proportion que représentent les francophones—plus précisément les personnes d'origine française—fluctue autour de 30 %. Cet équilibre séculaire est le résultat de l'action compensatrice de facteurs qui agissent dans des sens opposés. Grâce à leur forte fécondité, les francophones ont pu équilibrer, dans le long terme, les effets de la migration internationale, qui leur étaient défavorables. Mais par la suite, après la Seconde Guerre mondiale, la « surfécondité » des francophones a diminué rapidement et a même à peu près disparu au cours des années 1960. Cette évolution surprenante, ou en tout cas qui a surpris maints observateurs par sa rapidité, a fait craindre une sévère réduction du poids des francophones non seulement dans l'ensemble du Canada, mais aussi au Québec et en particulier dans la région de Montréal. Est-ce à dire que les francophones seraient menacés jusque dans leur bastion, le Québec, où ils tiennent 80 % de la population? Cette question et bien d'autres qui s'y rattachent sont étudiées dans le présent ouvrage.

Voici les principaux résultats auxquels nous sommes arrivés.

ÉVOLUTION DES COMPOSITIONS LINGUISTIQUES

1. Il est très probable que, dans l'ensemble du Canada, le poids démographique des francophones diminuera au cours des prochaines décennies, tandis que celui des anglophones augmentera. Cette tendance prolonge une évolution qu'on peut observer depuis vingt-cinq ans. La proportion que représente le groupe français (il s'agit des personnes dont le français est la langue maternelle, c'est-à-dire la première langue parlée et encore comprise) est en effet passée de 29,0 % en 1951 à 26,9 % en 1971 et à 26,0 % en 1976, pendant que le groupe de langue maternelle anglaise progressait de 59,1 % en 1951 à 61,5 % en 1976. Quant aux anglophones (il s'agit des personnes dont l'anglais est la langue d'usage, c'est-à-dire la langue le plus souvent parlée en milieu familial), ils détenaient déjà 67,0 % de la population canadienne en 1971 contre 25,7 % pour les francophones. Au début du vingt et unième siècle, le poids des anglophones pourrait varier entre 68 % et 72 %, celui des francophones entre 21 % et 24 %.

2. Il est très probable que les francophones et les anglophones seront de plus en plus concentrés, les premiers au Québec et les seconds ailleurs au Canada. De 1951 à 1976, la proportion des Canadiens de langue maternelle française qui résident au Québec est passée de 82,3 % à 84,8 %, tandis que celle des Canadiens de langue maternelle anglaise a diminué régulièrement : 5,6 % en 1976 contre 6,7 % en 1951. Si on utilise la langue d'usage au lieu de la langue maternelle, la concentration ressort avec encore plus de netteté, du moins pour les francophones. En 1971, le pourcentage d'entre eux qui résidaient au Québec était de 87,8 %; et, au début du vingt et unième siècle, cette proportion devrait être comprise entre 89 % et 92 %. Pour ce qui est des anglophones, la fraction de ceux qui habitent au Québec pourrait passer de 6,1 % en 1971 à une proportion comprise entre 3,2 % et 5,6 % trente ans plus tard.

3. Au Québec, il est probable que la fraction des francophones augmentera au cours des prochaines décennies, tandis que celle des anglophones diminuera. La proportion que représente le groupe de langue maternelle anglaise a diminué continûment de 1931 à 1976, passant de 14,9 % à 12,8 %. Quant au groupe français, son importance relative évolue en raison inverse de celle du tiers groupe. De 1931 à 1951, le poids du groupe français augmente de 79,8 % à 82,5 %, pendant que celui du tiers groupe diminue de 5,3 % à 3,7 %. Par la suite, la proportion détenue par le groupe français diminue jusqu'à 80,7 % en 1971, puis augmente à 81,1 % en 1976, tandis que celle du tiers groupe augmente rapidement jusqu'en 1971 (6,2 %) et diminue légèrement en 1976 (6,1 %). Au début du vingt et unième siècle, la proportion des francophones pourrait varier entre 81 % et 85 % et celle des anglophones entre 10 % et 13 %; rappelons que ces deux communautés représentaient respectivement, en 1971, 80,8 % et 14,7 % de la population du Québec. Les intervalles que nous venons de donner correspondent aux évolutions que nous jugeons probables. Si on élargit l'angle de l'éventail et que l'on considère des évolutions qui, tout en étant plausibles, sont moins probables, on est amené à envisager des intervalles beaucoup plus étendus. Par exemple, si la situation socio-économique du Québec demeurait médiocre pendant trente ans—ce qui serait fort surprenant—, et que les conditions sociolinguistiques des francophones devaient fortement s'améliorer, le poids des anglophones pourrait alors diminuer jusqu'à 9,1 % et celui des francophones atteindre 86,5 %. À l'opposé, si la situation socio-économique du Québec était bonne pendant trente ans—ce qui serait sans précédent—, et que les conditions sociolinguistiques des francophones ne s'amélioraient que légèrement, la proportion que détiennent les anglophones pourrait se hausser à 15,8 % et celle des francophones diminuer jusqu'à 79,3 %.

4. Dans les régions de contact du Québec (Cantons-de-l'Est, Montréal et Outaouais), il est probable que la proportion des francophones augmentera au cours des prochaines décennies et que celles des

anglophones se réduira. De 1951 à 1976, la fraction que représente le groupe anglais dans la région de Montréal a diminué de 23,3 % en 1951 à 20,0 % en 1976. Quant au groupe de langue maternelle française, il a vu son poids relatif diminuer de 1951 (69,5 %) à 1961 (68,4 %), pendant que le tiers groupe progressait de 7,2 % à 10,2 %; par la suite, la proportion tenue par le groupe français a augmenté jusqu'à 69,4 % en 1976 (68,9 % en 1971). Au début du prochain siècle, la proportion des francophones pourrait se situer entre 70 % et 79 %, et celle des anglophones entre 14 % et 23 %; en 1971, rappelons-le, ces communautés représentaient respectivement 68,8 % et 23,3 % de la population de la région de Montréal. En ce qui concerne les Cantons-de-l'Est, on y observe, depuis plus d'un siècle, une francophonisation toujours croissante, et on ne voit pas ce qui pourrait l'arrêter au cours des prochaines décennies. En 1871, les Britanniques d'origine y représentaient 56 % de la population et les Français d'origine 39 %; cent ans plus tard, en 1971, les proportions respectives étaient de 14 % et de 83 %. Et cette tendance ne se dément pas quand on considère la langue maternelle plutôt que l'origine ethnique. De 1941 à 1976, la proportion que détient le groupe anglais est passée de 24,0 % à 14,2 %, tandis que celle du groupe français a progressé de 75,0 % à 84,5 %. En Outaouais, toutefois, les mouvements récents de la composition linguistique rompent avec une évolution séculaire. En effet, de 1871 à 1971, la part du groupe d'origine britannique a diminué de 50 % à 16 %, tandis que celle des Français d'origine a augmenté de 46 % à 79 %. Mais de 1971 à 1976, on observe une baisse de la proportion des personnes de langue maternelle française, de 79,3 % à 78,5 %, pendant que le groupe anglais progresse très légèrement, de 18,8 % à 18,9 %. Il s'agit là sans doute d'un mouvement conjoncturel qui n'est pas sans rapport avec la politique d'aménagement de la capitale nationale (fédérale) qu'a mise en oeuvre le gouvernement fédéral au cours de cette période. Qu'en sera-t-il dans l'avenir? Il est plus difficile d'augurer l'évolution de la composition linguistique de l'Outaouais que celles des Cantons-de-l'Est et de Montréal. On peut néanmoins penser que la proportion des francophones devrait y augmenter au moins légèrement dans le long terme, sauf peut-être si cette région maintient encore longtemps un important solde migratoire positif.

    5. Dans le Canada moins Québec, il est très probable que la proportion des anglophones augmentera au cours des prochaines décennies, tandis que celle des francophones diminuera. À l'extérieur du Québec, l'importance relative de la population de langue maternelle française est passée de 7,2 % en 1951 à 5,4 % en 1976. Quant au groupe anglais, il a vu son poids diminuer de 1951 (77,6 %) à 1961 (76,8 %), puis augmenter jusqu'à 79,7 % en 1976. Et ces mouvements ne sont que le reflet inversé de ceux qu'on a observés chez le tiers groupe : la proportion que représentent les personnes de tierce langue maternelle a en effet progressé de 15,2 % à 16,7 % de 1951 à 1961, pour diminuer ensuite à 15,6 % en 1971 et 14,9 %

en 1976. Mais la composition selon la langue d'usage reflète mieux, sans doute, l'importance respective des communautés linguistiques. Cette information n'est disponible qu'au recensement de 1971. Les anglophones rassemblent cette année-là 87,2 % de la population du Canada moins Québec. Les francophones, eux, n'en regroupent que 4,4 %. Et, au début du vingt et unième siècle, leur proportion pourrait se situer entre 2,2 % et 3,5 %, tandis que celle des anglophones devrait être comprise entre 87,3 % et 91,7 %.

   6. Dans le Sud-Est comme dans le Nord-Est de l'Ontario, il est très probable que la proportion des francophones se réduira au cours des prochaines décennies, alors que celle des anglophones progressera. Ces deux régions limitrophes du Québec comportent d'importantes minorités francophones; celles-ci sont toutefois en déclin, en particulier dans le Sud-Est (la ville d'Ottawa appartient à cette région). En effet, de 1951 à 1976, la proportion que représentent les personnes de langue maternelle française est passée de 37,6 % à 34,5 % dans le Nord-Est et de 35,7 % à 25,7 % dans le Sud-Est. Et, dans le même temps, l'importance relative du groupe anglais a progressé de 49,5 % à 57,1 % dans le Nord-Est et de 61,3 % à 66,2 % dans le Sud-Est. On ne voit pas ce qui pourrait renverser durablement ces tendances au cours des prochaines décennies.

   7. Dans le Nord-et-Est du Nouveau-Brunswick, il est probable que la composition linguistique variera assez peu au cours des prochaines décennies. Cette autre région limitrophe du Québec abritait plus de 95 % des francophones du Nouveau-Brunswick en 1971. Mentionnons que la population de cette région était en majorité d'origine britannique (57 %) en 1871. Par la suite, les Britanniques d'origine ont vu leur proportion diminuer jusqu'à 34 % en 1961, pendant que le poids des Français d'origine progressait de 41 % en 1871 à 62 % en 1961. Mais si on considère la composition par langue maternelle au lieu de la composition selon l'origine ethnique, on constate que, pour le groupe français, le sommet a été atteint en 1951 (59,6 %); après quoi, la proportion qu'il détient diminue jusqu'en 1971 (58,0 %), puis se stabilise (également 58,0 % en 1976). Inversement, le poids du groupe anglais progresse de 39,4 % à 40,8 % de 1951 à 1971 et atteint 41,0 % en 1976. Les mouvements récents de la composition linguistique sont fort lents; il est probable qu'il en sera de même dans l'avenir.

VARIATIONS DES PHÉNOMÈNES DÉMOLINGUISTIQUES

   Quatre phénomènes agissent directement sur l'évolution de la composition linguistique : la mortalité, la fécondité, la mobilité linguistique et la migration. Ce sont leurs variations qui rendent compte des tendances que nous venons de présenter.

Mortalité

8. Les francophones ont une plus forte mortalité que les anglophones. Après s'être réduite, la surmortalité des francophones a augmenté au cours des derniers lustres. Toutefois, les différences de mortalité jouent dorénavant un rôle négligeable dans l'évolution des compositions linguistiques.

Fécondité

9. La surfécondité des francophones a presque disparu dans toutes les régions; à l'échelle du Canada tout entier, on observe même une sous-fécondité. Rappelons que les femmes de langue d'usage française nées entre 1906 et 1911 (elles appartenaient au groupe d'âges 60−64 ans en 1971) ont eu un nombre moyen d'enfants supérieur d'environ 50 % à celui de leurs concitoyennes anglophones; leur surfécondité était encore de 25 % chez celles qui sont nées entre 1921 et 1926, mais elle s'est transformée en sous-fécondité chez celles qui sont nées après 1935. D'ailleurs, au cours des deux derniers lustres (1966−1971 et 1971−1976), on a pu estimer que l'indice synthétique de fécondité du groupe français était, toujours à l'échelle du Canada tout entier, inférieur de 5 % à celui du groupe anglais. Mais, chose surprenante à première vue, cette sous-fécondité du groupe français ne se retrouve pas au Québec ni dans le reste du Canada. Il y a même encore, dans l'une et l'autre région, une légère surfécondité d'environ 10 %. La faible fécondité relative du groupe français dans l'ensemble du Canada résulte essentiellement de la concentration de ce groupe dans une région, le Québec, qui est caractérisée depuis le milieu des années soixante par une fécondité inférieure à la moyenne canadienne.

Mobilité linguistique

10. À l'échelle du Canada tout entier, la mobilité linguistique favorise nettement le groupe anglais, mais désavantage légèrement le groupe français, moyennement le groupe de langues endogènes (amérindiennes) et massivement le groupe de langues exogènes. Les personnes de langue maternelle autre qu'anglaise, française ou amérindienne adoptent en effet à plus de 80 % l'anglais pour langue d'usage, à l'âge adulte, quand elles sont nées au Canada. Ce groupe n'a donc pas d'existence linguistique proprement canadienne; il ne peut se maintenir que par des apports migratoires en provenance de l'étranger. C'est pourquoi nous l'avons désigné par l'expression *groupe de langues exogènes*. Au reste, chez les jeunes adultes, plus de 90 % des exophones (c'est-à-dire des personnes qui déclarent parler habituellement ces langues à la maison) sont nés à l'extérieur du Canada.

11. Le groupe français fait toujours des pertes appréciables dans ses échanges linguistiques avec le groupe anglais, sauf dans les régions du Québec où le groupe anglais ne constitue qu'une faible minorité. Du point de vue des effets démographiques de la mobilité linguistique, on peut distinguer cinq catégories de régions. La première catégorie rassemble les régions où les transferts linguistiques sont presque équilibrés entre les groupes anglais et français; il s'agit essentiellement des régions intérieure et périphérique du Québec dans lesquelles les personnes de langue maternelle anglaise forment moins de 5 % de la population. On peut également rattacher à cette catégorie les Cantons-de-l'Est, bien que la mobilité du groupe français y soit un peu plus forte que dans les régions précédentes. La région de Montréal forme à elle seule la seconde catégorie, en raison de l'importance qu'y représente le tiers groupe linguistique. Bien que le groupe anglais soit minoritaire dans cette région (il constitue environ 20 % de la population), il est non seulement favorisé dans ses échanges linguistiques avec le groupe français, mais encore il recueille plus de 70 % des transferts linguistiques émanant du tiers groupe. Pour équilibrer les gains du groupe anglais au chapitre des transferts linguistiques, les francophones devraient maintenir une surfécondité de 15 % à 20 % par rapport aux anglophones. Et il en va de même en Outaouais et dans la région Nord-et-Est du Nouveau-Brunswick, qui forment la troisième catégorie de régions. Mais, dans ces deux régions, la surfécondité des francophones devrait compenser à peu près uniquement les gains du groupe anglais au détriment du groupe français, le tiers groupe étant pratiquement inexistant, tandis que, dans la région de Montréal, elle compenserait en outre pour les gains que fait le groupe anglais aux dépens du tiers groupe, puisque les pertes du groupe français y sont plus faibles. Dans toutes les régions précédentes, les francophones forment la majorité de la population. La quatrième catégorie rassemble les régions Sud-Est et Nord-Est de l'Ontario, où ils représentent respectivement 25 % et 30 % de la population. Le groupe français y fait des pertes fort appréciables, à telle enseigne que, pour arriver à les contrebalancer, la surfécondité des francophones devrait être d'environ 50 %. La dernière catégorie regroupe toutes les autres régions du Canada. Il s'agit de régions à forte prépondérance anglophones. Les transferts linguistiques du groupe français y sont si importants qu'il est à peu près impossible d'en compenser les effets sans des apports migratoires appréciables en provenance des régions francophones.

12. Hors du Québec, la mobilité linguistique du groupe français a progressé au cours du temps, sauf peut-être au Nouveau-Brunswick, où elle semble avoir légèrement diminué de 1971 à 1976.

13. Au Québec, il y a tout à la fois augmentation de la mobilité linguistique du groupe anglais, stabilisation de celle du groupe français et progression de la part des transferts linguistiques du tiers groupe qui aboutissent à l'anglais, du moins jusqu'en 1976. Mais, en ce qui concerne les effets démographiques des transferts linguistiques, les changements

sont fort légers : le groupe anglais profite toujours très largement des transferts linguistiques, encore que l'écart entre le groupe anglais et le groupe français semble avoir tendance à diminuer légèrement.

14. **À proportion égale de l'autre groupe linguistique de langue officielle dans une région, le taux de bilinguisme du groupe français surpasse nettement celui du groupe anglais.** Cela tient non seulement à l'importance de l'anglais dans les communications internationales, mais surtout, semble-t-il, à la surreprésentation des anglophones dans les catégories supérieures de la hiérarchie socioprofessionnelle. C'est ce que nous avons appelé le bilinguisme d'inégalité.

Migration

15. **D'après les évaluations que nous avons pu faire, la migration internationale avantage nettement le tiers groupe linguistique, du moins de 1966 à 1976, et défavorise le plus souvent, en termes relatifs, les groupes anglais et français, au Québec comme dans le reste du Canada.** Précisons que, pour l'ensemble du Canada, la migration internationale désavantage plus le groupe français que le groupe anglais. S'il est fort probable que les effets démolinguistiques de la migration internationale aient connu par le passé d'importantes variations, on peut néanmoins penser que, pour la plupart des périodes caractérisées par une forte immigration nette, ils ont dû s'ordonner sensiblement de la même manière que ceux qui ont été évalués pour les deux derniers lustres.

16. **Dans presque toutes les régions, les échanges migratoires internes ont, en termes relatifs, favorisé le groupe français et défavorisé le groupe anglais au cours des deux derniers lustres.** Cette situation n'est probablement pas étrangère au fait que la population de langue maternelle française réside dans une proportion beaucoup plus élevée que la population de langue maternelle anglaise dans des régions ayant des soldes migratoires négatifs. Ce déséquilibre régional freine sans doute quelque peu la migration interne des personnes appartenant au groupe français, car celles-ci circulent surtout entre les régions à majorité francophone.

17. **Les propensions à quitter le Québec pour le reste du Canada sont beaucoup plus fortes pour les personnes de langue maternelle anglaise que pour celles dont le français est la langue maternelle; réciproquement, les membres du groupe français migrent bien plus du reste du Canada vers le Québec que les personnes qui appartiennent au groupe anglais.** En effet, pour les lustres 1966−1971 et 1971−1976, les propensions à migrer du groupe minoritaire (anglais au Québec, français ailleurs au Canada) sont de dix à quinze fois plus élevées que celles du groupe majoritaire de la même région.

18. **Il semblerait que les personnes qui adoptent l'anglais pour langue d'usage aient des propensions à quitter le Québec pour le reste du**

Canada beaucoup plus élevées que les personnes qui choisissent le français.

19. Quel que soit leur lieu de départ au Canada ou à l'étranger, les émigrants de langue maternelle française vont beaucoup plus que ceux des autres groupes vers les régions à majorité francophone; inversement, les émigrants de langue maternelle anglaise se dirigent toujours plus que ceux du groupe français vers les régions à majorité anglophone. Ainsi, il y aurait au Canada deux systèmes migratoires bien distincts, l'un étant polarisé par les régions à majorité francophone, l'autre par les régions à majorité anglophone. Certes, ils ne sont pas parfaitement juxtaposés. Dans certaines régions, le rattachement à l'un ou l'autre système se fait, pourrait-on dire, au second degré. Ainsi, les émigrants de langue maternelle française qui quittent la région Nord-Est de l'Ontario se dirigent un peu plus vers la région Sud-Est de cette province que vers les régions québécoises; mais, du Sud-Est de l'Ontario, les émigrants qui appartiennent au groupe français se portent massivement vers le Québec. Il y a aussi le cas des émigrants de langue maternelle anglaise de trois régions du Québec (Cantons-de-l'Est, Intérieur et Périphérie) qui s'établissent pour une bonne part dans la région de Montréal; partant de Montréal, les émigrants du groupe anglais se dirigent toutefois en quasi-totalité vers les régions à majorité anglophone. Le Sud-Est de l'Ontario et Montréal font office en quelque sorte de relais.

Introduction

(One must take constant precautions) to avoid easy solutions or the comfort of rigid ideas. (To achieve objectivity), one must have no fear of displeasing, or of risking one's reputation (Sauvy, 1966, p. 5). [1]

As with any scientific undertaking, the demographic study of language groups is in constant renewal. It evolves and changes shape, not only under the pressure of new theories, methods, and information, but in response and in reaction to changes that occur in the preoccupations and concerns of political agents. The researcher who undertakes to describe and analyse a concrete demographic situation, in this case that of Canada, must accordingly find a middle ground between two extremes: either make theory and demographic methodology the central point of his work, as data collected on the Canadian situation only provide an occasion for testing theories and applying methods, or confine himself to the socio-political interests of the moment and try to compensate for the lack of depth in his analysis by wide-ranging references and views, combining, more or less happily, demographic, economic, social, political, and cultural considerations. The first position is better suited to specialists, while the second calls for the talent and sensitivity of the generalist. For our part, although we have not overlooked the concerns expressed by the various socio-political agents regarding language issues, we have sought, in so far as possible, to adopt a strictly scientific point of view, that is, that of demography. By this we mean that the strategies and methods of description and analysis that we have used, as well as the theories that we have proposed, are quite general or, at least, can be extended to other situations than that of Canada. In other words, we have attempted to avoid both *ad hoc* procedures and *a posteriori* explanations. This has not always been easy or even desirable, in particular in the presentation of conclusions. To make the text more readable and certain analyses less formidable, we sometimes have modified the exact sequence actually followed; we also have suggested on occasion conclusions and explanations based on rather fragile scientific grounds. The more demanding reader will have little difficulty in retracing the orientation of our original approach, and distinguishing between the conclusions and results with a solid basis and those given only as an indication and necessarily requiring more extensive study.

1

Concerned as one may wish to be with rigour and precision, it is nonetheless necessary to choose a subject for study, a point of view from which to examine it, and a strategy for analysing it. These choices, for the most part, are arbitrary; this is inevitable. Doubtless no one will reproach us for having studied the demolinguistic situation in Canada, nor for having promoted, as demographers, the viewpoint of our discipline. However, it is possible, and rightly so, to question the strategy that we have adopted and to point out its limits. Let us examine this a little more closely.

Simplifying to a certain extent, it is possible to distinguish two conceptions of Canada. Some see the Canadian population as a vast ethnic or regional mosaic, in which no element has the majority; in this view of things, Canada is then a country of minorities. Others tend rather to bring out the dualist nature of Canada: linguistic dualism (anglophone/francophone) and, by extension, territorial dualism (Quebec/rest of Canada). The first view of the Canadian make-up is most frequently met with among those living outside Quebec or, more specifically, among non-francophones, while the second view is more often held by francophones, especially those living in Quebec. The existence of these largely contradictory views places the demographer in a rather delicate position. Should he, or can he, opt for one rather than the other? Assuming that his science enables him to make enlightened judgements, he may succeed in demonstrating that the facts and developments of demography are closer to one than the other. This conclusion would come only at the end of his study and could thus neither orient nor circumscribe his work. The demographer would thus be forced to study both the ethnic and the linguistic situation, and this assumes that he has the appropriate data at his disposal!

In the last decennial census, in 1971, three questions were asked regarding language and only one regarding ethnic origin. The latter was expressed as follows: "To what ethnic or cultural group did you or your ancestor (on the male side) belong on coming to this continent?" This question is aimed at discovering not ethnic sentiment or, in other words, the present feeling of belonging to an ethnic group, but rather ethnic *origin*, and then only in the paternal line. Unless it can be implicitly supposed that an individual cannot change his ethnic group during his lifetime and that ethnicity is unfailingly transmitted from one generation to another—by the paternal line—the demographer is certainly limited in his attempts to describe the present ethnic situation in Canada, or its evolution, using only census data, since no previous census provides any statistical information other than on ethnic origin. He must therefore fall back on the study of the demolinguistic situation. To do this, he has at his disposal a great deal of data on mother tongue ("language first spoken and still understood" in recent census questionnaires), home language (language most often spoken at home), and knowledge of English or French. He may also, under certain conditions, use data relating to ethnic origin.

Having made this choice or, rather, having had this choice imposed on us given the data presently available, we next had to develop and apply a regional breakdown, and decide on the number and nature of language groups to be considered in the study. Of course, all was not possible, but within the limits of available data, a number of options remained open. We nevertheless had to choose, since we could not do everything. Grasp all, lose all, as the saying goes. But what were we to set our nets for? We decided only to go for the bigger fish. This led us to concentrate our attention on the two numerically largest language groups, the anglophone and the francophone, and to consider mainly the larger regions. Our study, then, does not deal specifically with the demolinguistic situation of small minority enclaves within regions that are homogeneously French or English, nor do we examine the various groups that are neither French nor English, except in a general fashion. Occasionally, and exceptionally, we single out Amerindians, but never to take the investigation as far as we would have wished. The result of all this is that, on these subjects, hasty generalizations are to be avoided.

Throughout this study, we were faced with a very delicate problem, that of terminology. This is, of course, a difficulty encountered by all researchers, since they are led, by the particular nature of the questions they deal with, to make a much finer breakdown of reality than is normally done in everyday language. For the sake of precision, they are thus obliged to strike a delicate balance between the heaviness of circumlocution and the abuse of neologism. The terms that we have adopted are shown in Table I.1. We have tried to depart as little as possible from current usage, while aiming for precision, clarity, and concision. In certain cases, we have nevertheless proposed and used neologisms that appeared convenient in designating highly differentiated situations. It will be up to the speakers of the language to decide whether these are acceptable to them.

The book is divided into three parts. The first is devoted to describing the evolution of the demolinguistic situation over the past two centuries, and in particular over the past twenty-five years, from 1951 to 1976. We examine not only the situation of Canada as a whole as well as that of Quebec and the rest of Canada, but also changes in the ethnic and linguistic composition of several regions. The regional breakdown that we have used is described in Appendix *A*. The statistical data presented here are taken from the tables to be found in Appendix *B*.

The evolution of composition by language depends basically on four factors (or, more precisely, on the events to which they give rise): mortality, fertility, linguistic mobility, and migration. These are described and analysed in the second part. In each case, we have sought to show clearly the behavioural differences between the various language groups, to assess their evolution, and to evaluate their effects on changes in linguistic composition. Because of the leading role that linguistic mobility and migration have come

Table I.1
CLARIFICATION OF TERMINOLOGY

CATEGORY / VARIABLE	BRITISH/ENGLISH	FRENCH	Total	OTHER	
				Amerindian (Including Inuit)	"Other"
Ethnic Origin	Persons of British origin or stock. The British-origin or British-stock group. *British-origin persons*.	Persons of French origin or stock. The French-origin or French-stock group. *French-origin persons*.	Persons of other than British or French origin; of neither British nor French origin. Persons of other origin. *Third-origin persons*.	Persons of Amerindian origin. The *Amerindians*.	Persons of other than British, French, or Amerindian origin; of neither British, French, nor Amerindian origin. Persons of "other" origin. The *"other"-origin group*.
Mother Tongue	Persons of English mother tongue. The English mother-tongue group. The *English group*.	Persons of French mother tongue. The French mother-tongue group. The *French group*.	Persons of other than English or French mother tongue. Persons of other mother tongue. The *third-language group*.	Persons of Amerindian mother tongue. The Amerindian mother-tongue group. The *endogenous-language group*.	Persons of other than English, French, or Amerindian mother tongue. Persons of "other" mother tongue. The *exogenous-language group*.
Home Language	Persons of English home language. The English home-language group. *Anglophones*.	Persons of French home language. The French home-language group. *Francophones*.	Persons of other than English or French home language. The other home-language group. *Allophones*.	Persons of Amerindian home language. The Amerindian home-language group. *Endophones*.	Persons of other than English, French, or Amerindian home language. Persons of "other" home language. *Exophones*.

Note: The expressions we are inclined to prefer are shown in italics.

to play, we have paid very special attention to these phenomena and tried to present more detailed analyses of them.[2]

The next task is to combine the effects of all these phenomena, in short, to prepare a synthesis. As composition by home language was not available until 1971 and the data relating to mother tongue are not entirely comparable from one census to another, mainly because of shifts in mother tongue (see Chapter Six), it is almost impossible to ensure that the combined effects of all these demolinguistic phenomena coincide with actual changes in linguistic composition. If we admit certain hypotheses concerning the functioning of what might be called the demolinguistic system, it is nevertheless relatively simple, in principle, to simulate future developments in linguistic composition. This is because the future, by nature unknown and uncertain, lends itself more easily than the past to the inevitable simplification of analysis. In any case, the hypotheses on which our simulations are based are described in the third part, followed by our comments on the results of projections destined to delimit not only those situations that did not appear impossible, but above all those that we felt plausible or even probable. We also give some prospective views on the population of Canada as a whole, as well as that of Quebec and of the rest of Canada, and on trends in the demolinguistic situation in a number of regions.

What benefit can those concerned with these issues, political agents in particular, derive from our analyses and simulations? "What is going to happen?," we are often asked. "Are your forecasts scientific?" This last term is ambiguous, since, in the minds of those who ask the question, it often means "exact and certain." It is rare that rigorously scientific methods result in exact and certain conclusions. Additionally, there are degrees of precision that may sometimes be superfluous.

Coming back to our study, two things must be distinguished: (1) the description and analysis of past evolution; (2) future prospects. We feel that we have been as rigorous as possible as regards interpretation of past developments, and that we have succeeded in bringing out basic, and often very clear, tendencies relative to significant phenomena from the standpoint of the demolinguistic evolution of the Canadian population. We were obliged, as we have said, to confine ourselves to the "big fish." Some of these discoveries were surprising and at times in direct contradiction with well-established beliefs.

As regards the future, we cannot speak of forecasting, nor of certitude, nor of scientific method in the full sense of the term. Science interprets observations, and we certainly cannot observe the future. We could, in fact, only forecast it in so far as we had full knowledge of all the factors that act on a phenomenon. This is never the case for social change—far from it. This being said, forecasting can draw gainfully upon science. This is true in many ways: scientific knowledge enables us to properly identify the phenomena involved and to define them with the necessary precision; it also enables us to establish the limits of the probable (although not in every case); more important, a scientific frame of mind can add considerably to the quality of forecasting. The scientist is wary of prejudice, of his own sentiments and beliefs, of the temptation to please and to not displease, of extreme over-simplification, of empty words. Of course, even a virtuous man may err, but he tries his best not to. We feel that we have tried to avoid wrongdoing, and even misbehaviour, and we can only hope that we will be judged in the same spirit.

NOTE

[1] Our translation of Alfred Sauvy, *Théorie générale de la population*, Vol. II, *La vie des populations* (Paris: Presses universitaires de France, 1966).

[2] The analyses of linguistic mobility, migration, and also fertility often necessitate the use of unpublished data. Through the co-operation of Statistics Canada personnel, we were able to obtain many special tables based on the 1971 and 1976 censuses. These are much too voluminous, however, to be published. Additional information may be obtained either from the authors or from the appropriate Statistics Canada personnel.

Part One

Retrospective

Chapter One

Brief History of the Settlement of Canada

Successive waves of settlement fashioned the demographic structure of Canada and, even today, greatly influence the ethnic and linguistic make-up of its population, as well as the geographic distribution of the various groups of which it is composed. This is what we shall attempt to retrace briefly here, leaving aside, although not without regret, the Amerindians, about whom little is known. It is believed that the first men to cross from Asia into North America by the Bering Strait must have done so between 15,000 and 10,000 B.C., or even earlier. It is also thought that when white men came into contact with the native population of Canada, the latter numbered about 200,000, or only slightly less than in 1961. In 1871, it would have been 123,000 and, in 1901, 107,000, although these estimates may contain some major errors (Camu, Weeks, and Sametz, 1964, pp. 33–42).

White men first settled in Acadia, on the shores of the St. Lawrence River, and in Newfoundland at the beginning of the seventeenth century. In this chapter, we have divided the subsequent three and a half centuries into four periods:

a. The French colonization, which ended in 1760
b. The initial surge of British settlement, 1760–1871
c. Eight decades of linguistic balance, resulting from highly complex factors, 1871–1951
d. The past quarter-century, when this balance was upset, 1951–1976.

This chapter gives only a brief summary, and is limited to describing only those developments that are most significant from the viewpoint of the evolution of the ethnic and linguistic composition of the Canadian population. Statistical information on the first two periods is, in any case, scanty and often had to be supplemented by fairly rough estimates. Since 1871, however, these data have been more plentiful and more regularly kept, and Chapter Two will make good use of these data by going back over the study of the past hundred years in much greater detail.

A. FRENCH SETTLEMENT IN CANADA

History tells us that France had two main centres of settlement in Canada: Acadia and the St. Lawrence Valley. Both were founded at about the same time, at the very beginning of the seventeenth century, but they did not have equal lifespans: Acadia was surrendered to England in 1713, while New France was lost in 1760. The population of New France in 1760 was approximately 70,000, while that of Acadia was about 10,000.[1] After a hundred and a hundred and fifty years of colonization respectively, this was a rather meagre result. It was enough, however, with the help of natural growth, to ensure the development of a francophone society up to our time, and probably for some time to come, for those 80,000 or so descendents of French colonists multiplied themselves seventy-five times between 1760 and 1960! This in spite of heavy emigration towards the United States from 1830 on. It should also be recalled that the expulsion of the Acadians in 1755 inhibited their expansion in a most tragic manner. Some 6,000 out of 18,000 were banished, not to mention those who were chased from their villages and had to live in conditions hardly favourable to their demographic growth.

We have mentioned the poor showing of a century and a half of colonization. The mother country was not generous; it is estimated that during the French regime, approximately 10,000 colonists came to settle, or not quite 70 a year (Henripin, 1954). During the same period, the rival metropolis was doing much better. Towards 1760, there were around a million and a half inhabitants in New England: twenty times more than in Canada.

This disproportion deserves a closer examination, since it constitutes an excellent example of the great historical consequences of seemingly insignificant details. In the seventeenth and eighteenth centuries, France had within its grasp, through the St. Lawrence — Missouri — Mississippi River system, the better half of the North American continent. This territory was explored, but only about 80,000 people managed to settle there. It is interesting to speculate what might have happened if France, which at the time had a population three times that of England, had sent 1,400 colonists a year instead of 70. It, too, would have had a colony a million and a half strong, with, say, 500,000 along the St. Lawrence and the Great Lakes and a million in the centre of what is today the United States. The least that can be said is that the distribution of languages in North America would not be what it is today. Alfred Sauvy admirably describes the strange historical turnabout that resulted from France's lack of interest in its North American colonies.

> It sufficed that one of the two countries competing for a vast continent sent a few thousand settlers each year, while the other sent a few hundred, and the course of history was radically changed. This is both tragic and symbolic, since, just when the French language had reached international predominance in Europe, through its great demographic superiority, it was sealing its fate in the world at large because a few boats more, filled with illiterates, left England every year. (Sauvy, 1949, p. 12—our translation)

B. DEMOGRAPHIC COMPETITION BETWEEN ENGLISH AND FRENCH

In 1760, the British were starting from scratch in the St. Lawrence Valley, but they were already present in the Maritimes. The number of non-French can be estimated at 9,000 in Acadia and some 10,000 in Newfoundland. It probably took less than forty years, after 1760, to establish an anglophone majority throughout the territory of present-day Canada, and possibly even less time in Acadia and in Ontario. The American War of Independence caused the first great wave of British immigrants to leave the United States. They settled in the Maritimes, in Upper Canada and, in Lower Canada, in the Eastern Townships and near the Ottawa River and its tributaries. These first immigrants encircled the territory of the French Canadians and even occupied part of Lower Canada, as well as placing the British at the gateway to the West.

The great movement of immigration from the British Isles took place after the Napoleonic Wars, from 1816 on. It has been estimated that, from 1815 to 1840, 500,000 British settlers came to Canada (Canada, 1958, pp. 154−76). They seldom went much farther than Ontario, but it is to be noted that a Scottish colony was established in 1811 at Selkirk, on the Red River in southern Manitoba. At that time, there was no census covering the whole of Canada, but there were several, especially in Ontario, although the dates did not coincide from one colony to another. The first census of Upper Canada, in 1824, showed a population of 150,000. A year later, a census showed 480,000 inhabitants in Lower Canada. There must have been, at that time, some 280,000 people in the Atlantic colonies (including Newfoundland), and perhaps 2,000 white men in the West. The total number of whites in 1825, for the whole of present-day Canada, must have been around 925,000.

During this period, the French Canadians, obviously cut off completely from outside sources, could only count on natural growth to increase their numbers. It is known that they were extremely productive demographically, although perhaps no more so, at the time, than the other groups in North America (Henripin, 1972). What is less well known—although it seems an established fact—is that their rate of growth was a little faster during the eight or nine decades following the 1760 conquest than under the French regime. It can be estimated that from 1760 to 1850, their numbers doubled every twenty-six years; prior to 1760, they doubled about every thirty years (Henripin and Péron, 1972).

However, that was not enough to balance immigration from Britain: towards 1810, the French Canadians numbered about 250,000, but this number had probably been exceeded by the British. In 1825, in any case, they were clearly in the minority: approximately 400,000 out of a total white population of about 925,000, or only 43%. Quebec francophones were also to face another problem: towards 1830, it was found that the seigneuries they occupied could no longer support them all. There were a number of obstacles blocking the road to the Eastern Townships (Cartwright, 1980), and if they wished to remain in Quebec, they would have to move to the valleys (Gatineau, Rouge, St. Maurice) where they could combine farming and logging. Many did this, often together with recent British immigrants. A larger number, however, preferred jobs in the factories of New England. This did not slow down their growth (Henripin and Péron, 1972). It is estimated that for the whole of Canada, the number of French Canadians was approximately 750,000 in 1850, or about 30% of the total population. Almost 90% were in Quebec (670,000), 50,000 were in the Maritimes, and 26,000 were in Ontario. The number of those living further west is not known, but it cannot have been very large, as the white population of the Prairies can be estimated at around 6,000.

From 1851 to 1871, the total population of Canada (present territory) went from 2.5 to 3.8 million, principally through natural growth, which was, on the average, 2% a year; the first decade was characterized by a net immigration of about 120,000 and the second, by a net emigration of almost 200,000.[2] Here is how the ethnic balance sheet, by regions, would have looked in 1871.

	Population ('000s) and Percentage Breakdown							
	Total		French		English		Others	
	Number	%	Number	%	Number	%	Number	%
Atlantic (including Newfoundland)	917	100.0	100	10.9	754	82.2	63	6.9
Quebec	1,192	100.0	930	78.0	243	20.4	19	1.6
Ontario	1,621	100.0	75	4.6	1,333	82.2	213	13.2
West & Territories	110	100.0	9	8.2	33	30.0	68	61.8
Total	3,840	100.0	1,114	29.0	2,363	61.5	363	9.5

Some of these figures are approximate and were obtained by interpolation or rough estimates, in particular, distribution by ethnic origin for Newfoundland, the West, and the northern territories. However, it would not be far from the truth to say that for the present territory of Canada (including Newfoundland), there were about 62% British, 29% French, and 9% of other origins.

The West was beginning to develop, and there must have been between 45,000 and 60,000 whites living there. The British were almost four times as numerous as the French, of whom there cannot have been more than 10,000, or approximately 8% of the whole population of the West. They were slightly more numerous in the Atlantic region: 11% counting Newfoundland and 12% if this province is excluded. They began to settle in Ontario during the period 1851 1871, and their numbers tripled during this period but, in 1871, they still represented only 5% of the population. From 1851 to 1871, French Canadians had thus begun to move into the rest of Canada: 89% of them lived in Quebec in 1851, while in 1871 this fraction was 83.5%, and it was to continue to decrease until 1921. This reduction in concentration is probably due to two factors: expansion into Ontario and the West, but also the emigration of many French Canadians from Quebec to New England.

The growth rate of the French population apparently began to slow down towards 1850. Had this not been so, they would have numbered at least 200,000 more in 1871. This figure corresponds to the number of emigrants and their descendents. In addition, during these twenty years, approximately 400,000 people left Canada. If French Canadians had had as strong an urge to emigrate as other Canadians, some 120,000 of them would have left, but this is probably an underestimation, according to Yolande Lavoie (1973, pp. 74—79), who estimates net emigration for Quebeckers at about 170,000. A figure of this magnitude for French Canadians would be large enough to account for the 200,000 or so missing when the 1871 census was taken.

We have mentioned that French Canadians had occupied completely the seigneurial lands of the St. Lawrence Valley around 1830, and the towns were unable to absorb the excess. In 1825, Montreal had a population of 32,000, while Quebec had 22,000 residents; 10% of the Quebec population was thus urban. In 1851, the census showed 58,000 people in Montreal and 42,000 in Quebec. Canadians of French origin were, however, a minority in Montreal (45%) and a scant majority in Quebec (58%).[3] Twenty years later, the French had regained their majority in Montreal (53% of 107,000 residents) and improved it in Quebec (68% of 60,000 residents).

In Upper Canada, urbanization was taking place somewhat more rapidly. York, which was to become Toronto, had less than 2,000 residents in 1824; in 1851, there were 31,000 and, in 1871, 56,000.

C. A REMARKABLE DEMOGRAPHIC BALANCE: 1871—1951

From 1871 to 1951, the relative strength of French Canadians remained at around 30%, declining somewhat in periods of high immigration, and rising again when the flow of immigrants slackened. In actual fact, this fraction was already 30% in the mid-nineteenth century, but we have chosen 1871 as the cut-off date basically for three reasons:

1. Since Confederation, decennial censuses are available covering first the four original provinces, by far the most heavily populated at the time, and later the other provinces and territories, as they were integrated into the Canadian political system. The statistical basis for our estimates is thus stronger, and this is why, in the following chapter, the various series begin in this year and why we have judged preferable to keep it as the beginning of this third period.

2. Immigration was greater from 1871 on. From around 200,000 for each of the two preceding decades, it rose to 350,000 (1871—1881), then 900,000 (1881—1891), and 325,000 (1891—1901), after which is exceeded

the million mark during the first three decades of the twentieth century (Keyfitz, 1950). It was these waves of immigration that endangered the relative strength of French Canadians.

3. They were to reply with the *"revanche des berceaux"* (the revenge of the cradles). In effect, towards 1870, the excess fertility of francophones became evident. Before that, almost all groups had a natural fertility rate, since voluntary birth control appears to have begun about this time. French Canadians, however, joined the movement much later than the others, thus benefiting from an excess fertility that increased until around 1930, after which time it dropped off and finally disappeared during the 1960s, as will be seen in Chapter Four.

These, then, are the basic phenomena that make up the linguistic balance of this period of almost a century: two opposing forces whose effects, for the period as a whole, compensated each other. On the one hand, high immigration (offset to some extent by emigration) helped to swell the English forces; on the other, the excess fertility of French Canadians acted as a counterbalance in maintaining their relative strength, both in Canada as a whole and in the province of Quebec, where it remained around 80%.

To round out the picture, it should be added that this excess fertility was needed to compensate for another factor, the assimilation of Canadians of French origin into the ranks of the English, outside Quebec. As the French Canadians participated in the settlement of the rest of Canada, they became somewhat dispersed: 16.5% of them lived outside Quebec in 1871, and 23% in 1921. This proportion was maintained in the years that followed. In the rest of Canada (excluding Quebec), the percentage of French Canadians in the total population went from 6.9% in 1871 to 8.8% in 1901, where it remained until 1931, and then increased to 10.0% in 1951. This growth in relative size took place almost everywhere in Canada, but it was most noteworthy in certain regions, as shown in the following percentages:

	1871	1901	1931	1951
New Brunswick total	15.7	24.2	33.6	38.3
North-and-East New Brunswick[4]	40.6	50.1	57.7	61.4
Ontario total	4.7	7.3	8.7	10.4
Southeast Ontario[4]	23.6	37.1	39.5	39.9
Northeast Ontario[4]	20.0	42.6	38.0	41.6
West and Territories	8.2	4.6	5.0	5.8

Contrary to popular belief, then, French Canadians became stronger in New Brunswick and Ontario, and not in the West. They of course participated in the settlement of these new territories, but they lost ground between 1871 and 1901 and gained little back in the years that followed.

The demographic growth of French Canadians gave them an undeniable advantage, from a demographic standpoint: it gave them the majority in the

North-and-East region of New Brunswick, where they went from 40.6% in 1871 to 61.4% in 1951. Other considerable gains were made in the Southeast and Northeast regions of Ontario, where they went from around 20% in 1871 to 40% in 1951. However, French Canadians who settled outside Quebec came into contact with large anglophone populations, and many of them adopted English as their mother tongue. This assimilation can only be measured since 1921, as no general information existed prior to that year's census, which, for the first time, gave data on the mother tongue of persons ten years old and over. In 1921, the proportion of Canadians of French origin aged ten and over whose mother tongue was English was 1.0% for the whole of Canada, 0.1% for Quebec, 0.8% for New Brunswick, and from 1.6% to 12.6% in the other provinces (Henripin, Charbonneau, and Mertens, 1966). Since 1931, data are available for all age groups: the fraction of French Canadians who had become anglicized went from 4.7% in 1931 to 7.9% in 1951. In the latter year, it varied from province to province, between 1.3% (Quebec) and 78.0% (Newfoundland).

Time plays an important role in the increase of assimilation, as this phenomenon tends to be cumulative over generations. Its work is facilitated by urbanization. In an agricultural milieu, a great part of one's life is spent with family members. In addition, these francophone families were often concentrated in certain villages. Migration to the cities destroyed the supporting influence of these concentrations and forced many French Canadians to come into frequent contact with anglophones, both in work and in school settings. At the same time, the probability of marrying an anglophone was greatly increased; this is an important means of assimilation, as the children of a couple whose languages are different generally adopt the dominant language.[5]

As a result, although the proportion of Canadians of French origin living outside Quebec is about the same today as in 1921 (23.0%), the same does not hold true for those whose mother tongue is French; the proportion of members of the French group living outside Quebec went from around 19% in 1931 to 18% in 1951, then to 16% in 1971. It seems likely that this discrepancy is due to the difficulty French Canadians have had, over the years, in maintaining their mother tongue in other parts of Canada.

The relative strength of French-origin Canadians outside Quebec increased up until 1951, when it reached 10%. The peak for those of French mother tongue (7.8%), however, was reached in 1941. Even in New Brunswick, there were linguistic losses: in 1951, 38.3% were of French origin, compared to 35.9% of French mother tongue, which was the highest they had reached for at least a century.

We have already spoken of the French-Canadian expansion outside Quebec. But they also made impressive gains in two regions of their own province: the Outaouais and the Eastern Townships, where they represented a minority in 1871 and where they now have a clear majority. Here is how their situation evolved in those two regions.

	1871	1901	1931	1951
Outaouais	46.0%	60.5%	72.0%	77.3%
Eastern Townships	39.3%	55.6%	71.4%	79.7%

In the final analysis, it can be said that this eighty-year period (1871 to 1951) was a period of expansion for French Canadians. First in their own stronghold, Quebec, but also in North-and-East New Brunswick, as well as in the fringe areas of Ontario bordering on Quebec, although to a lesser extent. For the rest, we cannot really speak of gains; as we will see, outside the regions just mentioned, French Canadians have little resistance against the attraction of the English language.

Of course, all that is not French is not necessarily all of English mother tongue, much less of British origin. The British formed around 60% of the population in 1871. In Canada as a whole, their strength has declined constantly since then to the benefit of other origins, and they lost their absolute majority during the 1930s. In 1951, they accounted for 46.7% of the population, if we exclude Newfoundland, and 47.9% if this new province is included. On the whole, from 1871 to 1951, they lost an average of two percentage points every ten years. In no region, during this period, did they acquire a majority, which they did not already have, except in a few territories where Amerindians were still a majority in 1871. We should not be surprised that, around 1950, many people began to express concern regarding this trend, which had been on the rise since 1921, especially since francophones had been making marked progress since 1931. At the end of the Second World War, Canada was completely settled, and there was no question of immigration picking up at the same rate as during the first three decades of this century. Birth rates were down all over Europe, and a population decline was commonly predicted. It was even possible to imagine that without substantial immigration, the excess fertility of francophones would eventually give them a majority in the whole of Canada. It was only a matter of time.

As we know today, things did not happen quite that way. Immigration into Canada did pick up again. Doubtless, the British share was less than before, but from the viewpoint of English-language supremacy, that was not of prime importance: nine out of ten immigrants of other than British or French origin were potential anglophones. These immigrants of diverse origins obviously kept their mother tongues and, following a large wave of immigration, the percentage of third-language individuals increased. This could, however, be considered an investment in the future for the anglophone community, since the descendents of these immigrants are, or will be, for the most part, of English mother tongue. In 1951, only 48% of the population was of British origin, but 59% was of English mother tongue. Conversely, 20% of the population was of other than British or French origin, but only 12% gave their mother tongue as neither French nor English, and we may roughly estimate that less than 8% of the population used a third language at home.

The extent to which immigrants were anglicized could have been known around the 1950s, through the 1931 and 1941 censuses. But no doubt no one could have foreseen that immigration would be so heavy in the decades that followed, nor above all that the French Canadians were about to give up their legendary excess fertility. In short, the observer of 1950 had no idea that the century-old balance was about to be upset, on a nation-wide scale, to the detriment of the French group.

D. UPSETTING THE BALANCE

The balance that characterized the foregoing period was not immutable. There were many contributing factors, which varied continually. In any case, it is more the end result that leads us to speak of a balance than awareness of the factors that produced it, about which we often know next to nothing (for example, migratory currents by language). We do know, however, that there were two dominant factors: the birth rate and international immigration. The first favoured the French language, the second, the English language. If we are led to speak of upsetting the balance, it is because we know that one of these factors has almost disappeared and that there is little chance of its reappearing, at least to any great extent.

If we take a look at the whole of Canada, the simple fact that immigrants continue to settle here and adopt English in over 90% of cases seems to indicate that the century-old balance is upset, since there is no longer compensation through francophone excess fertility. The only other compensating factor that might be envisaged is somewhat unlikely: emigration would have to be just as great as immigration and almost entirely non-francophone. To understand this a bit better, we must distinguish three types of regions:

1. *The province of Quebec*. Many factors come into play, and their consequences are unpredictable. Most of this study will be devoted to these, and we will not attempt to summarize them here. We will simply mention the distinguishing features of this province: francophones form the great majority (81%) and even in the Montreal region, where some say they are threatened, they account for 69% of the population;[6] international immigration is less to the disadvantage of francophones, as many immigrants are already French-speaking and a sizeable number of the third-language group (around 30%) adopt French; emigration, at least based on recent periods, is very unfavourable to anglophones and even to allophones; transfers from French to English are few and partly compensated by transfers in the opposite direction; finally, the government has already established a fairly strong

policy in favour of French, and there is little likelihood it will return to a policy of *laissez-faire*.

2. *Regions outside Quebec with high concentrations of francophones*. Concentration is high from two points of view: numbers and the relative size of the francophone group, who are found in North-and-East New Brunswick, as well as in Ontario, along the Quebec border. Except for Southeast Ontario, which includes the city of Ottawa, these regions are generally not in highly developed areas and they often show sizeable net emigration; however, this often affects francophones to a lesser degree than anglophones, as we will see in Chapter Six. These francophone communities are nevertheless being eroded by a gradual transfer to English; these transfers are rather slow in North-and-East New Brunswick, but appreciable in Ontario. In the long term, this phenomenon leads to the gradual decline of such communities, although migratory currents may compensate this, as is possibly the case in North-and-East New Brunswick.

3. *Scattered francophones*. The other francophones in Canada are threatened by one dominant phenomenon: the adoption of English as the home language. This is occurring rapidly in almost all areas, although at varying rates. On the whole, each generation of French mother-tongue individuals loses almost half its members to English; that is to say, half of the people who spoke French as their first language (this is the mother tongue) will adopt English as their home language at some time in their lives, generally before the age of 40.[7] We fail to see how these scattered francophones could keep on using French for more than a couple of generations, at least a French language that would have any sort of social significance, without a very large influx of francophones from other areas.

The balance, in fact, has been upset to the detriment of French in all provinces with the exception of Quebec; in Quebec, it is probably to the detriment of English, although, in this case, the grounds for such a conjecture are less firm. Even in the region of North-and-East New Brunswick, which is by far the most resistant to assimilation and language transfers, the fraction of French mother-tongue persons has begun to decrease, dropping from 59.6% in 1951 to 58.0% in 1971 and 1976. It is much clearer in the other regions, as shown in the following table, drawn from Canadian census data, which gives the percentages of people of French ethnic origin (1951 and 1971), French mother-tongue (1951, 1971, and 1976) and French home language (1971 only):

| Regions | 1951 | | 1971 | | | 1976 |
	Ethnic Origin	Mother Tongue	Ethnic Origin	Mother Tongue	Home Language	Mother Tongue
Prince Edward Island	15.7%	8.6%	13.7%	6.6%	3.9%	5.6%
Nova Scotia	11.5%	6.1%	10.2%	5.0%	3.5%	4.5%
Southeast Ontario	39.9%	35.7%	32.0%	27.4%	24.0%	25.7%
Northeast Ontario	41.6%	37.6%	41.4%	35.7%	30.3%	34.5%
Manitoba	8.5%	7.0%	8.8%	6.1%	4.0%	5.4%

From 1951 to 1976, the percentage of those of French mother tongue decreased considerably in all regions, except Northeast Ontario. To fully appreciate the attraction of English, however, it is perhaps even more meaningful to compare the three percentages for 1971.

Take the case of Nova Scotia. The percentage of persons of French origin was 10.2%, while those of French mother tongue represented 5.0%. The difference between the two comes from the adoption of English by people of French descent during past generations, that is, the past two centuries: the loss is in the range of 50%. In Manitoba, this loss is relatively smaller, because the phenomenon is more recent. Let us now compare mother tongue and home language (the language most commonly used at home): the percentage declined from 5.0% to 3.5%. The difference, which is about a third, represents those who learned French as their first language as children but who most commonly speak English at home. This is therefore a recent loss: it is proper to those counted in the 1971 census. Losses in Prince Edward Island and Manitoba are of the same order of magnitude.

This phenomenon is much less pronounced in Southeast and Northeast Ontario, and even less in North-and-East New Brunswick. In the latter region, the figures for 1971 were as follows: French origin, 60.3%; French mother tongue, 58.0%, and French home language, 55.4%.

It is mainly because of the anglicization of francophones outside Quebec that we observe a concentration of francophones in the province of Quebec. In 1941, 81.0% of people of French mother tongue lived in Quebec, while, in 1976, this fraction was 84.8%.

The situation within Quebec is entirely different. There are, of course, some people of French origin who have adopted English, but this is more than compensated by those persons of other origins who have French as their mother tongue. In fact, although 79.0% of the 1971 population was of French origin, 80.7% gave French as their mother tongue (and 80.8% said French was their home language). The percentage of those whose mother tongue was French declined between 1951 and 1971, from 82.5% to 80.7%, as did the English mother-tongue fraction, from 13.8% to 13.1%, although this downward trend began in 1931. This is obviously the effect of high post-war immigration, which increased the relative strength of the third-language group from 3.7% in 1951 to 6.2% in 1971. In the medium term, these people adopt English or French, and their descendents will be anglophones or francophones. Here we touch on one of the key points in the problem of language-group evolution in Quebec. In the recent past, a little over two thirds of those whose mother tongue was neither English nor French adopted English in the long run (themselves or their children). In order for this factor to be neutral, that is, to have no effect on the linguistic balance, one fifth of these people would have to have adopted English, while all the others adopted French.

Up until recently, many specialists thought that this was the only real determining factor, but statistics on migration between provinces given in the 1971 census showed that these migratory currents played at least as important a part as did the linguistic choices of allophones. It was noted that anglophones and allophones lost heavily in migratory exchanges with other provinces, while francophones lost a great deal less.

The picture, then, is not as clear as it once seemed. We will not take this discussion any further for the moment, as a whole system of hypotheses and rather complicated calculations must be applied in order to see the possible effect of the various factors. It should be noted, however, that from 1971 to 1976, in spite of deficiencies in census statistics, it would appear that the percentage of those of French mother tongue increased from 80.7% to 81.1% in Quebec. The English-language group dropped from 13.1% to 12.8%, and the third-language group, from 6.2% to 6.1%. These figures are for mother tongue. But it is also worthwhile to look at the figures for home language in 1971: for 13.1% whose mother tongue was English, we find 14.7% whose home language is English. This difference is mainly due to persons of the third-language group adopting English.

This occurs especially in the Montreal region, where 80% of the anglophones and 90% of the allophones are concentrated. In this region, individuals of English mother tongue totalled 20.3% in 1971, but English was the home language for 23.3%. Conversely, other languages accounted for 10.8% (mother tongue) and 7.9% (home language) respectively.

There is much less to be said about the linguistic development of the rest of Canada: English clearly dominates and is well on its way to swallowing up all the others, except at the periphery of Quebec and in a few centres of francophone resistance. The percentage of English mother-tongue persons rose from 77.6% to 79.7% between 1951 and 1976 and, in 1971, anglophones as such represented 87.2% of the population. If there is doubt about Quebec becoming more French, it is certain that the rest of Canada is becoming more English: French as a dominant language is now only used by a little over 4% of the population. As for the 8% or so who still use a third language at home, we can safely say that most of them are doomed: they or their children will be using English at home within the next few decades.

These trends, both in Quebec and in the rest of Canada, have led some analysts to speak of the linguistic polarization of Canada, Quebec becoming more and more francophone and the rest of Canada, more and more anglophone. Trends observed since 1931 are certainly in this direction, although they are clearer for the rest of Canada than for Quebec. We would thus be heading towards a situation comparable to that of Belgium or Switzerland. It is also possible, however, to get a good idea of the situation by distinguishing between three types of regions: (1) those where French is used almost exclusively (the province of Quebec, except the regions of Montreal, the Outaouais, and the Eastern Townships); (2) contact regions where there are sizeable linguistic minorities (the three regions of Quebec already mentioned, plus North-and-East New Brunswick, and Southeast and Northeast Ontario; (3) the rest of Canada, where English is by far the dominant language. To see Canada as two territorial entities that are practically unilingual is to overlook some 800,000 anglophones in the contact regions of Quebec as well as 450,000 francophones in the contact regions of New Brunswick and Ontario; these figures are far from negligible.

E. SUMMARY

Lacking sufficiently strong inflows of French immigrants, the demographic strength of Acadia and New France was in a precarious state in 1760. Less than fifty years after the surrender of Canada to England, the British population had reached a dominant position in Canada. This position grew stronger until the middle of the nineteenth century. Since that time, the ebb and flow of strong migratory currents has brought about great ethnic diversity in the Canadian population, as well as the settlement of the West and the loss of many native Canadians and recent immigrants who were attracted to the United States by the earlier industrialization of that country. All this nevertheless left French-Canadian representation more or less intact, both in Canada as a whole and in Quebec. For eighty years, French Canadians counterbalanced by their legendary fertility the increases in the anglophone group due to the massive anglicization of immigrants of all origins. The percentage of British-origin persons in the Canadian population as a whole has, in fact, decreased since 1871, but the relative importance of the English language has generally remained the same and is even increasing through the attraction it has for non-British groups.

In the meantime, Canada had become urbanized, and francophones who settled outside Quebec and the periphery areas of Ontario and Acadia found themselves surrounded by an English environment and rapidly adopted the English language. To make things worse, francophone excess fertility is now a thing of the past, and French Canadians are losing ground in Canada as a whole and, indeed, in almost all regions of the country, with the exception of Quebec and the North-and-East region of New Brunswick. There are those who believe that the relative strength of francophones is even declining in Quebec, although this seems doubtful.

The century-old linguistic balance, which could be observed both for the whole of Canada and for Quebec as a whole, now seems much more precarious. This may always have been the case, but it has now been upset in almost all provinces in favour of English, and in Quebec in particular, preservation of the relative strengths of English and French appears to rest upon a delicate combination of migratory currents and propensities to adopt either French or English on the part of those having a different mother tongue.

A delicate combination indeed, since a large part of this study will be spent in attempting to elucidate this problem. We must, therefore, avoid jumping to conclusions, although we can nevertheless mention a few political problems. The basic demolinguistic phenomena we have just described are related to at least three aspects of language policy in Canada: the geographical and institutional extension of bilingualism, government intervention in favour of French in Quebec, and programmes of support for French minorities, particularly the largest ones: the Acadians and Franco-Ontarians.

If we leave aside for the moment some recent and relatively successful efforts aimed at strengthening the position of French in the federal public service, the phenomena we have described make it seem highly unlikely that everyday activities can be carried on in French in the country as a whole; outside Quebec, bilingual people are mainly French Canadians who have kept their original language but often no longer even speak it at home. This group is losing momentum and, in some cases, is on the decline (Beaujot, 1979; Castonguay, 1979a; De Vries and Vallee, 1980; Joy, 1967, 1978; Vallee and De Vries, 1978).

In Quebec, it does not seem likely that the relative strength of francophones will decrease, but the population of Quebec is declining in relation to the population of Canada as a whole, due to fairly unfavourable migratory currents, although these are not a new phenomenon. The disappearance of French Quebeckers' excess fertility might cause a reduction in their large majority if immigration, which favours the English group, was not compensated by emigration unfavourable to that group. It is true that this compensation occurred between 1966 and 1976, but it is not at all certain that it will last, and some Quebec francophones feel that their majority is threatened; this was one of the factors that led to the passing of stiff language laws in favour of French. By the same token, the importance of the anglophone community in Quebec appears threatened. If its members continue to emigrate at the same rate as between 1966 and 1976, and if the language laws cause it to lose the reinforcements it would normally get from immigrants of third-language groups, it seems fairly certain that English Quebeckers will lose their relative strength.

Acadians and Franco-Ontarians are, in general, sufficiently concentrated and numerous enough to carry on for quite some time, in particular the Acadians; however, they often live in regions that are not economically dynamic, which could cause many to move to anglophone regions, where they run the risk of assimilation into the English group. Even where they live presently, they do not always have the benefit of the means necessary to safeguard their language, much less make it possible to have a more active and more complete life in French in their region.

This brief summary raises a number of questions and, for a better understanding of the situation, it will be necessary to take the analysis much farther, especially with respect to migration and linguistic mobility and, to a lesser degree, fertility. In addition, we should keep in mind the particularities of certain regions. This concern will be reflected in the next chapter, which describes the demolinguistic evolution of the various regions of Canada over the past century in somewhat greater detail than in this first chapter.

NOTES

[1] For the period up to 1871, the numerical estimates we give in this chapter are almost all taken from the 1871 Canadian census, Volume IV. This volume is entirely devoted to censuses taken in various parts of the Canadian territory before 1871, including New France, Acadia, and Newfoundland. The statistical tables are preceded by an historical summary in which the author, J.-C. Taché, gives many valuable estimates, in particular regarding Amerindians and Acadians.

[2] These estimates are taken from Keyfitz (1950). According to this author, 86,000 people left Canada between 1851 and 1861, and 376,000, between 1861 and 1871.

[3] The 1851–52 census does give the number of French Canadians born in Lower Canada. This is a rather narrow definition of French-origin Canadians, but there cannot have been many born in Ontario or the Maritimes.

[4] These regions are defined in Appendix *A*.

[5] In this connection, see Chapter Five, which deals with linguistic mobility.

[6] This percentage corresponds to a larger definition of the Montreal region than the "metropolitan area" adopted by Statistics Canada for the census; in that area, the percentage is about 67%.

[7] It is this phenomenon that we call here "linguistic mobility"; an individual's mother tongue is replaced, at some time in his life, by another home language. This phenomenon is studied in Chapter Five.

Chapter Two

Size and Distribution of Ethnolinguistic Groups Since 1871

In the preceding chapter, we gave a general picture of the process of settlement in Canada, showing changes in the structure by ethnic origin and by language and making reference, although without analysing them, to the problems involved. Statistical information prior to 1871 is often incomplete and no doubt sometimes erroneous, although probably not to the point of invalidating the somewhat rough sketch we have drawn from this material.

These data become more plentiful and more regular, if not of better quality, from 1871 on. The concept of ethnic origin seems to take on a more definite form, and a good selection of data on mother tongue and official languages known (English and French) appears with the 1921 and 1931 censuses (Demers, 1979; Vallee and De Vries, 1978). Finally, the 1971 census gives us for the first time—and the only time to date—data on home language, that is, the language most commonly spoken at home.

Such a body of statistical data deserves a more precise, thorough, and systematic treatment than the outline in the preceding chapter, and this is what we intend to do in this chapter. Here again, our object is mainly to describe how these phenomena have evolved over the past century, as the demographic analysis as such will be dealt with in the following chapters. Our main interest is, of course, language groups, but it was not until 1921 that the Canadian census showed the mother tongue of individuals and, even then, children under 10 were excluded in that year. We will therefore only use this information from 1931 on; before that date, we must be satisfied with data on the ethnic origin of individuals, and we will continue to examine this information as well up to 1971. It can be observed that as we go back in time, the size of a given mother-tongue group comes closer to that of the corresponding ethnic-origin group, with the result that for earlier periods, membership in one of the three ethnic groups we use (British, French, or other) is a fairly good indicator of mother tongue.

We must also make clear what the census means by "ethnic origin." The concept of ethnicity is quite difficult to delimit. Criteria based on birthplace, language, religion, and somatic characteristics do not come near to covering all the ground. If individuals are questioned as to their feeling of belonging to an ethnic group, the replies may be difficult to classify and, in any case, yield classifications of limited usefulness for the study of demographic evolution.

To get around this difficulty, and lacking a more precise definition in ethnicity, censuses provide data on ethnic origin. This variable indicates the ethnic or cultural group of the first ancestor on the male side who came to this continent. Apart from the fact that it sometimes only takes the problem back in time, this variable is subject both to gaps in the individual's memory and to errors made in good faith when immigration took place a great many years ago and when the patronymic does not provide a reliable indication (Castonguay, 1977; De Vries and Vallee, 1975; Ryder, 1955). It should be added that ethnic identity may vary considerably from one generation to another, so past considerations may no longer correspond to the present ethnicity of the person questioned. This is why we should be cautious about hasty assimilation of the concept of ethnicity to that of ethnic origin, even if the latter is nonetheless one of the rare approximations of ethnicity possible, for the time being at least.

Language is no doubt an essential factor in ethnic differentiation in Canada. While census data do not enable us to cover exactly the concept of linguistic identity, they nevertheless give us information on mother tongue and, more recently, home language. In 1921 (in which year data are only available for persons 10 years old and over) and in 1931, mother tongue meant the first language learned and still spoken. This definition was modified in 1941 and has remained almost unchanged ever since: it is now the first language spoken and still understood. Home language corresponds to the language most often used at home, but this variable is only available for the 1971 census. Home language takes on special significance when we realize that it reflects a choice by the individual, while his mother tongue was, in a way, imposed on him. If we want to describe a linguistic situation, home language constitutes a much better indicator of the present linguistic distribution of the population than the mother-tongue variable, which refers to a past situation. Evolution over time of the distribution by mother tongue does, however, often give a good idea of what is happening to home language.

In order to describe the demolinguistic evolution, we must in any case make use of the composition by ethnic origin or by mother tongue. We will also examine population distribution by knowledge of the official languages (English and French).

This chapter is divided into four parts. The first will deal with the evolution of the ethnolinguistic composition of Canada as a whole. We will attempt to show trends, although without trying to analyse their component factors, except where changes are manifestly related to identifiable events, such as international immigration. The second section will emphasize the geographical aspects of linguistic dualism; in particular, it will be devoted to describing linguistic composition and its evolution from 1931 to 1976, comparing Quebec and the rest of Canada. In the third section, we will describe the situation of ethnolinguistic groups in Quebec. An examination of available data reveals a regional breakdown of the province into two types of regions: those where French is deeply rooted as by far the majority language, and those where the two official languages of Canada are in closer contact because of the existence of a larger proportion of anglophones. We will see how the relative strength of the various ethnolinguistic groups has evolved over the past century in different parts of Quebec. Finally, in the last section, we will make a comparable study of the other Canadian provinces. We have isolated those regions that have a larger proportion of francophones in order to spend some time discussing recent developments in these regions of contact between the country's two official languages.

A. EVOLUTION OF ETHNOLINGUISTIC COMPOSITION IN CANADA

The great periods of settlement have left their mark on the ethnic composition of the population. To the Amerindians were added first the French, then the British, and lastly a very mixed group, the "other ethnic origins." Since 1871, the population of these groups has been counted, regularly and with more or less satisfactory precision, through decennial censuses.

Statistical data concerning ethnic origin have thus been available for more than a century, while those dealing with mother tongue give us information for a period of about fifty years. We felt it would be interesting to combine these two types of data into one graph,[1] in order to better understand how the two notions are related and also to show the discrepancies that exist between them. In this way, we can study, in parallel, not only the composition of the population by origin from 1871 on, using the three principal groups (British, French, and other), but also the composition of the population by English, French, and other mother tongues from 1931 on (Figure 2.1).

The 1871 census included only the provinces that were then part of the Canadian Confederation (Nova Scotia, New Brunswick, Quebec, and Ontario). The population of these four provinces was then 3,486,000, of which 60.5% were British, 31.1%, French, and 8.2%, of other origins (0.2% had no declared origin). Statistics Canada, however, has made an estimate of the population of the rest of Canada (excluding Newfoundland): 203,500 persons should be added, half of them in Prince Edward Island, which gives a total population of 3,690,000. The 203,500 additional people do not significantly change the ethnic composition of Canada as a whole (excluding Newfoundland), so the proportions would be as follows: British, 60%; French, 30%; others, 10%. These estimates have been plotted in Figure 2.1

Figure 2.1
PERCENTAGE COMPOSITION OF THE POPULATION BY ETHNIC ORIGIN AND BY MOTHER TONGUE, CANADA, 1871 TO 1976

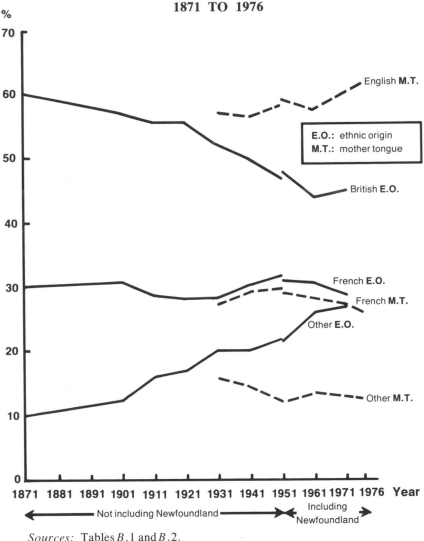

E.O.: ethnic origin
M.T.: mother tongue

English M.T.
British E.O.
French E.O.
French M.T.
Other E.O.
Other M.T.

1871 1881 1891 1901 1911 1921 1931 1941 1951 1961 1971 1976 Year

Not including Newfoundland — Including Newfoundland

Sources: Tables *B*.1 and *B*.2.

The 1901 census showed a population of almost 5,400,000. The great majority were still British (57.0%), while the French came next with 30.7%. Those of other origins, including Amerindians, constituted 12.3% of the population.

In three quarters of a century, the ethnic composition has changed radically. At first glance, there are two basic trends. From 1901 to 1971, the

British-origin component decreased from 57% to a little less than 45%. This reduction of the relative strength of the British was essentially to the advantage of the third-origin group, whose share of the population more than doubled in that period. The impact of migration on the relative strength of the more fertile French-origin group is also noteworthy: this proportion, which varied around 30%, increased in periods of emigration or low immigration and decreased in periods of heavy immigration.

Between 1901 and 1911, following the great wave of immigration at the beginning of the century, the population increased from 5,371,000 to 7,207,000, which corresponds to an annual growth rate of 3%. After the First World War, immigration stagnated until 1919. From 1901 to 1921, the British-origin component of the population decreased from 57.0% to 55.4%; the same occurred with the French-origin population, whose relative strength dropped from 30.7% to 27.9%. Conversely, the third-origin group increased from 12.3% to 16.7%.

Immigration picked up around 1920, but the economic crisis and the Second World War caused it to drop sharply between 1930 and 1945. From 1921 to 1951 (and especially after 1931), the French-origin component of the population was seen to increase, going from 28.2% to 31.6% between 1931 and 1951, while the British-origin component decreased from 55.4% in 1921 to 46.7% in 1951. From the beginning of the century, the fertility of French Canadians decreased more slowly than that of other Canadians, so that the variance between their fertility and that of other groups increased up until about 1930 and remained significant until the Second World War (Lieberson, 1970; Lachapelle, 1980). This excess fertility accounts, in fact, for the growth of the French-origin fraction of the population from the 1930s to the 1950s, when immigration, and thus the contribution of other groups, was relatively weak.

Newfoundland's entry into Confederation in 1949 increased the British-origin proportion of the population, while the other two groups decreased proportionately. From 1951 on, immigration kept a steady pace, and the third-origin group grew from 21.3% to 26.7% in 1971. This gain was mainly at the expense of the British-origin component, which decreased during the same period from 47.9% to 44.6%. At the same time, the French-origin group began to shrink, decreasing from 30.8% to 28.7% between 1951 and 1971. Their excess fertility decreased gradually, while the other groups felt the effects of the baby boom to a greater degree.

One thing should be noted when comparing ethnic origin data from the 1961 and 1971 censuses. Against all expectations, the British component increased from 43.8% to 44.6% between these two dates. Jacques Henripin (1974) has shown that this is a purely artificial and indeed almost impossible development, resulting from a change in the way statements about ethnic origin were made or treated in the 1971 census. He has attempted to make a rather arbitrary correction that at least has the merit of rendering things plausible. It would seem, in the final analysis, that the British-origin group continued to decrease from 1961 (43.8%) to 1971 (42.1%). As for the French-origin group, its share also decreased during this period (from 30.4% to 29.2%), but a little less than what is shown in the 1971 census (28.7%).

If we go on to compare changes in composition by mother tongue to those we have just described for ethnic origin, we first see that the constant reduction of the British share does not prevent the growth of the English mother-tongue group, which increased from 57.0% in 1931 to 61.5% in 1976. The gap gradually widens between the evolution of British ethnic origin and that of English mother tongue. The third-language component of the Canadian population decreased from 1931 (15.7%) to 1951 (12.1%), as well as from 1961 (13.4%) to 1976 (12.5%); however, it increased appreciably from 1951 to 1961, during which period international immigration was relatively heavy. Here, too, the gap widens between ethnic origin and mother tongue, but in the opposite direction to that of English. In other words, it is third-language immigrants who have been the main contributors to the constant increase in the English mother-tongue component, since French mother tongue evolves along a curve more or less parallel to that of French ethnic origin. It should be noted that from 1961 to 1971, French origin showed a sharper drop than French mother tongue, but this does not correspond exactly to reality, given the reservations expressed about the 1971 census; this results from a misleading comparison between the mother-tongue and ethnic-origin curves for French. It cannot really be said that there is true parallelism in the case of French, since even when the relative strength of the French-origin group rises, the proportion of French mother-tongue persons does not increase quite as rapidly (0.9% variance between French ethnic origin and mother tongue in 1931 as opposed to 1.8% variance in 1951). The French mother-tongue population has decreased constantly over the past twenty-five years, dropping from 29% in 1951 to 26% in 1976.

All these trends stand out even more clearly if we refer to the 1971 statistics, which introduced the variable "home language." Table 2.1 enables us to compare the composition of the population by ethnic origin, mother tongue, and home language. British origin was claimed by 44.6% of the population, while English mother tongue accounts for a higher percentage and English home language an even greater one (60.2% and 67.0% respectively). This means that a sizeable proportion of those of other than British origin have English as their mother tongue and an even larger proportion of them have English as their home language. The gap between ethnic origin and mother tongue is explained by changes involving the parents and grandparents of respondents. A comparison of mother tongue and home language, on the other hand, gives an idea of language shifts by individuals throughout their lifetime. The anglophone group displays an undeniable power of attraction, which acts especially on third-language groups, but also affects French.

Table 2.1
PERCENTAGE COMPOSITION OF THE POPULATION BY
ETHNIC ORIGIN (E.O.), BY MOTHER TONGUE (M.T.),
AND BY HOME LANGUAGE (H.L.), CANADA, 1971

VARIABLE	ORIGIN/LANGUAGE			
	Total	British/English	French	Other
E.O.	100.0	44.6	28.7	26.7
M.T.	100.0	60.2	26.9	12.9
H.L.	100.0	67.0	25.7	7.3

Sources: Tables *B*.1 and *B*.2.

It is also interesting to study the composition of the population by knowledge of the official languages; these data are shown in Table 2.2. The Canadian population is made up of a majority of unilingual English speakers: this proportion remained at more or less 67% between 1931 and 1971. It should be noted, however, that it decreased up until 1951, then rose during the next ten years, and finally went down again after 1961. Changes in the unilingual French component were the converse of those described for unilingual English speakers, except from 1961 on, when a downward trend also began. For all periods, the proportion of unilingual English persons is greater than that of English mother-tongue persons (67.5% and 57.0% in 1931, 67.1% and 60.2% in 1971). The opposite holds true for French: in all censuses, the proportion of unilingual French persons is much smaller than that of persons who declare French as their mother tongue (17.1% and 27.3% in 1931, and 18.0% and 26.9% in 1971). Apart from this, the unilingual French component varies in parallel with that of French mother-tongue persons, both of them increasing from 1931 to 1951 and then decreasing at the same rate from 1951 to 1971.

The proportion of persons knowing neither English nor French is a direct reflection of the varying intensity of immigration; the sizeable decrease in their relative strength between 1931 and 1951 (2.7% and 1.1%) is a good indicator of the slowing down of immigration. The proportion of bilingual persons varied around 12.5% between 1931 and 1961 and then rose sharply over the past ten years, going from 12.2% in 1961 to 13.4% in 1971. This recent increase in the bilingual component can no doubt be explained by the decrease in the relative numbers of young children (following the decline in

Table 2.2
PERCENTAGE COMPOSITION OF THE POPULATION BY
KNOWLEDGE OF OFFICIAL LANGUAGES, CANADA,
1931 TO 1971

YEAR	KNOWLEDGE OF OFFICIAL LANGUAGES				
	Total	English Only	French Only	Both English and French	Neither English nor French
1931[a]	100.0	67.5	17.1	12.7	2.7
1941[a]	100.0	67.2	19.0	12.8	1.0
1951[a]	100.0	66.2	20.1	12.6	1.1
1951[b]	100.0	67.0	19.6	12.3	1.1
1961[b]	100.0	67.4	19.1	12.2	1.3
1971[b]	100.0	67.1	18.0	13.4	1.5

Source: Table *B*.3.
Note: [a] Excluding Newfoundland.
      [b] Including Newfoundland.

fertility), since adults are more likely to be bilingual than are young children.

At the beginning of the century, Canada was a predominantly anglophone and British country. In the years that followed, immigration gradually transformed its demographic foundations. The newcomers did, however, give up their languages and adopt English to a great extent, first as a second language, then as their main language. Although Canada is no longer a mainly British country, it is nonetheless still a country with an anglophone majority, and that majority has a tendency to increase. The concepts of mother tongue and especially of home language give a better idea of this situation than the traditional concept of ethnic origin.

B. LINGUISTIC AND TERRITORIAL DUALISM

The Canadian population is made up, as we have seen, of two large language groups, anglophone and francophone. Other language groups obviously form part of the whole, but on a much smaller scale, as seen by the 1971 census statistics regarding home language. English and French account for 14,446,000 and 5,546,000 people respectively, while Italian is declared by only 425,000 people, German by 213,000, Ukranian by 145,000, Amerindian languages (including Inuktitut) by 137,000, Greek by 87,000, Chinese by 78,000, Portuguese by 75,000, Polish by 71,000, and Magyar by 51,000, to mention only those languages most frequently spoken in the home by more than 50,000 people. English and French together thus account for almost 93% of the Canadian population. The expression *linguistic dualism* describes this situation quite well and, in any case, better than the expression *linguistic diversity*, which is too vague and too general.

Anglophones form the majority in all provinces, except Quebec. In 1971, people whose home language was English accounted for 15% of the population of Quebec and 87% of that of the rest of Canada. Conversely, francophones are a minority everywhere but in Quebec, where they form the majority. In 1971, almost 81% of the population in that province had French as their home language, while elsewhere in Canada, French was most frequently spoken in the home by only a little over 4% of the population. This territorial dualism practically coincides with linguistic dualism: on one side, Quebec, where francophones are in the majority; on the other, the rest of Canada, where the great majority is anglophone.

Now let us look at the evolution of this territorial dualism between Quebec and the rest of Canada, first for the population as a whole, and then for each language group.

From the end of the eighteenth century to the beginning of the twentieth century, the lands situated to the west of Quebec were gradually settled. It is not surprising, then, that the demographic importance of Quebec should gradually decrease. The year 1921 marked the lowest point: the population of Quebec accounted for 26.9% of the Canadian population. In the decades that followed, the demographic weight of Quebec increased quite rapidly, due to strong natural growth resulting from "excess fertility" of (francophone) Quebec women. In 1951, Quebec held 29.7% of the Canadian population (28.9% if the residents of Newfoundland are added to the population of Canada). The situation remained stationary from 1951 to 1966, as the higher natural growth rates in Quebec compensated for lower immigration growth rates. This balance has since been upset. The demographic weight of Quebec went down from 28.9% in 1966 to 27.9% in 1971 and 27.1% in 1976. Not only are its natural growth rates now lower than those of the rest of Canada, but its migratory balance has become negative. Quebec still gains in its migratory exchanges with other countries, but it shows sizeable deficits in so far as interprovincial migration is concerned (Lachapelle, 1980).

The territorial dualism of the majority language groups has become more strongly marked over the past fifty years. The proportion of French mother-tongue Canadians living in Quebec rose from 80.9% in 1931 to 84.8% in 1976 (Figure 2.2). At the same time, the proportion of English mother-tongue persons living in the other provinces increased, going from 92.7% in 1931 to 94.4% in 1976. In other words, the French group is becoming more and more concentrated in Quebec, while the English group tends more and more to live in the rest of Canada. It should be noted that the proportion of French mother-tongue persons living in Quebec has always been greater than that of the French-origin group; the same holds true, in the other provinces, for the English language and British origin, which brings out the linguistic, rather than ethnic, nature of this dualism. While the proportion

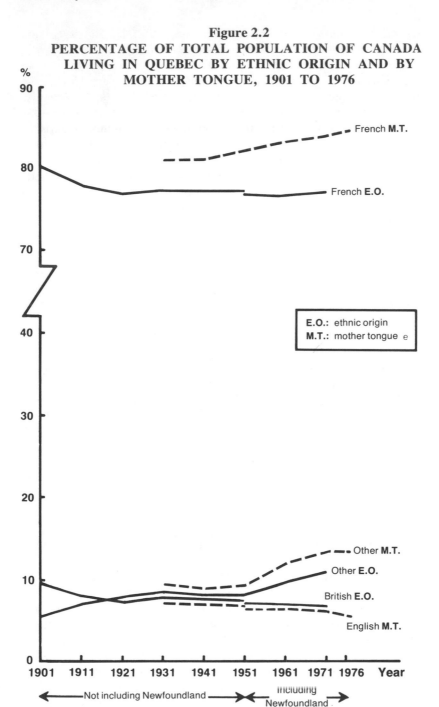

Figure 2.2
PERCENTAGE OF TOTAL POPULATION OF CANADA LIVING IN QUEBEC BY ETHNIC ORIGIN AND BY MOTHER TONGUE, 1901 TO 1976

French **M.T.**

French **E.O.**

E.O.: ethnic origin
M.T.: mother tongue e

Other **M.T.**

Other **E.O.**

British **E.O.**

English **M.T.**

Not including Newfoundland — Including Newfoundland

Sources: Tables *B*.1, *B*.2, and *B*.4.

of persons of French origin living outside Quebec has remained relatively stable since 1921 (around 23%), there has nevertheless been a regular decline in the proportion of French mother-tongue persons living outside Quebec (from 19.1% in 1931 to 15.2% in 1976). This is no doubt mainly because French Canadians maintain their original language much better in Quebec than elsewhere in Canada.

The tendency towards territorial dualism appears much more clearly in the light of data on knowledge of official languages. Table 2.3 shows that unilingual Frenchspeakers are increasingly found in Quebec: 94.6% of them lived there in 1971, as opposed to 90.8% in 1931. In the same period, unilingual English-speakers gathered increasingly in the other provinces: 94.3% in 1931 and 95.6% in 1971. It should be noted that Quebec invariably contains a proportion of bilingual persons much higher than its demographic share of Canada. It would appear, however, that bilingual Quebeckers represent a declining proportion of Canadians who speak English and French, dropping from 63.7% in 1931 to 57.4% in 1971.

Not only is there a very clear territorial concentration of the two large language groups, anglophone and francophone, but, in addition, this concentration has become even more clearly marked over the past half-century, no matter what linguistic variable is considered. This does not mean, however, that the proportion of francophones in Quebec is increasing, nor that anglophones in the rest of Canada are on the rise. To better understand what is happening, we must examine the evolution of the

Table 2.3
PERCENTAGE OF THE CANADIAN POPULATION LIVING IN QUEBEC, BY KNOWLEDGE OF OFFICIAL LANGUAGES, 1931 TO 1971

YEAR		KNOWLEDGE OF OFFICIAL LANGUAGES			
	Total	English Only	French Only	Both English and French	Neither English nor French
1931[a]	27.7	5.7	90.8	63.7	7.5
1941[a]	29.0	5.3	92.4	60.6	10.5
1951[a]	29.7	5.1	92.4	60.2	13.5
1951	28.9	4.9	92.4	60.1	13.4
1961	28.8	5.0	93.3	60.0	24.5
1971	27.9	4.4	94.6	57.4	19.9

Sources: Tables *B*.3 and *B*.5.
Note: [a] Canada does not include Newfoundland.

linguistic composition of Quebec, on the one hand, and that of the rest of Canada, on the other.

In order to satisfactorily describe and analyse the evolution of linguistic composition in each of the large regions, it would obviously be desirable to have a breakdown of the population by home language. Unfortunately, these data were only collected in the 1971 census. We do have, for a number of censuses, the composition of the population by mother tongue. This is better than nothing, but evolution of composition by mother tongue is not particularly sensitive, in the short term, to variations in linguistic mobility, except in an indirect fashion through births.[2] It is possible, in any case, to assume, as a first estimate, that *changes* in composition by mother tongue will basically reflect *changes* in composition by home language, although with a certain time lag. Another condition would be that composition by mother tongue be fairly comparable from one census to another. It would seem that figures from the 1941, 1951, and 1961 censuses may be compared approximately; however, there is some doubt about the comparability of composition by mother tongue from the 1931 and 1941 censuses (which did not define mother tongue in the same manner); the same applies to figures for 1961 and 1971. It appears that the methods of collecting and compiling data used in the 1971 census, compared to those used in the 1961 census, resulted in a slight overstatement of the size of the English group (see Chapter Six). A comparison of the two most recent censuses is also questionable, so we have attempted to adjust the 1976 census figures in order to make them approximately comparable to those of the 1971 census (Lachapelle, 1977*a*, 1980, 1982*a*). Caution should therefore be used in the interpretation of changes "observed" from 1931 to 1941, from 1961 to 1971, and from 1971 to 1976.

Two tendencies seem to remain constant through the last four or five decades, both of them related to minorities. In Quebec, the English mother-tongue proportion of the population decreased slowly and steadily (Figure 2.3), going from 14.9% in 1931 to 12.8% in 1976. This decline is the extension of a trend that began at least as far back as 1871 if ethnic origin, which should coincide more or less with mother tongue up until 1931, is any indication. By the same token, in the rest of Canada, following a temporary increase from 1931 to 1941 (Figure 2.4), the French mother-tongue fraction of the population decreased from 7.8% in 1941 to 5.4% in 1976. In addition, during the past five years, there has been a decrease in the French mother-tongue component of the population living outside Quebec, which went from 926,000 in 1971 to 908,000 in 1976. It would appear, then, that the size of minority groups has a tendency to decline gradually. The phenomenon is, however, more advanced and much more rapid in the rest of Canada than in Quebec.

The French group in Quebec and the English group elsewhere in Canada appear to vary in inverse proportion to changes in the population whose

Figure 2.3
PERCENTAGE COMPOSITION OF THE POPULATION BY ETHNIC ORIGIN AND BY MOTHER TONGUE, QUEBEC, 1871 TO 1976

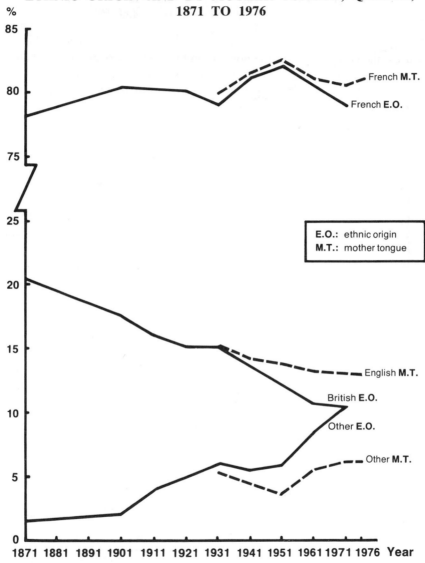

Source: Table B.4.

mother tongue is neither English nor French. In Quebec, the proportion of French mother-tongue persons increased from 79.8% to 82.5% between 1931 and 1951, while the third-language group saw its strength decrease from 5.3% to 3.7%. In the years following, the French group declined from 82.5%

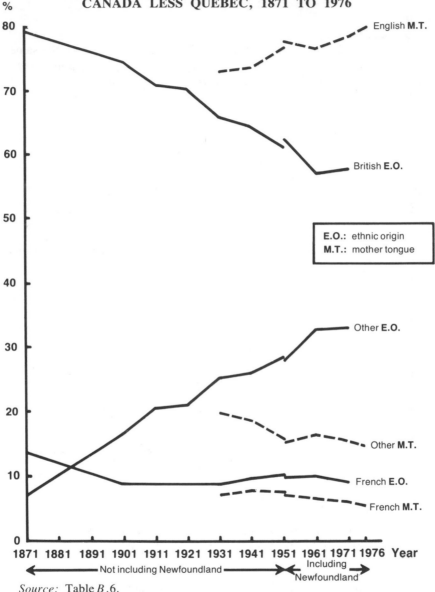

Figure 2.4
PERCENTAGE COMPOSITION OF THE POPULATION BY ETHNIC ORIGIN AND BY MOTHER TONGUE, CANADA LESS QUEBEC, 1871 TO 1976

Source: Table *B*.6.

in 1951 to 80.7% in 1971, then rose again to 81.1% in 1976, while the third-language group grew from 3.7% in 1951 to 6.2% in 1971 and decreased slightly in 1976 (6.1%). The same seesaw effect may also be observed elsewhere in Canada, between the English group and the third-language group (Figure 2.4). This is all a reflection of the important part international immigration plays in the evolution of linguistic composition.

While caution should be exercised in dealing with knowledge of the official languages, we can nevertheless distinguish some trends. First of all, in Quebec, the proportion of unilingual French speakers follows the rise and fall of the French group, at least from 1931 to 1971 (Table 2.4); the same is true for the unilingual English group, which varies along with the English mother-tongue proportion of the population, except for the period from 1951 to 1961, where the former increased slightly while the latter decreased. This type of relation does not appear to be as clearly defined in the rest of Canada between, on the one hand, the evolution of the unilingual English and unilingual French components and, on the other, corresponding changes in the English and French groups. However, it should be noted that the proportion of unilingual French speakers, already very small, has been declining steadily since 1951 (1.4% in 1971 as opposed to 2.1% in 1951).

Table 2.4
PERCENTAGE COMPOSITION OF THE POPULATION BY KNOWLEDGE OF OFFICIAL LANGUAGES, QUEBEC AND CANADA LESS QUEBEC, 1931 TO 1971

YEAR AND REGION	KNOWLEDGE OF OFFICIAL LANGUAGES				
	Total	English Only	French Only	Both English and French	Neither English nor French
1931[a] Q.	100.0	13.8	56.2	29.3	0.7
C.-Q.	100.0	88.0	2.2	6.4	3.4
1941[a] Q.	100.0	12.3	60.5	26.8	0.4
C.-Q.	100.0	89.6	2.0	7.1	1.3
1951[a] Q.	100.0	11.4	62.5	25.6	0.5
C.-Q.	100.0	89.3	2.2	7.1	1.4
1951 Q.	100.0	11.4	62.5	25.6	0.5
C.-Q.	100.0	89.7	2.1	6.9	1.3
1961 Q.	100.0	11.6	61.9	25.4	1.1
C.-Q.	100.0	90.0	1.8	6.9	1.3
1971 Q.	100.0	10.5	60.8	27.6	1.1
C.-Q.	100.0	89.0	1.4	8.0	1.6

Sources: Tables *B*.5 and *B*.7.
Note: Q.: Quebec.
    C.-Q.: Canada less Quebec.
    [a] Canada less Quebec does not include Newfoundland.

Unilingualism is much more prevalent in anglophone provinces than in Quebec. In 1971, for example, 60.8% of the residents of Quebec spoke only French, while 89.0% of those living elsewhere in Canada spoke only English. By correlation, bilingualism is a much more significant phenomenon in Quebec, where it has reached, at different periods, three to five times the frequency observed in all the other provinces together. A reduction of the bilingual fraction was, however, observed in Quebec from 1931 to 1961; during this period, the proportion of persons speaking English and French in the rest of Canada increased slightly or remained stable. From 1961 to 1971, the proportion of bilingual persons increased in all areas (Vallee and De Vries 1978). This may be due, as we have seen, to the decrease in the proportion of young children that followed the rapid decline in fertility during the 1960s.

C. DEMOLINGUISTIC SITUATION OF THE QUEBEC REGIONS

Although Quebec is, in the main, a francophone province, the demolinguistic situation is far from being homogeneous throughout its territory. To better illustrate the heterogeneous nature of language distribution throughout a geographical area such as Quebec, we have split the province into six regions: the Outaouais, Montreal, the Eastern Townships, the Interior, Gaspé, and the North. Appendix *A* gives a map showing these regions as well as an exact description of the census divisions that make them up.

Anglophones tend to concentrate mainly in the southeast portion of the province, that is, in the Outaouais, Montreal, and Eastern Townships regions. In 1971, these regions contained 91.4% of Quebec anglophones (Table 2.5), as well as 91.8% of the allophones, but only 52.4% of the francophones. Anglophones are found mostly in the Montreal region, as are allophones; this region contained 80.7% of Quebec anglophones and 90.2% of those whose home language was neither French nor English. In fact, almost all allophones lived in the centre of the Montreal region, since 85.5% of these Quebeckers were concentrated on Montreal Island and Île-Jésus.

It is interesting to note that the three Quebec regions having high concentrations of anglophones were predominantly British areas in the nineteenth century, at least if some geographical adjustments are made in the case of Montreal. As we saw in Chapter One, the British had an absolute majority in the *city* of Montreal in 1851 and 1861, although probably not in the area that today corresponds to Greater Montreal. However, the economic and social functions of this metropolitan area were probably carried out, a century ago, by the city of Montreal alone, where the British held their majority up until the 1860s. In the Outaouais, the British accounted for 49.7% of the population in 1871, and probably a little more before that time, and they are still in the majority in Pontiac County. The case of the Eastern Townships is even clearer, as we know that they were originally almost the

Table 2.5
REGIONAL BREAKDOWN OF THE POPULATION BY
HOME LANGUAGE, QUEBEC, 1971
(percentage)

REGION[a]	ALL LANGUAGES	ENGLISH	FRENCH	OTHER
Quebec Total	100.0	100.0	100.0	100.0
Contact Regions	59.9	91.4	52.4	91.8
Outaouais	3.6	5.2	3.5	0.9
Montreal	51.1	80.7	43.5	90.2
Montreal Island and Île-Jésus	36.3	64.5	28.4	85.5
Periphery	14.8	16.2	15.1	4.7
Eastern Townships	5.2	5.5	5.4	0.7
Predominantly French Regions	40.1	8.6	47.6	8.2
Interior	24.8	3.8	29.9	1.7
Gaspé	5.8	1.8	6.8	0.3
North	9.5	3.0	10.9	6.2

Source: Table B.9.
Note: [a] See Appendix A.

only inhabitants. In 1871, they still accounted for 56% of the population, and they were only to lose this majority status around 1880.

Up until 1871, there were few representatives of other origins in these three regions, so the number of anglophones should not have been much greater than the number of British-origin persons. Their geographical distribution was far removed from what it is today: in 1871, they were more numerous in the Eastern Townships and the Outaouais together (79,000) than on Montreal Island and Île-Jésus (55,000). In a hundred years, the withdrawal to Montreal has thus been considerable.

Three regions show high concentrations of francophones: the Interior, Gaspé, and the North.[3] In each, francophones make up more than 90% of the population (Table 2.6). The Eastern Townships, as well as the periphery area that rings the Montreal region, are also areas of francophone concentration. These two regions also have anglophone concentrations, as do the Outaouais and the subregion of Montreal Island–Île-Jésus, since all these regions show percentages of anglophones greater than 14.7%. Only the subregion Montreal Island–Île-Jésus shows a concentration of allophones. There are, then, three

Table 2.6

PERCENTAGE COMPOSITION OF THE POPULATION BY HOME LANGUAGE, QUEBEC AND REGIONS, 1971

REGION[a]	ALL LANGUAGES	ENGLISH	FRENCH	OTHER
Quebec Total	100.0	14.7	80.8	4.5
Contact Regions	100.0	22.5	70.7	6.8
Outaouais	100.0	21.0	77.9	1.1
Montreal	100.0	23.3	68.8	7.9
Montreal Island and Île-Jésus	100.0	26.2	63.3	10.5
Periphery	100.0	16.1	82.5	1.4
Eastern Townships	100.0	15.7	83.7	0.6
Predominantly French Regions	100.0	3.2	95.9	0.9
Interior	100.0	2.3	97.4	0.3
Gaspé	100.0	4.4	95.3	0.3
North	100.0	4.7	92.4	2.9

Source: Table *B*.9.
Note: [a] See Appendix *A*.

regions where francophones are the only group with high concentrations: the Interior, Gaspé, and the North. We will henceforth call them "predominantly French regions." They will be compared with the southeastern regions, which we will designate by the term "contact regions." As a whole, these contact regions are obviously regions with anglophone and allophone concentrations; however, as we have just seen, only the subregion Montreal Island–Île-Jésus shows an anglophone and allophone concentration, while there are low concentrations of anglophones and francophones in the Eastern Townships and the periphery of the Montreal region. This means that we cannot simply follow the evolution of linguistic composition in the contact regions as a whole; we must also study each one separately.

Following this, we will describe changes in composition by ethnic origin, by mother tongue, and by knowledge of French and English for the various regions or groups of regions. Ethnic origin of the population will be shown from 1931 to 1971 (and sometimes since 1871), and it should be borne in mind here that the compositions presented in the 1971 census cannot be compared to those provided by previous censuses. Composition by mother tongue will also be examined from 1941 to 1976, since it was not possible to obtain these data for 1931 because they were only available on a provincial basis. In addition, we will show the composition by knowledge of official languages from 1931 to 1971.

We will first discuss the evolution of the language situation in two groups of regions: contact regions and predominantly French regions. Following this, we will describe the evolution of each contact region: the Eastern Townships, Montreal, and the Outaouais, in that order. For the Montreal region, we will distinguish the centre (Montreal Island and Île-Jésus) from the periphery, when this appears useful.

1. Contact Regions and Predominantly French Regions

As we have seen, the English group in Quebec saw its strength decrease steadily, from 14.1% in 1941 to 12.8% in 1976. This decline occurred both in the predominantly French regions and in the contact regions (Figures 2.5 and 2.6). The proportion of English mother-tongue persons in the former regions went from 3.7% in 1941 to 2.7% in 1976 and, in the latter, from 23.5% to 19.4% during the same period. The evolution of the French group is, however, rather surprising. In the whole of Quebec as in the two largest regions, the proportions of French mother-tongue persons generally varied in much the same way: rising from 1941 to 1951, then falling from 1951 to 1961—following the influx of immigrants of neither English nor French mother-tongue—and then rising again from 1971 to 1976. There is, however, one disturbing exception during the period 1961 to 1971: the French component declined in the whole of Quebec (from 81.2% to 80.7%), while it increased not only in the predominantly French regions (from 95.4% to 95.6%), but also in the contact regions (from 70.3% to 70.8%). This was unexpected, since a rapid calculation would no doubt have led to the assumption that if the French position was deteriorating in Quebec as a whole, it should also be deteriorating in any one of its parts and most likely in the regions with anglophone concentrations, that is, in the contact regions. This sort of reasoning is, however, tantamount to taking for granted that population distribution among regions cannot change over time, which is obviously not always the case. Let us examine this more closely.

In any given census, the French component in Quebec as a whole is equivalent to the weighted average of its relative strength in each of the regions, the weight being, obviously, the regional distribution of the total population. Thus, in 1961, the contact regions contained 56.6% of the Quebec population. Consequently, the proportion of the French group in Quebec as a whole should satisfy the following equation:

$$81.2\% = (0.566 \times 70.3\%) + [(1 - 0.566) \times 95.4\%].$$

In 1971, there was a sizeable increase in the fraction of Quebeckers living in the contact regions; as we have seen, this fraction reached 59.9%. The

Figure 2.5
**PERCENTAGE COMPOSITION OF THE POPULATION BY
ETHNIC ORIGIN AND BY MOTHER TONGUE IN CONTACT
REGIONS COMBINED (EASTERN TOWNSHIPS, MONTREAL,
AND OUTAOUAIS), 1931 TO 1976**

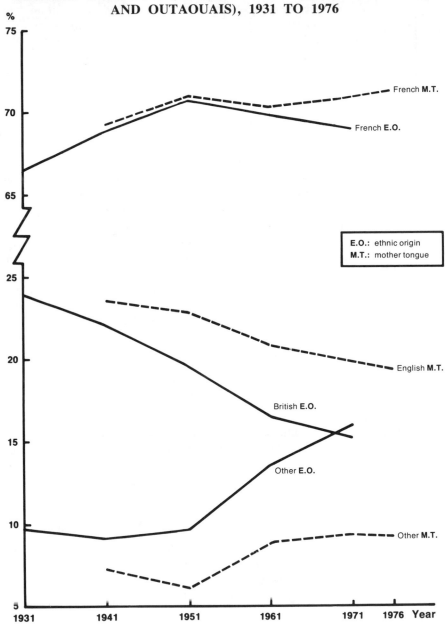

Sources: Tables *B*.12 to *B*.21.

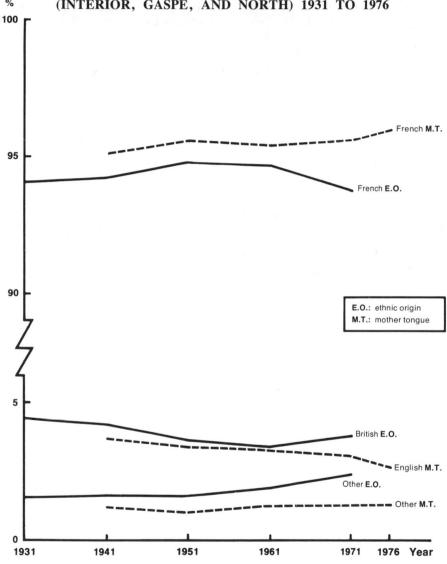

Figure 2.6
PERCENTAGE COMPOSITION OF THE POPULATION BY ETHNIC ORIGIN AND BY MOTHER TONGUE IN PREDOMINANTLY FRENCH REGIONS COMBINED (INTERIOR, GASPÉ, AND NORTH) 1931 TO 1976

French M.T.

French E.O.

E.O.: ethnic origin
M.T.: mother tongue

British E.O.

English M.T.

Other E.O.

Other M.T.

Sources: Tables *B*.12 to *B*.21.

proportion of French mother-tongue persons in Quebec as a whole in 1971, then, satisfies the following equation:

$$80.7\% = (0.599 \times 70.8\%) + [(1 - 0.599) \times 95.6\%].$$

This clearly explains why there is a variance between the evolution of the size of the French group in Quebec as a whole and that observed in the two regions under study. It is simply that the contact regions contain a growing number of Quebeckers.

There are other ways of demonstrating this rather surprising mathematical fact. One of them shows clearly, in concrete numerical terms, the way in which the differential growth of the various groups produces this result. If the size of all the language groups in every region of Quebec had varied at exactly the same rate from 1961 to 1971, the composition by mother tongue would have remained invariable in each region, as well as in Quebec as a whole. If we apply the growth rate for the total population of Quebec during this period (14.6%) to each group, we obtain the numbers ''expected'' in 1971. Then, by subtracting these ''expected'' numbers from the numbers actually observed, we can appreciate the effect of this differential growth of language groups. Shown below are the results of this calculation for each mother-tongue group in Quebec as a whole:

English	−10,100
French	−26,400
Other	+36,500

The sum of these values is obviously equal to zero. As might have been expected, they show that the English group and the French group have experienced growth rates lower than that of the total population. Let us now look at the results of the same calculation for the two largest regions of Quebec (in absolute terms and with the percentage distribution for each region):

	Contact Regions	Predominantly French Region	
English	+ 900 (0.4%)	− 11,000	(5.5%)
French	+157,300 (79.4%)	−183,700	(92.7%)
Other	+ 40,000 (20.2%)	− 3,500	(1.8%)
Total	+198,200 (100.0%)	−198,200	(100.0%)

All groups in the contact regions show surpluses and all those in the predominantly French regions show deficits. This is no doubt largely due to international migration as well as to migrant exchanges between these two groups of regions. The most important point here is that gains by the French group in the contact regions (79.4%) are comparatively larger than the relative strength of this group in these regions in 1961 (70.3%), while, at the same time, its deficit in the predominantly French regions is comparatively smaller (92.7%) than its relative strength in these regions in 1961 (95.4%).

This group has, then, come out ahead on both fronts. Conversely, the English group was behind in both groups of regions.

We now turn to the evolution of composition by knowledge of English and French (Figures 2.7 and 2.8). From 1941 to 1971, the increase in the fraction of French mother-tongue persons in the contact regions was quite small (from 69.3% to 70.8%), while the increase in the number of unilingual French speakers was fairly large (from 41.3% in 1941, and even 36.8% in 1931, to 46.5% in 1971). For the same period, the English mother-tongue fraction of the population shrank from 23.5% to 19.8%, while unilingual English speakers also decreased, from 21.1% in 1941 (23.2% in 1931) to 16.3% in 1971. The bilingual fraction declined steadily from 1931 to 1961 (from 39.1% to 34.4%), and then rose to 35.7% in 1971. This increase in the number of bilinguals between 1961 and 1971 appears to be linked to the rapid decrease in the unilingual English fraction during that decade.

In the predominantly French regions, there has been a slow but steady reduction of the unilingual English fraction, which was never, in any case, very large and which declined from 2.6% in 1931 to 1.8% in 1971. The unilingual French fraction has evolved in inverse proportion to the bilingual fraction. This is not surprising, since these two categories together account for between 97% and 98% of the population in any given year. However, it may be noted that from 1961 to 1971, bilingualism in these regions increased to the detriment of the unilingual French fraction, while in the contact regions, the growth in the bilingual fraction was at the cost of a decline in unilingual English speakers.

2. Eastern Townships

Following the American War of Independence, many Loyalists from New England were to settle in this region. By 1817, there were some 20,000 colonists in the area, almost all of them British (Cartwright, 1980). The Craig Road leading from Quebec City facilitated settlement, not only by the Loyalists, but also by immigrants from the British Isles. The region benefited from a favouritism that excluded many potential colonists, including many French Canadians who were also repelled by a property system that was unfamiliar to them. These colonists nevertheless began to settle in the region from about 1830 on, and according to Cartwright (1980), there were some 12,000 French Canadians in 1861, compared to 56,000 British. From that time on, there was almost an invasion. Our estimates from 1871 on are for a uniform area (as described in Appendix *A*). There were 36,000 French Canadians in 1871 (39%), and 72,000 in 1901, at which point they formed the majority, with 55.6% of the population.

French Canadians were attracted to this region by the availability of land, but also by jobs in the factories that the British (many of them original settlers who had made their fortunes) had set up beginning in the

Figure 2.7
PERCENTAGE COMPOSITION OF THE POPULATION BY
KNOWLEDGE OF OFFICIAL LANGUAGES IN CONTACT
REGIONS COMBINED (EASTERN TOWNSHIPS, MONTREAL,
AND OUTAOUAIS), 1931 TO 1971

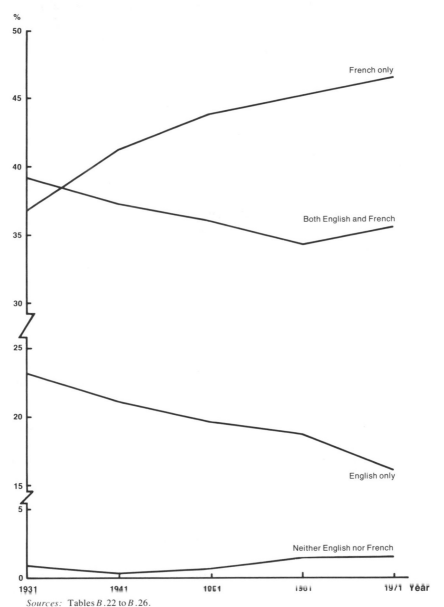

Sources: Tables *B* .22 to *B* .26.

Figure 2.8
PERCENTAGE COMPOSITION OF THE POPULATION BY KNOWLEDGE OF OFFICIAL LANGUAGES IN PREDOMINANTLY FRENCH REGIONS COMBINED (INTERIOR, GASPÉ, AND NORTH), 1931 TO 1971

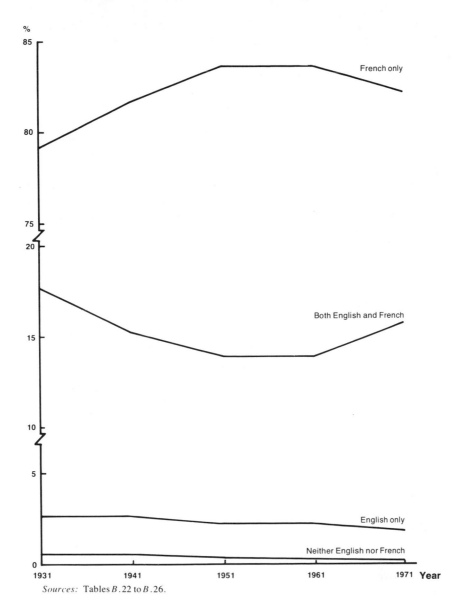

Sources: Tables *B*.22 to *B*.26.

mid-nineteenth century. There they frequently replaced British farmers who had preferred to seek their fortunes in the cities of Ontario or the United States. This settlement was apparently carried out under the active supervision of the Catholic clergy who had always ensured that, in such cases, the faithful had a parochial system not too far removed from the traditional model.

Figure 2.9 shows the astounding growth of francophone settlement in the Eastern Townships. In 1931, the British formed only 27% of the population and, in 1971, only 17%. The English mother-tongue group saw its strength decline in a similar manner, from 24.0% in 1941 to 14.2% in 1976. During the same period, a strong and steady increase in the French mother-tongue component can be observed, from 75.0% in 1941 to 84.5% in 1976.

The trends shown by the evolution of the composition by mother tongue hold true for the composition by knowledge of official languages. The unilingual English fraction decreased from 23.1% in 1931 to 9.8% in 1971, while the unilingual French component increased from 42.9% in 1931 to 61.0% in 1971 (Figure 2.10). The bilingual proportion first increased slightly between 1931 (33.9%) and 1941 (34.9%), then decreased until 1961 (28.2%), after which it increased again to 29.1% in 1971.

3. Montreal Region

The analysis of the ethnolinguistic composition of the Montreal region presents a special problem because of the territorial expansion of this region during the past few decades. The counties we have combined to form this region today would have no significance in the nineteenth century, or even at the beginning of the twentieth. While we were unable to make a detailed study of this problem, we feel that up until 1931, the city of Montreal as such should give a good idea of the evolution of ethnic groups in the metropolitan area. It is, however, possible that for 1931 as for 1941, it would be more meaningful to take the entire island of Montreal. Here, then, is the percentage breakdown of the population of Montreal from the 1871, 1931, and 1941 censuses:

Area and Ethnic Origin	1871	1931	1941
City of Montreal			
French	53.0	63.9	66.3
British	45.0	21.8	20.3
Other	2.0	14.3	13.4
Montreal Island			
French	—	60.2	62.6
British	—	26.3	24.5
Other	—	13.5	12.9

Figure 2.9
PERCENTAGE COMPOSITION OF THE POPULATION BY ETHNIC ORIGIN AND BY MOTHER TONGUE, EASTERN TOWNSHIPS, 1871 TO 1976

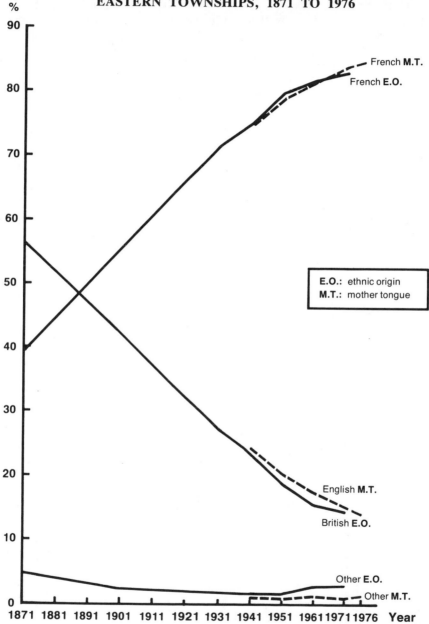

Sources: Tables *B*.10 to *B*.21.

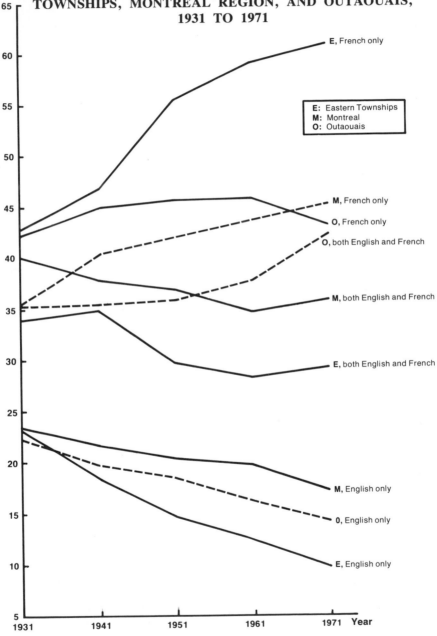

Figure 2.10
PERCENTAGE COMPOSITION OF THE POPULATION BY KNOWLEDGE OF OFFICIAL LANGUAGES, EASTERN TOWNSHIPS, MONTREAL REGION, AND OUTAOUAIS, 1931 TO 1971

E: Eastern Townships
M: Montreal
O: Outaouais

E, French only
M, French only
O, French only
O, both English and French
M, both English and French
E, both English and French
M, English only
0, English only
E, English only

Sources: Tables *B*.22 to *B*.26.

It can be seen that there was a sharp decline in the British fraction for the city of Montreal between 1871 and 1931; this group lost over half its relative strength. French-origin persons, who had a bare majority in 1871, totalled two thirds in 1931, in spite of a large increase in the number of other-origin persons. These trends continued from 1931 to 1941, except for a slight decrease in the third-origin component. This is as valid for the city of Montreal as for the whole of Montreal Island, although it might be noted that the British did a little better in the island as a whole than in the city itself.

From 1941 on, information is available on mother tongue, although the problem of the boundaries of the Montreal region between 1941 and 1976 is still a factor. We will examine this systematically in the annex to this chapter, where six different versions of the territory will be used. For the moment, we will limit ourselves to the Montreal region as we have defined it. The proportion of English mother-tongue persons decreased from 23.4% in 1941 to 20.0% in 1976 (Figure 2.11). The French group often evolved in inverse proportion to the group of persons whose mother-tongue was neither French nor English; this phenomenon is linked, as we have mentioned in speaking of Quebec as a whole, to variations in the amount of international immigration. There is, however, one exception. From 1961 to 1971, there was an increase in the French mother-tongue proportion (from 68.4% to 68.9%) and the third-language fraction (from 10.2% to 10.8%). The increase in the French group during this decade is no doubt a result of migratory gains by the Montreal region from other regions in Quebec. These gains were mainly for the French group, while the growth in the relative strength of the third-language group is probably due to international migration.

In the Montreal region, much as in the Eastern Townships, although at a slower rate, the proportion of unilingual anglophones declined from 23.3% in 1931 to 17.2% in 1971, while the unilingual francophone fraction increased from 35.5% to 45.2% (Figure 2.10) during the same period. The bilingual fraction decreased steadily from 1931 (40.1%) to 1961 (34.8%), then increased slightly between 1961 and 1971 (35.8%). This recent rise in bilingualism was, as in the Eastern Townships, at the expense of the unilingual English speakers.

4. Outaouais

This is another region where French Canadians gradually reached a dominant position in a region of Quebec where they had been a minority. In 1871, they accounted for only 46.0% of the population, compared to 49.7% for the British. According to Cartwright (1980), the British colonists were encouraged even prior to the nineteenth century to settle in this rather barren area, as well as in the rest of the semi-fertile fringe of the Canadian Shield, between Montreal and Trois-Rivières. These colonists were mainly Irishmen, who began fairly early on to abandon these unproductive lands and were

Figure 2.11
PERCENTAGE COMPOSITION OF THE POPULATION BY ETHNIC ORIGIN AND BY MOTHER TONGUE, MONTREAL REGION, 1931 TO 1976

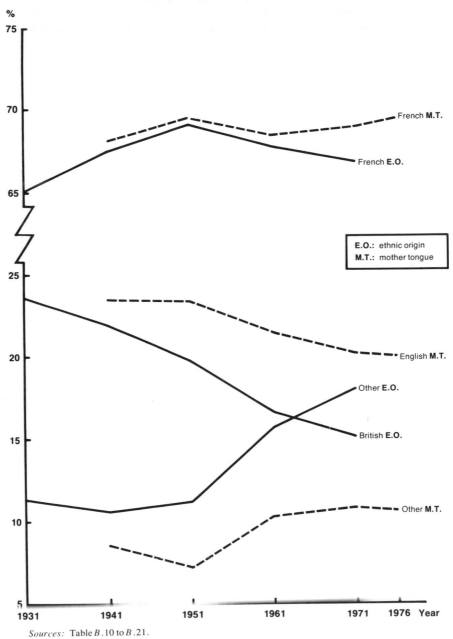

Sources: Table *B*.10 to *B*.21.

replaced around 1830 by French Canadians. The new settlers combined agriculture and logging, the whole remarkably planned by the authorities of the Catholic Church.

These authorities appear to have applied a type of economic planning to settlement that would be the envy of the most interventionist politicians of our time. Colonizer-priests would explore the most promising areas, encourage families from over-populated older parishes to go and settle there, and then do their best to make sure that these new settlements retained the traditional parish structure. This was not always easy, since work in the lumber camps was well paid and threatened to attract some of the faithful away from agriculture and the watchful eye of the clergy. The Church authorities had another concern as well, avoiding ethnic conflict between French and Irish Catholics. They appear to have been quite successful in separating them, the Irish settling in Ontario and the French, in Quebec. Finally, there was obviously competition between Catholics and Protestants for these lands.

Following the First World War, agricultural activity in this region gradually collapsed. The population became concentrated in the cities, and a growing number of those who remained in rural areas no longer made their living by farming. This trend took a sharp upward turn after the Second World War.

In 1931, French-origin persons exceeded 70% of the population, while the British had declined to less than 25%. These trends continued in the years that followed (Figure 2.12). The proportion of English mother-tongue persons decreased from 23.1% in 1941 to 18.8% in 1971, then stabilized (18.9% in 1976). In the same manner, the French mother-tongue fraction grew steadily from 75.1% in 1941 to 79.3% in 1971, and then dropped to 78.5% in 1976. The group formed by those whose mother tongue is neither French nor English showed little change from 1941 (1.8%) to 1971 (1.9%), but it grew rapidly from 1971 to 1976 (2.6%). All these recent changes, which broke with the trends of the past thirty years, may doubtless be linked, at least at first glance, to the development of the National Capital Region.

In the Outaouais, as in the other contact regions, a steady reduction in the unilingual English fraction may be observed; this fraction went from 22.2% in 1931 to 14.2% in 1971 (Figure 2.10). The proportion of unilingual French speakers increased only slightly between 1931 (42.2%) and 1961 (45.7%), then dipped to 43.1% in 1971. It should be recalled that this phenomenon was not observed in either the Eastern Townships or the Montreal region.

5. Some Problems of Interpretation

It would appear that the demographic status of the English group has deteriorated in all regions over the past thirty or forty years. There is one

Figure 2.12
PERCENTAGE COMPOSITION OF THE POPULATION BY ETHNIC ORIGIN AND BY MOTHER TONGUE, OUTAOUAIS, 1871 TO 1976

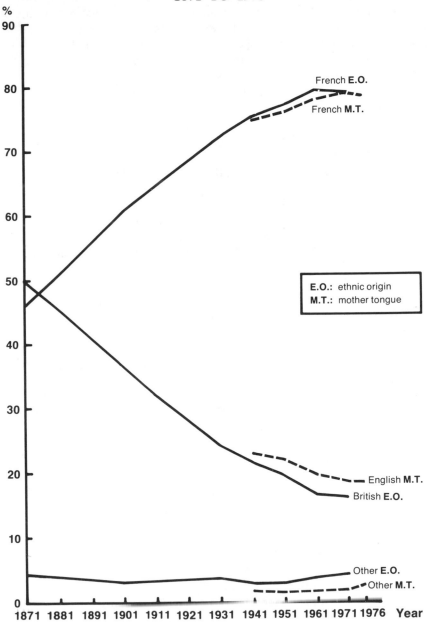

Sources: Tables *B*.10 to *B*.21.

exception to this rule, however; in the Outaouais, beween 1971 and 1976, the proportion of English mother-tongue persons remained stable or increased slightly. In the same period, the demographic position of the French group improved in almost all regions, especially in the contact regions. There were two exceptions to this trend. The first had to do with the Montreal region and was short-lived. From 1951 to 1961, the strength of the French group declined from 69.5% to 68.4% due to the arrival of a great number of persons during that period whose mother tongue was neither French nor English. The second exception concerns the Outaouais and is quite recent (1971 – 1976).

Many researchers, however, have presented a completely different description of the demographic situation. Why should this be so? Four hypotheses may be envisaged, none of which would exclude the others.

a. Due to lack of time and means, most researchers have been obliged to confine their examinations to the situation of Quebec as a whole. As we have seen, a quite different description will result, especially for the period 1961 – 1971, if we compile regional data.

b. The 1971 census did not publish interprovincial migratory flows for the period 1966 – 1971 by mother tongue. For this reason, many researchers supposed, implicitly or explicitly, that migratory transfers between Quebec and the rest of Canada were only slightly unfavourable to Quebec anglophones, while in fact they were very unfavourable (see Chapter Six).

c. Many researchers took advantage of the fact that the 1971 census gave data on mother tongue and home language to limit their studies to linguistic mobility. However, in Quebec, this factor was favourable to the anglophone group and unfavourable to the francophone group (see Chapter Five). But the evolution of the demolinguistic situation does not depend entirely on linguistic mobility; it is also the result of mortality, fertility and, above all, migration. If we confine ourselves to studying linguistic mobility, the picture we obtain of the demolinguistic situation is necessarily partial and incomplete.

d. In describing the evolution of the demolinguistic situation in the Montreal region, relatively small regions were used, that is, Montreal Island and Île-Jésus, or else the census metropolitan area, but in any case not a region that would include all the suburban areas. This brings up the delicate problem of a regional breakdown. We propose to deal with this question in the annex to this chapter.

As we have already seen, the centre of the Montreal region has a home language composition different from that of the surrounding areas (Table 2.6). To conclude this section, we will look quickly at the demolinguistic situation of each of these subregions (Figure 2.13). In the centre of the Montreal region (Montreal Island and Île-Jésus), the proportion of French mother-tongue persons declined slowly but steadily from 1951 (64.9%) to 1976 (62.3%), while the third-language group increased from 8.8% in 1951 to 14.5% in 1976. The English group experienced a decline from 1951

Figure 2.13
PERCENTAGE COMPOSITION OF THE POPLATION BY MOTHER TONGUE, MONTREAL REGION: MONTREAL ISLAND/ÎLE-JÉSUS AND PERIPHERY, 1941 TO 1976

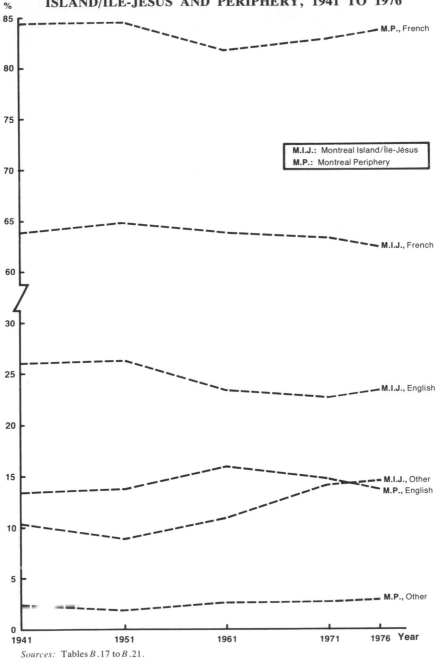

Sources: Tables *B*.17 to *B*.21.

(26.3%) to 1971 (22.6%) and then a slight increase to 23.2% in 1976. If we considered only this subregion, we might conclude, in good faith, that the situation of the French group had been deteriorating in ''Montreal'' for over twenty-five years, while that of the English group had improved since 1971.

It might be noted that the centre of the Montreal region lost 71,000 inhabitants between 1971 and 1976, while the periphery area increased by 171,000 persons. In Montreal Island and Île-Jésus, all language groups saw their numbers decrease over the past five years. The centre of the Montreal region is being depopulated in favour of its periphery, which, moreover, is constantly expanding. The move to the suburbs has a greater impact on the French group than on the English or third-language group. In the periphery areas, the proportion of French mother-tongue persons increased from 81.6% in 1961 to 83.5% in 1976, while the English group decreased from 15.8% in 1961 to 13.7% in 1976.

What, in the final analysis, is the ''Montreal region''? The annex to this chapter presents the reader with a number of possibilities among which to choose.

One basic criticism might be levelled at our description. In presenting the evolution of the various demographic situations, we have depended mainly on composition by mother tongue and by knowledge of official languages. It appears obvious, however, that it would have been preferable to use composition by home language, but, as we have mentioned, these data were only available for 1971. Although it is no doubt reasonable to assume that composition by mother tongue normally evolves in the same direction as composition by home language, this hypothesis is certainly not always satisfactory, particularly when variations are quite small. This remark is especially valid with regard to anglophones. It is accordingly not impossible that the picture drawn in our presentation is a little too black for them. It will be recalled that between 1941 and 1971, the English mother-tongue fraction decreased from 23.4% to 20.3% in the Montreal region as a whole, for a loss of 3.1%. This loss was, however, almost exactly counterbalanced by a surplus of 3.0% in the number of persons of English home language over those of English mother tongue (observed in 1971). This would seem to indicate that English mother-tongue losses over the past thirty years were recovered in home language, although this recovery may have been accumulating over a longer period. This cannot be verified due to lack of information on home language prior to 1971.

6. A Few Comments On Absolute Numbers

The strength of any social group depends not only on its relative size but also on its size in absolute terms. In Quebec, it is the English-language groups in certain regions that are in danger of being weakened by reductions in their absolute numbers. Are they actually decreasing in certain regions?

There is, so far, very little evidence of this. In the Montreal region and in the Outaouais, the number of English mother-tongue persons has increased considerably since 1941. A slight decline has recently been observed in the Eastern Townships; these persons numbered 46,000 in 1976. In the Interior region of Quebec and in the North, their numbers increased appreciably between 1941 and 1971, but there was a sharp drop from 1971 to 1976. Lastly, in the Gaspé region, where they are least numerous (around 15,000), there has been a slow decline since 1941, although the same has been true for the population as a whole since 1961.

These are obviously quite large regions, and it is possible that in certain areas of Quebec, their numbers are decreasing much more rapidly.

D. DEMOLINGUISTIC SITUATION OUTSIDE QUEBEC

Outside Quebec, as we have seen, the demographic position of the anglophone group as a majority is solidly established, and it is hard to imagine what might undermine it. The situation of the francophone group, on the other hand, appears much more delicate; indeed, this group has been declining for over a quarter of a century, the proportion of French mother-tongue persons having decreased from 7.8% in 1941 to 5.4% in 1976. This overall picture may, however, obscure regional changes that are less unfavourable, or even slightly favourable, to francophones. One way of getting a better idea of the true situation is to examine the regional distribution of the various language groups.

As we know, francophones are concentrated in the two provinces bordering on Quebec, that is, Ontario and New Brunswick. In 1971, these provinces contained 81.6% of those persons whose home language was French and who lived outside Quebec (Table 2.7). These francophones tended to live mainly in the regions closest to the Quebec border: North-and-East New Brunswick on one side, and Southeast and Northeast Ontario on the other. These are obviously the regions where the relative strength of francophones is highest (Table 2.8). They represent respectively 24.0% and 30.3% of the population of the Southeast and Northeast of Ontario; in North-and-East New Brunswick, they even form the majority (55.4%).

It should be noted that the regions having a high concentration of francophones all show a very low proportion of allophones. These persons are mainly concentrated in the Northwest and Interior of Ontario, as well as in Manitoba and the northern territories (although in the latter case they have one of the many Amerindian languages as their home language). This means, then, that in the western part of Canada, including the portion of Ontario west of the two regions bordering on Quebec, francophones consistently represent a very small fraction of regional or provincial populations. The same is true in the east, in the Atlantic provinces, with the obvious exception of the North-and-East region of New Brunswick.

Table 2.7
**REGIONAL DISTRIBUTION OF THE POPULATION BY
HOME LANGUAGE, CANADA LESS QUEBEC, 1971**
(percentage)

REGION[a]	ALL LANGUAGES	ENGLISH	FRENCH	OTHER
CANADA LESS QUEBEC	100.0	100.0	100.0	100.0
Newfoundland	3.4	3.8	0.3	0.2
Prince Edward Island	0.7	0.8	0.6	0.0
Nova Scotia	5.1	5.6	4.0	0.6
New Brunswick	4.1	3.2	29.5	0.4
North-and-East	2.2	1.1	28.4	0.2
South	1.9	2.1	1.1	0.2
Ontario	49.5	48.4	52.1	60.7
Southeast	3.8	3.2	21.1	1.9
Northeast	2.7	2.0	18.8	1.7
Interior	40.5	40.8	10.2	53.7
Northwest	2.5	2.4	2.0	3.4
Manitoba	6.4	6.0	5.9	10.1
Saskatchewan	6.0	6.1	2.4	6.0
Alberta	10.5	10.9	3.4	9.7
British Columbia	14.0	14.9	1.7	11.2
Northern Territories	0.3	0.3	0.1	1.1

Source: Table *B*.28.
Note: [a] See Appendix *A*.

Let us now describe the evolution of ethnic and linguistic composition in the various regions, bearing in mind once again that the composition by ethnic origin for 1971 is given simply as an indication, since it cannot be properly compared with compositions based on previous censuses.

1. Atlantic Provinces

There are no reliable data on the demolinguistic situation in Newfoundland prior to 1951, as this province only became part of Canada after the Second World War (1949). The population of Newfoundland is quite homogeneous: between 1951 and 1976, the proportion of English mother-tongue persons always remained close to 99.0%, while that of the French

Table 2.8

PERCENTAGE COMPOSITION OF THE POPULATION BY HOME LANGUAGE, CANADA LESS QUEBEC AND REGIONS, 1971

REGION[a]	ALL LANGUAGES	ENGLISH	FRENCH	OTHER
CANADA LESS QUEBEC	100.0	87.2	4.4	8.4
Newfoundland	100.0	99.1	0.4	0.5
Prince Edward Island	100.0	95.7	3.9	0.4
Nova Scotia	100.0	95.5	3.5	1.0
New Brunswick	100.0	67.9	31.4	0.7
North-and-East	100.0	43.7	55.4	0.9
South	100.0	96.9	2.5	0.6
Ontario	100.0	85.1	4.6	10.3
Southeast	100.0	71.9	24.0	4.1
Northeast	100.0	64.4	30.3	5.3
Interior	100.0	87.8	1.1	11.1
Northwest	100.0	85.0	3.5	11.5
Manitoba	100.0	82.6	4.0	13.4
Saskatchewan	100.0	89.9	1.7	8.4
Alberta	100.0	90.8	1.4	7.8
British Columbia	100.0	92.8	0.5	6.7
Northern Territories	100.0	70.8	1.4	27.8

Source: Table *B*.28.
Note: [a] See Appendix *A*.

group never exceeded 0.7%. The same situation exists, although in a less pronounced fashion, in Prince Edward Island and Nova Scotia (Figure 2.14).

In Prince Edward Island, the proportion of the French-origin population increased from about 10% in 1881 to 16.6% in 1961. This has not caused a corresponding increase in the French group, at least not since 1931, because of the growing number of French-origin persons who adopt English as their mother tongue. The French mother-tongue proportion of the population decreased steadily over the past forty-five years, going from 11.5% in 1931 to 5.6% in 1976. These trends may also be observed in Nova Scotia, where the French-origin group increased from 8.5% in 1871 to 11.9% in 1961, while the proportion of French mother-tongue persons declined from 7.6% in 1931 to 4.5% in 1976.

Figure 2.14
FRENCH-ORIGIN AND FRENCH MOTHER-TONGUE
PERCENTAGES OF THE POPULATIONS OF
NEWFOUNDLAND, PRINCE EDWARD ISLAND, NOVA
SCOTIA, AND NEW BRUNSWICK, 1871 TO 1976

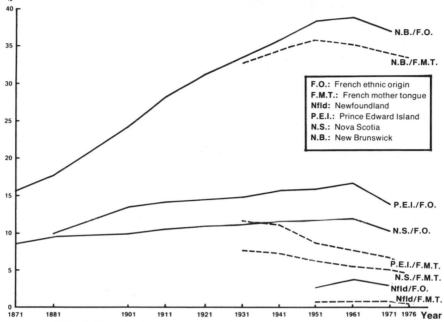

Sources: Tables *B*.29 to *B*.41; Canada, Royal Commission (1970), Tables *A*-8 and *A*-10.

New Brunswick stands out among the other Atlantic provinces because of the demographic importance of its francophone group. In this province, the French-origin proportion of the population increased rapidly from 1871 (15.7%) to 1951 (38.3%); there was also an increase in the French mother-tongue fraction of the population, which grew from 32.7% to 35.2% between 1931 and 1951. Over the past twenty-five years, there has nevertheless been a slow but steady reduction in the strength of the French group, which represented only 33.5% of the total population of New Brunswick in 1976.

As we have seen, francophones are not uniformly distributed over the territory of New Brunswick. In the North-and-East region, they form 55.4% of the population, as opposed to only 2.5% in the South region (Table 2.8). It would thus appear advisable to describe the demolinguistic evolution of each of these regions separately.

In the North-and-East, the French-origin, or Acadian, group, who were initially a minority in 1871 (40.6%), formed the majority of the population in

1901 (50.1%) and increased at least up until 1951 (61.4%). The following two decades, however, saw a steady decline in the French mother-tongue proportion of the population (Figure 2.15), which went from 59.6% in 1951 to 58.0% in 1971. Conversely, the English mother-tongue component increased from 39.4% in 1951 to 40.8% in 1971. Composition by mother tongue varied only slightly between 1971 and 1976: French remained at 58.0%, while English increased marginally to 41.0%.

In the South of New Brunswick, as we have seen, English is far in the lead. Contrary to what we have just described for the North-and-East region, the French mother-tongue proportion of the population progressed from 3.9% in 1951 to 5.2% in 1971 (Figure 2.16) and then dropped back to 4.6% in 1976, while the English mother-tongue fraction decreased from 95.1% in 1951 to 93.3% in 1971 and then rose to 93.9% in 1976. Changes in the size of the French group of this region are no doubt mainly due to migratory exchanges between the South and the North-and-East regions.

Figure 2.15
PERCENTAGE COMPOSITION OF THE POPULATION BY ETHNIC ORIGIN AND BY MOTHER TONGUE, NORTH-AND-EAST NEW BRUNSWICK, 1871 TO 1976

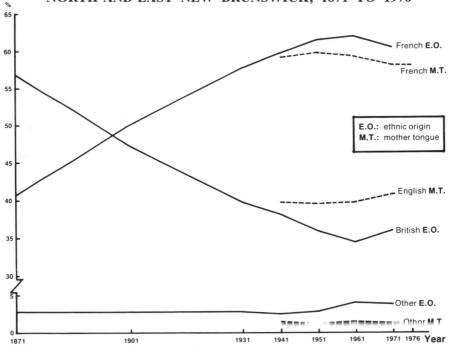

Sources: Tables *B*.29 to *B*.35 and *B*.37 to *B*.41.

Figure 2.16
PERCENTAGE COMPOSITION OF THE POPULATION BY ETHNIC ORIGIN AND BY MOTHER TONGUE, SOUTH NEW BRUNSWICK, 1871 TO 1976

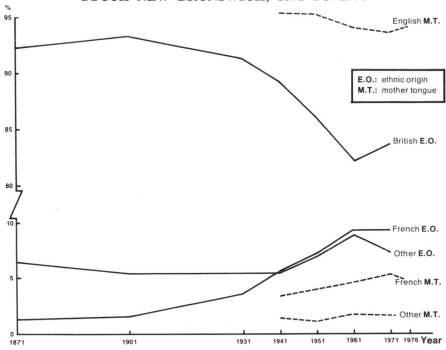

Sources: Tables *B*.29 to *B*.35 and *B*.37 to *B*.41.

Although francophones formed the majority of the population in the North-and-East in 1971, it can nevertheless be observed that the unilingual English fraction (37.5%) is much larger than the unilingual French component (28.8%). Indeed, after increasing from 29.1% in 1931 to 33.5% in 1951, the proportion of unilingual French speakers subsequently decreased until 1971 (Figure 2.17), while that of unilingual English speakers has not varied over the past two decades. This would indicate that the increase in the bilingual fraction from 1951 (29.0%) to 1971 (33.6%) was mainly accomplished to the detriment of the unilingual French group. In the South, on the contrary, the increase in bilingualism was essentially at the expense of the unilingual English group, although they still overwhelmingly outclassed the French unilinguals: in 1971, the first group constituted 92.5% of the population, compared to only 0.5% for the second group.

Figure 2.17
PERCENTAGE COMPOSITION OF THE POPULATION BY KNOWLEDGE OF OFFICIAL LANGUAGES, NEW BRUNSWICK AND REGIONS, 1931 TO 1971

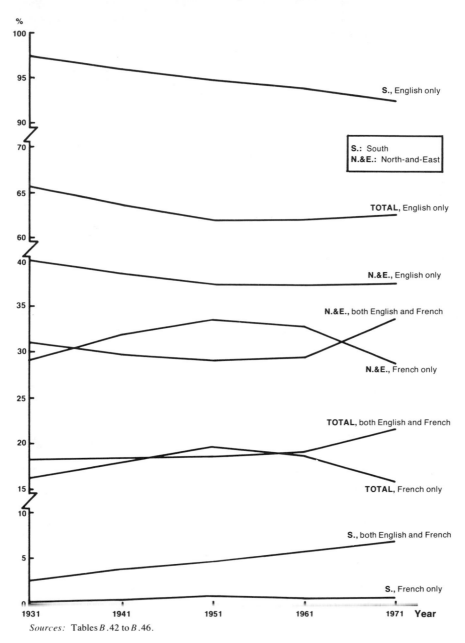

Sources: Tables *B*.42 to *B*.46.

2. Ontario

A little over 50% of the francophones living outside Quebec lived in Ontario in 1971 (Table 2.7). The relative strength of francophones is, however, quite small, as they represent only 4.6% of the total population of Ontario (Table 2.8). In addition, after increasing from 1931 to 1941, the proportion of French mother-tongue persons decreased constantly over the past thirty-five years, going from 7.6% in 1941 to 5.6% in 1976 (Figure 2.18). The English mother-tongue population has evolved essentially in inverse proportion to the group whose mother tongue is neither English nor French. The evolution of the English group in Ontario would thus appear to parallel that of the French group in Quebec. There is one major difference, however: in Ontario, English was the home language of 85% of the population in 1971 compared to 78% for English mother tongue, which is indicative of the attraction of the majority language, while in Quebec, French

Figure 2.18
PERCENTAGE COMPOSITION OF THE POPULATION BY ETHNIC ORIGIN AND BY MOTHER TONGUE, ONTARIO, 1871 TO 1976

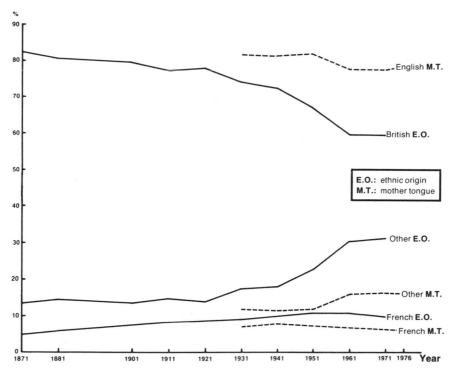

Sources: Tables *B*.29 to *B*.41; Canada, Royal Commission (1970), Table *A*-14.

as a home language accounts for the same proportion (81%) of the population as does French mother tongue.

Canadians of French origin had made significant gains between 1871 and 1901 in the Southeast and Northeast of Ontario. After 1931, however, a decline in the French group was observed in all regions of Ontario, and especially in the Southeast (Figure 2.19). In this region, the French mother-tongue proportion of the population dropped from 37.8% in 1941 to 25.7% in 1976. The reduction is much less pronounced in the Northeast, where it did not begin until 1951. The French group decreased from 37.6% in 1951 to 34.5% in 1976. In both these regions, it should be noted that the French mother-tongue proportion of the population evolved in much the same manner as did the French ethnic-origin population. This means that the sharp reduction observed in the Southeast is no doubt due to a great extent to

Figure 2.19
FRENCH-ORIGIN AND FRENCH MOTHER-TONGUE PERCENTAGES OF THE POPULATION OF THE SOUTHEAST, NORTHEAST, NORTHWEST, AND INTERIOR REGIONS OF ONTARIO, 1871 TO 1976

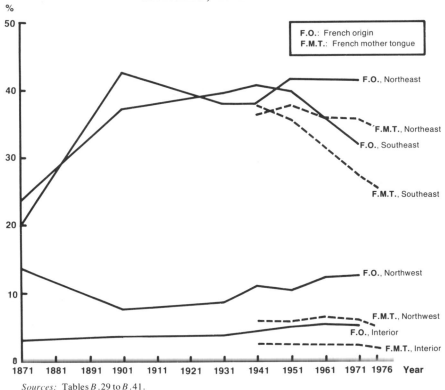

Sources: Tables *B*.29 to *B*.41.

migratory movements unfavourable to the French group; this is surely the case in relative terms and, for certain periods, in absolute terms as well. Elsewhere in Ontario, the strength of the French group varies between 5.0% and 6.0% in the Northwest and around 2.0% in the Interior.

In the two eastern regions closest to Quebec, the unilingual English fraction is relatively large: 62.1% in 1971 in the Southeast, where it is on the rise, and 57.2% in the Northeast for the same year, although with a downward tendency (Figure 2.20). The bilingual proportion is increasing in the Northeast, apparently at the expense of the unilingual English group, and bilingualism also went up slightly in the Southeast, after showing a marked reduction from 1941 (32.2%) to 1961 (29.1%). The unilingual French component has been decreasing constantly since 1951, especially in the Southeast, where it declined from 10.9% to 6.9% in 1971.

3. Western Provinces and Northern Territories

Contrary to popular belief, Canadians of French origin probably never represented a great proportion of the population in the West and the northern territories except, apparently, in Manitoba. In 1871, they must not have exceeded 8% of the total population, and the British were four times as numerous; by 1901, the British had exceeded the absolute majority (55%), while the French had dropped to less than 5%.

The English group has dominated the demographic scene in this vast region ever since, not only in percentage, but especially in terms of recent gains. Notwithstanding a decline in the British-origin component since 1931, English mother tongue has climbed from 63.1% in 1941 (62.3% in 1931) to 79.3% in 1976 (Figure 2.21). This upward trend was mainly at the expense of mother tongues other than English and French; the third-language group declined from 32.3% in 1941 (33.7% in 1931) to 18.0% in 1976. French mother tongue has only slight representation in this part of Canada; moreover, its importance has been slipping constantly for the past thirty-five years, going from 4.6% in 1941 to 2.7% in 1976.

These trends are also found in Manitoba, where the proportions of francophones and allophones are the highest in the western provinces (Table 2.8). Between 1941 and 1976, the English mother-tongue component progressed from 56.0% to 70.5%, while during the same period, the third-language fraction decreased from 36.9% to 24.1% (Figure 2.22). Conversely, the proportion of persons of French mother tongue declined from 7.1% in 1941 to 5.4% in 1976. It might be noted here that while this province is increasingly less British, it is becoming more and more anglophone. In 1971, 41.9% of the population claimed to be of British origin, while 82.6% stated they most often spoke English at home.

Although the western provinces were initially very diversified, both ethnically and linguistically, due to intensive and rapid colonization between

Figure 2.20
PERCENTAGE COMPOSITION OF THE POPULATION BY KNOWLEDGE OF OFFICIAL LANGUAGES, SOUTHEAST AND NORTHEAST ONTARIO, 1931 TO 1971

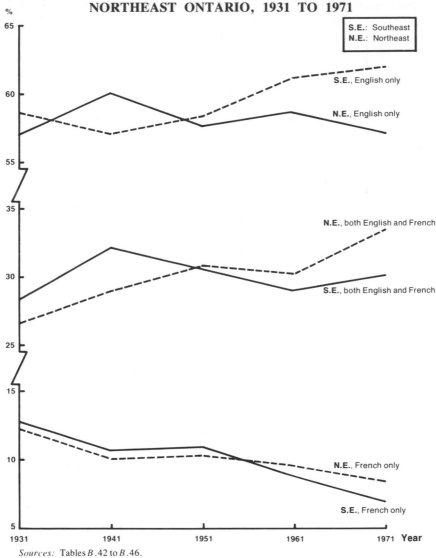

Sources: Tables *B* .42 to *B* .46.

1901 and 1931, they have become increasingly homogeneous with respect to language over the past four or five decades. This is explained by a massive adoption of English as their mother tongue by persons of other than British origin. Ethnic heterogeneity has nevertheless been maintained and has even become more pronounced; however, there is no guarantee that a person's

Figure 2.21
PERCENTAGE COMPOSITION OF THE POPULATION BY ETHNIC ORIGIN AND BY MOTHER TONGUE, WESTERN PROVINCES AND NORTHERN TERRITORIES, 1931 TO 1976

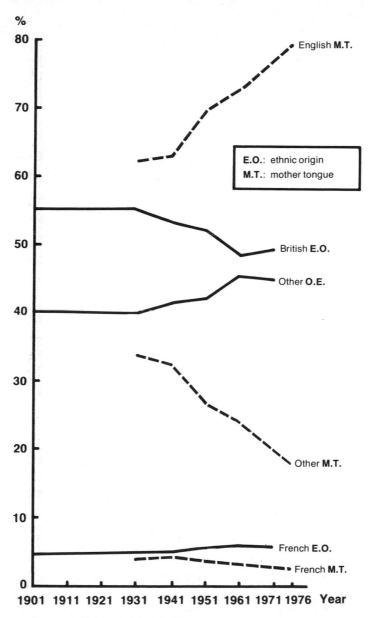

Sources: Tables *B*.30 to *B*.41.

Figure 2.22
PERCENTAGE COMPOSITION OF THE POPULATION BY ETHNIC ORIGIN AND BY MOTHER TONGUE, MANITOBA, 1881 TO 1976

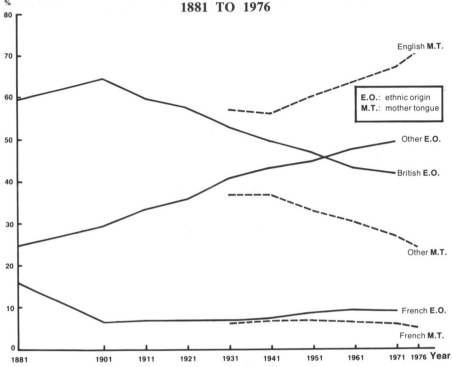

Sources: Tables *B*.30 to *B*. 41; Canada, Royal Commission (1970), Table *A*-16.

ethnic origin is a real indication of his own sentiment of belonging to a given ethnic group.

4. Comments on Absolute Numbers

Outside Quebec, the number of French mother-tongue persons has begun to decline: from 926,000 in 1971 to 908,000 in 1976. This decline has been observed in several of the regions where francophones are numerous: the Northeast and Northwest of Ontario and all the western provinces except British Columbia. In some cases, the decline began in 1961, for example, in the Northwest of Ontario and in Saskatchewan, each of these regions showing less than 30,000 persons of French mother tongue in 1976. A better indicator to consider in trying to evaluate the French group's chances for growth or their risk of decline would be home language. Table *B*.28, in Appendix *B*, clearly shows the weakness of certain regions: the Northwest of Ontario (13,455), Saskatchewan (15,930), Alberta (22,700), British Columbia

(11,505), and the northern territories (725). These francophones are often scattered, which obviously weakens their chances of retaining their language. They are, in fact, rapidly becoming anglicized, as we will see in the chapter dealing with linguistic mobility. There are, however, some groups that are sufficiently close-knit and large to be able to keep up their strength: these groups are found in North-and-East New Brunswick and in the Southeast and Northeast of Ontario, regions that in any case are home to some 70% of the francophones outside Quebec.

E. SUMMARY

We have adopted a purely descriptive approach in order to bring out the principal trends in the evolution of the demolinguistic situation. This approach does not, however, allow us to isolate the factors behind the changes observed, that is, variations in mortality, fertility, migration, and linguistic mobility. Nor were we able to include all the effects of linguistic mobility, since, due to lack of historical data on home language, we were obliged to use compositions by mother tongue; in addition, to complete and round out our description, we often brought in composition by ethnic origin and by knowledge of official languages.

From all this, we are nevertheless able to observe certain trends that have developed over the past quarter-century. The French group is becoming increasingly concentrated in Quebec, while the English group tends more and more to choose the rest of Canada. In Quebec, a growing fraction of English-language persons live in the contact regions (the Outaouais, Montreal, and the Eastern Townships): from 88.3% in 1951, this fraction grew to 91.5% in 1976. Outside Quebec, there is a steady increase in the proportion of French mother-tongue persons living in Ontario and in New Brunswick (76.4% in 1976 compared to 73.0% in 1951). There is thus concentration of both majorities and minorities.

In six regions, the anglophone and francophone groups both form appreciable fractions of the population. Three of these regions are in Quebec (the Outaouais, Montreal, and the Eastern Townships) two in Ontario (Southeast and Northeast), and one in New Brunswick (North-and-East). This is what Joy (1967) called the "bilingual belt." In the southeastern part of Ontario, the French minority has seen its strength decline rapidly over the past twenty-five years; a comparable evolution has been observed for the English minority in the Eastern Townships. The decrease took place more slowly for the French minority in the Northeast of Ontario, as for the English minority in the Montreal region. In the North-and-East region of New Brunswick, the French group, which formed the majority, declined between 1951 and 1971, but maintained its strength from 1971 to 1976. The same was generally true for the English minority in the Outaouais. All these apparent analogies may, of course, be misleading. They indicate descriptive likenesses, but not analytical similarities. The true picture could only be arrived at through study of the various demolinguistic phenomena, that is, mortality, fertility, migration, and linguistic mobility.

What we have examined in this chapter, as in the preceding one, has at least been useful in that it has enabled us to show the present situation in the light of historical trends. Some of these trends go against popularly held beliefs based on mere observation; it is also possible that certain of them speak so compellingly that we are strongly tempted to follow them into the future in order to make forecasts. This would be an error, as we cannot reasonably predict the future if we have not examined all the factors governing the evolution of these groups. These factors are numerous, often complex, and their interactions even more so. The chapters that follow examine the four basic phenomena that determine variations in the strength of language groups.

Annex

LINGUISTIC DISTRIBUTION IN THE MONTREAL REGIONS

1. Definition

As might be expected, there is no universally accepted definition of the Montreal region. The one we have chosen goes a little further than the definition adopted by Statistics Canada for the "metropolitan area" in the 1976 census. The population of that metropolitan area was, at the time, 2,802,485, while the population of "our" region was 3,180,810. Our region, compared to that of Statistics Canada, included, in addition, the counties of Argenteuil, Soulanges, Beauharnois, Saint-Jean, Huntingdon, and Napierville, as well as parts (mainly rural) of Vaudreuil, Terrebonne, Verchères, Rouville, Laprairie, and Châteauguay counties. These additions add less than 400,000 inhabitants to the total, although this figure can certainly not be considered negligible. The reader who prefers a definition of the Montreal region closer to that used in the census could refer to Region IV, defined below, which would be quite similar. Our region is, however, smaller than the "census region" proposed by the Quebec Planning and Development Bureau (Office de planification et de développement du Québec) (Quebec, O.P.D.Q., 1976), which in 1976 had a population of 3,532,280 (Region VI described below).

The problem is even more complicated because the boundaries of this region have changed over time. If we keep to the Statistics Canada definition, the "metropolitan area" of Montreal in 1941 included little more than Montreal Island and Île-Jésus. According to that year's census, the metropolitan area had a population of 1,139,121: Montreal Island had 1,116,800 residents, and if we add Île-Jésus, which had only 21,631, the total is 1,138,431, or very close to the population given for the metropolitan area. Of course, the boundaries of the metropolitan area do not necessarily correspond to the combined area of the two islands, and these indications are only given to clarify the figures.

In order to trace the evolution of the situation in "Montreal," we would ideally have to continually modify the boundaries of that region, at the cost of a more or less arbitrary decision at each new census. The problem is even more delicate because linguistic distribution would not be the same for all sets of boundaries. The larger the territory, the greater the proportion of francophones; thus, in 1976, the fraction of French mother-tongue persons is only 59.7% if we consider only Montreal Island, 69.4% if we adopt our regional definition, and 71.6% if we add nine more counties (Region VI).

We do not propose to cut all these Gordian knots, but rather to maintain a certain degree of neutrality in determining the evolution of linguistic distribution since 1941 for six different definitions of the Montreal region. Indeed, one of the remarkable results of this exercise is that no matter which definition is chosen, the situation almost always evolves in the same direction: the English language has been losing ground since 1961, while French has been gaining, except if we limit our analysis to Montreal Island and Île-Jésus. The other languages have been gaining ground since 1951, but their progress is beginning to slow down.

Let us now define our six regions. They are all formed by the combination of census divisions (in this case, counties). From smallest to largest, here then are the census divisions that must be added, with their populations in 1976:

Region Number	Census Division Added	Population Added in 1976	Total Population in 1976
I	Montreal Island	1,869,640	1,869,640
II	Île-Jésus	246,240	2,115,880
III	Chambly and Laprairie	370,345	2,486,225
IV	Châteauguay, Deux-Montagnes, L'Assomption, Terrebonne, and Vaudreuil	409,555	2,895,780
V	Argenteuil, Beauharnois, Huntingdon, Iberville, Napierville, Rouville, Saint-Jean, Soulanges, and Verchères	285,030	3,180,810
VI	Bagot, Berthier, Brome, Joliette, Missisquoi, Montcalm, Richelieu, Saint-Hyacinthe, and Shefford	351,470	3,532,280

The region we have adopted, in general, is Region V, which is in between the census metropolitan area used by Statistics Canada and the administrative region of Montreal, approximately as proposed by the O.P.D.Q. We have on occasion split the region into two parts, the centre (Montreal Island and Île-Jésus) and the periphery (the other sixteen divisions). Some readers might prefer another definition, but it seemed to us that if we want to get a clear, overall picture of the Montreal agglomeration, the lowest we could go would be Region IV.

2. Mother Tongue

Figures 2.A.1 to 2.A.3 illustrate the evolution of the relative size of each language group.[4] This can be most clearly seen for the English group: no matter which regional definition is used, the fraction of persons with this mother tongue decreases over the period as a whole. For the three smallest areas, however, there is an increase between 1971 and 1976, and the smaller the region, the greater the increase. It should be recalled that in 1976, the question on mother tongue was answered in such a way that the English strength was overstated, and this could mean that the increase shown between

Figure 2.A.1
PERCENTAGE OF ENGLISH MOTHER-TONGUE PERSONS FOR SIX DIFFERENT DEFINITIONS OF THE MONTREAL REGION, 1941 TO 1976

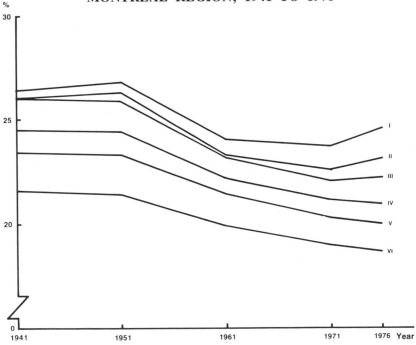

Sources: Census of Canada, 1941, 1951, 1961, 1971, and 1976.

1971 and 1976 is partly artificial (see Chapter Six, and Lachapelle and Gervais, 1982). The fact remains that English did lose ground during this period in Regions IV to VI. It appears obvious that English mother-tongue persons have tended to be concentrated in the two central islands, especially Montreal Island. As we adopt more and more "realistic" definitions of the Montreal agglomeration, the decline is seen to continue.

The French mother-tongue group made gains between 1941 and 1951 and experienced losses between 1951 and 1961, no matter what regional definition we use. The decrease in the latter period is essentially due to the growth in the third-language group, which accompanied the high immigration of that period. Following 1961, there is a considerable decline in Regions I and II, as French mother-tongue persons tended to move to the periphery. This is clearly illustrated by the fact that the proportion of these persons in Regions IV and VI has increased.

The percentage of third-language persons has become a significant factor in all regions. These persons also tend to be concentrated on the two

Figure 2.A.2
PERCENTAGE OF FRENCH MOTHER-TONGUE PERSONS
FOR SIX DIFFERENT DEFINITIONS OF THE
MONTREAL REGION, 1941 TO 1976

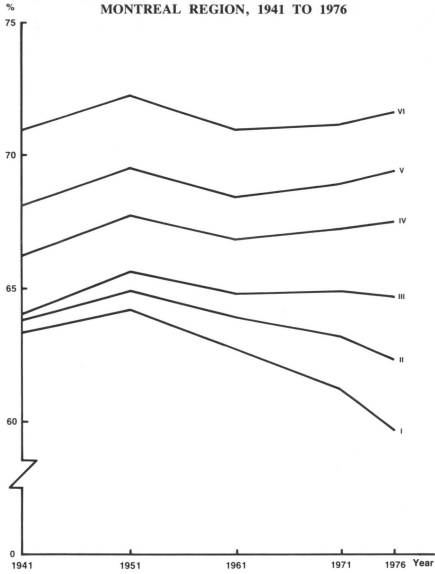

Sources: Same as for Figure 2.A.1.

islands, to an even greater degree than the English-language persons. It should be added here that their numbers are probably underestimated for 1976. If it were possible to correct this, their strength might be shown to have

Figure 2.A.3
PERCENTAGE OF OTHER MOTHER-TONGUE PERSONS
FOR SIX DIFFERENT DEFINITIONS OF THE
MONTREAL REGION, 1941 TO 1976

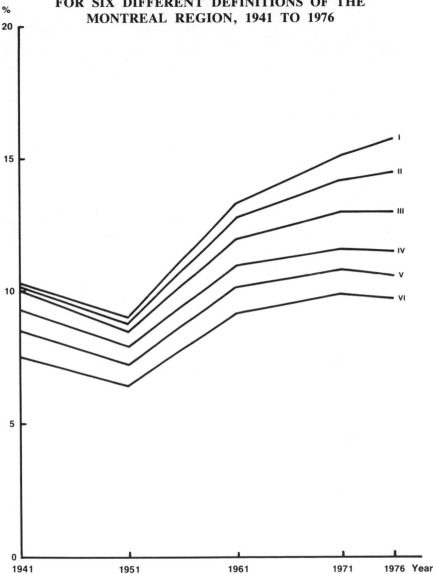

Sources: Same as for Figure 2.*A*.1.

increased up to 1976 in all regions. There was, nevertheless, a real slow-down in their relative growth, particularly if we adopt a larger definition of the Montreal region.

One additional point should be made here, to take into account the expansion of the Montreal area between 1941 and 1976. Generally speaking, the evolution is from Region II to Region V, and we must consequently move progressively from Curve II to Curve V in order to follow this evolution. If we do this, English mother tongue decreases from 26% to 20%, while French mother tongue increases from 64% to 69%, and other languages increase from 10% to 11%. Some readers may prefer to finish up on Curve IV or Curve VI; this will make little difference in the overall trends. All in all, it is hard to see how it can be claimed that the French language has lost its relative importance in the Montreal region over the past quarter-century.

3. Knowledge of English and French

The trends, in this connection, are quite clear, as may be seen from Figures 2.*A*.4 to 2.*A*.6. The curves on each graph are remarkably parallel, which means that variations are much the same no matter what definition of the region is used. For the period as a whole, unilingual French speakers gained approximately nine percentage points, unilingual English speakers lost about five, and bilinguals almost as much (the group of those who knew neither English nor French increased by almost a point). It should be noted that there was a slight improvement in bilingualism between 1961 and 1971, although this can probably be explained by the relative reduction in the number of young children, who are more rarely bilingual.

A progressive shift from Curve II to Curve V would yield the following results: a reduction in the strength of unilingual English speakers from 26.3% in 1931 to 17.2% in 1971; a reduction in the percentage of bilingual persons from 43.5% to 35.8%; and an increase in the percentage of French unilingual persons from 29.0% to 45.2%.

4. Conclusion

These trends were a surprise to us, as they will no doubt be to many of our readers. It might have been imagined that if, in Quebec as a whole, the francophone fraction was heading for, or already in, a period of decline, in Montreal, in any event, the situation was clear: there could be no question but that their share of the population was decreasing. This was asserted on the basis of perfectly reliable statistics, but using a definition of the Montreal region that appears somewhat limited. All we have to do is adopt a reasonable definition of this region, and the case is clear indeed, except that it is French that is making progress and not English.

If we consider mother tongue, English only shows an increase for the most limited definitions of the Montreal region, and then only between 1971

Figure 2.A.4
PERCENTAGE OF PERSONS KNOWING ONLY ENGLISH
FOR SIX DIFFERENT DEFINITIONS OF THE
MONTREAL REGION, 1931 TO 1971

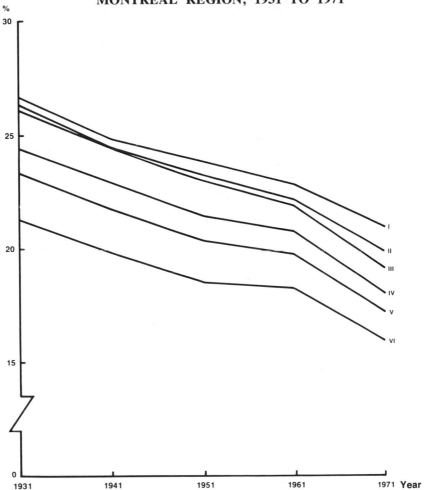

Sources: Census of Canada, 1931, 1941, 1951, 1961, and 1971.

and 1976. In addition, there is a very good chance that this increase in the relative strength of English as a mother tongue is due to shifts in mother tongue[5] between 1971 and 1976 attributable to the particular circumstances of that period. As for French, apart from the period 1951−1961, its relative strength increased, except in the central part of the Montreal region. The other languages saw their relative strength grow from 1951 on, especially on Montreal Island. This growth is due to high immigration rates during the

Figure 2.A.5
PERCENTAGE OF PERSONS KNOWING ONLY FRENCH FOR SIX DIFFERENT DEFINITIONS OF THE MONTREAL REGION, 1931 TO 1971

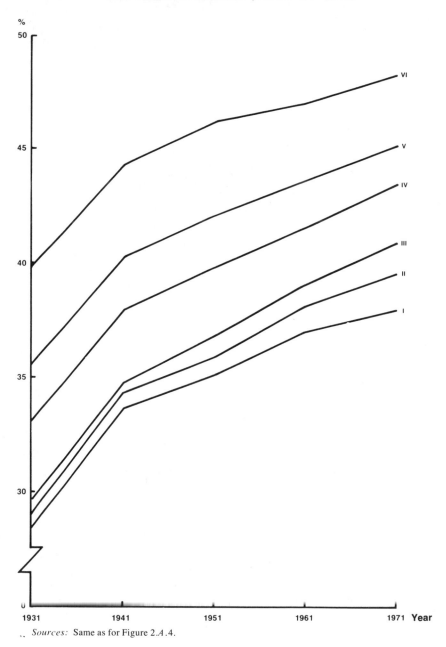

Sources: Same as for Figure 2.*A*.4.

Figure 2.A.6
PERCENTAGE OF PERSONS KNOWING BOTH FRENCH AND ENGLISH FOR SIX DIFFERENT DEFINITIONS OF THE MONTREAL REGION, 1931 TO 1971

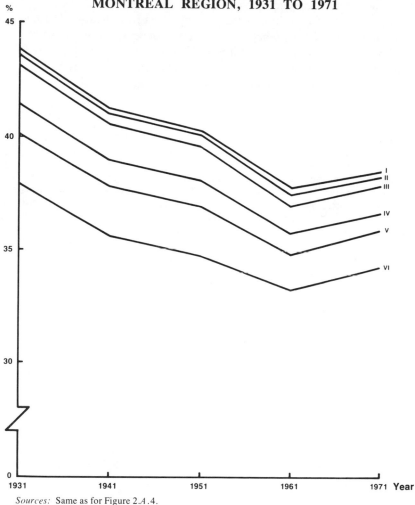

Sources: Same as for Figure 2.*A*.4.

period 1951–1971. In the enlarged Montreal region, the third-language group nevertheless declined slightly from 1971 to 1976, probably due to shifts to English mother tongue. It should be noted that a great many persons whose mother tongue was neither French nor English have already chosen one of these languages as their home language, and their descendants will become part of the English or French mother-tongue group. In the past, these shifts indubitably tended to favour English over French. Despite this, French has nonetheless gained ground.

If we turn our attention to the breakdown by knowledge of English and French, the upswing in French unilingualism and the decline in English unilingualism could not be clearer, and it is hard to see what artifice could explain such clearly marked and persistent trends.

The conclusion to all this is that over the past forty years, Montreal has become more and more French. This may not necessarily hold true for the future, but it would require a great effort, in our view, to find trends in the recent past that are favourable to English, at least in so far as the evolution of the relative strength of each language group is concerned.

NOTES

[1] The figures in this chapter (except those in the Annex) were plotted using the statistical tables in Appendix *B*.

[2] A person whose mother tongue is x and who adopts another language at some point in his lifetime will always keep x as his mother tongue and be classified accordingly (unless he can no longer understand it). His children, however, if they learn the new language first, will have that new language as their mother tongue. It is through the children that the language transfer will take place.

[3] In a sense, there is a concentration of francophones almost everywhere in Quebec. We give a special meaning to this term, however: we may say that a group is concentrated in a particular region of a larger territory when the fraction this group represents in the region considered is greater than the fraction it represents in the territory as a whole. More concretely, this means that a region of Quebec is said to have a concentration of francophones when the francophone component in that region is greater than 80.8%. If we were speaking of Canada as a whole, all regions having more than 25.7% francophones would be said to have concentrations of francophones.

[4] The figures that appear in this Annex were prepared using data taken from tables published in the various censuses.

[5] See the discussion in Chapter Six.

Part Two

Demolinguistic Phenomena

Chapter Three

Mortality

Through the death statistics and life tables that Statistics Canada has now been publishing regularly for over forty years, we have a fairly good idea of the extent and evolution of mortality variations at the provincial level. It is more difficult, however, to assess differences in mortality between language groups, due to lack of data. We are consequently obliged to do our best with what is available.

Two different types of approach are often used to evaluate differences in mortality between language groups. The first is based on the idea that if there are appreciable differences in mortality between, for example, francophones and anglophones, these should show up when we compare the mortality of predominantly French regions with that of regions having high proportions of anglophones. This approach obviously gives rise to some rather delicate methodological questions, but it does enable us to draw conclusions under certain conditions. This is the method we will use, with all due precautions, in the first section. Apart from regional data on mortality, we also have information that allows us to evaluate mortality by ethnic origin. The second approach is based on the hypothesis that the mortality of the French-origin population is equal to that of francophones; this hypothesis appears quite acceptable, especially for Quebec. It is, however, more difficult to admit that the mortality of the British-origin population can be identified with that of anglophones, due to the ethnic diversity of the English-language population. This is why, in the second section, we will confine ourselves to comparing, for Quebec only, the mortality of the French-origin population to that of the rest of the population.

To assess differences in mortality between populations, the normal method is to compare average lifespan (or life expectancy at birth). Although such indices are a reasonably good reflection of inequality with respect to death, they do not allow us to pin-point the effects of differential mortality on demographic growth. For this reason, in the last section, we will consider instead an index of excess fertility, which cancels out the unfavourable effects of excess mortality on demographic growth.

A. REGIONAL VARIANCES

If we wish to make a rapid evaluation of differences in mortality between language groups, we can compare the mortality of regions that present contrasting linguistic compositions. It is obvious that the differences shown in these comparisons are not only the result of variations in linguistic composition; they also depend on a number of other factors, whose variations are linked to variations in linguistic composition. This remark is an indication of the difficulties involved in determining the causes of differential mortality. As a consequence, in the pages that follow, we will confine ourselves to assessing differences in mortality between francophones and anglophones, whatever the causes may be. To do this, we will first compare Quebec mortality to that of Ontario and then, within the census metropolitan area of Montreal, the mortality of zones having high proportions of francophones to that of zones having low proportions of francophones.

In Ontario, the English mother-tongue proportion of the population varied between 77% and 82% over the past forty years, while in Quebec, the French mother-tongue proportion of the population hovered between 79% and 83% during the period 1931−1976. This means that if there are noteworthy differences between anglophone and francophone mortality, these should show up when we compare the mortality of Ontario to that of Quebec.

Table 3.1 shows life expectancy at birth for men and women in Ontario and Quebec from 1931 to 1976. We can see the great progress that has been made in combatting death: in Ontario, average life expectancy increased by 9.3 years for men and 13.8 years for women between 1931 and 1976, while in Quebec it had increased by 12.9 years for men and 18.7 years for women during the same period. Gains by women largely exceed those of men: the differences between the average lifespans of women and men increased from 1.6 and 2.6 years respectively in Quebec and Ontario in 1931 to 7.4 and 7.1 years in 1976. This is not a purely Canadian phenomenon, but can be observed in many other countries (I.N.E.D., 1977; Preston, 1977). But while there has been an increase in the difference in mortality between the sexes, the variances between average lifespans in Ontario and Quebec have narrowed: for men, this variance declined from 5.1 years in 1931 to 1.5 years in 1976, while for women, it decreased from 6.1 years to 1.2 years. It should be noted, however, that after declining from 1931 to 1966, the difference between the average life expectancies of Ontario and Quebec men has increased over the past ten years, while continuing to decrease slightly for women.

Although Quebec is still trailing Ontario in so far as the battle against death is concerned, the average life expectancy of Quebeckers, both men and women, is nonetheless quite close to that of French men and women (Table 3.1); life expectancy at birth for the Quebec population was also slightly

Table 3.1
EVOLUTION OF LIFE EXPECTANCY AT BIRTH, CANADA, FRANCE, GREAT BRITAIN, ONTARIO, AND QUEBEC, 1931–1976
(in years)

YEAR	CANADA	FRANCE	GREAT BRITAIN	ONTARIO	QUEBEC	ONTARIO MINUS GREAT BRITAIN (4)−(3)	QUEBEC MINUS FRANCE (5)−(2)	ONTARIO MINUS QUEBEC (4)−(5)
	(1)	(2)	(3)	(4)	(5)	(6)	(7)	(8)
Males								
1931[a]	60.0	54.5	58.4	61.3	56.2	2.9	1.7	5.1
1951	66.3	63.2	66.2	66.9	64.4	0.7	1.2	2.5
1961	68.4	67.5	67.9	68.3	67.3	0.4	−0.2	1.0
1966	68.8	67.7	68.5	68.7	67.9	0.2	0.2	0.8
1971	69.3	68.3	68.6	69.6	68.3	1.0	0.0	1.3
1976[b]	70.2	69.0	69.3	70.6	69.1	1.3	0.1	1.5
Females								
1931[a]	62.1	59.1	62.5	63.9	57.8	1.4	−1.3	6.1
1951	70.8	68.8	71.2	71.9	68.6	0.7	−0.2	3.3
1961	74.2	74.3	73.8	74.4	72.8	0.6	−1.5	1.6
1966	75.2	75.1	74.7	75.5	73.9	0.8	−1.2	1.6
1971	76.4	75.9	74.9	76.8	75.3	1.9	−0.6	1.5
1976[b]	77.5	76.9	75.6	77.7	76.5	2.1	−0.4	1.2

Sources: Canada (1978); Great Britain (1974, 1977); I.N.E.D. (1977).
Note: [a] Canada did not include Newfoundland in 1931.
  [b] Figures for France correspond to 1975 and those for Great Britain, to 1974.

greater at the beginning of the 1970s than the average for European and Anglo-Saxon countries (Vallin and Chesnais, 1974).

Let us now consider the situation within the census metropolitan area of Montreal, a region that is home to over 75% of the non-francophones of Quebec. A recent study (Loslier, 1976) enables us to compare the mortality of areas with high proportions of francophones to that of areas with low proportions of francophones. It can be seen from Table 3.2 that the population of predominantly francophone areas has a markedly higher mortality than the rest of the population of the Montreal metropolitan area. This region would thus have, or so it would seem, an excess mortality of francophones compared to non-francophones (see also Henripin, 1961). We can probably extend this conclusion to the population of Quebec as a whole without running too much risk of error.

To sum up briefly, then, an examination of the regional variances in mortality appears to indicate that there exists an excess mortality for Quebec francophones compared to, on the one hand, Ontario anglophones and, on the other, Quebec non-francophones. This conclusion, interesting though it may

Table 3.2
INFANT MORTALITY RATE AND MORTALITY INDEX FOR AREAS OF THE MONTREAL METROPOLITAN REGION HAVING HIGH OR LOW PROPORTIONS OF FRANCOPHONES, AROUND 1971

TYPE OF AREA	% OF THE POPULATION WHOSE HOME LANGUAGE IS FRENCH	INFANT MORTALITY RATE IN °/oo	COMPARATIVE MORTALITY INDEX[a]	
			All ages	*35−64 years*
High proportion of francophones	85.5	16.9	1.05	1.04
Low proportion of francophones	48.3	14.0	0.95	0.92

Source: Loslier (1976, pp. 39 and 68).
Note: [a] The comparative index is equal to the ratio of actual deaths to deaths calculated by applying the age-group mortality rate for the whole of Quebec to the populations of the areas in question.

appear, nevertheless remains quite general, since it is difficult to calculate the magnitude of francophone excess mortality using the available regional data.

B. ETHNIC DIFFERENCES

Although we cannot measure mortality by mother tongue or by home language, we do have, nevertheless, many estimates of mortality by ethnic origin (Charbonneau and Maheu, 1973; Henripin, 1961; Roy 1975a, 1975b). In Quebec, the French-origin group coincides almost exactly with the population whose mother-tongue or home language is French. This means that we can, for all practical purposes, take the mortality of the French-origin group for that of francophones. Because of the great ethnic heterogeneity of the group whose mother-tongue or home language is English, however, it would be an error to identify the mortality of the British-origin group with that of anglophones. We may assume, though, that the mortality of the population whose origin is other than French is equivalent to the mortality of non-francophones.

Table 3.3 shows life expectancy at birth for the population of Quebec, by sex and ethnic origin, for the three-year periods having as their central points the last three decennial censuses. According to calculations made by Laurent Roy, these show that from 1950−1952 to 1970−1972, the

Table 3.3
LIFE EXPECTANCY AT BIRTH BY SEX AND BY ETHNIC ORIGIN,
QUEBEC, 1950–1952 TO 1970–1972
(in years)

	MALES			FEMALES		
PERIOD	French	British	Other	French	British	Other
	Charbonneau and Maheu Study					
1950–1952	63.7	66.9	65.1	67.8	71.8	68.8
1960–1962	66.9	68.3	70.4	72.4	74.4	74.9
	Roy Study					
1950–1952	64.1	66.3		68.2	71.1	
1960–1962	67.0	68.8		72.5	74.3	
1970–1972	67.4	71.5		74.5	77.6	

Sources: Charbonneau and Maheu (1973, p. 148); Roy (1975*b*, p. 1).

French-origin population made slower gains in average life expectancy than did the rest of the Quebec population. Here is how the gap between life expectancy at birth for these two segments of the population has evolved:

	Women	**Men**
1950–1952	2.9 years	2.2 years
1960–1962	1.8 years	1.8 years
1970–1972	3.1 years	4.1 years

After decreasing from 1950–1952 to 1960–1962, the gap between the average life expectancies of francophones and non-francophones increased greatly from 1960–1962 to 1970–1972, to the point of being more pronounced in 1970–1972 than in 1950–1952. In fact, except for new-borns, this increase in the excess mortality of the French-origin group can be observed for almost all age groups (Table 3.4), particularly among men.

The great increase in excess mortality for francophones between 1960–1962 and 1970–1972 appears somewhat surprising. It is also possible that it is, to some degree, artificial (Lachapelle, 1982*b*). It would appear that by comparison with the 1961 census, the French-origin population was underestimated and, by the same token, the population of non-French origin, overestimated in the 1971 census (Castonguay, 1977; Henripin, 1974; Rochon-Lesage and Maheu, 1975). According to Laurent Roy (1975*b*, p. 75), gaps in average life expectancy between the French-origin group and

Table 3.4

**EXCESS MORTALITY INDEX,[a] FRENCH-ORIGIN
POPULATION OVER NON-FRENCH-ORIGIN POPULATION,
BY SEX, QUEBEC, 1951 TO 1971**

Age Group	FEMALES			MALES		
	1951	1961	1971	1951	1961	1971
0−1	142	132	129	156	134	117
1−5	163	141	132	145	128	180
5−15	106	130	152	119	140	150
15−35	158	145	156	122	127	167
35−65	112	109	128	100	111	141

Source: Roy (1975*a*), Appendix *E*, Tables 25 and 26.

Note: [a] $\dfrac{\text{Mortality risk of French-origin population}}{\text{Mortality risk of non-French-origin population}} \times 100$

the rest of the Quebec population might have been 2.0 years instead of 3.1 years for women and 2.3 years instead of 4.1 for men in 1970−1972.

Although it is difficult to measure exactly the rate and evolution of differential mortality by ethnic origin, much less by mother tongue or by home language, some conclusions can be drawn from the foregoing description. Francophones in Quebec exhibit an excess mortality compared to the rest of the population and, far from decreasing, this high death rate had a tendency to increase slightly between 1960−1962 and 1970−1972. It would appear that by 1971, the gap between the average life expectancies of francophones and non-francophones would be, at the least, two years, and, at the most, four years.

C. EFFECTS ON DEMOGRAPHIC GROWTH

As we have seen, the population of Quebec has a higher mortality than that of Ontario. This excess mortality in Quebec obviously has the effect of slowing the growth of the Quebec population compared to that of the Ontario population. For the rate of demographic growth in Quebec to be equal to that of Ontario , in the absence of migration, the fertility of Quebec women would have to be greater than that of Ontario women. Table 3.5 gives the results of calculations showing how the excess fertility of Quebeckers enables them to cancel out the effect of their excess mortality compared to Ontarians. This excess fertility index varies with mortality conditions and the average age of

Table 3.5
EXCESS FERTILITY CANCELLING OUT THE EXCESS
MORTALITY OF QUEBEC OVER ONTARIO, BY VARIOUS
MORTALITY CONDITIONS AND BY VARIOUS AVERAGE AGES AT
CHILDBIRTH
(Fertility of Ontario Women = 100.0)

MORTALITY CONDITIONS (FEMALE MORTALITY TABLES)	AVERAGE AGE AT CHILDBIRTH		
	27 Years for All	30 Years for All	27 Years in Ontario and 30 Years in Quebec
1930−1932	108.4	109.0	110.0
1950−1952	102.6	102.8	103.1
1960−1962	101.0	101.0	101.2
1965−1967	100.7	100.7	100.9
1970−1972	100.6	100.7	100.9
1975−1977	100.4	100.4	100.6

Source: Lachapelle (1982*b*), Table 8.

childbearing (Lachapelle, 1982*b*). The second factor appears to be negligible compared to the first, except when mortality is very low, in which case both factors are negligible.

Based on mortality conditions observed in Quebec and Ontario in the early 1930s, Quebec women should have attained an excess fertility of around 9% in order to counterbalance their excess mortality compared to that of Ontario. More specifically, this means that if Ontario women had an average of 3 children, Quebec women would have had to have 3.3 to enable the Quebec population, in the absence of migration, to progress at the same rate as that of Ontario. An excess fertility rate of 9% is certainly not negligible, but this percentage does seem a little low, at least when compared to actual behaviour. The excess fertility of Quebec women over that of Ontario varied between 45% and 60% during the 1920s and 1930s (Lachapelle, 1974).

As hygiene conditions improve, the excess fertility required of Quebec women decreases. To counterbalance the excess mortality of Quebec women over Ontario women, an excess fertility of only 3.0% would be required according to mortality conditions observed around 1951, 1.0% based on conditions observed around 1961, and approximately 0.5% based on 1976 conditions. The effects of mortality variances have thus become completely negligible compared to those that may result from fertility variances. This conclusion applies not only to the excess mortality of Quebec over Ontario, but also to differential mortality by ethnic origin (Table 3.6).

If we considered only the life expectancies at birth, which appear in Table 3.3, and the excess mortality indices shown in Table 3.4, we would be inclined to suggest that the excess mortality of French-origin persons increased greatly between 1960–1962 and 1970–1972. Excess fertility of about 1.0% would be sufficient, however, to compensate for the excess mortality observed around 1971, while excess fertility must have been approximately 1.3% to arrive at the same result based on mortality conditions observed around 1961 (Table 3.6). It might seem a little paradoxical that higher excess mortality could be neutralized by lower excess fertility. These diverging developments are due to the fact that in measuring the effects of mortality, the index used varies not with differential mortality but with differential survival. A simple example will help explain what happens. Say we have two populations whose risk of death between birth and 30 years is calculated at 9.0% and 7.0% respectively during year 0. Hygiene conditions then subsequently improve, and these risks then drop to 4.0% and 3.0% during year n. Excess mortality thus increased between year 0 (9/7 = 1.29) and year n (4/3 = 1.33). Conversely, the relative difference between probabilities of survival from birth to 30 years decreased between these two years from 2.2% in year 0 (93/91 = 1.022) to 1.0% in year n (97/96 =

Table 3.6

EXCESS FERTILITY CANCELLING OUT THE EXCESS MORTALITY OF THE FRENCH-ORIGIN POPULATION COMPARED TO THE REST OF THE QUEBEC POPULATION, BY VARIOUS MORTALITY CONDITIONS AND BY VARIOUS AVERAGE AGES AT CHILDBIRTH

(Fertility of Non-French-Origin Population = 100.0)

MORTALITY CONDITIONS (FEMALE MORTALITY TABLES)	AVERAGE AGE AT CHILDBIRTH		
	27 Years for All	30 Years for All	27 Years for Non-French Origin and 30 Years for French Origin
1951	102.3	102.5	102.8
1961	101.2	101.3	101.4
1971	100.9	101.0	101.1

Source: Lachapelle (1982*b*), Table 9.

1.010). This explains why if the average age at childbirth is around 30 years, the excess fertility necessary to compensate the excess mortality in question is lower for year n (1.0%) than for year 0 (2.2%).

D. SUMMARY

Canada does not have the statistics necessary to measure the state and evolution of differential mortality by mother tongue or home language. We thus had to resort to indirect methods. These methods all give results that are similar, or at least in agreement, and enable us to suggest that in Canada as in Quebec, francophones definitely have a higher mortality than anglophones.

Judging from the differences in mortality between Quebec and Ontario, the excess mortality of Quebec francophones over Ontario anglophones seems to have declined gradually from the beginning of the 1930s to the mid-1960s. For the past ten years, however, except (fortunately) in the case of new-born children, this converging trend has been interrupted, and a sharp increase in the excess mortality of francophone men has even been observed. This recent worsening of excess mortality among Quebec francophones stands out even more clearly if we compare the mortality of this group with that of the rest of the Quebec population.

Recent changes in differential mortality between language groups is a matter for concern. Due to a lack of detailed studies on this subject, we are unfortunately unable to pin-point the factors responsible. There is, in fact, little study done in Canada on inequality in the face of death, whether this is based on ethnic or social group membership (Billette, 1977). This is a regrettable gap that should be filled.

While it is difficult, in the present state of statistical documentation, to determine factors of differential mortality according to ethnic origin or mother tongue, we can, however, easily measure their effects on the demographic growth of ethnolinguistic groups. These effects have no doubt always been rather weak, at least if we compare them to those exerted in the past by differences in fertility. Nowadays, the effects of differential mortality on the rate of demographic growth have become so slight that it is hardly worth mentioning them. We would no doubt be surprised that a still-sizeable differential mortality could have negligible effects on demographic growth. This is fairly easy to explain. Risk of death among young people has decreased for all groups. Although this reduction was smaller among francophones than for the rest of the population, reflecting the increase in their excess mortality, risk of death before 30 years is now so small that differences in survival are now negligible. The effects of mortality on demographic growth depend essentially on survival rates between birth and the thirtieth birthday. This means that if we are to pursue the fight against death, and especially against inequality in the face of death, we cannot expect these efforts to have a noticeable effect on demographic growth in the future (Coale, 1959; Preston, 1977).

Chapter Four

Fertility

Our objective in this chapter is to make an analysis of recent trends in the fertility of language groups, mainly with a view to supporting reasonable hypotheses on the future evolution of this phenomenon. Our intention is thus not to make a study of fertility as such, but rather to concentrate on differences between language groups. This is not easy, as these differences have been far from stable in the past, and the recent upsets add further confusion to the picture as it once appeared. For example, Quebec, which maintained its remarkable excess fertility for a hundred years, is now characterized by a lower fertility than the rest of Canada, and this holds true for each of our three language groups: the English, French, and third-language groups in Quebec all have lower fertility than the corresponding groups in the rest of Canada. In addition, francophones formerly had a much higher fertility rate than the rest of the population, while now, in many regions, their fertility is outranked by that of allophones and occasionally even by that of anglophones.

It is to emphasize the unexpected nature of recent developments that we will spend some time in the beginning of this chapter on the evolution of fertility since 1900 (Section A). Section B is much longer and will deal with recent trends, which are somewhat more difficult to assess and whose interpretation requires a few adjustments. We will end the chapter with some remarks about future prospects.

We will distinguish three language groups: English, French, and others. We will also examine a number of regions, and the regional breakdown will vary with each case. For the greater part of the analysis (Section B), the three regions that serve as a basis for projections will be used: Montreal, Quebec less Montreal, and Canada less Quebec. A more detailed breakdown will occasionally be used.

A. A LOOK AT HISTORY

It is always enlightening to place the recent evolution of a phenomenon in an earlier historical perspective. Going back in time generally explains recent trends, or at least gives a better idea of how they developed. When we set out to examine differences in fertility between the various language groups or even between various regions of Canada, we are forced to admit that the earlier periods show a sharp contrast with the last two or three decades. Either the relative positions are reversed—this is the case of Quebec compared to the rest of Canada—or else large and seemingly long-lasting variances have practically disappeared—this is the case of the legendary excess fertility of French Canadians.

It is hard to determine when the remote past ends and the recent past begins, but this is necessary if we are to reach a clear understanding. This point may conveniently be established in terms of cohorts.[1] From this point of view, it corresponds more or less to the women born around 1935; these persons were about 10 at the end of the last war and most of them married between 1953 and 1965. In this section, then, we will examine the fertility of women born before 1936.

The easiest and also the most meaningful way of measuring their fertility is derived from an observation made during certain censuses (1941, 1961, and 1971): ever-married women (that is, those who had already been married) were asked how many children they had borne throughout their lives. We will use mainly information from the 1971 census. At that date, women over 65 were born before 1906, while those 45−49, who were at the end of their period of fertility, were born between 1921 and 1926; the last two cohort groups that will be studied in this section, 1926−1931 and 1931−1936, were respectively 40−44 and 35−39 years old. These women had thus not completed their fertility, but nowadays very few women give birth to a child after 40, and relatively few between 35 and 40, so that the number of children born to women aged 35−39 gives a fairly good idea of their ultimate family size.

For Canada as a whole, women born before 1896 and married at some time in their lives had an average of 4.0 children (see Table 4.1).[2] English-speaking women had 3.2, while the French had twice as many, and the third-language women were between the two with 4.7 children. In succeeding cohorts, these variances tended to decrease sharply. A comparison of English and French women shows this in a striking way: compared to the fertility of the English, French women show a rate 97% higher for women born before 1896. This excess is subsequently reduced little by little: dropping to 52% for the 1911−1916 cohort, 18% for those born in 1926−1931, and 6% for those of 1931−1936.

The fertility of women of other mother tongues first occupied an intermediate position, the oldest cohorts having an excess fertility of 46% compared to English women. Starting with the 1921−1926 cohorts, however, the third-language group goes to last place, although we will see that it was not to remain there.

The fertility measured here is that of women who are married, while women who did not marry are excluded from the calculations. From a population-growth viewpoint, it would be better to measure the fertility of all women, of whatever marital status. Censuses give us no information on the

Table 4.1
NUMBER OF CHILDREN PER EVER-MARRIED WOMAN, BY MOTHER TONGUE, CANADA, COHORTS OF WOMEN BORN BETWEEN PRE-1896 AND 1931–1936

COHORTS	MOTHER TONGUE			
	English	French	Other	All Languages
Pre-1896	3.23	6.37	4.70	4.04
1896–1901	2.90	5.58	3.81	3.65
1901–1906	2.62	4.62	3.34	3.23
1906–1911	2.55	4.23	3.14	3.06
1911–1916	2.65	4.03	2.99	3.04
1916–1921	2.87	4.13	2.92	3.19
1921–1926	3.09	4.12	2.90	3.32
1926–1931[a]	3.24	3.84	2.97	3.35
1931–1936[a]	3.16	3.36	2.87	3.16

Sources: Census of Canada, 1961 for cohorts born before 1901, and Census of Canada, 1971 for succeeding cohorts.

Note: [a] The fertility of these women was not complete in 1971; for example, women born in 1931–1936 were 35–40 years old in 1971.

children born to women who have never married. We would not err too much if we presumed that all children are born to women who were married at some time; on the one hand, births outside of marriage are not very numerous and, on the other, a fraction (unknown) of these births are eventually taken into account by censuses because the mother, although single at the time of giving birth, subsequently married. A satisfactory estimate of the fertility of women of all marital statuses can thus be obtained by multiplying the average number of children of ever-married women by the fraction of ever-married women in the total number of women of their cohort.

This operation obviously reduces the average number of children born per woman, but does not significantly change the relative variances between language groups. The reason for this is simple: differences in nuptiality (the fraction of ever-married women) are almost negligible compared to fertility differences among women who have married. This can be seen from Table 4.2. These differences are not altogether insignificant, however; in particular, they contribute to reducing the fertility of French-language women by 5% or 6% compared to that of English-language women. It should be noted that

Table 4.2

FRACTION OF EVER-MARRIED WOMEN AMONG ALL WOMEN OF THEIR COHORT, BY MOTHER TONGUE, CANADA, COHORTS 1906–1911 TO 1931–1936

COHORTS	MOTHER TONGUE			
	English	French	Other	All Languages
1906–1911	0.90	0.84	0.96	0.90
1911–1916	0.92	0.86	0.96	0.91
1916–1921	0.93	0.88	0.96	0.92
1921–1926	0.94	0.89	0.96	0.93
1926–1931	0.94	0.89	0.95	0.93
1931–1936	0.94	0.89	0.95	0.93

Source: Census of Canada, 1971, special tables.

the nuptiality of the third-language group was formerly extremely high; it has remained so, but that of English-language women is now quite close.

Let us now make the conversion we explained above, in order to pass from the fertility of ever-married women to that of women of all marital statuses. The results are shown in Figure 4.1 (Panel 1). The other panels show comparable results for various regions of Canada, and some of these deserve further comment.

a. For almost all regions, the relative position of languages is similar to that of Canada as a whole.

b. The excess fertility of French-speaking women was of the same order of magnitude in Quebec as in the rest of Canada; however, it was lower and then reversed in the "Other Atlantic Provinces." In all areas, this excess fertility has declined, if not reversed.

c. Almost everywhere, the relative position of other languages has deteriorated and dropped to last place.

d. Finally, for all languages combined, Ontario is characterized by low fertility and the Atlantic provinces by high fertility. Quebec maintained its fertility above that of the rest of Canada until the 1926–1931 cohorts, but succeeding cohorts have given this province an under-fertility (see Panel 8).

It would thus appear that the last cohorts studied exhibit a substantial attenuation of these once-considerable differences. It should be mentioned in passing that there is one rather paradoxical aspect of the fertility of French mother-tongue women that we will come across in an amplified version a little later on. In all areas, their fertility is greater than that of English-language women, even for the youngest cohorts (the exception of the "Other Atlantic Provinces" does not significantly change this); however, in Canada as a whole, this excess fertility disappears. This is because Quebec, where French-language women are highly concentrated, is now characterized by a particularly low level of fertility.

Figure 4.1
AVERAGE NUMBER OF CHILDREN BORN PER WOMAN (ALL MARITAL STATUS) BY MOTHER TONGUE, COHORTS 1906 TO 1936, CANADA AND SELECTED REGIONS

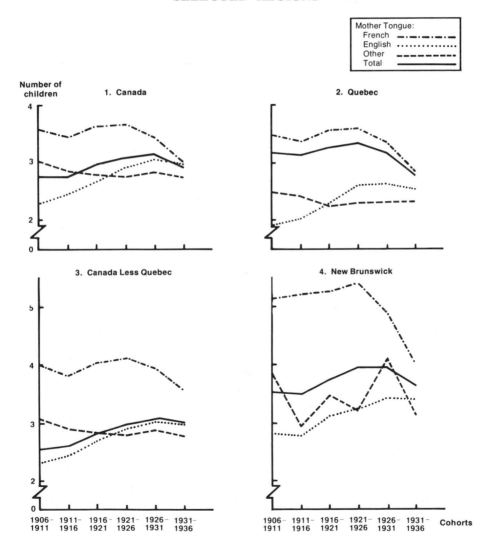

Figure 4.1 *(cont'd.)*

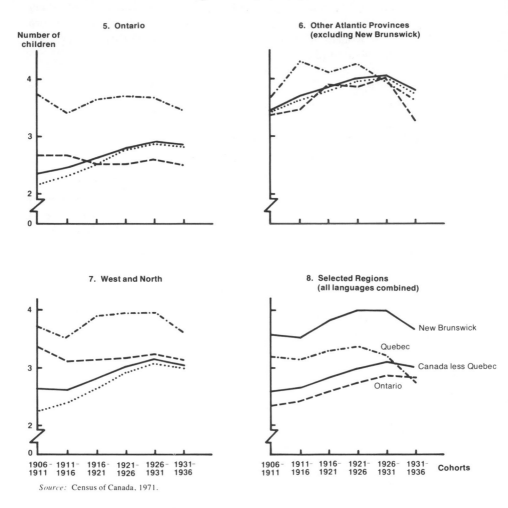

Source: Census of Canada. 1971.

This reversal of Quebec's relative position compared to the rest of Canada is confirmed by the results of an analysis made by Réjean Lachapelle (1974, pp. 14–15), based on vital statistics. This study deals only with Ontario and Quebec. For both provinces, the estimates he arrives at are a little higher than those obtained by using census data, but, more important, fertility is shown to be lower in Quebec than in Ontario beginning with the 1931–1936 cohorts (3.0 and 3.2 children per woman respectively).

It is hard to tell if we should be more surprised by the high rate of French fertility in the past or by its near disappearance. In any case, it would appear that this fertility cannot be explained by characteristics systematically attributed to the French group. In the first place, it was observed for all types of habitat: urban, rural non-farm, and rural farm (Henripin, 1972, p. 180). In addition, in her monograph on Canadian fertility, Enid Charles showed that for women born between 1886 and 1896, French mother tongue was associated with an excess fertility in the range of 50% compared to English, independently of the influence of such factors as religion, schooling, and habitat (Charles, 1948, p. 68). A comparable study for women born between 1906 and 1916 showed that this excess fertility had nevertheless almost disappeared, except in rural areas (Henripin, 1972, p. 192).

B. RECENT TRENDS IN FERTILITY

We will now take a closer look at the fertility of the younger cohorts, those born between 1931 and 1951 and who were 20 to 40 years old in 1971, which is the last year the Canadian census gave information on the number of children born. We will use our three main regions: Montreal, the rest of Quebec, and the other Canadian provinces combined. We have data by home language and by mother tongue, but there is very little difference between the fertility of a given mother-tongue group and that of the corresponding home-language group. The only notable exception is the third-language group in the region "Quebec less Montreal": in this case, the fertility of the other home-language group is 0.5 to 0.6 children higher than that of the third-language group. In any case, it might have been expected that in this group, which includes many Amerindians, home language would be a more important factor than mother tongue. We will consequently concern ourselves, in principal, with home language only.

1. Fertility of Ever-Married Women

Table 4.3 gives the average number of children born per ever-married woman between 20 and 40 years old, by five-year age groups, according to the 1971 census. A number of facts stand out.

a. In the whole of Canada, allophones, who had the lowest fertility, now hold first place among women 20 to 24 years old.[3] Francophones have switched from first to last place.

b. The Montreal region and Canada less Quebec experienced the same phenomena, except that, in both regions, francophones maintained a higher fertility than anglophones.

c. The region "Quebec less Montreal" is somewhat of a special case: anglophones are not numerous and the allophones are mainly Amerindians. The fertility of francophones here is lower than that of the other two groups, which is somewhat surprising.

d. The province of Quebec is characterized by a systematic under-fertility. Shown below are the average number of children by home language and by age group, for Quebec.

Table 4.3

AVERAGE NUMBER OF CHILDREN BORN PER EVER-MARRIED WOMAN AGED 20–40, BY HOME LANGUAGE, CANADA AND SELECTED REGIONS, 1971

REGION AND HOME LANGUAGE	AGE GROUP IN 1971			
	20–24	25–29	30–34	35–39
Canada				
English	0.92	1.74	2.66	3.14
French	0.82	1.61	2.60	3.35
Other	1.10	1.74	2.39	2.76
All languages	0.91	1.71	2.62	3.16
Montreal				
English	0.67	1.38	2.20	2.59
French	0.74	1.48	2.33	2.88
Other	0.98	1.56	2.04	2.34
All languages	0.75	1.47	2.27	2.76
Quebec less Montreal				
English	0.96	1.85	2.85	3.41
French	0.83	1.63	2.70	3.60
Other	1.91	2.88	4.12	4.60
All languages	0.84	1.65	2.72	3.60
Canada less Quebec				
English	0.93	1.76	2.68	3.17
French	1.08	2.02	3.21	4.08
Other	1.11	1.75	2.43	2.82
All languages	0.95	1.77	2.68	3.17

Source: Census of Canada, 1971, special tables.

	20–24	25–29	30–34	35–39
English	0.73	1.47	2.31	2.73
French	0.79	1.56	2.53	3.26
Other	1.06	1.68	2.19	2.50
All languages	0.79	1.55	2.48	3.14

For every language and for all age groups, the fertility is lower than that of the rest of Canada. This explains one curious phenomenon: while francophones have a *higher* fertility than anglophones, both in Quebec and in the rest of Canada, their fertility is *less* in the country as a whole because they are concentrated in a province that has been associated with low fertility.

The trend that began to take shape in the last section thus becomes more clearly defined: a double see-saw motion, both from a language viewpoint and from the point of view of the distinction between Quebec and the rest of Canada. Francophones have become less fertile since the cohort of women who were 30 to 35 in 1971, while Quebec fell behind the rest of Canada a little earlier, with the women aged 35 to 40. This sort of break with the past occurred around the year 1960.

These unprecedented changes in the respective positions of the various language groups led us to examine the situation in smaller regions. The rest of the province of Quebec (that is, excluding the Montreal region) was divided into four regions: the Eastern Townships, the Outaouais, the Interior of Quebec, and the Periphery.[4] In the Eastern Townships and the Periphery, anglophone women had a slightly higher fertility than francophones, while in the two other regions, the Outaouais and the Interior, these groups were almost equal. With respect to allophones, it can be observed that they were clearly ahead of francophones and anglophones, except in the Eastern Townships.

The province of Ontario was also divided into four regions: Northwest, Northeast, Southeast, and Interior.[5] In all regions, francophone fertility was slightly higher than that of anglophones, except for women 20 to 30 years old (in 1971) in the Interior. Women of other home languages have a lower fertility after 30 and almost the same as anglophones before 30. There is one exception, however: in the Northwest, allophones, whose fertility was less than that of francophones over 30, are far ahead of francophones in the under-30 group.

In the two regions of New Brunswick, the South and the North-and-East,[6] anglophones and francophones are quite similar. The same is true for the other Atlantic provinces combined.

Finally, we have formed one region made up of the western provinces and the northern territories. Here, francophone fertility is higher than that of anglophones, although this difference tends to get smaller with the younger cohorts. Allophones, who were once in an intermediate position between francophones and anglophones, are now slightly ahead of these two groups.

2. Fertility of Women of All Marital Status

In the foregoing section, we only dealt with the number of children born per ever-married woman, and we thus only considered women who had been married. In fact, the great majority of women were still married, since widows and divorcées were not frequent at these ages. However, the fertility of a population also depends on the number of women who marry. We must therefore estimate the number of children born to women of all marital status.

We have already described, in the preceding section, the method used in making this conversion, which uses the fraction of ever-married women. Table 4.4 shows this fraction for various categories of women.

It is clear that francophones have a slightly lower tendency to marry than the rest of the population and, in any case, marry later. At 20−24 years, 48% of francophone women are married, while this fraction is 60% for anglophones and 62% for allophones, It should be noted, however, that in Quebec—these figures do not appear here—anglophones and francophones tend to marry in about the same way, that is, less frequently and later. The allophone women in that province are, on the contrary, similar to those in Canada as a whole.

For Quebec women and Canadian francophones, there are then two low-fertility factors that combine their effects: not only do these women have fewer children when they marry, but in addition they marry slightly less frequently and later.

The number of children born to women of all marital status is shown in Table 4.5. This table is much the same as Table 4.3, except that we have added the figures for Quebec as a whole. The respective positions of the various language groups are not very different from those we described previously for ever-married women. Generally speaking, variances are a

Table 4.4
PROPORTIONS OF EVER-MARRIED WOMEN, FOR CERTAIN AGE GROUPS, BY HOME LANGUAGE, CANADA AND SELECTED REGIONS, 1971

REGIONS	AGE GROUP IN 1971			
	20−24	25−29	30−34	35−39
Canada				
English	0.600	0.864	0.922	0.943
French	0.476	0.804	0.868	0.882
Other	0.620	0.860	0.930	0.954
All languages	0.568	0.847	0.909	0.928
Montreal	0.487	0.796	0.867	0.891
Quebec less Montreal	0.450	0.800	0.874	0.885
Canada less Quebec	0.608	0.868	0.925	0.944
Province of Quebec	0.468	0.796	0.870	0.891

Source: Census of Canada, 1971, special tables.

Table 4.5

AVERAGE NUMBER OF CHILDREN BORN PER WOMAN OF ALL MARITAL STATUS, AGED 20–40, BY HOME LANGUAGE, CANADA AND SELECTED REGIONS, 1971

REGION AND HOME LANGUAGE	AGE GROUP IN 1971			
	20–24	25–29	30–34	35–39
Canada				
English	0.55	1.50	2.46	2.96
French	0.39	1.30	2.26	2.96
Other	0.68	1.50	2.22	2.63
All languages	0.52	1.44	2.38	2.93
Montreal				
English	0.29	1.06	1.89	2.34
French	0.36	1.18	2.01	2.53
Other	0.59	1.34	1.88	2.25
All languages	0.36	1.17	1.97	2.46
Quebec less Montreal				
English	0.56	1.58	2.61	3.22
French	0.37	1.30	2.35	3.17
Other	1.06	2.34	3.75	4.36
All languages	0.38	1.32	2.38	3.18
Canada less Quebec				
English	0.57	1.53	2.49	2.99
French	0.62	1.73	2.84	3.70
Other	0.69	1.51	2.27	2.69
All languages	0.58	1.54	2.48	2.99
Quebec				
English	0.34	1.15	2.01	2.48
French	0.36	1.24	2.19	2.87
Other	0.63	1.42	2.02	2.40
All languages	0.37	1.24	2.15	2.80

Source: Census of Canada, 1971, special tables.

little larger, since low fertility in married women goes hand in hand with later nuptiality, and vice versa. Francophones in particular lose ground, as they tend to marry a little less frequently and also later.

These differences in nuptiality have a considerable effect on the fertility of women 20 to 24 years old, so that statistics for this age group do not give a good idea of the final birth cohorts, that is, the number of children these women will have had by the end of their fertile lives. In the following section, we will attempt to make some corrections to this picture.

3. Adjustments in Fertility for 20−24 Year-Old Women

Ever-married women between 20 and 24 have had less than half of the children they will eventually have throughout their lives, so that their fertility at that age is not a very good indication of their final fertility. Their behaviour is, however, important, since they are the last cohort whose fertility we can measure. It is thus worthwhile to make the best use possible of the information available with a view to estimating their final fertility. The results will obviously not be forecasts, but we can make an adjustment that takes into account two factors.

a. Ever-married women 20−24 years old—these women are almost all married—had not all been married for the same length of time. Obviously, these differences in marriage duration have an effect on the number of children they have borne.

b. In estimating the cumulative fertility per woman of *all marital status*, we simply multiplied the cumulative fertility of ever-married women by the fraction of ever-married women. This is as good a method as any, but it is clear that the fractions of ever-married women will increase rapidly past this age. In fact, they tend to become more uniform from one group to another, as the variances between the ever-married fractions in the 20−24 age group are much greater than in the 25−29 age group. This fact cannot be neglected when using the cumulative fertility of ever-married women of 20−24 years of age in calculating differences in lifetime fertility of women of all marital status.

A more detailed description of the methods we used in making the appropriate adjustments will be found in a separate study (Henripin and Lachapelle, 1982).

Table 4.6 gives the corrected estimates of the number of children born to women 20−24 years old, both for ever-married women and for women of all marital status. Only the first adjustment was made for ever-married women, while both adjustments were applied to women of all marital status. It can be seen that, in general, these adjustments reduced variances in fertility.

4. Evolution of Variances in Fertility

What we are interested in here are differences in fertility between geolinguistic groups and changes in these variances over recent years. The

Table 4.6
AVERAGE NUMBER OF CHILDREN BORN, ADJUSTED FOR DURATION OF MARRIAGE AND DELAYED MARRIAGE, EVER-MARRIED WOMEN AND WOMEN OF ALL MARITAL STATUS AGED 20−24 IN 1971

REGION AND HOME LANGUAGE	EVER-MARRIED WOMEN		WOMEN OF ANY MARITAL STATUS	
	Unadjusted	Adjusted[a]	Unadjusted	Adjusted[b]
Canada				
English	0.92	0.82	0.55	0.47
French	0.82	0.82	0.39	0.44
Other	1.10	0.96	0.68	0.56
All languages	0.91	0.84	0.52	0.48
Montreal				
English	0.67	0.69	0.29	0.36
French	0.74	0.73	0.36	0.40
Other	0.98	0.87	0.59	0.50
All languages	0.75	0.74	0.36	0.40
Quebec less Montreal				
English	0.96	0.87	0.56	0.50
French	0.83	0.85	0.37	0.45
Other	1.91	1.78	1.06	1.00
All languages	0.84	0.86	0.38	0.46
Canada less Quebec				
English	0.93	0.82	0.57	0.48
French	1.08	0.99	0.62	0.56
Other	1.11	0.96	0.69	0.56
All languages	0.95	0.84	0.58	0.49
Quebec				
English	0.73	0.74	0.34	0.40
French	0.79	0.80	0.36	0.43
Other	1.06	0.94	0.63	0.54
All languages	0.79	0.80	0.37	0.43

Sources: Census of Canada, 1971, special tables, and authors' estimates.
Note: [a] Adjusted for duration of marriage only.
[b] Adjusted for duration of marriage and for delayed marriage.

simplest way of analysing this is to convert the cumulative fertility of each geolinguistic group into an index, with the base value of 100 being assigned to each age group for Canada as a whole. These indices will be found in Table 4.7 and, for women of all marital status only, in Figure 4.2. If we look at the first panel in Figure 4.2, which gives a regional breakdown for all languages

Table 4.7
AGE-SPECIFIC INDEX OF AVERAGE NUMBER OF CHILDREN BORN, EVER-MARRIED WOMEN AND WOMEN OF ALL MARITAL STATUS, 1971
(For Each Age Group, Canada as a Whole = 100.0)

REGION AND HOME LANGUAGE	EVER-MARRIED WOMEN				WOMEN OF ALL MARITAL STATUS			
	$35-39$	$30-34$	$25-29$	$20-24^a$	$35-39$	$30-34$	$25-29$	$20-24^b$
Canada								
English	99	102	102	98	101	103	104	99
French	106	99	94	98	101	95	90	93
Other	87	91	102	114	90	93	104	118
All languages	100	100	100	100	100	100	100	100
Montreal								
English	82	84	81	82	80	79	74	76
French	91	89	86	87	86	84	82	83
Other	74	78	91	104	77	79	93	106
All languages	87	87	86	88	84	83	81	84
Quebec less Montreal								
English	108	109	108	104	110	110	110	104
French	114	103	95	101	108	99	90	94
Other	146	157	168	212	149	158	162	210
All languages	114	104	96	102	108	100	92	95
Canada without Quebec								
English	100	102	103	98	102	105	106	100
French	129	122	118	118	126	119	120	118
Other	89	93	102	114	92	95	105	118
All languages	100	102	104	100	102	104	107	102
Quebec								
English	86	88	86	88	85	84	80	83
French	103	97	91	95	98	92	86	89
Other	79	84	98	112	82	85	99	114
All languages	99	95	91	95	96	90	86	90

Sources: Tables 4.3, 4.5, and 4.6.

Notes: ^{a} Adjusted for duration of marriage only.

^{b} Adjusted for duration of marriage and for delayed marriage.

combined, three noteworthy trends stand out: first, the Montreal region is always well below Canada as a whole; next, the rest of Quebec, which was above the other regions for women over 35, is now lower than the rest of Canada; and last, there appears to be a convergence in fertility levels when we go from women 25−29 years old to those 20−24. This last observation, however, is due to the adjustments we have made and may possibly be less reliable. Let us see, nevertheless, what are the main conclusions we can draw from Figure 4.2.

Francophones are ahead of anglophones in all areas, except in "Quebec less Montreal," where there are very few anglophones. In the country as a whole, francophones are well below anglophones because of their concentration in Quebec, a region of low fertility. Francophone excess fertility is best seen in the rest of Canada, and this situation seems to be stable.

Allophones have followed the same general trend in almost all areas: women 35−39 years old had a lower fertility than those of the other two groups, but the younger women gradually surpassed them, except in the rest of Canada, where they reached the same level as the francophones. We do not consider the case of allophones in "Quebec less Montreal" here; these women have exceptionally high fertility levels, since they belong mainly to the endophone group, that is, they are mainly women whose home language is one of the many Amerindian languages.

In each of the three regions (Montreal, rest of Quebec, and rest of Canada), francophones and anglophones generally maintained their respective positions. The same was not true for Canada as a whole, because of the downward pressure of Quebec fertility, which affected mainly francophones. As for the allophones, their rise is astounding, and it is quite difficult to say what might be the reason for it, or if they can maintain this excess fertility.

We wanted to see if the examination of differences in fertility in the smaller regions might not bring out some unexpected aspects. We examined the five regions of Quebec, the four of Ontario, and the two of New Brunswick. As there was no question of adjusting the number of children born to women 20−24 years old, we looked mainly at the fertility of ever-married women. Nothing new or significant came from this analysis, but a few minor points are of interest.

a. In Quebec, it is only in the Montreal region that francophone fertility is higher than that of anglophones, at least for women aged 20−35 in 1971, and the gap in any case is not very large. Elsewhere, the two language groups are almost equal, except in the "periphery" region, where anglophones are in the lead.

b. In Ontario, francophone fertility is higher than that of anglophones in all areas, but only slightly so for women under 35 in 1971; in the Interior of Ontario, in fact, this difference is negligible.

c. In New Brunswick, francophones are slightly ahead in the North-and-East and slightly behind in the South, for women under 35.

Figure 4.2
AGE-SPECIFIC INDEX[a] OF AVERAGE NUMBER OF
CHILDREN BORN, WOMEN OF ALL MARITAL STATUS, 1971

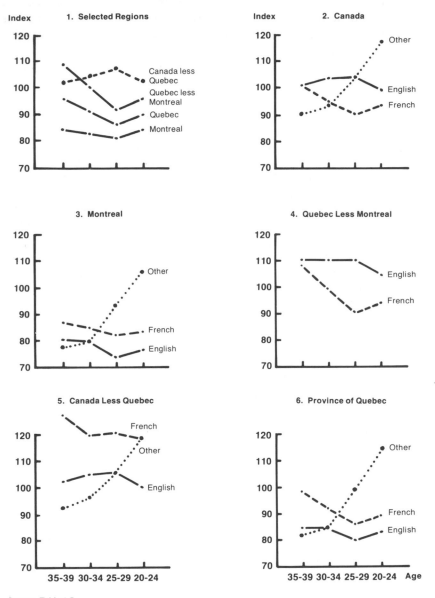

Source: Table 4.7.
Note: [a] Total Canada = 100. For the 20–24 age group, a double adjustment was made (see text).

d. The fertility of allophone women is less stable; it is moving ahead of that of other groups (for women under 25 or 30 depending on the region), but the difference is not very large, except in those regions where the high fertility of Amerindian women is a factor.

Finally, we examined differences in fertility for women of all marital status aged 25−29, leaving aside the 20−24 age group whose more or less early nuptiality might seriously distort our comparisons. Nothing noteworthy was discovered in this examination.

If we had to sum up recent trends in fertility in just a few words, from the viewpoint of differences between language groups, the following points stand out: (*a*) francophones generally have a slightly higher fertility than anglophones, but this is not valid for the whole of Canada because of the concentration of francophones in Quebec, a province in which none of the language groups is especially productive; (*b*) allophone fertility, once extremely low, now tends to exceed that of the other two groups.

5. Changes Between 1966−1971 and 1971−1976

From 1971 on, information comparable to that we have used up to now is no longer available: the question on the number of children was not asked in the 1976 census. We were not completely without resources, however, since the 1976 census gave the distribution of children under 5 years old by mother tongue and by the age of their mothers or those who performed this function. Children 0−4 years old are the survivors of births during the preceding five years, so this gives us a fairly good idea of the fertility of the period 1971−1976. For each age group of women, we simply divided the number of their children 0−4 years old by the number of women in the group, and we obtained a sort of age-specific, five-year fertility rate.[7] It is then relatively easy to derive total fertility rates.[8]

We have calculated these rates not only for the period 1971−1976, in which we are mainly interested, but also for the preceding five-year period, using the same method. The results of our calculations appear in Table 4.8. We were unable to make this calculation for the Montreal region and had to limit ourselves to the whole of Canada, Quebec, and the rest of Canada.

The most interesting aspect of this calculation of fertility levels is the period 1971−1976: we wished to determine if there were any appreciable differences compared to our previous estimates, which were based on 1971 census data on the number of children born. It might also be worthwhile, though, to try to relate these to the period 1966−1971. In the first place, it is during this period that the last ''children born'' to women counted in the 1971 census came into the world, and second, this enables us to see, using the same calculation method, if the relative fertility levels of the different geolinguistic groups have changed from one period to another. We should point out here that the total fertility rate is a different sort of measurement than that which we have been using up to now: the number of children born.

Table 4.8
ESTIMATED TOTAL FERTILITY RATE, BY MOTHER TONGUE, CANADA, QUEBEC, AND CANADA LESS QUEBEC, 1966−1971 AND 1971−1976

PERIOD AND REGION	MOTHER TONGUE			
	English	French	Other	All Languages
1966−1971				
Canada	2.46	2.34	2.86	2.48
Quebec	2.08	2.25	2.56	2.25
Canada less Quebec	2.48	2.81	2.91	2.58
1971−1976				
Canada	1.95	1.85	2.34	1.97
Quebec	1.64	1.80	2.20	1.80
Canada less Quebec	1.97	2.14	2.37	2.04

Source: Henripin and Lachapelle (1982).

The former is related to definite periods (here 1966−1971 and 1971−1976), while the latter depicts the whole fertility history of women observed at a given age in any census.

The majority of women who had children between 1971 and 1976 were between 15 and 30 years old in 1971. It is therefore interesting to see if their behaviour after 1971 is different from what it was prior to 1971, or to be more exact, if relative differences between geolinguistic groups have changed significantly. In Table 4.9, fertility statistics have been converted into indices (Canada, all languages = 100) to facilitate comparisons. The first point that stands out is the strong similarity between the indices showing the relative values of the total fertility index for the two periods (first two columns). This means that even though fertility declined considerably between 1966−1971 and 1971−1976, the drop was proportionately almost equal for all groups. This is already an indication that there have been few changes in relative fertility levels from one group to another since 1971.

If we now compare these indices with those for cumulative fertility in 1971 for women 20−24 and 25−29, we see that there is very close correlation in the case of women 20−24 years old. The cumulative fertility of these women corresponds to births that in almost all cases took place during the period 1966−1971, and it is thus not surprising that we find a strong correlation with the total fertility index for this period. Correlation with the 1971−1976 total fertility index is also very strong, indicating that, as we saw

Table 4.9
INDICES SHOWING RELATIVE VALUES OF TOTAL FERTILITY
RATE FOR PERIODS 1966−1971 AND 1971−1976, AND
CUMULATIVE FERTILITY OF WOMEN OF ALL MARITAL
STATUS, AGED 20−24 AND 25−29 IN 1971, BY HOME
LANGUAGE OR MOTHER TONGUE, CANADA, QUEBEC,
AND CANADA LESS QUEBEC
(Whole of Canada, All Languages = 100)

REGION AND LANGUAGE[a]	TOTAL FERTILITY INDEX		CUMULATIVE FERTILITY IN 1971		
	1966−1971	1971−1976	Age 20−24[b]	Age 25−29	Mean
Canada					
English	99	99	99	104	101.5
French	94	94	93	90	91.5
Other	115	119	118	104	111.0
All languages	100	100	100	100	100.0
Quebec					
English	84	83	83	79	81.5
French	91	91	89	86	87.5
Other	103	112	114	99	106.5
All languages	91	91	90	86	88.0
Canada less Quebec					
English	100	100	100	106	103.0
French	113	109	118	120	119.0
Other	117	120	118	105	111.5
All languages	104	104	102	106	104.5

Sources: Tables 4.7 and 4.8.
Note: [a] Mother tongue for total fertility index and home language for cumulative fertility.
[b] Adjusted for duration of marriage and delayed marriage.

earlier, the recent behaviour of women as regards fertility has been such that the relative positions have remained practically unchanged over the past two five-year periods.

Correlation is less good, however, between total fertility indices and cumulative fertility in 1971 for women between 25 and 29, and yet, these women also had children during the period 1966−1971. The explanation is simple: the weaker correlation is due to the fact that these women had a sizeable number of their children *prior to* 1966. Their cumulative fertility in 1971 should thus be related to the total fertility indices for 1961−1966 and 1966−1971. We were unable, however, to estimate the total fertility index for the period 1961−1966.

We may therefore conclude that nothing, during the five years that followed the 1971 census, suggests that the respective positions of geolinguistic groups had changed appreciably. This may not hold true for the decades to come, but it does nevertheless constitute a stable element that reinforces the basis on which forecasts about the future will be made.

C. SOME INDICATIONS ON FORECASTING FERTILITY

In order to predict how a phenomenon will evolve, we must understand the effect of factors that cause it to vary. It would be foolhardy to pretend that we have such knowledge with respect to fertility, as this is far from being the case. However, we can make an attempt at understanding what we observe. Let us begin by examining the most noteworthy points.

The relative positions of francophone and anglophone women appear remarkably constant, when we examine them region by region. In Montreal and in "Canada less Quebec," the superiority of French fertility appears to persist. This can probably be explained by francophone adhesion to Catholicism, by a lower level of schooling, and by the fact that many of these people live in rural areas (in New Brunswick in particular). The reverse can be observed for the region "Quebec less Montreal," but the number of anglophones involved is very small, and many of them live in rural areas.

The relative increase in the fertility of the third-language group is surprising, to say the least. This higher fertility among women born outside Canada, and this is the case for most of them, existed in the past for certain language or ethnic groups: Russian, Polish, and Dutch women born around the beginning of the century. This subsequently disappeared and, up until recently, foreign-born women were generally less fertile than were native-born Canadians. The return of this group to a relative excess fertility could be explained, at least in part, by the countries of origin of these "new" allophones: they are less likely to come from Europe and more likely to come from other continents where fertility is markedly higher than in Canada. If this hypothesis is found to be true, the excess fertility of allophones could persist for some time to come. There must, however, be more determining factors than the one mentioned above. We are inclined to believe that at least part of this excess fertility is of a temporary nature and that it will decline.

Perhaps the most unforeseen discovery is that Quebec has become an area of under-fertility for all three language groups. In the case of anglophones and allophones, this can be at least partly explained by the fact that the majority of them live in the Montreal region, but the low fertility of francophones living in Quebec, even outside Montreal, is most surprising. There is one possible explanation: it might be advanced that as long as French Quebeckers lived in obedience to the dictates of their specific culture, they were led to have many children. This culture was strongly impregnated with Catholicism, gave little importance to schooling but a great deal to family life and, above all, gave little encouragement to those seeking social and financial success. As French Quebeckers opened their minds to a more modern concept of life, they may have been inspired to place new goals and new satisfactions above having children. Or the explanation may be even more prosaic: their recent access to material comfort may have changed them more radically than would have been the case with other groups who were better able to defend themselves and who were armed with a moral code based on something other than a discarded religion. These are more questions than statements or even hypotheses, but we must be satisfied with them, for the moment. They are products of imagination, and we must not yield to the temptation to carry them too far.

What can we draw from all this that might be useful in trying to predict what lies ahead? Obviously, within the limits of our biological system, nothing is impossible. But all is not equally plausible, and social constraints significantly limit the range of biological possibilities. It appears likely that francophones, in each region, will maintain their excess fertility during the next decade or two (no doubt excepting the region "Quebec less Montreal"). The same will probably hold true for the even higher excess fertility of allophones, but in our view, this should decline somewhat. We are left with the under-fertility that characterizes Quebec as a whole. This too will no doubt diminish as, in all probability, will all differences. It is worth noting here that by 1975, fertility in Quebec had become equal to if not greater than that of Ontario, as well as moving closer to that of the whole of Canada (Henripin and Lachapelle, 1982).

NOTES

[1] A birth cohort is the group of individuals born during a given period, generally a year.

[2] Strictly speaking, these are women counted in the 1961 census. This excludes those who emigrated or died and, conversely, includes women who immigrated or who gave birth to their children in a different region from that in which they were counted.

[3] The fertility of this age group is dependent on the duration of the marriage and should be interpreted with caution. This question will be examined further on.

[4] See Appendix *A* for the description of these regions.

[5] *Ibid.*

[6] *Ibid.*

[7] These "rates" have been adjusted to take into account both children who died and those children whose mother tongue was known but whose mother's age and mother tongue were unknown (Henripin and Lachapelle, 1982).

[8] The total fertility rate is a measurement that is the sum of fertility rates by age; it represents the number of children a woman would have in her lifetime if she was subject, between 15 and 50, to the age-specific fertility rates observed in a given period.

Chapter Five

Linguistic Mobility

The study of what was once, and still is, called linguistic assimilation was traditionally based on comparison of census data on ethnic origin and mother tongue (Arès, 1975; Charbonneau and Maheu, 1973; Gryz, 1977; Henripin, Charbonneau, and Mertens, 1966; Joy, 1967; Lieberson, 1970; Maheu, 1968, 1970; Vallee and Shulman, 1969). These data do not, however, enable us to estimate the language transfers made by census respondents; they can only perceive transfers made by their ancestors, more specifically their male ancestors, since ethnic origin is determined by the male side. Some quite ingenious methods have certainly been proposed for estimating the real assimilation rate (Maheu, 1968) or, more precisely, the rate of retention of French in a French mother-tongue population that knows English (Lieberson, 1970). These methods are, however, based on somewhat fragile hypotheses (Gryz, 1977) and in the final analysis are useful only in appreciating the rate of language transfer in groups having a high assimilation rate.

In view of the obvious insufficiency of data dealing only with ethnic origin and mother tongue, the Royal Commission on Bilingualism and Biculturalism suggested that an additional question be included in the 1971 census. This question should, according to the Commission, deal with "the main language of each Canadian" (Canada, Royal Commission, 1967, p. 18). This suggestion is not easy to implement, since for some persons the same language does not take precedence in the family and at work, or at home and at school. Statistics Canada decided to limit itself to home language, that is, the language most often spoken within the family group. Since the publication of the 1971 census statistics, studies on linguistic mobility have drawn mainly upon data on mother tongue and home language (Bernard, 1978; Cartwright, 1976; Castonguay, 1974, 1976a, 1976b, 1979b; Castonguay and Marion, 1974; De Vries, 1977b; De Vries and Vallee, 1975, 1980; Henripin, 1974; Joy, 1975, 1978; Kralt, 1976; Lachapelle, 1979, 1980; Rochon-Lesage and Maheu, 1975; Vallee and Dufour, 1974; Veltman, 1976). Most of them do little more than present statistics taken from the 1971 census, without explaining the hypotheses that justify linking linguistic mobility to tables that cross mother tongue and home language. Charles

Castonguay (1976*b*), John De Vries (1977*b*), and Réjean Lachapelle (1980) nevertheless did try to clarify the concept of linguistic mobility and to bring out the possibilities offered by census data, as well as the difficulties they entail when one wishes to describe trends and variations in linguistic mobility. Lachapelle (1982*c*) also demonstrated that there is a formal relationship between linguistic mobility and regional mobility and, in addition, should we admit certain hypotheses, between linguistic mobility and nuptiality. This enabled us not only to propose a precise definition of linguistic mobility and the events it produces, language transfers, but also, taking our inspiration from demographic methods, to lay down a broad outline for analysis of linguistic mobility.

As in the case of the other demolinguistic phenomena, we will be interested mainly in changes over time and variations in space with respect to linguistic mobility. Because of the limitations imposed by availability of data, we will have to confine ourselves, in all cases, to assessing changes in completed linguistic mobility from one cohort to another and more specifically for those persons who were over 30 at the time of the 1971 census. Variations in linguistic mobility over space will be described and analysed for those regions displaying contrasting linguistic compositions. Five of these regions are in Quebec, four in Ontario, and two in New Brunswick. The regional breakdown used is described in Appendix *A*.[1] We have added two regions to the eleven mentioned above: one includes Newfoundland, Prince Edward Island, and Nova Scotia, while the other takes in the western provinces and northern territories (Yukon and Northwest Territories).

Linguistic mobility may be considered from two points of view (Lachapelle, 1982*c*); on the one hand, to use statistical terminology, as a dependent or explainable variable whose variations must be measured and explained and, on the other, as an independent or explanatory variable likely to account for some of the changes in linguistic composition. For this reason, we will try to distinguish clearly between statements dealing with *propensities* to make a language transfer and those dealing with the *effects* of linguistic mobility. In estimating propensities, we will often use a linguistic mobility rate, that is, the proportion of persons with a given mother tongue who use a different language at home. Effects will be evaluated mainly by use of an index of linguistic continuity (Lachapelle, 1980, 1982*c*), which corresponds to the ratio between the number of persons using a given home language and those using the corresponding mother tongue.

Changes over time and variations over space will be described and analysed first for linguistic mobility rates and then for continuity indices. The first section will deal with the evolution in various regions of linguistic mobility rates from one cohort to another. We will also try to evaluate changes that took place between 1971 and 1976. The following two sections will describe regional variations in linguistic mobility rates observed among young adults. In the second section, we will study the frequency of bilingualism and the linguistic mobility of bilingual persons, while the third section will deal with linguistic homogamy as well as the linguistic mobility of persons forming homolinguistic or heterolinguistic couples.[2] These two sections are at times rather technical, and it would perhaps be advisable in the first reading to scan them rapidly, and then come back and read them more thoroughly should the need be felt. Our main findings are in any case presented in a simpler form at the end of the chapter. In the last section, we will consider the effects of linguistic mobility on linguistic composition in various regions.

A. TRENDS IN LINGUISTIC MOBILITY

The terms of reference underlying our description of changes in linguistic mobility are quite simple. They assume that the linguistic mobility rate depends, first, on the *degree* of risk that a language transfer will take place and, second, on the *length of exposure* to the risk of changing languages. This way of breaking down the linguistic mobility rate is aimed at isolating the intensity of the phenomenon, which is our only interest here, from the length of exposure to risk, which interferes with comparisons and renders them ambiguous. This is why we will introduce two control variables: age and place of birth.

We will first consider, for the whole Canadian population, age-specific variations in 1971 of the linguistic mobility rate for the English and French groups, and then examine the changes in the linguistic mobility of each group. As can be seen in Figure 5.1, the curve representing the French group shows three distinct phases: an ascending phase from the 0−4 age group to the 35−39 age group, then a stabilization phase that continues until the 50−54 age group is reached, and finally a descending phase for the older age groups. The ascending phase basically illustrates the length of exposure to the risk of language transfers. After a certain age, however, no doubt between 30 and 50 years, linguistic mobility apparently becomes so weak that the effects of continued exposure can be considered negligible. Consequently, if the process of linguistic mobility had been more or less stationary over the decades preceding the 1971 census, we might have expected that the linguistic mobility rate would not vary noticeably past 30 or 40 years of age, that is, for those cohorts born before 1941 or 1931. And this is precisely what can be observed from the 1916−1921 cohorts to the 1931−1936 cohorts, whose linguistic mobility rate fluctuates slightly around 8.8%. This recent stabilization of the linguistic mobility of the French group does, however, follow a sizeable increase: the overall rate increased from 6.7% for the cohorts born between 1901 and 1906 (65−69 years old in 1971) to 8.8% for the 1916−1921 cohorts.

This means that the linguistic mobility of the French group increased from the 1901−1906 cohorts to the 1916−1921 cohorts and varied only slightly thereafter, at least until the 1931−1936 cohorts. It should be emphasized that these facts are not immediately evident from the observations made during the 1971 census. Data, as we know, never speak for themselves. Their meaning and implications are always derived through a model (Coleman, 1964), and this model requires some explanation. In the present case, it had to be assumed that for all the cohorts involved, language transfers were negligible after 30 or 35 years of age; in addition, we formed the hypothesis that language transfers are one-time occurrences, which means that there is no return transfer that would enable a person who had adopted a home language different from his mother tongue to once again change his home language in favour of his mother tongue.[3] If this hypothesis and several others are approximately satisfied, we can then liken the linguistic mobility rate of persons over 30 or 35 to the frequency of the completed linguistic mobility of the cohorts to which these persons belong (Lachapelle, 1982c). This enables us to give a fairly simple description and interpretation of changes in the linguistic mobility of the cohorts from 1901−1906 (65−69 years old in 1971) up to 1931−1936 (35−39 years old in 1971), and sometimes to 1936−1941 (30−34 years old in 1971). It should be borne in mind, however, that the model on which our descriptions are based is only an approximation of reality and that, moreover, this reality is far from perfectly depicted by any given census.

Variations in the linguistic mobility rate for those under 30 are manifestations, as we have seen, of the combined effects of degree of risk of linguistic mobility and length of exposure to the risk of changing languages. If we are to conclude that there is an increase in linguistic mobility in the younger cohorts, the overall rate must be seen to decrease from one age group to another or, at the very most, to increase very slowly. This would involve a very sharp increase in the degree of linguistic mobility from one cohort to another, since it would have to counterbalance the length of exposure to the risk of changing languages.[4] This is precisely what we can see in Figure 5.1: a reduction in the linguistic mobility rate for the younger segment of the English group, from 1.6% for the 0−4 age group to 1.0% for those 15−19. It seems unlikely that this change is indicative of a recent increase in the linguistic mobility of the English group. Both the level and the age-specific variations in the rate for the English group reflect not only the linguistic mobility of those persons whose true mother-tongue is English, but also of those persons to whom an English mother-tongue has been artificially attributed.[5] These fictitious language transfers probably represent a sizeable fraction of the transfers "observed" in the English group, particularly among young people and mainly outside Quebec. For this reason, we will in future limit our examination to the linguistic mobility of adults.

Figure 5.1
LINGUISTIC MOBILITY RATE (IN %) FOR PERSONS OF ENGLISH OR FRENCH MOTHER TONGUE, BY AGE GROUP (OR COHORT GROUP), CANADA, 1971

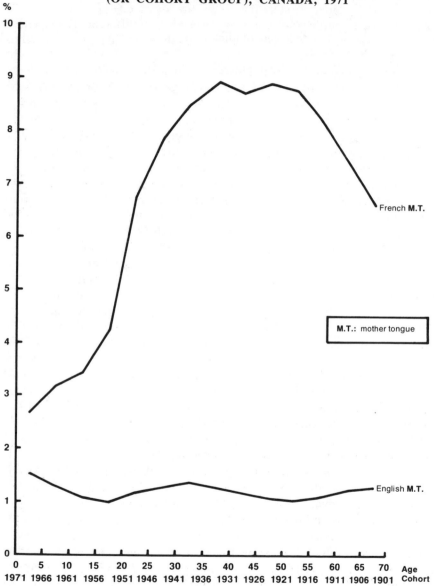

Strictly speaking, we are not concerned here with language transfers made by persons counted in the Canadian census, but rather with language transfers made within Canada. The latter correspond to the linguistic mobility prevalent in the country, while the former are also a reflection of linguistic mobility elsewhere in the world, as well as of differential migration. Therefore, we will give special attention to the linguistic mobility of persons born in Canada.[6]

Figure 5.2 shows that the linguistic mobility of the third-language group is much higher, for all age groups, among persons born in Canada than among those born outside Canada. This is not surprising. For a given age group, the length of residence in Canada, and thus the period of exposure to the risk of language transfer, is always longer for the population born in Canada than for those born outside Canada. Moreover, there appears to have been a sizeable increase over the years in the linguistic mobility of third-language persons born in Canada. Their overall rate increased from 58% to 80% between the 1901—1906 cohorts and those of 1931—1936.[7] This rise in the linguistic mobility can be observed for both the Amerindian group and the "other" group, but at quite different levels (Table 5.1). Among those of Amerindian mother tongue, the rate increased from 29% to 35% between the 1906—1916 cohorts (55—64 in 1971) and the 1926—1936 cohorts (35—44 in 1971), while the rate for the corresponding cohorts in the "other" mother-tongue group went from 78% to 86%. This means that only 15% to 20% of young adults in the "other" group keep their mother tongue as their home language if they are born in Canada, for an extremely low level of language maintenance. Under such conditions, only 15% to 20% of the children would have the same mother tongue as their parents, and less than 5% of the children in the following generation would have the same mother tongue as their grandparents. It would thus appear that these languages do not have any real *linguistic existence* in Canada; they barely outlast the generation that brought them into Canada. Moreover, in the 1971 census, 92% of the young adults (25—44 years old) who claimed to normally speak these languages at home were born outside Canada.

The term *allophone* (from the prefix *allo-*, other) is frequently used to designate those persons whose home language is neither French nor English. It presents the advantage of being short and relatively neutral. It does, however, have two disadvantages: (1) it does not translate satisfactorily the fact that these languages have always had a transitory existence in Canada and that their centre of development is elsewhere, and (2) depending on the context, it either includes or excludes those persons who normally speak one or another of the Amerindian languages. As we have just seen, the Amerindian group has a level of linguistic maintenance much higher than that of the "other" group; moreover, as opposed to the "other" languages, the centre of development of most of the Amerindian languages is in Canada. We therefore propose the expression *endophone* (from *endo-*, within) to

Figure 5.2
LINGUISTIC MOBILITY RATE (IN %) FOR PERSONS OF OTHER THAN FRENCH OR ENGLISH MOTHER TONGUE, BY PLACE OF BIRTH AND BY AGE GROUP (OR COHORT GROUP), CANADA, 1971

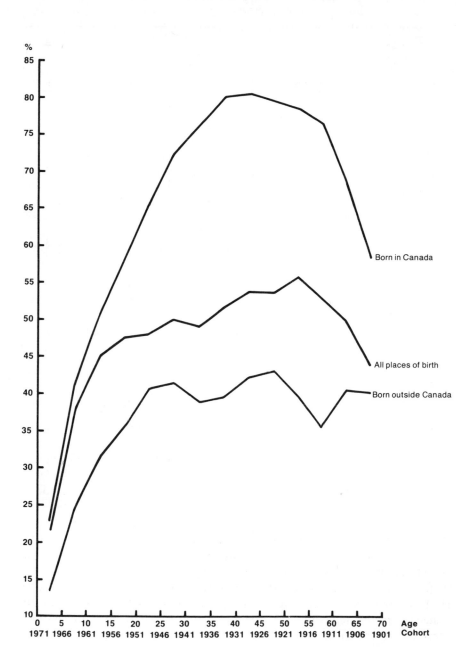

Table 5.1
LINGUISTIC MOBILITY RATE BY MOTHER TONGUE, AGE GROUP, AND PLACE OF BIRTH, CANADA, 1971
(percentage)

AGE GROUP AND PLACE OF BIRTH	MOTHER TONGUE				
	English	French	Neither English nor French	Amerindian[a]	"Other"
15−24 years					
All countries	1.1	5.4	47.9	31.9	49.5
Canada	0.8	5.2	61.0	31.7	68.8
Abroad	4.0	20.9	38.7	48.2	38.7
25−34 years					
All countries	1.3	8.1	49.5	36.3	50.2
Canada	1.0	7.8	74.5	35.9	82.9
Abroad	3.5	19.1	40.2	52.8	40.1
35−44 years					
All countries	1.2	8.8	52.8	34.9	53.4
Canada	0.9	8.5	80.3	34.5	86.3
Abroad	3.1	20.5	40.9	60.0	40.9
45−54 years					
All countries	1.0	8.8	54.6	31.0	55.4
Canada	0.9	8.5	79.0	30.3	83.7
Abroad	2.0	21.7	41.8	75.0	41.8
55−64 years					
All countries	1.2	7.8	50.9	29.7	51.6
Canada	1.0	7.4	73.5	29.3	77.6
Abroad	2.1	21.5	38.2	61.5	38.2

Source: Census of Canada, 1971, special tables.
Note: [a] In census terminology, this includes Eskimo and (North American) Indian languages.

designate those persons who normally speak an Amerindian language at home. Conversely, we could use the term *exophone* (from *exo-*, outside) to describe persons whose home languages is neither French, English, nor an Amerindian language. In line with the usage that has become current in recent years, we will use the expression *allophones* only when speaking of the group formed by endophones and exophones.

We will now describe changes in linguistic mobility for the English and French groups in Quebec and in the rest of Canada. In estimating the frequency of completed linguistic mobility in the cohorts aged over 30 in 1971, we will use the linguistic mobility rate observed for persons born in Canada. This choice is of course partly arbitrary. We might have confined ourselves to the mobility rate from English to French or from French to

English, but in most cases this would have yielded only slight variations in estimates of the completed linguistic mobility of cohort groups, since transfers from the French group are almost exclusively to English and those from the English group almost all towards French, at least in Quebec.[8] We might also have used, in place of the population born in Canada and living in one region or the other in 1971, the population born either in Quebec or in the rest of Canada and living anywhere in Canada, or else the total population counted by the census in one region or the other, or again the population born and living in each of these regions. No matter how this is done, while *levels* of linguistic mobility may often show sizeable variations depending on the sub-population under study, *changes* in the linguistic mobility rate from one cohort group to another are almost always parallel. This means that the developments we describe in the following paragraphs have a fairly high degree of reliability.

It can be seen, from Figure 5.3, that the linguistic mobility rate of the English group in Quebec decreased from 7.9% for the 1901−1906 cohorts (65−69 in 1971) to 7.0% for the 1911−1916 cohorts (55−59 in 1971), then rose steadily to 11.0% for the 1936−1941 cohorts (30−34 in 1971). In the rest of Canada, however, the rate for the English group varied little from one cohort group to another; indeed, it is so low (0.4%) that we can almost regard it as negligible. By comparison, still outside Quebec, the rate for the French group (Figure 5.4) climbed steadily from 27.0% in the 1901−1906 cohorts (65−69 in 1971) to 41.0% in the 1931−1936 cohorts (35−39 in 1971). Within Quebec, the mobility rate of the French group is obviously much lower. It first increased, from 1.5% for the 1901−1906 cohorts to 2.2% for the 1916−1921 cohorts (50−54 in 1971), then varied around 2.0−2.1% until the 1936−1941 cohorts (30−34 years old).

In Quebec, the completed linguistic mobilities for the English and French groups have evolved almost symmetrically. While the mobility of the French group rose from the 1901 cohorts to the 1921 cohorts, that of the English group decreased up to the 1911−1916 cohorts. The mobility of the English group then increased progressively up to the 1936−1941 cohorts, while that of the French group remained practically stationary. These trends can be found, with only slight difference one way or the other, in the various regions of Quebec (Table 5.2). By the same token, outside Quebec, the upward trend in linguistic mobility for the French group can be observed in most regions (Table 5.3).

To calculate the linguistic mobility rates, we must have at our disposal tables that divide the population by mother tongue and home language. If we assume, however, that women transmit home language as a mother tongue to their children, we can get an approximation of the linguistic mobility of women of child-bearing age if we know the mother tongue of young children and that of their mothers. It is possible to have these statistical data not only for the 1971 census, but also for the 1976 census, where we only have

Figure 5.3
**RATE OF COMPLETED LINGUISTIC MOBILITY (IN %) FOR THE
ENGLISH MOTHER-TONGUE POPULATION BORN IN CANADA,
BY COHORT GROUP, QUEBEC AND CANADA LESS QUEBEC, 1971**

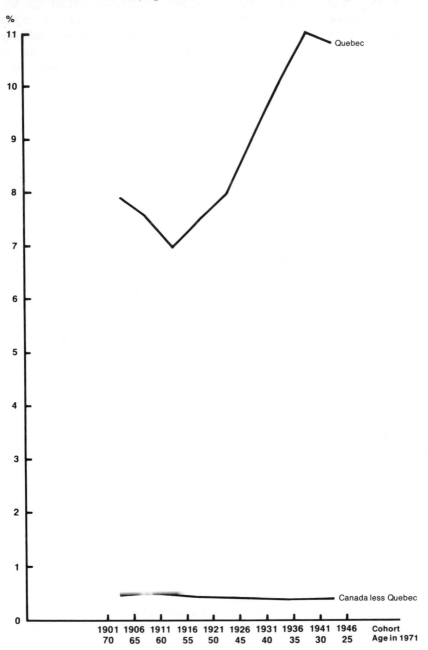

Figure 5.4
RATE OF COMPLETED LINGUISTIC MOBILITY (IN %) FOR THE FRENCH MOTHER-TONGUE POPULATION BORN IN CANADA, BY COHORT GROUP, QUEBEC AND CANADA LESS QUEBEC, 1971

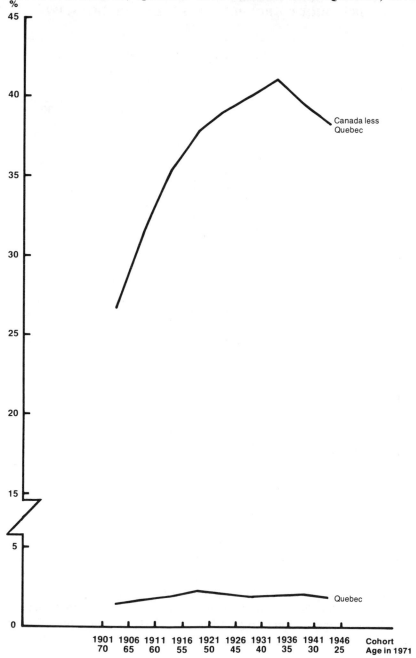

Table 5.2
RATE OF COMPLETED LINGUISTIC MOBILITY OF POPULATION
BORN IN CANADA, BY MOTHER TONGUE AND AGE GROUP
(OR COHORT GROUP), QUEBEC AND REGIONS, 1971
(percentage)

REGION[a] AND MOTHER TONGUE	COMPLETED LINGUISTIC MOBILITY BY AGE GROUP *(or Cohort Group)*			
	60–69 (1901–1911)	50–59 (1911–1921)	40–49 (1921–1931)	30–39 (1931–1941)
QUEBEC TOTAL				
English	7.7	7.3	8.5	10.5
French	1.6	2.1	2.0	2.1
Outaouais				
English	5.0	6.3	7.0	8.9
French	4.4	4.7	4.5	5.0
Montreal				
English	6.0	5.3	6.6	7.9
French	2.4	3.3	3.1	3.0
Eastern Townships				
English	4.7	6.6	6.2	14.2
French	2.3	2.6	2.1	1.8
Interior				
English	30.6	34.5	37.4	40.8
French	0.6	0.6	0.7	0.8
Periphery				
English	14.3	13.4	16.1	18.0
French	0.7	1.0	0.8	1.1

Source: Census of Canada, 1971, special tables.
Note: [a] See Appendix A.

mother-tongue statistics. The tables we were able to obtain divide children under 5 living in husband-wife families both by their mother tongue and that of the wife, who of course is not necessarily the mother in the biological sense of the word. While we are obliged, for the 1976 census, to use such tables to estimate the linguistic mobility of women of child-bearing age, we can however use other methods for the 1971 census. By comparing the results thus obtained with those obtained using the mother tongue of young children, we can form an appreciation for this estimation procedure.

Almost all mothers of children under 5 are between 20 and 45 years old. It would thus appear natural to compare, for 1971, the linguistic mobility of women in the 20–44 age group with that of wives living in husband-wife

Table 5.3
RATE OF COMPLETED LINGUISTIC MOBILITY FOR THE FRENCH MOTHER-TONGUE POPULATION BORN IN CANADA, BY AGE GROUP (OR COHORT GROUP), CANADA LESS QUEBEC AND REGIONS, 1971
(percentage)

REGION[a]	COMPLETED LINGUISTIC MOBILITY BY AGE GROUP *(or Cohort Group)*			
	60–69 (1901–1911)	50–59 (1911–1921)	40–49 (1921–1931)	30–39 (1931–1941)
CANADA LESS QUEBEC	29.6	36.8	39.8	40.4
Atlantic less				
New Brunswick	39.1	41.5	44.5	45.9
New Brunswick	9.7	12.0	13.5	13.9
North-and-East	7.0	8.3	9.1	9.6
South	47.9	53.0	58.5	55.6
Ontario	29.7	36.5	39.6	39.8
Southeast	13.6	17.8	20.9	23.1
Northeast	14.8	22.5	23.5	22.8
Northwest	53.8	60.7	54.2	50.3
Interior	58.3	63.6	66.6	66.9
West-and-North	47.2	58.2	62.1	64.4

Source: Census of Canada, 1971, special tables.
Note: [a] See Appendix *A*.

families having at least one child under 5. The results of this comparison appear in the first two columns in Table 5.4. As in both cases we have the home language of the women, variances between the two series of estimates should be quite small if we assume that for a given mother tongue, there is little difference in fertility by home language, and also that the linguistic mobility of women who have young children does not vary too greatly from that of women who do not. These variances are, in fact, often negligible, except for the third-language group as well as for the French group in Ontario and, above all, in the western provinces and northern territories.

To see if the mother tongue of children is a good approximation of the home language of their mothers, we have only to compare the linguistic mobility rates calculated using these two types of data. These calculations were made for wives living in husband-wife families having at least one child under 5. Whether we use the home language of these women or the mother tongue of their young children, we get essentially the same rates of linguistic mobility for the English group. For the French group, however, linguistic mobility is slightly lower when we measure it using the mother tongue of

Table 5.4
ESTIMATED LINGUISTIC MOBILITY RATE FOR WOMEN OF
CHILD-BEARING AGE, BY MOTHER TONGUE, CANADA AND REGIONS,
1971 AND 1976
(percentage)

REGION AND MOTHER TONGUE	FEMALE POPULATION AGED 20−44 IN 1971	WIVES LIVING IN HUSBAND-WIFE FAMILIES WHERE THERE IS AT LEAST ONE CHILD UNDER 5		
		Estimated Rate Based on Home Language of Wives in 1971	Rate Based on Mother Tongue of Children 1971	1976[a]
Canada				
English	1.1	0.9	0.9	1.2
French	7.9	8.4	7.4	6.8
Other	48.9	42.5	41.8	44.7
Quebec				
English	8.5	8.4	8.5	11.4
French	2.1	2.0	1.6	1.6
Other	31.1	22.5	17.9	22.4
Canada less Quebec				
English	0.7	0.7	0.5	0.7
French	38.6	35.4	31.8	31.8
Other	51.7	45.6	45.3	48.1
New Brunswick				
English	1.0	1.0	1.1	1.6
French	13.2	12.7	11.1	10.7
Other	55.3	41.4	43.3	48.6
Other Atlantic Provinces				
English	0.2	0.1	0.2	0.2
French	43.4	44.4	42.4	46.1
Other	57.7	47.4	51.6	46.3
Ontario				
English	0.8	0.8	0.6	0.8
French	38.8	35.2	31.5	32.3
Other	41.6	36.4	41.0	45.1
West-and-North				
English	0.6	0.7	0.5	0.6
French	62.9	49.4	53.2	56.7
Other	64.7	56.3	50.2	52.4

Source: Census of Canada, 1971 and 1976, special tables.
Note: [a] We have assumed, for any given mother tongue of wives, that children whose mother tongue is unknown follow the same distribution as those for whom mother tongue is reported.

young children, except in the western provinces and northern territories. Finally, for the third-language group, variances between the two series of rates are greater and not always in the same direction. In any case, we will confine ourselves in the following pages to examining the linguistic mobility of the English and French groups, since the methods of estimation we use do not lend themselves to even an approximate evaluation of linguistic mobility accomplished in Canada by women belonging to the third-language group.

All in all, it would appear that the linguistic mobility of women of child-bearing age may often be satisfactorily estimated using only data on mother tongue, provided we have access to tables giving the breakdown of young children both by their mother tongue and by that of their mothers.

We look next at changes in linguistic mobility between 1971 and 1976 for women of child-bearing age or, more specifically, for women living in husband-wife families having at least one child under 5. On the whole, the estimates given in Table 5.4 correspond fairly well with the trends in linguistic mobility of cohorts we described above, especially in Quebec. As we saw, the linguistic mobility of the English group increased regularly between the 1911−1916 cohorts and the 1936−1941 cohorts (30−34 years old in 1971); the linguistic mobility rate of women having young children appears to continue along these lines, increasing from 8.5% to 11.4% between 1971 and 1976. The same is true for the French group: linguistic mobility varied only slightly between the 1916−1921 cohorts and the 1936−1941 cohorts, and the rate for women with young children remained stationary at 1.6% in 1971 and 1976. It will be recalled that, outside Quebec, the linguistic mobility of the French group increased slowly in New Brunswick and in Ontario among the cohorts from 1921−1931 to 1931−1941, and more rapidly in other areas (Table 5.3). These rates of evolution can also be found in changes in the linguistic mobility rate for women with young children between 1971 and 1976. There is one exception, however; this rate decreased slightly, from 11.1% to 10.7%, in New Brunswick. Could this be the beginning of a new trend or simply a variation caused by circumstances particular to that period, or even an artificial variation?

The language transfers of third-language women, based on the mother tongue of children under 5, were to French in 31% of cases[9] in 1971 and in 27% of cases in 1976, in Quebec. This downward movement is in line with the trend observed for recent cohort groups, where the proportion of transfers from the third-language group towards French increased from 21% to 36% from the 1901−1906 cohorts (65−69 years old in 1971) to the 1941−1946 cohorts (25−29 in 1971), then dropped to 24% for cohorts born between 1956 and 1961 (10−14 in 1971). It should be noted that these proportions were calculated on the total population living in Quebec in 1971. If we were to look only at those residents of Quebec who were born in Canada, however, the changes are less clearly defined. The percentage of transfers from the third-language group towards French fluctuates between 30% and 35% from the 1901–1906 cohorts to the 1951–1956 cohorts (15–19 years old in 1971), then falls to 25% among the 1956–1961 cohorts.[10] All told, the distribution of third-language group transfers between English and French perhaps varied little in the past, with the exception of a quite recent trend towards English as shown by the comparison of situations observed in the 1971 and 1976 censuses. The situation is much clearer in the rest of Canada. Language transfers from the third-language group have, in over 99% of cases, always been towards English.

So far, we have described changes in linguistic mobility for the main groups in various regions of Canada. We have not attempted to explain them, as we felt it was preferable to first try to measure them properly; as can be seen from the above paragraphs, this is not an easy task, due both to the limited observations available to us and to the inevitably slow development of trends. We were also obliged to forgo the description and analysis of differences in linguistic mobility between regions. This aspect of linguistic mobility will be examined in the next two sections.

B. BILINGUALISM AND LINGUISTIC MOBILITY

Linguistic mobility, as we have seen, evolves very slowly from one cohort group to another. This is not surprising, since the factors that may influence linguistic mobility no doubt themselves evolve, almost without exception, quite slowly. The socio-linguistic conditions in which persons born around 1930 lived, in a given region, cannot have been very different from those that influenced the linguistic mobility of persons born in the same region around 1935. It is a quite different picture when we look at regional variations in linguistic mobility. Thus, in 1971, the rate of mobility from French to English among young adults (25–44 years old) reaches 64.5% in the Interior region of Ontario, but only 0.7% in the Interior region of Quebec, while in these two regions the rate of mobility from English to French is 0.1% and 38.3% respectively. These great variations would seem to be related to the contrasting demolinguistic situations that characterize these regions. The English and French groups represent 73.0% and 3.0% respectively of the young adults living in the Interior region of Ontario, while the proportions are reversed in the Interior region of Quebec: 2.0% for the English group and 97.0% for the French group. This indicates that it might be worthwhile to examine the relations between linguistic mobility and linguistic composition on a regional basis.

Linguistic mobility is, as we know, the product of two processes, bilingualism and the linguistic mobility of bilingual persons (Lieberson, 1970; Lachapelle, 1982c). If a person is to be able to make a language transfer, he must obviously have first learned the language he will adopt as his home language. In other words, bilingualism is a necessary condition of linguistic mobility. It is not, however, a sufficient condition. This is why, for the English and French groups, we will describe and analyse in turn regional variations in bilingualism, the linguistic mobility of bilingual persons and, lastly, the combination of these two phenomena, general linguistic mobility. All the figures we will use are taken from the 1971 census and are for young adults (25−44 years old).

1. Regional Variations in Bilingualism

In the whole of Canada in 1971, 7.0% of young adults of English mother tongue claimed they could carry on a conversation in French. Bilingualism is, however, much more frequent in the French group, since 46.0% of those in the 25−44 age group said they could converse in English. These frequencies are nonetheless a poor reflection of the situations prevailing in the various regions (Table 5.5). The bilingualism rate in the English group varies, depending on the region, from 2.5% (Other Atlantic Provinces) to 77.2% (Interior of Quebec), while that of the French group varied from 20.5% (Periphery of Quebec) to 97.4% (western provinces and northern territories). If the variation range between bilingualism rates in the English group (74.7 = 77.2 − 2.5) differs only slightly from that of bilingualism rates in the French group (76.9 = 97.4 − 20.5), it can nevertheless be seen that the lowest and highest rates of bilingualism in the French group are much higher than the corresponding rates in the English group. It would also appear that regional variations in bilingualism rates are somehow linked to variations in composition by mother tongue (Table 5.6).

Let us examine all this systematically. We will call b_e and b_f the bilingualism rates of the English and French groups, and p_e and p_f the proportions of the population whose mother tongue is English and French respectively. Using only the thirteen distinct regions for which the values of these variables are shown in Tables 5.5 and 5.6, we will attempt to estimate the extent to which bilingualism and linguistic composition are related. In doing this, we will often make use of a coefficient of correlation. This has been calculated, on the one hand, between the bilingualism rate of the English group (b_e) and the proportion represented by the French group (p_f) and, on the other, between the bilingualism rate of the French group (b_f) and the relative strength of the English group (p_e). These coefficients work out to 0.92 and 0.93 respectively. There is nothing really surprising here, unless it is the close relation between the two factors. Normally, we learn a language when it appears worthwhile, that is, when we are likely to have frequent contacts with persons whose mother tongue is that language. This is valid for the English group and for the French group, but not necessarily to the same extent. Shown below are the two applicable regression lines:

$$b_e = -0.02 + 0.59 p_f. \qquad (1)$$
$$b_f = 0.33 + 0.80 p_e. \qquad (2)$$

Table 5.5

GENERAL LINGUISTIC MOBILITY RATE, PROPORTION OF BILINGUAL PERSONS, AND LINGUISTIC MOBILITY RATE OF BILINGUAL PERSONS IN THE POPULATION AGED 25–44, BY MOTHER TONGUE, CANADA AND REGIONS, 1971

(percentage)

REGION[a]	ENGLISH MOTHER TONGUE			FRENCH MOTHER TONGUE		
	General Rate of Linguistic Mobility Towards French	Proportion of Bilingual Persons	Linguistic Mobility Rate of Bilingual Persons Towards French	General Rate of Linguistic Mobility Towards English	Proportion of Bilingual Persons	Linguistic Mobility Rate of Bilingual Persons Towards English
CANADA	0.7	7.0	10.0	8.3	46.2	18.0
Quebec	8.6	44.9	19.2	2.1	37.8	5.6
Outaouais	9.5	36.0	26.4	4.8	66.1	7.3
Montreal	6.2	43.1	14.4	3.0	50.0	6.1
Eastern Townships	11.2	52.4	21.4	1.8	39.8	4.6
Interior	38.3	77.2	49.6	0.7	23.7	3.0
Periphery	18.2	47.5	38.3	1.0	20.5	4.8
Canada less Quebec	0.2	4.4	3.9	39.9	88.8	44.9
New Brunswick	0.9	6.9	13.0	13.4	71.2	18.8
North-and-East	2.3	13.0	17.7	8.9	68.6	13.0
South	0.2	3.8	5.3	55.7	95.0	58.6
Other Atlantic Provinces	0.1	2.5	4.0	45.2	94.8	47.7
Ontario	0.2	5.5	3.6	39.6	90.8	43.6
Southeast	1.2	15.9	7.4	22.2	88.1	25.2
Northeast	1.2	12.2	9.8	23.6	86.8	27.2
Northwest	0.2	4.4	4.6	49.1	88.2	55.7
Interior	0.1	4.5	2.0	64.5	96.4	66.9
West-and-North	0.1	3.2	3.1	62.9	97.4	64.6

Source: Census of Canada, 1971, special tables.
Note: ^a See Appendix A.

Table 5.6
COMPOSITION BY MOTHER TONGUE OF THE POPULATION IN THE 25−44 AGE GROUP, CANADA AND REGIONS, 1971
(percentage)

REGION[a]	MOTHER TONGUE			
	Total	English	French	Other
CANADA	100.0	55.2	27.9	16.9
Quebec	100.0	12.1	80.1	7.8
Outaouais	100.0	16.9	80.5	2.6
Montreal	100.0	18.0	69.0	13.0
Eastern Townships	100.0	12.2	86.1	1.7
Interior	100.0	2.3	96.8	0.9
Periphery	100.0	4.3	93.4	2.3
Canada less Quebec	100.0	72.9	6.5	20.7
New Brunswick	100.0	64.6	33.3	2.1
North-and-East	100.0	40.9	57.5	1.6
South	100.0	90.6	6.7	2.7
Other Atlantic Provinces	100.0	93.6	4.0	2.4
Ontario	100.0	71.0	6.9	22.1
Southeast	100.0	61.2	27.4	11.4
Northeast	100.0	50.6	37.5	11.9
Northwest	100.0	69.0	7.8	23.2
Interior	100.0	73.3	3.1	23.6
West-and-North	100.0	71.7	3.7	24.6

Source: Census of Canada, 1971, special tables.
Note: [a] See Appendix *A*.

When the strength of the French group increases by 10 percentage points, the percentage of bilingual persons to the English group will have a tendency to increase by 5.9 points. The bilingualism of the French group is even more sensitive: it increases by 8.0 points when the English-group proportion rises by 10 percentage points. It should be borne in mind, however, that the above equations occasionally yield incoherent results. When p_f approaches 0 and p_e approaches 1, b_e is in the area of -0.02 (or -2%), which is obviously impossible, and b_f is nearly 1.13 or (113%), which is equally impossible.

These impossibilities lead us to question not the relation between bilin-gualism and linguistic composition, but rather the linear form we have assumed this relation to have. Moreover, there is no apparent reason why the relation should necessarily be linear.

To our knowledge, there is no theory that enables us to determine the form of a function g such that $b_e = g\,(p_f)$ and $b_f = g\,(p_e)$. We can nevertheless suggest several hypotheses concerning the properties this function should have. In the first place, it most likely shows a minimum for the English group when $p_f = 0$, and a minimum for the French group when $p_e = 0$. Let m_e and m_f represent these minimum bilingualism rates for the English and French groups. These rates should, by definition, be equal to or greater than zero. In addition, because of the geopolitical context that characterizes Canada and the importance of English in international communications, it is plausible to suppose that the minimum bilingualism rate of the French group exceeds that of the English group ($m_f > m_e$). In the second place, we can no doubt assume that the function g is increasing monotonically, and that the maximum is less than or equal to one.

Let us now attempt to determine the precise nature of the function g, or rather to constitute a function whose parameters can be given a worthwhile interpretation. We will base our reasoning on a group of regions that are quite similar from all points of view except linguistic composition. Our first assumption is that individuals belong to only two language groups, groups e and f. We will also assume that two categories of social relations can be distinguished, those where an individual is in a "supply" position and those where his situation is one of "demand," and that only the latter can constitute an incentive to bilingualism. More precisely, we will assume that the propensity towards bilingualism of the unilinguals in group e (or group f as the case may be) is proportional to the fraction of social relations in which they are in a position of demand *vis-à-vis* persons belonging to group f (or group e respectively). Let us in addition hypothesize that the two language groups are distributed in the same fashion between the social positions, that is, that there is social equality between groups e and f. The bilingualism rate of group e would then correspond to the sum of the following terms:

- m_e, which does not depend on the regional demolinguistic situation
- $(1 - m_e)u_e\,p_f$, where $1 - m_e$ designates the fraction of unilinguals in the absence of group f within the region, p_f is identified with the fraction of social relations where the unilinguals of group e are in a position of demand in relation to members of group f, and u_e corresponds to a proportionality coefficient.

We thus have $b_e = m_e + k_e\,p_f$, where $k_e = (1 - m_e)u_e$. In the same way, for the bilingualism rate of group f, we obtain:

$$b_f = m_f + k_f\,p_e.$$

These equations were estimated above, but the results were judged unsatisfactory.

Let us now put aside the hypothesis of social equality between groups e and f. Let the proportion of "suppliers" be s_e for group e and s_f for group f. The "suppliers" then are divided between the two language groups as follows:

$$p_e^o = \frac{p_e\, s_e}{p_e\, s_e + (1 - p_e)\, s_f} = \frac{p_e}{p_e + (1 - p_e)\, d_{fe}}$$

and

$$p_f^o = \frac{p_f\, s_f}{p_f\, s_f + (1 - p_f)\, s_e} = \frac{p_f}{p_f + (1 - p_f)\, d_{ef}},$$

where $d_{fe} = s_f/s_e$ and $d_{ef} = 1/d_{fe}$. If we maintain all the other hypotheses stated in the foregoing paragraph, we finally arrive at the following functions for the bilingualism rates of groups e and f:

$$b_e = m_e + k_e\, p_f^o = m_e + \frac{k_e\, p_f}{p_f + (1 - p_f)\, d_{ef}}$$

and

$$b_f = m_f + k_f\, p_e^o = m_f + \frac{k_f\, p_e}{p_e + (1 - p_e)\, d_{fe}}.$$

Each equation contains three unknown parameters, but we only have to determine a total of five parameters, since, as we saw, $d_{fe} = 1/d_{ef}$.[11]

In order to estimate the above equations for the French and English groups, we had to proceed by trial and error. We first chose various plausible values for d_{fe}. This enabled us at once to determine d_{ef}, as well as the values that p_e^o and p_f^o would take in each of the thirteen regions under study. Then, using the method of least squares, we estimated first m_e and k_e, and then m_f and k_f. On the whole, the results are quite satisfactory when d_{fe} is between 0.2 and 0.4. Shown below are the equations we have obtained by using $d_{fe} = 0.3$:

$$b_e = 0.03 + \frac{0.71 p_f}{p_f + 3.33\,(1 - p_f)} \tag{3}$$

and

$$b_f = 0.16 + \frac{0.85 p_e}{p_e + 0.3\,(1 - p_e)}. \tag{4}$$

The fit is generally excellent, as can be seen from Figures 5.5 and 5.6. In addition, it should be noted that the correlation coefficient between b_e and p_f^o is equal to 0.96, and that between b_f and p_e^o is 0.98, which is also a good indication of the quality of fit.

Let us now interpret rapidly equations (3) and (4). We will assume a region in which $p_e = p_f = 0.5$. In such a region, the bilingualism rate of the English group would be approximately 19.4% ($0.194 = 0.03 + (0.71 \times$

Figure 5.5
RELATION, AT THE REGIONAL LEVEL, BETWEEN THE PROPORTION OF BILINGUAL PERSONS IN THE FRENCH MOTHER-TONGUE POPULATION AND THE PROPORTION OF THE POPULATION HAVING ENGLISH AS THEIR MOTHER TONGUE, 1971

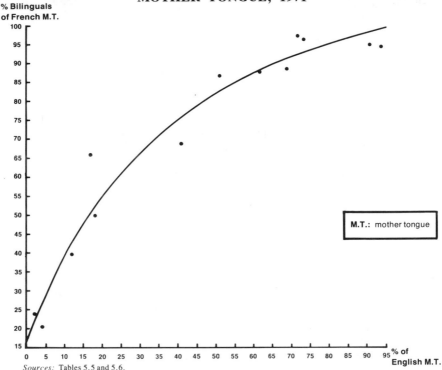

Sources: Tables 5.5 and 5.6.

0.231)), while that of the French group would be 81.4% (0.814 = 0.16 + (0.85 × 0.769)). The difference between these rates is 62 percentage points, which is far from negligible. This difference may be due to the combined effect of three more or less distinct factors.

a. The geopolitical context and the importance of English in international communications; the impact of this can probably be seen through the difference between m_f and m_e.

b. Social inequality between the English and French groups; this is translated by the parameters d_{ef} and d_{fe}.

c. The intensity of the reaction of English or French mother-tongue persons to contacts with members of the other group; this is approximately reflected by the coefficients k_e and k_f.

The first factor alone would bring about a difference of 13 percentage points (0.13 = 0.16 − 0.03) in favour of the English group. It accounts for

Figure 5.6
RELATION, AT THE REGIONAL LEVEL, BETWEEN THE PROPORTION OF BILINGUAL PERSONS IN THE ENGLISH MOTHER-TONGUE POPULATION AND THE PROPORTION OF THE POPULATION HAVING FRENCH AS THEIR MOTHER TONGUE, 1971

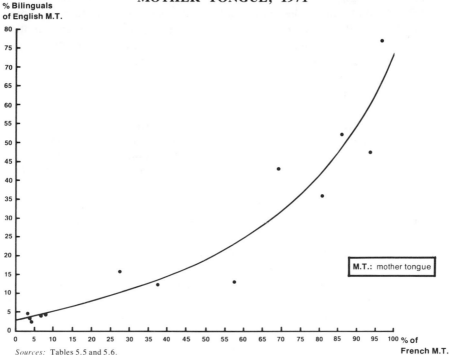

% Bilinguals
of English M.T.

M.T.: mother tongue

% of
French M.T.

Sources: Tables 5.5 and 5.6.

about 20.0% of the difference between the bilingualism rates of the French and English groups (0.21 = 0.13/0.62). To approximately isolate the specific effect of the second factor, we calculate the bilingualism rate that corresponds to a situation of social equality between the English and French groups. This is the same as assuming that $d_{ef} = d_{fe} = 1$. Under this hypothesis, the bilingualism rate of the English group would be 38.5% (0.385 = 0.03 + (0.71 × 0.5)) and that of the French group, 58.5% (0.585 = 0.16 + (0.85 × 0.5)). The difference here is only 20 percentage points. This means that social inequality between the language groups would cause a difference of 42 percentage points between the bilingualism rates of the French and English groups. The effect of the third factor would obviously be much weaker. If we suppose that the reaction of the French group is identical to that of the English group, the bilingualism rate of the French group would drop from 81.4% to 70.6% (0.706 = 0.16 + (0.71 × 0.769)), for a difference of 10.8 percentage points. It will be noted that the sum of the effects of the three factors (65.8) is slightly greater than the total variance (62). This is due to interaction between the second and third factor. We can nevertheless consider that in a region where the two groups were equally represented, the difference between the bilingualism of the French group and that of the English group would be 20.0% due to the international context, 60.0% to 70.0% due to the favourable social positions of the English group, and 10.0% to 20.0% due to a stronger reaction by persons of French mother tongue to intergroup contacts. These are obviously orders of magnitude, and are in any case based on an interpretation of the facts that may seem somewhat fragile and highly speculative, particularly with respect to the third factor. We nevertheless felt that this interpretation was possible.[12]

We have just seen that bilingualism rates appear to vary under the influence of three factors. Let us assume that a distinct category of bilingual persons can be associated with each of these factors, with membership in one category or another depending on the factor that prevailed in the decision to learn the second language. The first category would thus be made up of persons whose bilingualism is mainly motivated by their relations with individuals or organizations outside the region in which they live. We would call this external or international bilingualism. The second category would contain persons whose bilingualism is principally due to unequal social relations in which they are engaged with members of another language group; we can reasonably assume that this type of social relation would mainly be found in work situations. This type of bilingualism would be designated as inequality bilingualism. Finally, the third category would correspond to persons who have learned a second language essentially because of the equal social relations that they have with the members of another language group; it can be imagined that such social contacts frequently take place in the home as well as in relations with neighbours. In this case, we would speak of proximity bilingualism.

The observations we have obviously do not enable us to assign numbers to the categories of bilingualism we have just described. For many bilingual persons, it would in any case be quite difficult to determine to which category they belong: international, inequality, or proximity bilingualism. These types of bilingualism do not represent clearly identifiable categories, but rather latent classes. They are intellectual constructions with no immediate interest. Their usefulness is mediate, through the light they shed or the clarification they bring, as well as through the interpretations they permit of situations and facts that can be observed or measured. Let us then see what use we can make of the three types of bilingualism we have just described.

If we go back to equation (4), we see that it describes satisfactorily the variations in the bilingualism rate of the French group as a function of the proportion of persons of English mother tongue. When the English group is not present in a region, the frequency of bilingualism is nonetheless 16% for the French group.[13] This could only be the type of bilingualism we have designated as external or international. When the strength of the English group increases, the two other categories of bilingualism appear. To get an approximate idea of the respective size of the three categories, we have assumed that international bilingualism would correspond to m_f (0.16), while proximity bilingualism would be equal to $k_f p_e$ and inequality bilingualism would be equal to the remainder of the estimated bilingualism rate $(b_f - m_f - k_f p_e)$. It can then easily be seen that the proportion of international bilingualism decreases as the rate of bilingualism increases, while that of proximity bilingualism increases constantly. The relative importance of inequality bilingualism first increases more and more slowly, then decreases and becomes zero when the French group represents a very small fraction of the population. The turning point would correspond to a proportion of English mother-tongue persons of 18% and a bilingualism rate in the French group of 52%. Of course, such precision is quite deceptive. It might be preferable to speak of a zone rather than a turning point. This zone would probably include three or four regions: the Eastern Townships, Montreal, the Outaouais, and perhaps also North-and-East New Brunswick. It is in these regions that inequality bilingualism[14] would be the most widespread, and not, as we might be inclined to believe, in regions where the French group constitutes only a small fraction of the population. This cannot be explained by a reduction in social inequality in predominantly anglophone regions, since equation (4) assumes that inequality is identical in all regions, but rather by the fact that the factors acting on proximity bilingualism take on such importance that they leave little scope for inequality bilingualism.

The English group does not appear to experience inequality bilingualism, at least based on equation (3). In addition, social inequality between the English and French groups would have the effect of reducing the impact of factors acting on proximity bilingualism. The proportion of proximity bilingualism would nevertheless tend to increase quite rapidly with an increase in the bilingualism rate of the English group, because of the low degree of international bilingualism.

2. Regional Variations in the Linguistic Mobility of Bilingual Persons

The three types of bilingualism we have described above apparently lead to very different linguistic mobility rates. International bilingualism no doubt causes little change in linguistic behaviour within the family group, and we can thus assume that it seldom leads to language transfers. Conversely, proximity bilingualism is likely to cause high linguistic mobility, since this type of bilingualism is due to factors that act directly on the family milieu. With respect to inequality bilingualism, we can assume that it is associated with an intermediate linguistic mobility, because this type of bilingualism results from factors that influence social contacts in work situations, and these factors probably have only an indirect impact on linguistic behaviour in the family milieu.

The foregoing considerations enable us to propose certain hypotheses regarding variations in the linguistic mobility rates of bilingual persons depending on the rates of bilingualism. Let us assume that, for a given language group, linguistic mobility rates are invariable within each category of bilingualism. This is the same as making the hypothesis that variations in the linguistic mobility rates of bilingual persons depend solely on the distribution of bilingual persons among the three categories of bilingualism. We have seen, however, that this distribution varies with the rate of bilingualism, although the evolution will be quite different depending on whether we study the English group or the French group.

For the English group, there would be only two types of bilingualism: international bilingualism and proximity bilingualism. When the rate of bilingualism increases, the share of proximity bilingualism first increases very rapidly, then more and more slowly. We may thus expect, all other things being equal, that the linguistic mobility rate of bilingual persons will evolve in a similar manner, depending on the rate of bilingualism. This, however, is not exactly what we see from Figure 5.7, where we have plotted

Figure 5.7
RELATION, AT THE REGIONAL LEVEL, BETWEEN THE LINGUISTIC MOBILITY RATE OF BILINGUAL PERSONS OF ENGLISH MOTHER TONGUE TOWARDS FRENCH AND THE PERCENTAGE OF BILINGUAL PERSONS IN THE ENGLISH MOTHER-TONGUE POPULATION

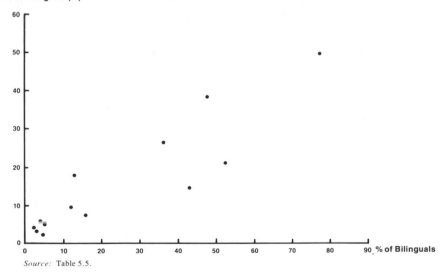

Source: Table 5.5.

the observations made in thirteen regions. Although the linguistic mobility rate of bilingual persons ($r(b)_e$) increases when the bilingualism rate rises, this increase appears to follow a constant and rather gentle slope. The regression line that would best fit the data in this case would be as follows (the coefficient of correlation is equal to 0.91):

$$r(b)_e = 0.02 + 0.55b_e. \tag{5}$$

The gap between observation and "theory" is scarcely surprising, since, in order to state a fairly precise theoretical proposition, we had to make a number of hypotheses, some of which were quite obviously implausible. To be truthful, our objective was not to develop a theory in the strongest sense of the word. What we were after was rather a bench-mark, or frame of reference, that would enable us to interpret observations. Let us then attempt to suggest an interpretation of the gap between the bench-mark proposition and equation (5). The deviation is, in fact, twofold: the linguistic mobility rate of bilingual persons increases more slowly than expected for low rates of bilingualism, but more rapidly than supposed when the bilingualism rates are higher. The first variance can easily be explained if we admit the assumption that the linguistic mobility of proximity bilinguals differs little from that of international bilinguals. In addition, it is unlikely that these linguistic mobilities would not increase when the proportion represented by the French group rises, with a consequent rise in the bilingualism rate of the English group. This could account for the second variance.

The next step is to develop a bench-mark proposition for the French group, using hypotheses similar to those made about the English group. Here again, when the rate of bilingualism rises, there is an increase in the proportion of proximity bilingualism, but a decrease in that of international bilingualism. The part left for inequality bilingualism increases more and more slowly, until it reaches a bilingualism rate of almost 50%, then decreases more and more rapidly. If the linguistic mobility rate of inequality bilinguals is much lower than that of proximity bilinguals, we should observe, depending on the rate of bilingualism, first a very slow increase in the linguistic mobility rate of all bilingual persons, then a markedly faster increase. This is exactly what we can see in Figure 5.8, where we have plotted data observed in thirteen regions. It should be mentioned, however, that the sharp progression in the linguistic mobility rate of bilingual persons, when the bilingualism rate is greater than 80%, is difficult to explain unless we put aside the hypothesis that the linguistic mobility rate of inequality bilinguals does not vary. Apart from this, the agreement between the observations and the bench-mark proposition is excellent. This result alone obviously does not authorize us to conclude that the mobility rate of inequality bilinguals is lower than that of proximity bilinguals. Other observations support this hypothesis. If we assume that, given equal levels of bilingualism, the linguistic mobility rates of proximity bilinguals are much

Figure 5.8
RELATION, AT THE REGIONAL LEVEL, BETWEEN THE
LINGUISTIC MOBILITY RATE OF BILINGUAL PERSONS OF
FRENCH MOTHER TONGUE TOWARDS ENGLISH AND THE
PERCENTAGE OF BILINGUAL PERSONS IN THE
FRENCH MOTHER-TONGUE POPULATION

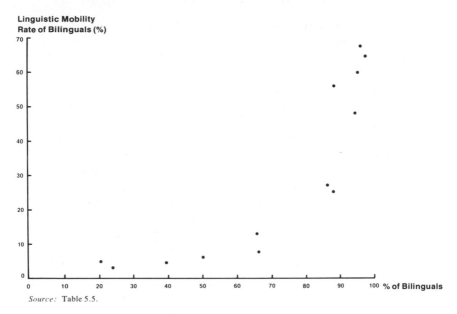

Source: Table 5.5.

the same for the English and French groups, we may expect that due to the lower relative frequency of proximity bilingualism in the French group, the mobility rate of all bilingual persons, bearing in mind the identical levels of bilingualism, would be much higher for the English group than for the French group. This is exactly what can be seen by comparing Figures 5.7 and 5.8. When bilingualism rates are between 30% and 50%, the mobility rate of French mother-tongue bilinguals is around 5%, while that of English mother-tongue bilinguals fluctuates between 14% and 38% (Table 5.5).

Based on the foregoing results, we may suggest that the linguistic mobility rate of inequality bilinguals in the French group is no doubt much lower than that of proximity bilinguals. This conclusion is valid mainly for the Quebec regions. It accounts for the fact that overall linguistic mobility rates for the French group are rather low in that province, in spite of high rates of bilingualism.

3. Regional Variations in Overall Linguistic Mobility

As we have seen, the overall linguistic mobility rate of the English group (r_e) or the French group (r_f) corresponds to the product of the bilingualism rate and the linguistic mobility rate of bilingual persons, that is:

$$r_e = b_e \times r(b)_e$$

and

$$r_f = b_f \times r(b)_f.$$

Bearing in mind the relations we demonstrated between, on the one hand, the bilingualism rate and linguistic composition and, on the other, the linguistic mobility rates of bilingual persons and the rate of bilingualism, it might be expected that the overall linguistic mobility rate would vary according to an exponential function of the proportion of the other language group, or, which amounts to the same thing, that the logarithm of the overall linguistic mobility rate corresponds to a linear function of the proportion of the other language group. Observations are fairly well in line with this prediction, as can be seen from Figures 5.9 and 5.10. This is not simply an impression, because the correlation coefficient between Log r_f and p_e is equal to 0.955,

Figure 5.9
RELATION, AT THE REGIONAL LEVEL, BETWEEN THE OVERALL MOBILITY RATE TOWARDS ENGLISH OF THE FRENCH MOTHER-TONGUE POPULATION AND THE PROPORTION OF THE POPULATION WHOSE MOTHER TONGUE IS ENGLISH, 1971

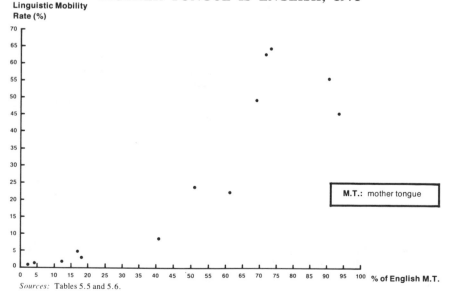

Sources: Tables 5.5 and 5.6.

Figure 5.10

RELATION, AT THE REGIONAL LEVEL, BETWEEN THE OVERALL MOBILITY RATE TOWARDS FRENCH OF THE ENGLISH MOTHER-TONGUE POPULATION AND THE PROPORTION OF THE POPULATION WHOSE MOTHER TONGUE IS FRENCH, 1971

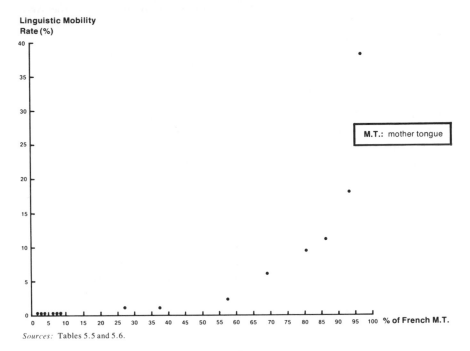

Sources: Tables 5.5 and 5.6.

and it rises to 0.987 between Log r_e and p_f, which is entirely satisfactory. We would point out here that the fit is better in the first case if we replace p_e by $1-p_f$; the correlation between Log r_f and $1-p_f$ is then 0.979. This might mean that the third-language group reinforces the drawing power of the English group. The regression lines we have estimated are as follows:

$$\text{Log } r_e = -6.800 + (5.683p_f) \qquad (6)$$
$$\text{Log } r_f = -4.445 + (4.845p_e) \qquad (7)$$
$$\text{Log } r_f = -4.603 + [4.136\,(1-p_f)]. \qquad (8)$$

So far we have described and analysed linguistic mobility as if it were a phenomenon proper to a group or a series of groups examined separately, one after another. We have considered that each group generates language transfers, while the other groups are seen as passive recipients. Each group is in fact both an issuer and a recipient of language transfers. We can thus only appreciate the effects of linguistic mobility on linguistic composition if we consider simultaneously all the language transfers that take place between all the groups involved. This aspect of linguistic mobility will be dealt with in the last section. We will thus confine ourselves here to approaching it schematically, using the equations estimated above.

To simplify the analysis, let us assume that equations (6), (7), and (8) correspond to regions made up of only two language groups, French and English. It is then easy to divide the regions into two subgroups, the first including the regions where English benefits from language transfers ($p_f r_f > p_e r_e$), the second taking in those where language transfers are mainly towards French ($p_f r_f < p_e r_e$). Using equations (6) and (7), we can determine that language transfers favour English when the French group component is less than 77%. If we use equations (6) and (8) instead, the threshold goes up to 85%. Based on this last estimate, language transfers should be favourable to French in three regions of Quebec—the Eastern Townships, the Periphery, and the Interior. In fact, this situation was only observed in the Interior region, where the French group in any case takes in almost 97% of the population.

C. HOMOGAMY AND LINGUISTIC MOBILITY

In describing and analysing regional variations in linguistic mobility up until now, we have broken this phenomenon down into two processes: bilingualism and the linguistic mobility of bilingual persons. Good results might also be obtained by using other types of breakdown (Lachapelle, 1982c). For instance, it is quite possible that the propensity to make a language transfer varies greatly depending on whether we consider members of homolinguistic couples or those belonging to heterolinguistic couples. In order to test this method of breaking down linguistic mobility, we will first examine regional variations in linguistic homogamy and then the differences in linguistic mobility depending on the mother tongue of the spouse.

1. Regional Variations in Linguistic Homogamy

Table 5.7 shows observed frequencies of linguistic homogamy in various regions of Canada. These frequencies were calculated for husband-wife families where the husband is in the 25–44 age group. They basically reflect choices of partner that took place during the two decades prior to the 1971 census. It should be noted, however, that some of the couples observed in 1971 were married abroad. This remark is valid mainly for the third-language group. In this group, the homogamy of men and women is 76.7% and 85.0% respectively for all couples questioned in 1971, while it drops to 48.3% for men and 61.7% for women if we exclude those couples where both partners were foreign-born. On the whole, the data we have available make it quite difficult to compare the homogamy of the third-language group with that of the French or English group.

Table 5.7
OBSERVED FREQUENCY OF LINGUISTIC HOMOGAMY IN THE ADULT POPULATION MADE UP OF COUPLES WHERE THE HUSBAND IS IN THE 25–44 AGE GROUP, BY SEX AND MOTHER TONGUE, CANADA AND REGIONS, 1971
(percentage)

REGION[a]	MALES			FEMALES		
	English	French	Other	English	French	Other
CANADA	92.9	92.2	76.7	90.6	91.2	85.0
Quebec	78.4	97.1	81.6	79.1	96.1	89.7
Outaouais	66.4	94.0	55.4	69.6	92.4	68.1
Montreal	81.8	96.0	83.3	82.1	94.3	91.2
Eastern Townships	78.5	96.8	43.1	76.5	96.5	63.8
Interior	46.9	98.7	53.4	50.0	98.5	59.5
Periphery	66.0	98.5	77.9	69.9	98.0	85.9
Canada less Quebec	93.8	67.5	76.0	91.3	66.5	84.3
New Brunswick	92.8	88.7	62.2	93.7	87.2	61.6
North-and-East	86.9	92.0	65.1	88.7	90.8	63.6
South	95.7	57.3	60.3	96.1	54.3	60.3
Other Atlantic Provinces	97.7	60.1	66.5	97.6	58.9	69.9
Ontario	93.9	67.9	80.4	91.6	66.6	87.8
Southeast	88.0	80.1	71.4	88.0	76.7	78.8
Northeast	83.5	80.8	65.8	81.9	79.6	75.6
Northwest	92.2	59.4	71.5	88.0	63.5	81.1
Interior	95.0	49.1	81.7	92.5	48.1	88.9
West-and-North	92.6	49.0	70.5	89.0	49.2	79.9

Source: Census of Canada, 1971, special tables.
Note: [a] See Appendix A.

Although the homogamy of the English group is almost the same as that of the French group in Canada as a whole, fairly large differences can be seen at the regional level. In the Interior region of Quebec, for example, the rate of homogamy in the French group is 98.7% for men and 98.5% for women, while that of the English group is 46.9% and 50.0% respectively. Conversely, in the Interior region of Ontario, homogamy in the English group is 95.0% for men and 92.5% for women, while it is much lower in the French group, at 49.1% for men and 48.1% for women. Let us see if there is any way we can account for these large regional variations.

Let us assume a population made up of only two language groups, group e and group f. We also assume that in each group the number of men is equal to the number of women and that marriage is universal. In each group, the rate of homogamy would therefore be the same for men and for women. Let h_e and h_f be the rates of homogamy of groups e and f. If there is neither segregation between the language groups nor preference associated with the mother tongue of potential spouses, in short, if mother tongue has no significance or social weight, then the choice of spouse will be made in a haphazard manner in so far as the mother-tongue variable is concerned. This is what we call, in population genetics, random mating (Jacquard, 1970). We would thus have $h_e = p_e$ and $h_f = p_f$, where p_e and p_f denote the proportions of the population respectively represented by the groups e and f. It is then fairly easy to calculate the expected frequency of homogamy for each language group and for each sex. These are shown in Table 5.8. We do not have to do a great deal of testing to conclude that the expected frequencies are

Table 5.8
EXPECTED FREQUENCY OF LINGUISTIC HOMOGAMY BASED ON THE RANDOM-MATING MODEL, IN THE ADULT POPULATION MADE UP OF COUPLES WHERE THE HUSBAND IS IN THE 25−44 AGE GROUP, BY SEX AND MOTHER TONGUE, CANADA AND REGIONS, 1971
(percentage)

REGION[a]	MALES[b]			FEMALES[c]		
	English	French	Other	English	French	Other
CANADA	56.7	27.4	15.9	55.3	27.0	17.7
Quebec	11.6	80.9	7.5	11.6	80.1	8.3
Outaouais	15.8	81.8	2.4	16.6	80.4	3.0
Montreal	17.2	70.0	12.8	17.3	68.7	14.0
Eastern Townships	12.1	86.7	1.2	11.8	86.5	1.7
Interior	2.1	97.1	0.8	2.3	96.8	0.9
Periphery	4.3	93.7	2.0	4.5	93.3	2.2
Canada less Quebec	74.4	6.4	19.2	72.4	6.3	21.3
New Brunswick	64.8	33.2	2.0	65.4	32.6	2.0
North-and-East	40.8	57.6	1.6	41.7	56.8	1.5
South	90.7	6.8	2.5	91.0	6.5	2.5
Other Atlantic Provinces	93.9	3.8	2.3	93.9	3.7	2.4
Ontario	72.0	6.9	21.1	70.1	6.8	23.1
Southeast	61.5	27.6	10.9	61.6	26.4	12.0
Northeast	52.1	37.9	10.0	51.1	37.4	11.5
Northwest	72.3	7.3	20.4	69.0	7.9	23.1
Interior	74.2	3.0	22.8	72.2	3.0	24.8
West-and-North	74.5	3.5	22.0	71.5	3.6	24.9

Source: Census of Canada, 1971, special tables.
Note: [a] See Appendix *A*.
    [b] This is simply the composition by mother tongue in the female population.
    [c] This is also the composition by mother tongue in the male population.

systematically lower than the observed frequencies of homogamy (Table 5.7). The random-mating model must therefore be rejected. This is not too surprising, as it is highly unlikely that mother tongue would not be taken into account when choosing a spouse.

Let us assume instead that individuals exhibit a marked preference for a spouse with the same mother tongue and examine the choices of spouse made by persons in group e. We further assume that their potential spouses are distributed in the same fashion as the population of the opposite sex, that is, that a fraction p_e of potential spouses have e as their mother tongue and a fraction p_f of them belong to group f. Let us now assume that the members of group e marry with a proportion t_{ee} of the potential spouses with mother tongue e, and with a proportion t_{ef} of those whose mother tongue is f, t_{ee} being greater than t_{ef}. The homogamy rate of group e would then be equal to

$$h_e = \frac{t_{ee}p_e}{t_{ee}p_e + t_{ef}(1 - p_e)}$$

$$= \frac{p_e}{p_e + v_e(1 - p_e)} \qquad = \frac{p_e}{v_e + p_e(1 - v_e)}, \qquad (9)$$

where $v_e = t_{ef}/t_{ee}$. If we invert each member of the above equation, we obtain

$$1/h_e = (1 - v_e) + v_e/p_e. \qquad (10)$$

We can obviously set up a similar equation for each language group.

Judging from equation (10), we would expect there to be a linear relation between the reciprocal of the homogamy rate of a given group on the one hand and, on the other, the reciprocal of the proportion this group represents in the population of the opposite sex or, which is the same thing, the reciprocal of the expected frequency of homogamy based on the random-mating model. We accordingly calculated the correlation coefficients between these variables for both sexes as well as for the three language groups, with the following results:

	English	**French**	**Other**
Men	0.951	0.950	0.708
Women	0.945	0.947	0.778

The fit appears to be quite satisfactory, especially for the French and English groups. It should be borne in mind that these correlation coefficients correspond to a model that may, and in fact does, always exhibit slight inconsistencies. What we have done is to proceed to fit the equation $1/h = u + v/p$, without putting any constraint on the parameters u and v. If we impose the constraint $u = 1 - v$, we obtain the following estimates for v coefficients:[15]

	English	**French**	**Other**
Men	0.025	0.032	0.011
Women	0.025	0.036	0.008

A reminder of the meaning of coefficient v. An individual belonging to a given language group is deemed likely to meet potential partners whose mother tongue is either the same as his or different. When a potential partner is homolinguistic, the probability that he will be chosen is not necessarily identical to that of a heterolinguistic partner. Coefficient v designates the ratio of the second probability to the first. It is equal to 1 under conditions of random-mating and to 0 when the propensity to form a couple with a potential heterolinguistic partner is nil. The coefficients calculated above are obviously much closer to 0 than to 1. They indicate the tendency of members of each language group to form homolinguistic couples. This tendency is especially marked in the third-language group, which is not surprising, since, as we have seen, a large proportion of these couples were formed outside Canada. Comparison of the coefficients for the English and French groups, however, yields quite surprising results, at least based on popular belief: homolinguistic preferences are more pronounced in the English group than in the French group. Before accepting this conclusion, we should take a closer look at the v coefficients.

We have estimated the parameter v in an equation of the type $1/h = (1-v) + v/p$ for each sex and all three language groups. We now have to see if these equations give reasonable approximations of the observed frequencies of homogamy. Figures 5.11 to 5.13 show these comparisons for each language group, for female homogamy only. It can be seen that the estimated frequencies of homogamy correspond fairly well to the observed frequencies when the relative size of the language group in question (or the expected frequency of homogamy based on the random-mating model) is less than 10%. Past this percentage, estimated frequencies are systematically greater than observed frequencies. This inconsistency is also found in the adjustment equation for male homogamy. This weakness could of course be partly remedied by using more refined methods of estimation, but there is another, more serious problem. The estimates we have undertaken are based on the implicit hypothesis that the v coefficients are constant for all language groups and consequently independent of linguistic composition, which is impossible.

Rather than undertake a demonstration that, while simple, would be rather cumbersome, let us look instead at a few examples. We will assume that v_e is constant and equal to 0.025, and calculate h_e in a region where $p_e = 0.05$ and $p_f = 0.95$. If we apply equation (9), we obtain $h_e = 0.678$. When p_e, p_f, and h_e are known, h_f can be calculated quite simply, on the condition that $p_e + p_f = 1$. This is because the number of couples where the man is of e mother tongue and the woman of f mother tongue is always equal to the

Figure 5.11
RELATION, AT THE REGIONAL LEVEL, BETWEEN THE OBSERVED FREQUENCY OF HOMOGAMY IN THE ENGLISH MOTHER-TONGUE FEMALE POPULATION AND THE EXPECTED FREQUENCY BASED ON THE RANDOM-MATING MODEL, 1971

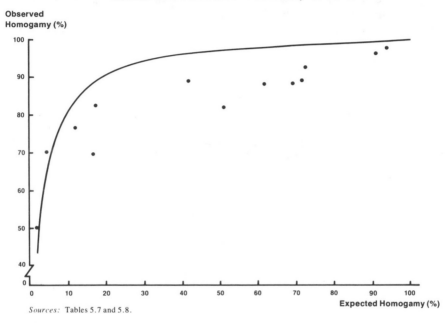

Sources: Tables 5.7 and 5.8.

number of couples where the women is of f mother tongue and the man of e mother tongue. We then always have $(1-h_e)\,p_e = (1-h_f)\,p_f$, which enables us to calculate h_f. This is equal to 0.983. Knowing h_f and p_f, we can also determine the value of v_f. We have, in effect, assumed that $h_f = p_f/[p_f + v_f (1-p_f)]$. Thus:

$$v_f = p_f(1-h_f)/(1-p_f)h_f.$$

In the population under study, v_f equals 0.329. If we repeat the same calculations for a region with the composition $p_e = 0.95$ and $p_f = 0.05$, still assuming that $v_e = 0.025$, we first obtain the value of h_e (0.9987), then that of h_f (0.9753), and finally that of v_f (0.0013). It is thus clear that v_f is dependent on both the value chosen for v_e and the linguistic composition. We therefore cannot assume that the parameters v_e and v_f are *both* invariable,

The above considerations lead us to question the conclusion we drew from the comparison of parameters v for the French and English groups, that is, that the English group seems to display a stronger homolinguistic preference than does the French group. We nevertheless did see that the

Figure 5.12
RELATION, AT THE REGIONAL LEVEL, BETWEEN THE OBSERVED FREQUENCY OF HOMOGAMY IN THE FRENCH MOTHER-TONGUE FEMALE POPULATION AND THE EXPECTED FREQUENCY BASED ON THE RANDOM-MATING MODEL, 1971

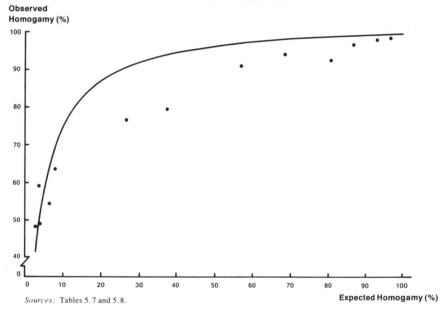

Sources: Tables 5.7 and 5.8.

estimated frequencies are close to the observed frequencies when the groups involved represent less than 10% of the population. Might we not then consider that the above conclusion is at least valid for these situations? To better appreciate the problem, let us take two regions that are symmetrical from the point of view of linguistic composition. Let $p_e = 0.05$ and $p_f = 0.95$ in region 1, while in region 2 the linguistic composition would correspond to $p_e = 0.95$ and $p_f = 0.05$. Let us further assume, in line with estimates already made, that v_e equals 0.025 in region 1 and that v_f is equal to 0.034 in region 2. We first calculate the rates of homogamy for each group in the two regions. For region 1, we obtain $h_e = 0.678$ and $h_f = 0.983$, while in region 2 we have $h_e = 0.979$ and $h_f = 0.608$. These values are fairly close to the homogamy frequencies observed in the English and French groups in the Periphery region of Quebec, where the linguistic composition resembles that of region 1, and in the region "Other Atlantic Provinces," which is quite similar to region 2. We then calculate the unknown v parameters. In region 1, $v_f = 0.329$, and in region 2, $v_e = 0.408$. Are we to conclude that the English group has a lower homolinguistic preference than the French group, and that

Figure 5.13
**RELATION, AT THE REGIONAL LEVEL, BETWEEN THE
OBSERVED FREQUENCY OF HOMOGAMY IN THE
THIRD-LANGUAGE FEMALE POPULATION AND THE
EXPECTED FREQUENCY BASED ON THE
RANDOM-MATING MODEL, 1971**

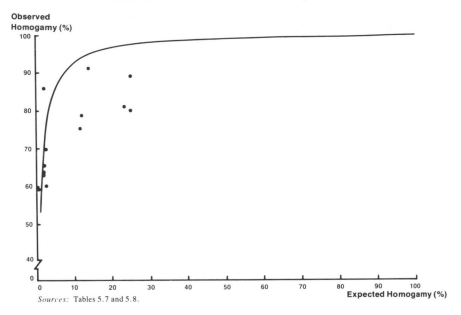

Sources: Tables 5.7 and 5.8.

this conclusion only applies to situations where one group or the other represents more than 90% of the population? We would then have two diametrically opposite conclusions, one valid in minority situations, the other in majority situations. Moreover, and this should be emphasized, either one implies the other, and it would be impossible to observe one without noticing the other.[16]

Our brief look at linguistic homogamy in Canada leaves us with several general conclusions. Members of the various language groups appear to have a marked preference for homolinguistic partners, that is, having the same mother tongue as themselves. The expression *homolinguistic preference* here describes the *results* of the process of choosing a partner, and not an *intrinsic disposition* to prefer a partner having the same mother tongue, if all other things are equal. In addition, in all language groups, the rate of homogamy varies in direct proportion to the relative share of the population held by the group in question. This conclusion bears out the theory proposed by Blau (1977, p. 23). Lastly, and with some reservations, we might advance two symmetrical conclusions. The English group appears to have a stronger homolinguistic preference than the French group, judging from situations where one group or the other forms a small minority. Conversely, when either group forms a large majority, the homolinguistic preference of the English group will be weaker than that of the French group. These conclusions obviously only deal with preferences that can be observed once the choice of partner has been made; our analysis does not enable us to speculate, even indirectly, on pre-existing homolinguistic preferences.

2. Linguistic Mobility Based on Partner's Mother Tongue

In Tables 5.9 and 5.10, we show the rates of linguistic mobility from English to French and from French to English according to the partner's mother tongue. These rates have been calculated for various regions, based on data concerning young adults forming husband-wife families where the husband is in the 25−44 age group. It will be seen that the overall linguistic mobility rates are not very different from those given previously for the total population between 25 and 44 years old (Table 5.5). We may therefore occasionally base our reasoning on these data as representative of the total population.

We would obviously expect linguistic mobility to be much greater when the partner is heterolinguistic than when he is homolinguistic. This in fact is what can be observed in all regions, in the English group as in the French group. Thus, for the whole of Canada, the linguistic mobility rate from English to French is only 0.2% when a partner's mother tongue is English; it rises to 14.4% when a partner's mother tongue is French and drops back down to 0.2% if one partner belongs to the third-language group. In the case of the rate of mobility from French to English, it is 2.6% in homolinguistic situations, rises to 58.3% when husband or wife claims a mother tongue other than English or French, and reaches 76.9% when one partner belongs to the English group. Although rate levels vary greatly from one region to another, this type of gradation is nevertheless common to all regions.

Although there is a certain similarity between the linguistic mobility of the English group and that of the French group, there are nonetheless a number of differences. For French mother-tongue persons, the risk of adopting English as the home language is as high, whether they marry a member of the English group or of the third-language group, while for the English group, linguistic mobility towards French varies little whether the partner is of English or third-language mother tongue. While we will not go so far as to assimilate the third-language group to the English group, we can nevertheless advance the assumption that with respect to repercussions on linguistic mobility, the third-language group is much closer to the English group than to the French group, even in the various regions of Quebec. In addition, in cases of heterolinguistic couples made up of a partner of English mother tongue and one of French mother tongue, linguistic mobility[17] is clearly to the benefit of English in almost all regions, except in three Quebec

Table 5.9

RATE OF MOBILITY TOWARDS FRENCH OF ENGLISH MOTHER-TONGUE PERSONS IN HUSBAND-WIFE FAMILIES WHERE THE HUSBAND IS IN THE 25−44 AGE GROUP, BY PARTNER'S MOTHER TONGUE, CANADA AND REGIONS, 1971

(percentage)

REGION[a]	PARTNER'S MOTHER TONGUE			
	All Languages	English	French	Other
CANADA	0.6	0.2	14.4	0.2
Quebec	8.5	2.2	38.4	3.0
Outaouais	9.1	3.1	23.7	3.0
Montreal	6.1	1.7	33.8	2.2
Eastern Townships	11.5	2.9	44.5	3.7
Interior	36.2	11.4	61.3	19.4
Periphery	18.3	4.7	48.6	16.0
Canada less Quebec	0.2	0.1	3.5	0.1
New Brunswick	0.8	0.3	9.3	0.0
North-and-East	2.1	0.6	13.6	0.0
South	0.2	0.2	1.7	0.0
Other Atlantic Provinces	0.1	0.0	2.4	0.0
Ontario	0.2	0.1	3.9	0.1
Southeast	1.0	0.4	8.1	0.4
Northeast	1.2	0.6	5.6	0.3
Northwest	0.2	0.1	2.8	0.0
Interior	0.1	0.1	2.0	0.1
West-and-North	0.1	0.0	1.3	0.0

Source: Census of Canada, 1971, special tables.
Note: [a] See Appendix A.

regions: the Eastern Townships, the Interior, and the Periphery, where it is French that benefits. It will be recalled that in these regions the English group forms only a small fraction of the population, 12%, 2%, and 4% respectively. Outside Quebec, French-Englishcouples adopt English as their home language in the vast majority of cases, although to a slightly lesser degree in regions where the French group forms a sizeable part of the population (North-and-East New Brunswick as well as Southeast and Northeast Ontario).

Table 5.10

RATE OF MOBILITY TOWARDS ENGLISH OF FRENCH MOTHER-TONGUE PERSONS IN HUSBAND-WIFE FAMILIES WHERE THE HUSBAND IS IN THE 25−44 AGE GROUP, BY PARTNER'S MOTHER TONGUE, CANADA AND REGIONS, 1971

(percentage)

REGION[a]	PARTNER'S MOTHER TONGUE			
	All Languages	French	English	Other
CANADA	8.5	2.6	76.9	58.3
Quebec	2.1	0.8	45.7	24.4
Outaouais	5.1	1.5	56.2	40.0
Montreal	3.1	1.0	50.7	24.6
Eastern Townships	1.7	0.6	39.0	14.0
Interior	0.7	0.4	24.4	20.8
Periphery	1.0	0.5	34.4	22.9
Canada less Quebec	40.3	15.7	91.1	85.8
New Brunswick	13.9	4.9	80.6	61.8
North-and-East	9.3	3.3	73.2	52.0
South	57.0	28.3	93.7	80.0
Other Atlantic Provinces	48.3	18.8	92.1	81.0
Ontario	39.5	15.6	89.8	80.5
Southeast	23.0	7.2	81.9	69.6
Northeast	23.8	8.9	84.1	81.1
Northwest	48.7	21.9	92.4	86.1
Interior	64.3	34.3	94.5	82.3
West-and-North	64.6	32.8	96.4	91.9

Source: Census of Canada, 1971, special tables.
Note: [a] See Appendix *A*.

The dissymmetry between the linguistic mobility of the English and French groups can be demonstrated by comparing the situations observed for English-French couples in two regions having contrasting linguistic compositions: the Interior of Quebec and the Interior of Ontario. In the predominantly French region, the rate of mobility from English to French is as high as 61.3%, as compared to 24.4% for the rate from French to English;

conversely, in the strongly anglophone region, 94.5% of French mother-tongue persons adopt English as their home language, while only 2.0% of English mother-tongue persons speak French more often than English at home. The situation is thus favourable to French in the Interior region of Quebec: the difference between the two rates is 37 percentage points (36.9 = 61.3−24.4) while, in the Interior region of Ontario, the difference between the rates is in favour of English and much higher: 92.5 percentage points (92.5 = 94.5−2.0). It may also be noted that quite similar gradations can be observed, although at a lower level, when we consider the linguistic mobility rate of homolinguistic couples in both regions. Does this mean that, for both groups, attenuation and amplification would be constant for homolinguistic couples on the one hand and for English-French couples on the other, in relation to the overall situation proper to each group? A simple statistical model will help us see this more clearly.

The following notation will be used:

- $r_{ef}(ee)$ Rate of mobility from English to French for individuals forming homolinguistic English couples
- $r_{ef}(ef)$ Rate of mobility from English to French for persons forming French-English couples
- $r_{fe}(ff)$ Rate of mobility from French to English for individuals forming homolinguistic French couples
- $r_{fe}(fe)$ Rate of mobility from French to English for persons forming French-English couples.

These rates are known. Let us assume that they are dependent on unknown rates for the situation that would be observed if all these individuals lived alone. Let $\tilde{r}_{ef}$ be the rate for the English group and $\tilde{r}_{fe}$ that of the French group. These rates, which vary from one region to another, reflect the overall situation of each language group. The fact of forming a homolinguistic couple would appear to bring about a sizeable reduction in the risk of language transfer, while on the other hand it is possible that being part of a French-English couple would considerably increase the risk of language transfer. There are obviously any number of ways to state these hypotheses as equations. We have chosen equations that appeared simple and easy to interpret.

$$r_{ef}(ee) = l_e \tilde{r}_{ef} \tag{11}$$
$$r_{ef}(ef) = (\tilde{r}_{ef})^{m_e} \tag{12}$$
$$r_{fe}(ff) = l_f \tilde{r}_{fe} \tag{13}$$
$$r_{fe}(fe) = (\tilde{r}_{fe})^{m_f}. \tag{14}$$

The parameters l_e, l_f, m_e, and m_f must of course have values between 0 and 1. The lower the value of parameter l, the greater the reduction in linguistic mobility caused by forming a homolinguistic couple. Conversely, the increase in linguistic mobility brought about by forming a French-English couple is less when parameter m has a high value. It is therefore interesting to compare, on the one hand, l_e to l_f and, on the other, m_e to m_f; however, these still remain to be estimated.

Simple manipulations of equations (11) and (12) allow us to eliminate the variable $\tilde{r}_{ef}$, leaving

$$r_{ef}(ef) = l_e^{-m_e} \times [r_{ef}(ee)]^{m_e} \tag{15}$$

or

$$\text{Log } r_{ef}(ef) = -m_e \text{Log } l_e + m_e \text{Log } r_{ef}(ee). \tag{16}$$

In the same way, for the French group, we would have

$$r_{fe}(fe) = l_f^{-m_f} \times [r_{fe}(ff)]^{m_f} \tag{17}$$

which is equivalent to

$$\text{Log } r_{fe}(fe) = -m_f \text{Log } l_f + m_f \text{Log } r_{fe}(ff). \tag{18}$$

Using the rates given in Tables 5.9 and 5.10, and confining ourselves to the thirteen distinct regions in those tables, we can easily estimate[18] the parameters involved. The following results were obtained:

$$r_{ef}(ef) = 4.223[r_{ef}(ee)]^{0.747} \tag{19}$$

and

$$r_{fe}(fe) = 1.403[r_{fe}(ff)]^{0.253} \tag{20}$$

These equations[19] fit quite well with the observed results: the correlation coefficient between the logarithms of the rates is equal to 0.955 for the English group and 0.944 for the French group.

In so far as their respective situations are concerned, forming a French-English couple causes a greater increase in linguistic mobility for the French group ($m_f = 0.253$) than for the English group ($m_e = 0.747$). To give a numerical example, let $\tilde{r}_{ef} = \tilde{r}_{fe} = 0.1$. In this hypothetical situation, English mother-tongue persons belonging to French-English couples would have a mobility rate of 17.9%, while the mobility towards English of their French mother-tongue partners would be 55.8%. Turning to the values taken by l_e and l_f, we find that they are equal[20] to 0.145 and 0.262 respectively. Still in relation to the overall situation of each group, this means that belonging to a homolinguistic couple brings about a greater reduction in linguistic mobility for the English group than for the French group. The French group would thus be at a twofold disadvantage in comparison with the English group: they benefit less from homogamy and lose more in heterolinguistic situations.

D. EFFECTS OF LINGUISTIC MOBILITY

In the foregoing sections, we have described and analysed the various developments over time and the regional variations in linguistic mobility or, more precisely, in the propensity to make a language transfer. In order to do this successfully, we had to use either rates of mobility from one language to another or rates of mobility from one language towards all other languages, which we called overall linguistic mobility rates. These rates are based on the statistical concept of risk, in this case the risk of making a language transfer. Useful though it may be in studying the characteristics and factors of linguistic mobility, the concept of risk does not allow us to perceive or measure, except in an indirect manner, the impact of linguistic mobility on the linguistic composition of the population. Of course, changes in linguistic composition do not only depend on linguistic mobility; they are also due to mortality, fertility, and differential migration or, more exactly, to the events generated by each of these phenomena. We can nevertheless attempt to estimate the specific effects of linguistic mobility.

How do we go about measuring the effects of linguistic mobility on the linguistic composition of the population? Although this question does not appear ambiguous, it could nevertheless have several meanings, depending on the way in which we understand, measure, and thus distinguish the effects of linguistic mobility from those of other demolinguistic phenomena, and above all on whether we consider changes in linguistic composition from one period to another or from one generation to the next. Limitations imposed on us by the available data on language transfers mean that we are obliged to look mainly at the effects of linguistic mobility on intergenerational variations in linguistic composition. In measuring these, we have up to now used net language transfer rates (Castonguay and Marion, 1974), or else comparisons of limit compositions with observed linguistic compositions (Bernard, 1978) or, lastly, continuity indices (Lachapelle, 1980). Following detailed analysis of the advantages and disadvantages of these methods of measuring the effects of linguistic mobility, Lachapelle (1982c) concluded that continuity indices yielded richer and more varied interpretations, while fitting in better with the particular ways in which demography perceives reality.

By continuity index, we mean the ratio of the number of persons claiming a given home language to the number of persons with the corresponding mother tongue. When language transfers favour a group, its continuity index is greater than 1: this group gives up less transfers than it obtains. Conversely, the continuity index is less than 1 for a group that gives up more language transfers than it receives. To get a more concrete picture of this, let us look at the continuity indices of various language groups for Canada as a whole in 1971 (Table 5.11). We shall confine ourselves here to young adults (25−44 age group) born in Canada, that is, a population in which linguistic mobilities are pretty well definitive and approximately comparable. The continuity index for the English group is 1.114 (or 111.4%), showing its drawing power, while that of the French group is less than 1 at 0.936 (or 93.6%). This means that the French group experiences sizeable losses in its linguistic exchanges with the rest of the population; as

Table 5.11
CONTINUITY INDEX FOR THE POPULATION IN THE 25-44 AGE GROUP, BY MOTHER TONGUE AND PLACE OF BIRTH, CANADA, 1971
(percentage)

MOTHER TONGUE	PLACE OF BIRTH		
	Total	Canada	Abroad
English	118.1	111.4	160.4
French	94.0	93.6	109.5
Other	50.9	24.7	61.5

Source: Census of Canada, 1971, special tables.

we know, these are mainly with the English group. The continuity index of the third-language group is only 24.7%; however, this low figure clearly underestimates the linguistic continuity of the endogenous-language group (Amerindians), which is around 65.0%, and slightly overestimates that of the exogenous-language group, which is between 15.0% and 20.0%. Thus we see that only the English group is favoured by linguistic mobility, while all other groups experience losses, although to a greater or lesser degree. The French group nevertheless shows much stronger linguistic continuity than does the endogenous-language group, which in turn is well ahead of the exogenous-language group.

Our next step is to attempt to interpret the continuity indices. Let us assume we have a population that is closed to migratory exchanges and in which all language groups have the same mortality rate. Let F_r correspond, in this population, to the lifetime fertility (average number of children per woman) that just enables the generations to replace themselves. It has been shown (Lachapelle, 1982c) that in these conditions any group i will ensure the replacement of its generations if its lifetime fertility (F_i) is equal to F_r/c_i, where c_i stands for its continuity index. This model gives an interpretation of the continuity index in terms of fertility. It also makes it possible to estimate the lifetime fertility that will enable a language group to replace itself, providing of course that we can first establish the value of F_r.

Under the present mortality conditions prevailing in Canada, the generation-replacement threshold is approximately 2.1 children per woman. This threshold is however much higher for the endogenous-language group (Amerindians) because of its high mortality rate. It would be about 2.6 children per woman. Using these estimates, we can calculate the lifetime fertility rates that would ensure replacement of the various language groups, taking into account language transfers, but assuming no migratory exchanges with other countries. The English group could be content with a lifetime fertility of 1.9 children per woman (2.1/1.114), since it gains from language transfers. The average number of children per woman in the French group would have to be 2.2 (2.1/0.936), which is slightly higher than the generation-replacement level assuming no linguistic mobility. It would have to be as high as 4.0 (2.6/0.65) for the endogenous-language group and at least 10.5 (2.1/0.2) for the exogenous-language group. This last figure is almost a biological impossibility; it has never, in any case, been observed in a human population (Coale, 1972, pp. 7−8). We must once again conclude that the exogenous-language group has no specifically Canadian existence: its strength can only be kept up with the help of massive and regular input from other countries.

This interpretation of continuity indices will serve to enrich our presentation of regional variations in the effects of linguistic mobility. More specifically, we will study the joint impact of fertility and linguistic mobility when examining changes in linguistic continuity from one generation to another.

1. Regional Variations

In Tables 5.12 and 5.13, we show the continuity indices for the English group and the French group, among young adults in various regions of

Table 5.12
LINGUISTIC CONTINUITY INDEX FOR THE POPULATION IN THE 25−44 AGE GROUP, BY PLACE OF BIRTH AND MOTHER TONGUE, QUEBEC AND REGIONS, 1971
(percentage)

REGION[a]	ENGLISH			FRENCH		
	All Places of Birth	Population Born in		All Places of Birth	Population Born in	
		Canada	*Quebec*		*Canada*	*Quebec*
Quebec Total	118.3	111.1	112.8	100.2	99.6	99.7
Outaouais	119.2	116.1	117.9	97.5	97.2	97.9
Montreal	120.7	112.8	114.8	100.2	99.2	99.4
Eastern Townships	105.4	102.7	103.2	100.3	99.9	99.9
Interior	99.3	95.7	94.5	100.5	100.2	100.2
Periphery	108.6	105.6	106.7	100.2	100.0	100.0

Source: Census of Canada, 1971, special tables.
Note: [a] See Appendix *A*.

Table 5.13

LINGUISTIC CONTINUITY INDEX FOR THE POPULATION IN THE 25–44 AGE GROUP, BY MOTHER TONGUE AND PLACE OF BIRTH, CANADA LESS QUEBEC AND REGIONS, 1971

(percentage)

REGION[a]	ENGLISH			FRENCH		
	All Places of Birth	Population Born in		All Places of Birth	Population Born in	
		Canada	Canada Less Quebec		Canada	Canada Less Quebec
CANADA LESS QUEBEC	118.0	111.4	110.9	62.5	62.4	61.1
New Brunswick	107.7	106.7	106.4	88.5	88.5	88.6
North-and-East	111.6	111.0	110.6	92.9	92.8	92.9
South	105.7	104.6	104.3	46.9	47.2	45.2
Other Atlantic Provinces	103.2	102.2	102.0	57.3	57.2	57.2
Ontario	116.5	108.2	107.3	63.3	63.2	60.4
Southeast	117.7	112.1	110.5	81.2	80.7	80.4
Northeast	128.7	123.8	122.3	78.3	78.3	75.1
Northwest	121.7	115.5	114.5	53.2	52.9	37.5
Interior	115.7	106.6	105.9	38.7	37.1	31.0
West-and-North	125.4	118.9	118.7	39.0	37.6	35.6

Source: Census of Canada, 1971, special tables.
Note: [a] See Appendix *A*.

Quebec and of Canada less Quebec. Our comments will deal mainly with continuity indices calculated for the population born in Canada.

Roughly speaking, we can distinguish six categories of geolinguistic groups.

a. Groups with sizeable surpluses. These clearly benefit from language transfers. Their continuity index is always greater than 1.02 (or 102%). The English group is in this category in almost all regions, including the Quebec regions, with the exception of the Interior region.

b. Neutral groups. These gain or lose little in linguistic exchanges. Their continuity index falls between 0.98 (or 98%) and 1.02 (or 102%). The French group is in this category in the various regions of Quebec, except in the Outaouais, where its continuity index is 0.97.

c. Groups with slight deficits. Their continuity index is somewhere between 0.90 and 0.98. If we assume that the average number of children to ensure replacement of generations in the absence of linguistic mobility is about 2.1, these geolinguistic groups can replace themselves when their completed fertility is between 2.14 (2.1/0.98) and 2.33 (2.1/0.9) children per woman. They are thus at a slight handicap, from a demographic viewpoint. The French groups in the Outaouais and the North-and-East region of New Brunswick are in this category, as is the English group in the Interior region of Quebec. It should be noted, however, that the French group in the Outaouais, like the English group in the Interior of Quebec, could probably have been included in the second category. The boundary lines between categories are, in any case, drawn somewhat arbitrarily.

d. Groups with moderate deficits. Their continuity index is greater than 0.7 but less than 0.9. The French groups in Southeast and Northeast Ontario are in this category. In order to ensure the replacement of generations in spite of their handicap with respect to linguistic mobility, their completed fertility should be in the order of 2.6 (2.1/0.8) children per woman.

e. Groups with large deficits. In this category are the French groups in the Northwest region of Ontario, the South of New Brunswick, and in the Atlantic provinces other than New Brunswick. Their continuity index is always less than 0.7. It varies between 0.57 and 0.47 from one region to another. These groups would need lifetime fertilities in the order of 3.7 to 4.5 children per woman in order to just barely replace themselves. Fertility rates like this were certainly observed in the past, but they appear less and less likely today.

f. Groups with insurmountable deficits. The French group in the western provinces and in the Interior region of Ontario belong in this category. In order to compensate for the great losses they experience due to language transfers, the average number of children per woman should be slightly more than 5.5. It should be remembered that this number would just ensure replacement of the generation. Although this kind of fertility is not biologically impossible, it is nevertheless not socially feasible under present conditions. This means that these groups have no specific linguistic existence. They can only keep up their strengths by calling on outside sources. In this they are similar to the exogenous-language group, although that group always shows an even smaller continuity index for the population born in Canada.

To sum up, then, the English group benefits from language transfers in all areas, except in the Interior region of Quebec, where in any case it only represents 2% of the population. As for the French group, its gains or losses are negligible in all regions of Quebec, except in the Outaouais, where its losses, while noticeable, are slight. Elsewhere in Canada, the situation of the French group deteriorates as the distance from Quebec increases. In the regions adjacent to Quebec (North-and-East New Brunswick as well as Southeast and Northeast Ontario), where the French group represents a sizeable fraction of the population, it certainly shows noticeable deficits in so far as language transfers are concerned, but these are not so great that they would irreparably jeopardize replacement of generations. This group may effectively maintain its strength if the average number of children per woman is greater than 2.2 in the North-and-East region of New Brunswick and 2.6 in the regions of Ontario nearest to Quebec. In the other regions of Canada, with the exception of a few small, isolated language groups, it is almost impossible, or at least very unlikely, that the French group would keep its numbers up without large contributions from outside.

Judging only from the foregoing analysis, we would be inclined to conclude, with respect to the French group, that linguistic mobility has a rather weak effect, sometimes negligible and at worst slightly unfavourable, not only in the various regions of Quebec but also in the regions bordering on this province. This conclusion is not incorrect, but it is incomplete. In fact, we have not attempted up to now to assess the effects of linguistic mobility on linguistic composition, since we have studied each geolinguistic group separately. All groups, without exception, were measured by the same minimum standard—maintenance of their strengths or, more precisely, replacement of generations, taking into account the language transfers observed but assuming no migration. Based on the standard of generation replacement, the French group, in regions where it represents an appreciable fraction of the population, displays linguistic continuity that is either slightly favourable or somewhat unfavourable. But how does this compare with the English group in these regions?

For the relative strength of the French and English groups to remain unchanged from one generation to the next, if there were no migration, it would be enough if the ratio of the continuity index of the English group to that of the French group were equal to the ratio of the completed fertility of the French group to that of the English group (Lachapelle, 1982c). This ratio gives a normative index of relative fertility, or more exactly the excess fertility the French group must achieve compared to the English group if it is to counterbalance the effects of linguistic mobility. We have calculated this normative index for the regions under study (Table 5.14).

The eight regions involved can be divided into four categories.

a. Regions where the anglophone group is far in the lead. The Northeast and Southeast of Ontario belong in this category. To balance the favourable effects of language transfers on the anglophone group, francophones would need an excess fertility of 60% in the Northeast and 40% in the Southeast. In other words, if the completed fertility of anglophones is close to the generation-replacement threshold (2.1 children per woman), francophones would have to have 3.4 and 2.9 children per woman respectively in order to cancel out the effects of linguistic mobility.

b. Regions where the anglophone group has a moderate lead. In this category are the Outaouais and Montreal regions, as well as the North-and-East region of New Brunswick. In these regions, francophones would need an excess fertility of 15% to 20% to counteract gains made by the anglophones from language transfers. This means that the completed fertility of francophones would have to be in the order of 2.4—2.5 children per woman if

Table 5.14

RATIO OF THE ENGLISH GROUP CONTINUITY INDEX TO THAT OF THE FRENCH GROUP, FOR THE POPULATION IN THE 25–44 AGE GROUP, BY PLACE OF BIRTH, FOR SELECTED REGIONS, 1971

(percentage)

REGION[a]	ALL PLACES OF BIRTH	POPULATION BORN IN CANADA
Northeast Ontario	164	158
Southeast Ontario	145	139
North-and-East New Brunswick	120	120
Outaouais	122	119
Montreal	120	114
Eastern Townships	105	103
Periphery of Quebec	108	106
Interior of Quebec	99	96

Sources: Tables 5.12 and 5.13.
Note: [a] See Appendix *A*.

that of anglophones is equal to 2.1. It should be noted that much of the excess fertility that Montreal francophones must achieve goes to offset gains made by the anglophone group at the expense of the third-language group. If we consider only those language exchanges between the French group and the English group (Table 5.15), francophones could cancel out the effects of linguistic mobility by an excess fertility of 7% or 8%.

  c. Regions where the anglophone group is slightly ahead. Two regions are in this category: the Eastern Townships and the Periphery of Quebec.

  d. Regions where the francophone group is slightly ahead. The only region in this category is the Interior of Quebec.

  In short, linguistic mobility has little effect on the respective situations of the English and French groups in three Quebec regions: the Eastern Townships, the Interior, and the Periphery. Whether the norm we use is replacement of generations or maintenance of the relative size of the French and English groups makes little difference to our conclusions about the effects of linguistic mobility in these regions. This is not the case for the other two regions in Quebec: Montreal and the Outaouais. Although the French group can replace itself with no more difficulty, or not too much more, than the total population (all language groups combined), it

Table 5.15
RATIO OF THE ENGLISH GROUP CONTINUITY INDEX TO THAT OF THE FRENCH GROUP, FOR THE POPULATION IN THE 25−44 AGE GROUP WITH FRENCH OR ENGLISH MOTHER TONGUE AND HOME LANGUAGE, BY PLACE OF BIRTH, FOR SELECTED REGIONS, 1971
(percentage)

REGION[a]	ALL PLACES OF BIRTH	POPULATION BORN IN CANADA
Northeast Ontario	149	150
Southeast Ontario	135	137
North-and-East New Brunswick	119	119
Outaouais	117	118
Montreal	107	108
Eastern Townships	102	102
Periphery of Quebec	103	103
Interior of Quebec	92	94

Source: Census of Canada, 1971, special tables.
Note: [a] See Appendix *A*.

nevertheless exhibits a marked disadvantage when compared with the English group. The North-and-East region of New Brunswick is in the same situation. The overall effects of linguistic mobility are similar in these three regions, but the causes for this are quite different. In the Outaouais and North-and-East New Brunswick, the francophone excess fertility of about 20% goes mainly to cancel out imbalances in language transfers between the English group and the French group. In Montreal, however, half of the francophone excess fertility must counterbalance gains made by the English group at the expense of the third-language group. As for the Ontario regions closest to Quebec, the francophones there are always at a clear disadvantage, no matter what indicator we use.

2. Changes Between Generations

We have confined ourselves so far to establishing the lifetime fertility that would enable a language group either to ensure generation replacement or to maintain its relative strength in the population. We can go further than this, since the 1971 census gives us the average number of children per woman, by home language, for the various cohort groups. Using these data, we will attempt to follow the development of linguistic reproduction through successive cohorts.

We will assume that there is no migration nor any mortality differences between language groups and lay down the following notation for the female population in any given age group:

$P_i.$ Number of women of i mother tongue

$P._i$ Number of women of i home language

$c_i = P._i/P_i.$ Continuity index of group i

$P..$ Total number of women in the age group considered

$p_i. = P_i./P..$ Proportion of women of i mother tongue in this age group

$M._i$ Number of ever-married women of i home language

$m._i = M._i/P._i$ Proportion of ever-married women in the female population of i home language

$m..$ Proportion of ever-married women in the total female population in the age group considered

$n_i = m._i/m..$ Differential nuptiality index of women of i home language

$F._i$ Average number of children born to ever-married women of i home language

$F..$ Average number of children born to all ever-married women in the age group under study

$f_i = F._i/F..$ Differential fertility index of ever-married women of i home language

R_i Reproduction index of group i.

If we assume that the fertility of single women is negligible and that the mother tongue of children corresponds to the home language of their mothers, we can then estimate approximately the proportion of children born to women in the age group under study who will have i as their mother tongue. This proportion is equal to $p_i. R_i$, where $R_i = c_i n_i f_i$. The linguistic reproduction index thus corresponds to the product of the indices of continuity, differential nuptiality, and differential fertility of ever-married women.

These indices have been calculated for the total female population living in Canada in 1971 (Table 5.16). It should be noted at the outset that the indices for allophones cannot in any case be compared with those for anglophones and francophones, since a large proportion of the women in the third-language group were not born in Canada. This is why in the following paragraphs we will limit ourselves to comparing the indices for anglophones to those for francophones.

It can be seen from Table 5.16 that the continuity and differential nuptiality indices for anglophones and francophones varied little between the 1906–1911 cohorts and the 1936–1941 cohorts. These indices show the effects of linguistic mobility and nuptiality on inter-cohort variations in linguistic composition. These two phenomena always favour the English group and invariably work to the detriment of the French group. It is a

Table 5.16
INDICES OF CONTINUITY (*c*), DIFFERENTIAL NUPTIALITY (*n*), DIFFERENTIAL FERTILITY OF EVER-MARRIED WOMEN (*f*), AND LINGUISTIC REPRODUCTION (*R*) IN THE FEMALE POPULATION, BY AGE GROUP (OR COHORT GROUP) AND LANGUAGE, CANADA, 1971
(percentage)

AGE GROUP (*or Cohort Group*) AND INDEX	ENGLISH	FRENCH	OTHER
30−34 *(1936−1941)*			
c	116.9	93.6	55.4
n	101.5	95.5	102.4
f	101.6	99.3	91.1
R	120.6	88.8	51.7
35−39 *(1931−1936)*			
c	119.5	93.2	51.9
n	101.6	95.1	102.9
f	99.5	106.2	87.4
R	120.8	94.1	46.7
40−44 *(1926−1931)*			
c	119.7	93.6	49.1
n	101.4	95.5	102.7
f	96.3	115.1	85.8
R	116.9	102.9	43.3
45−49 *(1921−1926)*			
c	118.3	93.5	49.2
n	101.4	95.2	103.3
f	93.2	125.4	85.9
R	111.8	111.6	43.7
50−54 *(1916−1921)*			
c	115.8	93.3	46.7
n	101.4	94.7	104.2
f	90.5	131.3	93.1
R	106.3	116.0	45.3
55−59 *(1911−1916)*			
c	115.1	94.1	51.0
n	101.6	93.6	106.2
f	88.5	134.4	102.9
R	103.5	118.4	55.7
60−64 *(1906−1911)*			
c	115.0	95.1	57.6
n	101.2	93.4	108.2
f	85.3	139.8	107.3
R	99.3	124.2	66.9

Source: Census of Canada, 1971, special tables.

completely different story, however, for the differential fertility of ever-married women. For the cohorts born between 1906 and 1911 (60−64 years old in 1971), the excess fertility of francophones over anglophones is as high as 64% (1.639 = 139.8/85.3). It decreases steadily among succeeding cohorts and even develops into under-fertility for francophones in the 1936−1941 cohorts (30−34 in 1971). It is no surprise, then, that the reproduction index of the French group shows such a rapid drop from one generation to another.

If we consider only the combined effects of the linguistic mobility, nuptiality, and fertility of ever-married women, inter-cohort variations in linguistic composition are first, for the 1906−1911 cohorts, clearly favourable to francophones (R_f = 1.242) and slightly unfavourable to anglophones (R_e = 0.993). Following this, the reproduction indices for anglophones and francophones move closer and closer together as the excess fertility of the latter over the former declines; they meet in the 1921−1926 cohorts (45−49 years old), when both are equal to 1.12. The gap then widens increasingly in favour of the English group as francophone excess fertility is less and less able to compensate for the unfavourable effects of nuptiality and, above all, linguistic mobility. Starting with the 1931−1936 cohorts, the French group is no longer able to maintain its relative strength in the total population, since its reproduction index is less than 1. In the final analysis, the sharp reduction in the reproduction index of the French group between the 1906−1911 cohorts and the 1936−1941 cohorts, and the rise in that of the English group, are almost entirely due to the evolution in the differential fertility indices of ever-married women.

The above conclusion is valid not only for the total Canadian population, but also, to a large degree, for the Quebec population as well as for that of the rest of Canada (Table 5.17). In Quebec, the excess fertility of francophones compared to anglophones fell from 86% in the 1906−1911 cohorts to 48% for the 1921−1926 cohorts, then to 9% for the 1936−1941 cohorts. The slight excess fertility of francophones is no longer sufficient to counter-balance gains made by anglophones through language transfers. Although the reproduction index of the French group is slightly greater than 1 for the 1936−1941 cohorts, it is far less than that of the English group. If there were no migration, the French group would succeed in maintaining or slightly increasing its relative strength, while the English group would see its proportion increase quite rapidly.

It might come as somewhat of a surprise that the continuity index of the English group decreases very little in Quebec between the 1921−1926 cohorts (119.0%) and the 1936−1941 cohorts (118.1%), since it was shown, in Section *A*, that the linguistic mobility rate of the English group increased quite rapidly there starting with the 1911−1916 cohorts. This disparity in evolution is due to the fact that the continuity index depends not only on the

Table 5.17
INDICES OF CONTINUITY (c), DIFFERENTIAL NUPTIALITY (n), DIFFERENTIAL FERTILITY OF EVER-MARRIED WOMEN (f), AND LINGUISTIC REPRODUCTION (R) IN THE FEMALE POPULATION, BY LANGUAGE AND FOR SELECTED AGE GROUPS (OR COHORT GROUPS), QUEBEC AND CANADA LESS QUEBEC, 1971
(percentage)

REGION, AGE GROUP (or Cohort Group) AND INDEX	ENGLISH	FRENCH	OTHER
QUEBEC			
30–34 *(1936–1941)*			
c	118.1	99.8	75.2
n	99.9	99.6	106.1
f	93.4	102.1	88.4
R	110.2	101.5	70.5
45–49 *(1921–1926)*			
c	119.0	99.6	67.8
n	103.0	98.9	106.8
f	73.2	108.1	68.8
R	89.7	106.5	49.8
60–64 *(1906–1911)*			
c	113.7	100.0	69.6
n	102.2	98.6	114.6
f	59.9	111.6	74.8
R	69.6	110.0	59.7
CANADA LESS QUEBEC			
30–34 *(1936–1941)*			
c	116.8	62.2	52.3
n	100.1	95.5	100.8
f	100.2	119.9	90.8
R	117.2	71.2	47.9
45–49 *(1921–1926)*			
c	118.3	63.3	46.7
n	99.9	96.7	101.8
f	98.6	154.3	91.8
R	116.5	94.4	43.6
60–64 *(1906–1911)*			
c	115.1	70.9	56.1
n	97.0	95.7	105.9
f	93.5	175.1	119.0
R	104.4	118.8	70.7

Source: Census of Canada, 1971, special tables.

linguistic mobility rate but also on the composition by mother tongue (Lachapelle, 1982c). This deserves a closer examination.

Between the 1921−1926 cohorts and the 1936−1941 cohorts, the rate of mobility from English to French for the total female population of Quebec increased from 5.9% to 7.9%, while the rate of mobility from French to English remained almost stationary, going from 2.1% to 2.0%. In addition, the 1971 census showed that the strength of the English mother-tongue group declined, between these two groups of cohorts, from 14.0% to 11.9%, while the relative strength of the French mother-tongue group rose from 78.6% to 80.1%. We shall attempt to isolate the impact of changes in rates of linguistic mobility from that of variations in linguistic composition on the evolution of the continuity indices. To do this, we will apply the linguistic mobility rates of the 1921−1926 cohorts to the composition by mother tongue observed in 1971 among the 1936−1941 cohorts. This will enable us to calculate the continuity indices that would have been observed in the 1936−1941 cohorts if the propensity to change languages had not varied from that of the 1921−1926 cohorts. The indices thus calculated are shown below, with the observed indices in brackets:

English	1.251	(1.181)
French	0.995	(0.998)
Other	0.674	(0.752)

If there had been no variation in linguistic mobility rates, the continuity index of the English group would nevertheless have increased from 1.190 to 1.251 between the 1921−1926 cohorts and those of 1936−1941, while that of the French group would have decreased slightly, from 0.996 to 0.995. The stabilization of linguistic mobility rates[21] would thus have caused the gap between the continuity index of the English group and that of the French group to widen. The increase in the rate of mobility from English to French allowed the gap to close somewhat.

E. SUMMARY

For Canada as a whole, linguistic mobility clearly favours the English group, but is slightly unfavourable to the French group, quite unfavourable to the endogenous-language group (Amerindians), and extremely unfavourable to the exogenous-language group. Persons whose mother tongue is neither French nor English nor an Amerindian language adopt English in more than 80% of cases on reaching adulthood if they were born in Canada.[22] This group thus has no specifically Canadian existence; it can only maintain itself by migratory inflow from other countries. This is why we have called it the "exogenous-language group." The high rate of linguistic mobility in this group is not exceptional; it appears that the same phenomenon is observed in the United States.[23]

Although the French group always shows much lower linguistic mobility than the exogenous-language group,[24] it nevertheless experiences sizeable losses in its linguistic exchanges with the English group, except in the Interior region of Quebec, where it is slightly favoured. Looking at the demographic effects of linguistic mobility, we can roughly distinguish five categories of regions. The first category would include regions where language transfers are almost balanced between the English and French groups; these are mainly the Interior and Periphery regions of Quebec, where persons of English mother tongue form less than 5% of the population. The Eastern Townships may also be placed in this category, although here the mobility of the French group is a little greater than in the other two regions. The Montreal region in itself forms the second category, because of the size of its third-language group. While the English group is a minority in this region (forming about 20% of the population), it is not only favoured in linguistic exchanges with the French group, it also receives more than 70% of the language transfers from the third-language group. As for the French group, it sets off its losses to the English group by its gains from the third-language group. To counterbalance gains by the English group with respect to language transfers, francophones would have to maintain an excess fertility of 15% to 20% compared to anglophones. The same is true of the Outaouais and the North-and-East region of New Brunswick, which form the third category of regions. In these two regions, however, francophone excess fertility only has to compensate for English-group gains from the French group, since the third-language group is almost non-existent, while in the Montreal region it must also offset the sizeable gains the English group makes from the third-language group. All told, the effects of linguistic mobility are quite similar in the Montreal region, the Outaouais, and the North-and-East of New Brunswick. If we look only at language transfers between the English and French groups, however, the situation observed in the Montreal region is closer to that seen in the Eastern Townships. In all the foregoing regions, francophones form the majority of the population. The fourth category takes in the Southeast and Northeast regions of Ontario, where francophones form 25% and 30% respectively of the population. The French group experiences quite heavy losses in these regions, to the point where francophone excess fertility would have to be around 50% to counterbalance them. The last category includes all the other regions of Canada. These are predominantly anglophone regions. Language transfers from the French group are so large that it is almost impossible to offset them without the help of sizeable migratory inflow from francophone regions.[25] In these regions, the situation of the French group is quite similar to that of the exogenous-language group, although the latter displays even weaker linguistic continuity.

This of course is only a very brief description of linguistic mobility, or rather of its demographic effects. It does not include some highly varied local situations, and it passes over some factors that might account for regional variations in linguistic mobility. In addition, it is much too static.

Outside Quebec, the linguistic mobility of the French group increased over time in almost all regions, except in New Brunswick, where it appears to have declined slightly between 1971 and 1976. This increase in linguistic mobility is not unexpected, since persons of French mother tongue have effectively had to adjust to many socio-economic changes. They get more and more schooling, which increases the risk of a scholastic language shuttle,[26] and tend less and less to choose agricultural work; they must accordingly often accept English as their working language and thus carry out occupational language shuttles.[27] All these factors—increased schooling, urbanization, and industrialization—multiply the occasions for contact with anglophones, add to bilingualism, encourage the forming of French-English heterolinguistic couples and, as a consequence, increase the risk of linguistic mobility. The measures taken to improve the situation of the French group, notably in the area of schooling, have no doubt partly offset the effect of these factors. They may have even stopped the spread of linguistic mobility in New Brunswick.

Within Quebec, recent developments in linguistic mobility may at first glance appear somewhat surprising. There has been a simultaneous increase in the linguistic mobility of the English group, stabilization of linguistic mobility in the French group, and decrease in the proportion of language transfers from the third-language group to French. The increase in linguistic mobility in the English group among recent cohorts and between 1971 and 1976 is no doubt partly artificial. Part of the increase in the rate of mobility from English to French would appear to be due to differential emigration, as English mother-tongue persons who adopt French are less likely to leave Quebec than the others.[28] In addition, since the relative strength of the English group decreases from one cohort group to another, we would expect the rate of homogamy in the English mother-tongue population to go down. If all other factors remain unchanged, we should consequently observe at least a slight increase in linguistic mobility in the English group. Whatever the case may be, when we consider the effects rather than the evolution of the risks of linguistic mobility, changes are very slight: the English group still derives considerable benefit from language transfers, although the gap between the linguistic continuity of the English group and that of the French group does appear to be narrowing with the more recent cohorts.

There exists, then, a strong dissymmetry between the French and English groups in Canada, with the latter always having an advantage over the former when it comes to linguistic mobility, except when the French group forms more than 95% of the population of a region. To get a better understanding of this situation, we considered two different ways of analysing linguistic mobility. The first way was to break down the phenomenon into two processes: bilingualism and the linguistic mobility of bilingual persons, who are the only ones able to make a language transfer. The second approach was to study the process of choosing a mate or, more specifically, linguistic homogamy, as well as the linguistic mobility of the various categories of couples. In either case, when we wished to be particularly rigorous and precise, we have used the language of mathematics. This language is obviously nothing more than a tool that helps us to better understand the processes related to linguistic mobility. We should consequently be able to express the results of these analyses in plain language.

In order to describe regional variations in the bilingualism rates of the English and French groups, we have distinguished three categories of bilingualism. In the first place, we have assumed that in a region that was perfectly homogeneous from the point of view of language, there would nevertheless be bilingual persons, mostly due to the many interregional and international exchanges that characterize modern life. This can be called external or international bilingualism. Because of the geopolitical situation of Canada and the importance of English in international communications, it is plausible to assume that this type of bilingualism is more common in the French group than in the English group. We were able to make an approximate estimate of the proportion of international bilinguals among young adults in 1971: it would be 3% in the English group and 16% in the French group. The second type of bilingualism is linked to contacts with neighbours as well as communication within the family. This is what we called proximity bilingualism. In both the English and French groups, this type of bilingualism varies in direct relation to the relative strength of the other language group in a given region. We have also tried to isolate a third type of bilingualism, which would be related to the respective positions of the two groups involved in the socio-professional hierarchy, and thus in the work setting. We may assume that the group that is underrepresented in the higher ranks must accept what we have called inequality bilingualism. In Canada, this type of bilingualism is essentially characteristic of the French group. Moreover, it would appear that inequality bilingualism is most prevalent in regions where the English group constitutes a large minority, as in the contact regions of Quebec (the Eastern Townships, Montreal, and the Outaouais) and in North-and-East New Brunswick. In the largely French regions (the Interior and the Periphery of Quebec), the bilingualism of the French group would instead be mainly of the external or international type, while in predominantly anglophone regions, proximity bilingualism takes on such importance that it almost entirely prevents the occurrence of inequality bilingualism in the French group.

As we have seen, bilingualism is a necessary condition of linguistic mobility. It is not enough, however, to be simply bilingual. It might well be assumed that the external or international type of bilingualism gives rise to few language transfers, since the second-language group is not physically present in the immediate surroundings. Conversely, proximity bilingualism, due to the very factors that cause it, no doubt gives rise to many more language transfers. Inequality bilingualism most probably occupies an intermediate position, since the socio-linguistic situation of work environments has only an indirect effect on the dominant language of the family (home language). The observations we have been able to collect certainly do not disagree with this hypothesis.

It is a well-known fact that there is great socio-economic as well as socio-linguistic inequality between the anglophones and francophones of Quebec (Canada, Royal Commission, 1969; Quebec, Commission of Inquiry, 1973; Porter, 1965). In an attempt to correct this situation, the Quebec government has been led, over the past twenty years, to pass legislation in a number of fields, notably to allow a greater degree of schooling for francophones and to improve the position of French in work situations. These measures have had, and will no doubt continue to have, the effect of reducing inequality bilingualism in the French group. With francophones being better represented in the higher ranks of the occupational hierarchy and therefore having to deal with a larger share of the communications with the rest of Canada and the United States, it seems plausible that the external or international type of bilingualism will take on greater importance in the future. It nevertheless seems likely that, in the medium term, the first effect will be stronger than the second; as a consequence, we will probably see a reduction in the proportion of bilingual persons in the French group, this reduction being the logical extension of a trend in this direction that has been observed over the past few decades (Duchesne, 1977).

Analysing the process of choosing a mate, as well as the language choices of partners, enables us to take another look, from a different point of view, at regional variations in linguistic mobility. No matter which language group we study, we observe that in homolinguistic couples, that is, those where the partners have the same mother tongue, linguistic mobility is always much lower than among heterolinguistic couples. Moreover, it would appear that from the viewpoint of the risks of language transfer for the two main groups, we may almost assimilate the third-language group to the English group. For French mother-tongue persons, the risk of adopting English as their home language is effectively just as high, or almost, when they marry a member of the English group or of the third-language group, while for the English group, linguistic mobility towards French varies little whether the other partner is of English or other mother tongue. This observation is valid for almost all regions, including those of Quebec. We have also been able to establish that, with reference to an overall situation specific to each group, the fact of belonging to a homolinguistic couple brings about a greater reduction in linguistic mobility in the English group than in the French group. Moreover, it would appear that forming part of a French-English couple gives rise to a greater increase in linguistic mobility for the French group than for the English group.

Because of the low linguistic mobility of homolinguistic couples, it is important to describe and analyse variations in linguistic homogamy and, more precisely, regional variations, for each group, in the proportion of persons whose partner has the same mother tongue. We have showed that, as might have been expected, the homogamy of a language group varies directly with the proportion this group holds in the region in question. In addition, but not more unexpectedly, we have seen that the members of any given language group always exhibit a marked "preference" for a partner having the same mother tongue. The term "preference" here refers to the *results* of the process of choosing a mate rather than to an *intrinsic disposition* to choose a mate of the same mother tongue, all other things being equal. We have also tried to determine whether the English or the French group displayed a stronger homolinguistic "preference." We were unable to come to a firm conclusion in this respect, mainly because of the difficulties we encounter when we attempt to ensure that the clause "all other things being equal" is properly respected.

NOTES

[1] The two periphery regions of Quebec—Gaspé and the North—have been combined.

[2] In any couple, the partners may have the same mother tongue or different mother tongues. In the first case, we would speak of a homolinguistic couple and, in the second, of a heterolinguistic couple.

[3] In actual fact, it is enough to say that, past 30 or 35 years of age, initial transfers and return transfers almost cancel one another out. While this hypothesis is not necessarily always true (De Vries, 1974, 1977*a*), it nevertheless appears plausible, at least in Canada (Castonguay, 1979*b*).

[4] This reasoning is obviously based on the hypothesis that the distribution by age—in demographic jargon, the timing—of language transfers does not show very significant variations from one cohort group to another.

[5] In the 1971 census, mother tongue was taken to mean the first language spoken and still understood. Home language is the language most often spoken in the home. Certain persons sometimes declared more than one mother tongue or home language, and it is even possible that several responses were given to one question or the other. Statistics Canada applied precise rules to these cases of multiple response (Lachapelle, 1982*a*), and these sometimes have the effect of creating fictitious language transfers. For example, if a thousand persons claimed English and German as their mother tongue, and English and German as their home language as well, when the census results were compiled, English or German would be chosen as the mother tongue with a probability equal to about 0.5. Next, without reference to the choice of mother tongue, English or German would be selected as the home language, again with a probability of about 0.5. These thousand persons would then be broken down as follows in the final figures:

Mother Tongue	Home Language		
	English	**German**	**Total**
English	250	250	500
German	250	250	500
Total	500	500	1,000

For the five hundred persons of English mother tongue who will be added to those who claimed only English as their mother tongue, we have a linguistic mobility rate of 50%. This rate obviously does not correspond to an observation; it is simply the result of the rules applied to cases of multiple responses to the questions dealing with mother tongue and home language.

[6] The linguistic mobility observed for the population born in Canada does not correspond exactly to the linguistic mobility that occurs in Canada, mainly because of differential emigration. For lack of more precise data, we will nevertheless assume that the one is approximately equal to the other.

[7] Approximately 97% of third-language group transfers are made towards English and 3% towards French.

[8] Outside Quebec, less than 50% of language transfers for English mother-tongue adults who were born in Canada are towards French.

[9] Language transfers measured by the home language of women having young children were towards French in 30% of cases in 1971. If we instead consider all women between 20 and 44, third-group transfers in 1971 were 29% towards French. The difference between these percentages and 100 obviously gives the percentage of transfers towards English home language.

[10] We felt it was preferable not to take into account language transfers among the third-language group for children under 10, because it is no doubt around these ages that we find most of the multiple responses to questions on mother tongue and home language. For those who are interested, here then are the percentages of third-group language transfers to French: 27% at 5−9 years and 36% at 0−4 years. These percentages are valid both for the total population and for the population born in Canada and living in Quebec.

[11] As will have been noticed, the foregoing two equations correspond to homographic functions. They are below their respective reference lines ($b = m + kp$) when the parameter d is less than 1 and above them when it is greater than 1.

[12] This cautious phrasing is indispensable, since it is impossible to draw upon experience. Ideally, we should be able to vary the linguistic composition of a region and then estimate, all other things being equal, the changes these variations would bring about in the rate of bilingualism. All we have available, however, is a series of observations in which the condition "all other things being equal" is in all probability not respected.

[13] This percentage is, of course, quite approximate and would be likely to vary from one region to another.

[14] According to equation (4), inequality bilingualism would be greater than 30% when the proportion of the English group is between 5% and 50% or, which comes to the same thing, when the bilingualism rate of the French group varies between 30% and 80%. It is obvious that the relative importance of inequality bilingualism is given here only as an indication. The data we have do not enable us to measure the exact level.

[15] Methods of estimation in models where the parameters must satisfy one or more linear constraints are presented in most textbooks on econometrics (Johnston, 1972; Theil, 1971).

[16] These conclusions are obviously questionable, since they are derived from a model where the parameter to be estimated cannot be constant, even in theory. We have attempted to conceive a more satisfactory model, and we feel we have been successful. In theory at least, the parameters of this model may be constant from one region to another, and may be calculated using equations of the type $1/(1 - h) = b_0 + [b_1/(1 - p)]$. The conclusions to be formed using this model are quite similar to those we have already presented, and we therefore felt it was not necessary to describe the model in detail.

[17] The sum of the rates for the English group and the French group is always less than 100. This is essentially due to the fact that in a certain number of English-French couples, the partners both state their mother tongue as their home language.

[18] We have assumed that linguistic mobility rates were never less than 0.0005.

[19] The attentive reader will remark that the estimated values of parameters display somewhat surprising relations. For example, $0.747 + 0.253 = 1.000$, and $0.747/0.253 \simeq 4.223/1.403 \simeq 3$. We were unable to make a model capable of accounting for this, nor is there any way of being sure that these relations are not purely fortuitous.

[20] To calculate these values, we only have to remember that $l_e^{-m_e} = 4.223$ and $l_f^{-m_f} = 1.403$.

[21] If we stabilize only the linguistic mobility rates of the English and French groups, while allowing that of the third-language group to vary, we obtain the following continuity indices for the 1936−1941 cohorts: English, 1.210; French, 0.995; and other, 0.735.

[22] No matter what regions and language groups (German, Ukranian, and Italian) we consider, the rates of linguistic endurance are always very low; according to the 1971 census, they are almost always between 5% and 30% for young adults born in Canada. We should also emphasize the fact that endurance rates vary little with the birthplace of the father or mother, except in the case of very young children.

[23] In 1976, the American government collected data that enabled it to make approximate measurements of the linguistic mobility of the principal minority groups (Veltman, 1979). Looking only at adults born in the United States, the linguistic endurance in the German, French, Italian, and Portuguese groups appears as low as, if not lower than, that observed in the exogenous-language groups in Canada. The only exception is the Spanish group, and then only in certain southern states (Arizona, New Mexico, and Texas), where linguistic endurance would appear to be much the same as that observed in the French group in predominantly anglophone regions of Canada. We should mention the fact that the American data differ from the Canadian data in that the former overestimate linguistic mobility compared to the latter (Veltman, 1979). Whatever the case may be, it is no doubt possible to suggest that the linguistic mobility of the Spanish group shows a greater increase from one generation to another than does the French group in any given region in Canada.

[24] This statement of course only applies to those born in Canada. It is true not only for Quebec but also for the rest of Canada, even if we limit the French group to persons born outside Quebec (Lachapelle, 1980).

25 This conclusion is valid for the total French mother-tongue population in these regions. It does not necessarily apply to all local groups. In many small pockets of francophones scattered over the country, the linguistic mobility of the French group is often relatively low and occasionally even less than 15% or 20% for the young adults questioned during the 1971 census.

26 We speak of a scholastic language shuttle when a person is educated in a different language than his home language (Lachapelle, 1982*c*).

27 By occupational language shuttle we mean a situation characterized by the fact that the language of work is different from the home language (Lachapelle, 1982*c*).

28 Although highly plausible, this hypothesis is difficult to verify. For further discussion, see Chapter Six and also Chapter Seven.

Chapter Six

Migration

Although considerable literature exists in Canada on international and internal migration (Desrosiers, Gregory, and Piché, 1978; Richmond and Kalbach, 1980; Stone, 1974, 1976, 1978a, 1979), little is known about the components and linguistic factors of migration streams. Most studies generally confine themselves to stating that because of their specific culture and language, Quebeckers display migratory behaviour different from that of other Canadians (Stone, 1969; Termote and Fréchette, 1979). It has even been suggested that "language and culture act as deterrents to mobility" (Canada, Dept. of Manpower, 1975, p. 50), although no really detailed analysis is made of this question.

The limited quantity of statistical data available up until recently may no doubt be the reason for the very general and occasionally rather ambiguous statements found in many studies. For international immigrants, in the legal sense, the only data available from the mid-1960s on is the breakdown by knowledge of official languages. The rare estimates available with respect to international emigrants deal only with the population as a whole (Canada, Statistics Canada, 1977) and, in any case, are not always very reliable (Kelly, 1977; Lachapelle and Gervais, 1982). The situation regarding internal migration, especially interprovincial migration, is somewhat better. For the past few years, Statistics Canada has been using family allowance records to measure migratory movements between provinces (Canada, Statistics Canada, 1977; Kasahara, 1963; Termote and Fréchette, 1979). Some researchers (Courchesne, 1974; Grant and Vanderkamp, 1976; Vanderkamp, 1973) have also drawn upon the central files of the Unemployment Insurance Commission in studying internal migration. It does not appear, however, that these two sources can provide language data on migrants. In the final analysis, there is only one source from which we can obtain migration statistics for the characteristics that interest us here, and this is the census. We effectively find, in the 1971 and 1976 censuses, a wealth of statistical information, by mother tongue, on international immigration and on internal migratory movements that occurred in the periods 1966–1971 and 1971–1976. To date, little use has been made of these data in studying the demolinguistic aspects of migration (Lachapelle, 1979, 1980; Stone 1978a, 1979; Stone and Fletcher, 1977).

For a given region and period, we must have the external migration balance (or net migration) by mother tongue if we are to grasp the overall demolinguistic effects of migration. The external migration balance of a region is the result of two partial balances: an internal balance (or net internal migration), the balance of its migratory exchanges with other regions in Canada; and an international balance (or net international migration), the balance of its migratory exchanges with other countries. While it is sometimes possible to obtain statistics that enable us to determine the internal balances, especially for the last two five-year periods, it is never easy to calculate the international balance by mother tongue, since we do not know the linguistic composition of international emigration. We must therefore proceed on the basis of hypotheses. These hypotheses, for Quebec and the rest of Canada, will be presented in the first section. We will also analyse the internal and international balances, by mother tongue, of these two regions in 1966−1971 and 1971−1976.

The second section will describe the evolution of migratory exchanges between Quebec and the rest of Canada, by mother tongue between 1966−1971 and 1971−1976, and by ethnic origin between 1956−1961 and 1966−1971. Our main interest here will be the evolution of the demolinguistic effects of internal migration. In the third section, we will attempt to show the factors that influence migration between Quebec and the rest of Canada. We will examine, for each mother tongue in turn, the propensity to leave Quebec for other regions of Canada, as well as the reverse propensity, by age, schooling, place of birth, ethnic origin, and home language. We will again take up the study of the demolinguistic effects of internal migration in the fourth section, this time for the thirteen regions often used in the foregoing chapters. The linguistic structure of interregional migratory exchanges in Canada will also be described. Finally, in the last section, we will give a brief analysis of the linguistic composition of recent international immigration.

A. NET EXTERNAL MIGRATION BY MOTHER TONGUE

When statistical information is found lacking for one or another of the migratory streams, we can employ two strategies to estimate the net external migration of a region. In the first strategy, we attempt to identify net migration with the residue of an equation in which all the other terms are known or can be estimated with a low margin of error, while the second strategy is simply to attempt to evaluate the missing data. Both of these methods have been used in Canada to estimate the net external migration of ethnolinguistic groups. We will present each in turn, then briefly examine the overall demolinguistic effects of migration from 1966 to 1971 and from 1971 to 1976. Readers for whom methodological considerations are of little interest would perhaps be well advised to skip directly to the last sub-section, at least for the first reading.

1. Estimates Based on a Residue

There are many methods by which, faced with a lack of satisfactory migration statistics, we can develop a more or less precise estimate of net migration (United Nations, 1970; Shryock and Siegel, 1973). We obviously do not intend to describe them all here, especially as a number of them are of only limited interest to us in estimating the migratory balances of ethnolinguistic groups in Canada. The first method we will describe is a very simple one, in addition to being the one most frequently employed. Let us assume that we have the population by mother tongue for two successive censuses. We can then easily calculate the demographic growth of each language group in the intercensal period for a given region. Assume that, in addition, we know, from vital statistics, the births and deaths by mother tongue, which enables us to establish, for the region and period under study, the natural increase (difference between births and deaths) of each language group. As we know, demographic increase is equal to the sum of natural increase and migratory increase, the latter obviously being equal to the net migration or external migratory balance. On condition that census data and vital statistics are both reliable and comparable, we can estimate net migration by mother tongue.

In Canada, vital statistics are unfortunately not available by mother tongue. We do, however, have births and deaths by ethnic origin for certain periods. This is why we have most often confined ourselves to estimating net migration by this variable.[1] For the period 1951−1961, Robert Maheu (1968) made estimates by province of the migratory growth of the French-origin group and of the rest of the population. This type of estimate has also been made for French, British, and other origins in Quebec only, from 1951 to 1961 (Charbonneau and Maheu, 1973) and also from 1961 to 1971 (Rochon-Lesage and Maheu, 1975).

There is another method we could use to estimate net migration by mother tongue. This method does not require that we know births and deaths by mother tongue, but we must have a fairly precise idea of the differences in mortality between language groups and population statistics by age and mother tongue for two censuses, say, ten years apart. If net migration is nil for each language group during the period in question, the survivors of the population observed in the first census are equal to the population 10 years old and over in the second census. The difference between the population actually counted in the census and these survivors thus provides an estimate of net migration[2] by mother tongue in the population aged 10 and over at the end of the period. This method has been used to estimate the external migration balance of Quebec, by mother tongue, from 1951 to 1961 (Charbonneau and Maheu, 1973) and from 1961 to 1971 (Rochon-Lesage and Maheu, 1975).

How good are all these estimates? In theory, they are perfect. In practice, however, they are as good as the data used to arrive at them, or rather, since they are residues, these estimates may include significant errors, even if the source data are relatively reliable. This can obviously pose a serious problem. In addition, the methods we have just described implicitly assume that there are no statistics on migration, while in Canada we often know the ethnic and linguistic composition of international immigration. If we assume that estimates of net external migration are reasonably precise, we can then calculate the ethnic or linguistic composition of international emigration. It is quite likely that these calculations, being the residues of residues, will not bear much resemblance to reality. They can nevertheless be used to test the preciseness and, above all, the coherence of estimates of net migration by ethnic origin or by mother tongue, since by definition the number of emigrants must always be equal to or greater than zero. By our calculation, however, there would have been, for the total Canadian population, approximately −300,000 emigrants of British origin and about −100,000 emigrants of English mother tongue between 1961 and 1971![3] For the following five-year period, from 1971 to 1976, we again obtained a negative international emigration, in the order of −70,000 for the English mother-tongue group. We can also calculate international emigration by mother tongue at the provincial level from 1971 to 1976, since we have data on internal migratory exchanges by mother tongue. It would appear that the number of English mother-tongue emigrants was slightly less than zero in the Quebec population and that it reached −70,000 in the English mother-tongue population of the rest of Canada.[4]

All this would lead us to believe that indirect estimates of net migration by ethnic origin or by mother tongue are not very reliable and that they tend to overstate considerably the British or English group balance at the expense of that of the French origin or mother-tongue group and, especially, that of the third ethnic origin or language group. This does not mean, however, that these estimates are of no interest, but only that they must be interpreted for what they are—residues—and that we must avoid identifying them with external migratory balances without taking the appropriate precautions (Lachapelle, 1979).

How are these many anomalies to be explained? Part of the explanation may perhaps lie in changes in differential under-enumeration from one census to another,[5] but this can hardly account for the degree of inconsistency we have demonstrated. It is likely that, at least since 1961, there have been a great many substitutions of ethnic origin and also of mother tongue, with individuals claiming a different ethnic origin or even a different mother tongue in two successive censuses. These substitutions[6] are for the most part to the benefit of British origin—or more precisely English ethnic origin (Kralt, 1977)—and of English mother tongue. Like language transfers, they are proof of the drawing power of the anglophone group.

2. Estimates Based on the Assessment of Missing Data

Indirect methods of estimating net migration give rather unreliable results, but we are left with at least one recourse: we can tackle the problem head-on, without trying to avoid the issue, and try to assess the missing data. Basically, what we have to do is form hypotheses regarding the number and the ethnic or linguistic composition of international emigrants. This is how Henripin (1974) estimated net migration by ethnic origin between 1961 and 1971 for Canada as a whole. We used the same method to calculate external migratory balances,[7] by mother tongue, for Quebec and the rest of Canada from 1966 to 1971 and from 1971 to 1976 (Lachapelle and Gervais, 1982). These estimates appear in Tables 6.1 to 6.4

For each period, we considered two hypotheses: hypothesis *A* corresponds to fairly low international emigration, while hypothesis *B* assumes higher international emigration. Apart from the number of international emigrants, other elements also vary from one hypothesis to the other. Thus, under hypothesis *A*, we simply accepted the estimates of internal balances

Table 6.1

EXTERNAL MIGRATORY BALANCE AND COMPONENTS THEREOF, BY MOTHER TONGUE, FOR THE POPULATION 5 YEARS OF AGE AND OVER AT THE END OF THE PERIOD, CANADA, QUEBEC, AND CANADA LESS QUEBEC, 1966–1971 (HYPOTHESIS *A* CORRESPONDS TO RELATIVELY LOW INTERNATIONAL EMIGRATION)

REGION AND MOTHER TONGUE	EMIGRANTS REMAINING (1)	IMMIGRANTS REMAINING (2)	MIGRATORY BALANCE		
			International (2)−(1)=(3)	Internal (4)	External (3)+(4) =(5)
Canada					
English	192,000	414,000	222,000	—	222,000
French	51,000	52,000	1,000	—	1,000
Other	97,000	359,000	262,000	—	262,000
Total	340,000	825,000	485,000	—	485,000
Quebec					
English	37,000	38,000	1,000	−52,000	−51,000
French	41,000	39,000	−2,000	−14,000	−16,000
Other	27,000	63,000	36,000	−10,000	+26,000
Total	105,000	140,000	35,000	−76,000	−41,000
Canada less Quebec					
English	155,000	376,000	221,000	52,000	273,000
French	10,000	13,000	3,000	14,000	17,000
Other	70,000	296,000	226,000	10,000	236,000
Total	235,000	685,000	450,000	76,000	526,000

Sources: Census of Canada, 1971, and estimates by Lachapelle and Gervais (1982).

Table 6.2

EXTERNAL MIGRATORY BALANCE AND COMPONENTS THEREOF, BY
MOTHER TONGUE, FOR THE POPULATION 5 YEARS OF AGE AND
OVER AT THE END OF THE PERIOD, CANADA, QUEBEC, AND
CANADA LESS QUEBEC, 1971–1976 (HYPOTHESIS *A* CORRESPONDS TO
RELATIVELY LOW INTERNATIONAL EMIGRATION)

REGION AND MOTHER TONGUE	EMIGRANTS REMAINING (1)	IMMIGRANTS REMAINING (2)	MIGRATORY BALANCE		
			International (2)−(1)=(3)	Internal (4)	External (3)+(4) =(5)
Canada					
English	149,000	398,000	249,000	—	249,000
French	37,000	54,000	17,000	—	17,000
Other	54,000	268,000	214,000	—	214,000
Total	240,000	720,000	480,000	—	480,000
Quebec					
English	21,000	33,000	12,000	−52,000	−40,000
French	29,000	40,000	11,000	−4,000	+7,000
Other	10,000	37,000	27,000	−6,000	+21,000
Total	60,000	110,000	50,000	−62,000	−12,000
Canada less Quebec					
English	128,000	365,000	237,000	52,000	289,000
French	8,000	14,000	6,000	4,000	10,000
Other	44,000	231,000	187,000	6,000	193,000
Total	180,000	610,000	430,000	62,000	492,000

Sources: Census of Canada, 1976, and estimates by Lachapelle and Gervais (1982).

and international immigrants remaining, which we took directly from the 1971 and 1976 censuses, while under hypothesis *B*, we assumed, based on the rates of under-enumeration of migrants (Blackstone and Gosselin, 1974; Théroux, 1976) that the above estimates were understated by about 5%.

In determining the number of international emigrants, we were also guided by the estimates arrived at in studies aimed at testing the quality of the 1971 and 1976 censuses (Gosselin, 1975; Théroux and Gosselin, 1978). Under hypothesis *A*, we used slightly lower numbers, in particular for 1971−1976, while under hypothesis *B*, we used much higher numbers, especially, this time, for 1966−1971. It will no doubt be noticed that the differences between hypotheses *A* and *B* are much greater for the period 1966−1971 than for the period 1971−1976. This is because we have reason to believe that international emigration was more seriously underestimated for the period 1966−1971 (Lachapelle and Gervais, 1982).

These international emigrants still have to be classified by mother tongue, and we have very little information on which to base this. We do know, however, that all situations are not equally plausible. Our reasoning

Table 6.3
EXTERNAL MIGRATORY BALANCE AND COMPONENTS THEREOF, BY
MOTHER TONGUE, FOR THE POPULATION 5 YEARS OF AGE AND
OVER AT THE END OF THE PERIOD, CANADA, QUEBEC, AND
CANADA LESS QUEBEC, 1966–1971 (HYPOTHESIS *B* CORRESPONDS TO
RELATIVELY HIGH INTERNATIONAL EMIGRATION)

REGION AND MOTHER TONGUE	EMIGRANTS REMAINING (1)	IMMIGRANTS REMAINING (2)	MIGRATORY BALANCE		
			International (2)−(1)=(3)	Internal (4)	External (3)+(4) =(5)
Canada					
English	347,000	434,000	87,000	—	87,000
French	54,000	54,000	0	—	0
Other	109,000	377,000	268,000	—	268,000
Total	510,000	865,000	355,000	—	355,000
Quebec					
English	67,000	39,000	−28,000	−55,000	−83,000
French	47,000	40,000	−7,000	−15,000	−22,000
Other	46,000	66,000	+20,000	−10,000	+10,000
Total	160,000	145,000	−15,000	−80,000	−95,000
Canada less Quebec					
English	280,000	395,000	115,000	55,000	170,000
French	7,000	14,000	7,000	15,000	22,000
Other	63,000	311,000	248,000	10,000	258,000
Total	350,000	720,000	370,000	80,000	450,000

Sources: Census of Canada, 1971, and estimates by Lachapelle and Gervais (1982).

was as follows. It is no doubt conceivable that the propensity to emigrate from Canada is much stronger for foreign-born persons than for those born in Canada. Migratory studies carried out in Canada as elsewhere in the world do in fact show that every stream has its corresponding counter-stream and that a significant part of the latter is composed of persons making a return migration (Lee, 1966). Thus, under hypothesis *A*, we have assumed that foreign-born persons have a propensity to leave Canada that is four times as strong as that of Canadian-born persons. Under hypothesis *B*, we have assumed that these propensities were in a 5 to 1 ratio. We felt that these ratios were plausible, at least as preliminary estimates. They do not suffice, however, to establish the linguistic composition of international emigrants. Some conjectures must be made about the ratios between propensities to leave Canada for persons of English, French, or other mother tongue. We postulated a ratio for Quebec of 4:1:3 under hypothesis *A* and 6:1:4 under hypothesis *B*. These estimates, obviously somewhat arbitrary, are based on the following considerations. The propensity to leave Quebec for a given country is no doubt as strong as the ethnic or linguistic characteristics of the group in question are close to

Table 6.4

EXTERNAL MIGRATORY BALANCE AND COMPONENTS THEREOF, BY MOTHER TONGUE, FOR THE POPULATION 5 YEARS OF AGE AND OVER AT THE END OF THE PERIOD, CANADA, QUEBEC, AND CANADA LESS QUEBEC, 1971–1976 (HYPOTHESIS B CORRESPONDS TO RELATIVELY HIGH INTERNATIONAL EMIGRATION)

REGION AND MOTHER TONGUE	EMIGRANTS REMAINING (1)	IMMIGRANTS REMAINING (2)	MIGRATORY BALANCE		
			International $(2)-(1)=(3)$	Internal (4)	External $(3)+(4)$ $=(5)$
Canada					
English	224,000	420,000	196,000	—	196,000
French	38,000	57,000	19,000	—	19,000
Other	48,000	283,000	235,000	—	235,000
Total	310,000	760,000	450,000	—	450,000
Quebec					
English	33,000	34,000	1,000	−54,000	−53,000
French	33,000	42,000	9,000	−4,000	+5,000
Other	14,000	39,000	25,000	−7,000	+18,000
Total	80,000	115,000	35,000	−65,000	−30,000
Canada less Quebec					
English	191,000	386,000	195,000	54,000	249,000
French	5,000	15,000	10,000	4,000	14,000
Other	34,000	244,000	210,000	7,000	217,000
Total	230,000	645,000	415,000	65,000	480,000

Sources: Census of Canada, 1976, and estimates by Lachapelle and Gervais (1982).

those of the country of destination, but, due to geographical and socio-economic proximity, the majority of Quebeckers, when they emigrate, move to the United States. Nowadays, moreover, international emigration is a selective phenomenon that affects mainly persons having a high level of schooling; in Quebec especially, anglophones hold an overwhelming share of this category. All this would lead us to think that the propensity to leave Quebec and move to another country should be greater among anglophones than among francophones. This is what we have postulated, while the third-language group was assigned an intermediate position, although closer to that of the English group than that of the French group. In the rest of Canada, the differences are no doubt less marked, because of the near-universal use of English. We have assumed a ratio of 1:1:1 for propensities to emigrate to another country of the English, French, and other groups under hypothesis A and 4:1:2 under hypothesis B.

If we further assume that the ratios between these propensities for the three language groups are identical for the Canadian-born and foreign-born populations, we can then calculate the composition by mother tongue of international emigrants, based on the population breakdown by place of birth and mother tongue observed in the 1971 census. The results thus obtained were used for the period 1966—1971. We made slight adjustments to the following five-year period in order to allow for the decline in the number of emigrants between 1966—1971 and 1971—1976. When the number of emigrants is low, it can be assumed that those who belong to the majority language group in each region make up a larger proportion of emigrants, since the greater part of international emigration involves temporary emigrants (students, voluntary service workers, etc.) who will eventually return to their place of origin. This assumption was included in calculating the mother-tongue composition of international emigrants during the period 1971—1976.

This rather lengthy presentation of our estimates is destined to emphasize their hypothetical nature. Due to lack of data, we had to fall back on speculation, some of it based on theory, some based on the general knowledge we have been able to acquire on the migration phenomenon. While we feel that our estimates are plausible, we had the impression, looking back on them, that we may have somewhat underestimated the number of emigrants from the third-language group, as well as slightly overestimated the French mother-tongue emigrants in Quebec and those of English mother tongue in the rest of Canada. This is only an impression, however, and we felt its basis in fact was so weak as to rule out the idea of going through the entire estimation process again. International migratory balances by mother tongue should nonetheless be interpreted with care as, by the same token, should the external migratory balances of the various language groups.

3. Demolinguistic Effects of Migration

There are many ways of assessing the demolinguistic effects of migration, and more specifically of net external migration, since, from a demographic point of view, it is the balance that is important. For example, it might be suggested that between 1971 and 1976, migration in Canada as a whole was favourable to the English, French, and other groups; based on hypothesis A, these figures were respectively 249,000, 17,000, and 214,000 (Table 6.2). In this type of statement, we consider each language group separately from the other groups or, more exactly, independently of the linguistic composition of the region under study. What we are in fact interested in is the specific effect of migration on linguistic composition. To measure this, we can compare the migration balances to the corresponding population at the beginning of the period, that is, calculate what we will henceforth call a migration ratio. The effect of migration will be to increase the proportion held by a language group in a region when the migration ratio of this group is higher than that of the total population. If this is not the case, migration will tend to decrease the strength of the language group involved.

Tables 6.5 to 6.7 show the migration ratio by mother tongue, calculated according to hypotheses *A* and *B*, for Canada, Quebec, and the rest of Canada in 1966–1971 and 1971–1976. In Canada as a whole, only the third-language group benefits, relatively speaking, from international migration, while the English and French groups show, for 1966–1971 as for 1971–1976, a migration ratio lower than those for the total population. It should be added that the English-group ratios are much higher than those of the French group. This means that if we consider only the effects of international migration, and assuming that natural increase ratios[8] do not vary from one language group to another, the relative strength of the third-language group should have increased between 1966 and 1976, that of the English group declined slightly, and that of the French group decreased even more rapidly. This situation is probably not particular to the decade under study, and it is likely that it has been characteristic of periods of high immigration for some time.

Let us now look at the effects of migration on the linguistic composition of the Quebec population (Table 6.6). On the whole, migration benefits the French and third-language groups (the latter more than the former) and is

Table 6.5
INTERNATIONAL NET MIGRATION RATIO,[a] BASED ON TWO HYPOTHESES, BY MOTHER TONGUE, CANADA, 1966–1971 AND 1971–1976
(percentage)

PERIOD AND HYPOTHESIS	MOTHER TONGUE			
	Total	English	French	Other
1966–1971[b]				
Hypothesis *A*	2.4	1.9	0.0	10.1
Hypothesis *B*	1.8	0.7	0.0	10.4
1971–1976				
Hypothesis *A*	2.2	1.9	0.3	7.6
Hypothesis *B*	2.1	1.5	0.3	8.4

Sources: Census of Canada, 1966 and 1971; Tables 6.1 to 6.4
Note: [a] Ratio of migration balance by population at beginning of period.
　　　 [b] A quick estimate of population by mother tongue for 1966 was made by applying the compositions observed in 1971, in Quebec and in the rest of Canada, to total populations counted in the census in these two regions in 1966.

Table 6.6
INTERNATIONAL, INTERNAL, AND EXTERNAL NET MIGRATION RATIOS,^{a} BASED ON TWO HYPOTHESES, BY MOTHER TONGUE, QUEBEC, 1966–1971 AND 1971–1976
(percentage)

PERIOD, HYPOTHESIS, AND BALANCE	MOTHER TONGUE			
	Total	English	French	Other
1966–1971^b				
HYPOTHESIS *A*				
International	0.6	0.1	0.0	10.1
Internal	−1.3	−6.9	−0.3	−2.8
External	−0.7	−6.7	−0.3	7.3
HYPOTHESIS *B*				
International	−0.3	−3.7	−0.1	5.6
Internal	−1.4	−7.3	−0.3	−2.8
External	−1.6	−11.0	−0.5	2.8
1971–1976				
HYPOTHESIS *A*				
International	0.8	1.5	0.2	7.3
Internal	−1.0	−6.6	−0.1	−1.6
External	−0.2	−5.1	0.1	5.7
HYPOTHESIS *B*				
International	0.6	0.1	0.2	6.7
Internal	−1.1	−6.8	−0.1	−1.9
External	−0.5	−6.7	0.1	4.8

Sources: As for Table 6.5.
Note: ^{a} Ratio of migration balance by population at beginning of period.
^{b} An approximate estimate of population by mother tongue in 1966 was obtained by applying compositions observed in 1971 to total population according to the 1966 census.

clearly unfavourable to the English group, both between 1966 and 1971 and between 1971 and 1976. The unfavourable effects on migration on the proportion held by the English group in Quebec are basically the result of migratory exchanges with the rest of Canada. Although the internal balances are negative for all language groups in Quebec, these exchanges clearly favour, in relative terms, the French group and are just as clearly to the disadvangage of the English group and, to a lesser degree, the third-language group, over the past two five-year periods. The third-language group,

Table 6.7
INTERNATIONAL, INTERNAL, AND EXTERNAL NET MIGRATION RATIOS,[a] BASED ON TWO HYPOTHESES, BY MOTHER TONGUE, CANADA LESS QUEBEC, 1966–1971 AND 1971–1976
(percentage)

PERIOD, HYPOTHESIS, AND BALANCE	MOTHER TONGUE			
	Total	English	French	Other
1966–1971[b]				
HYPOTHESIS A				
International	3.2	2.0	0.4	10.2
Internal	0.5	0.5	1.6	0.4
External	3.7	2.4	2.0	10.6
HYPOTHESIS B				
International	2.6	1.0	0.8	11.1
Internal	0.6	0.5	1.8	0.4
External	3.2	1.5	2.6	11.6
1971–1976				
HYPOTHESIS A				
International	2.8	1.9	0.6	7.7
Internal	0.4	0.4	0.4	0.2
External	3.2	2.4	1.1	7.9
HYPOTHESIS B				
International	2.7	1.6	1.1	8.6
Internal	0.4	0.4	0.4	0.3
External	3.1	2.0	1.5	8.9

Sources: As for Table 6.5.
Note: [a] Ratio of migration balance by population at beginning of period.
[b] An approximate estimate of population by mother tongue in 1966 was obtained by applying compositions observed in 1971 to total population according to the 1966 census.

however, benefits overwhelmingly from international migration, and this is why it derives an overall benefit from migration, both in Quebec and in the rest of Canada. Still in relative terms, the English and French groups gain or lose little, under the hypotheses considered, in migratory exchanges between Quebec and other countries.

In the rest of Canada, the situation is a little less complex (Table 6.7). On the whole, migration clearly favours the third-language group and is unfavourable, in relative terms, to the English group and the French group, the latter a little more than the former, except for the period 1966–1971 and then only under hypothesis *B*. The effects of internal migration being fairly weak, this situation reflects the effects of international migration, which clearly favours the third-language group and is at the expense of the English group as well as the French group, again the latter more than the former. Internal migration was somewhat favourable to the French group between 1966 and 1971, but had almost no demolinguistic effects during the following five-year period.

In Canada as a whole, as in Quebec and in the rest of Canada, migration by and large is overwhelmingly in favour of the third-language group and more or less clearly unfavourable to the English group and the French group, except in Quebec, where the French group benefits slightly. This exception can be explained by the specific effects of internal migration and deserves a more detailed examination.

B. STABILITY AND EVOLUTION IN MIGRATORY EXCHANGES BETWEEN QUEBEC AND THE REST OF CANADA

Because of gaps in statistical data on international emigration, we had to be content with partly arbitrary estimates of the demolinguistic effects of international migration. Information on internal migration is, however, more varied and much more satisfactory, particularly with respect to migration streams between provinces. Using these data, we will attempt here to bring out consistent trends and to show the evolution of internal migration, by mother-tongue, between Quebec and the rest of Canada during the periods 1966–1971 and 1971–1976. These two five-year periods are somewhat special, as Quebec experienced much greater losses in its migratory exchanges with the rest of Canada than during the preceding fifteen years.[9] This is why, for the sake of comparison, we will also examine migrant exchanges by ethnic origin between Quebec and the rest of Canada during the periods 1956–1961 and 1966–1971.

1. From 1966–1971 to 1971–1976

In Table 6.8, we show the number of migrants between Quebec and the rest of Canada, by mother tongue, for the periods 1966–1971 and 1971–1976. It can be seen that the linguistic composition of the streams is almost identical from one period to another, while varying considerably during both periods, from the linguistic composition of the region of origin as well as from that of the region of destination. Let us try to imagine a simple model that would explain this.

We will assume two regions, *E* and *F*, the first made up mainly of persons of mother tongue *e* and the second having a majority of persons of

Table 6.8

MIGRATORY EXCHANGES[a] BETWEEN QUEBEC AND THE REST OF CANADA, BY MOTHER TONGUE, FOR THE POPULATION 5 YEARS OF AGE AND OVER AT THE END OF THE PERIOD, 1966–1971 AND 1971–1976

MIGRATION STREAM	MOTHER TONGUE			
	Total	English	French	Other
1966–1971				
Quebec to Rest of Canada	160,400	99,100	46,900	14,400
	(100.0)	*(61.8)*	*(29.2)*	*(9.0)*
Rest of Canada to Quebec	84,900	46,900	33,400	4,600
	(100.0)	*(55.2)*	*(39.3)*	*(5.5)*
Balance for Quebec	−75,500	−52,200	−13,500	−9,800
	(100.0)	*(69.1)*	*(17.9)*	*(13.0)*
1971–1976				
Quebec to Rest of Canada	145,800	94,100	41,300	10,400
	(100.0)	*(64.6)*	*(28.3)*	*(7.1)*
Rest of Canada to Quebec	83,800	41,900	37,200	4,700
	(100.0)	*(50.0)*	*(44.4)*	*(5.6)*
Balance for Quebec	−62,000	−52,200	−4,100	−5,700
	(100.0)	*(84.2)*	*(6.6)*	*(9.2)*

Sources: Census of Canada, 1971 and 1976, special tables.

Note: [a] Migrants who did not state their prior place of residence in Canada were distributed proportionately between intraprovincial and interprovincial migrants. In addition, in 1976, persons who did not state their mother tongue were distributed in the same manner as those who did state it.

mother tongue f. Chances for migration are constantly being created, both in region E and in region F (these are often job opportunities), and these opportunities may be taken up by persons living in the other region. For a migration opportunity to give rise to a migration, potential migrants must obviously be informed of it, and it would also be necessary that, for at least one of them, expected gains exceed the costs foreseen—gains and costs being taken in a broad sense. We can no doubt assume that, in region F, persons of mother tongue e would be better informed than those of group f of migration opportunities offered in region E. In addition, if two persons, one from group e and the other from group f, had knowledge of migration opportunities in region E that entailed considerable advantages, the former would be more likely to migrate than the latter, since the group *f* person would have to agree to subject himself and his family not only to the "normal" costs involved in migrating, but also to the costs of linguistic and cultural adaptation and integration. All in all, it would be expected that the propensity to migrate from region *F* to region *E* would be much higher for group *e* than for group *f* and vice versa.

These propositions are in no way negated by the facts, as can be seen from Table 6.9. Thus, between 1971 and 1976, the propensity[10] to migrate

Table 6.9
OUT-MIGRATION AND NET INTERNAL MIGRATION RATIOS,[a] BY MOTHER TONGUE, QUEBEC AND THE REST OF CANADA, 1966–1971 AND 1971–1976
($^o/_{oo}$)

TYPE OF RATIO AND PERIOD	MOTHER TONGUE			
	Total	English	French	Other
OUT-MIGRATION				
Quebec to Rest of Canada				
1966–1971	29.3	133.4	10.5	49.7
1971–1976	25.4	124.2	8.8	32.8
Rest of Canada to Quebec				
1966–1971	6.3	4.4	40.1	2.3
1971–1976	5.7	3.5	44.6	2.2
NET INTERNAL MIGRATION				
Quebec				
1966–1971	−13.8	−70.3	−3.0	−33.9
1971–1976	−10.8	−68.9	−0.9	−18.0
Rest of Canada				
1966–1971	5.6	4.9	16.2	4.9
1971–1976	4.2	4.4	4.9	2.8

Sources: Census of Canada, 1971 and 1976, special tables; Table 6.8.
Note: [a] These are the ratios of out-migrants, or of the internal balance of the region and mother tongue considered, to the corresponding numbers of persons who lived in Canada at the end of the period and were in the region considered at the beginning of the period.

from Quebec (a predominantly francophone region) to the rest of Canada (a predominantly anglophone region) was 12.4% for the English group and only 0.9% for the French group, while the propensity to migrate from Canada less Quebec to Quebec reached 4.5% for French mother-tongue persons, as opposed to 0.4% for those of English mother tongue. Note that, in both cases, the propensity of the minority group is ten to fifteen times greater than that of the majority group.

Let us assume that, in each region, migratory opportunities are distributed proportionately among language groups. We will further assume that information regarding migratory opportunities only passes from one region to the other among members of the same language group. This is the same as assuming that the propensity to migrate of the various language groups is proportional to the linguistic composition of the region of destination. If we know the linguistic composition of the region of origin and that of the region of destination, it is then fairly easy to determine the "expected" linguistic composition of the migrant streams, which must in any case be equal to one another. We can thus estimate the "expected" composition of migrants going from Quebec to the rest of Canada and from the rest of Canada to Quebec by basing our calculations on the composition by mother tongue of Quebec and the rest of Canada in 1971. The results of our calculations are as follows: English, 64%; French, 30%; and other, 6%.

The expected composition is very close to the composition observed among migrants going from Quebec to the rest of Canada during the last two five-year periods (Table 6.8) In the stream from the rest of Canada into Quebec, however, the English group is underrepresented in comparison with the expected proportion, while the French group is overrepresented. This may be due to the fact that, in the rest of Canada, the French group is highly concentrated in the regions bordering on Quebec, and French mother-tongue migrants would thus, on the average, have shorter distances to cover than would those of English mother tongue.

Using a very simple model, we are thus able to establish the linguistic composition of migratory exchanges between Quebec and the rest of Canada. This model also provides an interpretation of the stability in the linguistic composition of migrant streams from one period to another. Since mother-tongue compositions of regions evolve fairly slowly, it is to be expected that the compositions of migration streams would also show little variance.[11]

We turn now to the demolinguistic effects of internal migration. To do this, we must consider internal migration balances[12] (Table 6.8) and more specifically, as we have seen, internal migratory increase ratios (Table 6.9). There are obviously a number of methods by which we can estimate the effects of internal migration, from both a regional viewpoint and a linguistic one. The first method we will consider is quite simple.[13] We have to calculate, using migration propensities assumed to be invariable over time, first the limit distribution of the Canadian population between Quebec and the rest of Canada and, second, the limit linguistic composition of each of these regions. These calculations also entail the assumption that there are no migratory exchanges with other countries and that natural increase rates for the various geolinguistic groups are identical. These hypotheses illustrate the somewhat artificial nature of the proposed method. It nevertheless enables us to determine the direction in which the effects of a set of migration propensities act and to get a very approximate idea of the extent of these effects.

The out-migration ratios shown in Table 6.9 will henceforth be considered as propensities to migrate. Let us first postulate, by way of illustration, that propensities to migrate from Quebec to the rest of Canada and from the rest of Canada to Quebec do not vary with mother tongue, which boils down to making the hypothesis that the migration propensities of each language group are equal to those of the total population of the region concerned. It is then easy to calculate the limit distribution of the Canadian population between Quebec and the rest of Canada. Based on the migration propensities we estimated for the period 1966−1971, Quebec's strength at the limit would be 17.7%; should we use those for 1971−1976 instead, we would obtain 18.3%. It should be recalled that in 1976 Quebec was home to 27.1% of the Canadian population. In addition, according to the hypotheses we have made, the linguistic composition of Quebec would be equal, at the limit, to that of the rest of Canada. To estimate this common linguistic composition, all we have to do is agree on an initial mother-tongue composition for the whole of Canada. This composition would obviously be invariable and, consequently, would correspond to the limit composition of Quebec, as well as to that of the rest of Canada.

Let us put aside the hypothesis that the migration propensities of the various language groups are equal and adopt the propensities by mother tongue that appear in Table 6.9. If we are to calculate both the limit distribution of the Canadian population between Quebec and the rest of Canada and the limit linguistic composition of each region, we must obviously adopt an initial mother-tongue composition for all of Canada. We have chosen that of 1976: as already seen, the English group formed 61.5% of the population, the French group, 26.0%, and the third-language group, 12.5%. In line with our hypotheses, this composition will again be invariable in this model. The limit proportion of Quebec in the whole of Canada will of course vary depending on which migration propensity is adopted: 23.1% if we base our calculations on those for 1966−1971 and 24.2% if we use those of the following five-year period. We should also give the limit compositions by mother tongue for Quebec and the rest of Canada that result from these two different migration propensities:

	Quebec		Canada Less Quebec	
	1966–1971	**1971–1976**	**1966–1971**	**1971–1976**
English	8.5%	7.0%	77.5%	78.9%
French	89.1%	89.7%	7.0%	5.6%
Other	2.4%	3.3%	15.5%	15.5%

These compositions may be compared with those observed in 1976:

	Quebec	Canada Less Quebec
English	12.8%	79.7%
French	81.1%	5.4%
Other	6.1%	14.9%

It would appear that, on the whole, internal migration has only a slight effect on the linguistic composition of Canada less Quebec. It should nevertheless be pointed out that the English group is always at a slight disadvantage, while the French group made noteworthy gains if we use the migratory regime observed in 1966–1971, but only negligible gains based on migration propensities observed in 1971–1976. The third-language group is at a slight advantage. In Quebec, however, the effect of internal migration is much greater. This phenomenon is clearly to the advantage of the French group, while being unfavourable to both the English and third-language groups.

All, or almost all, of these conclusions were already established in the preceding section, when we described the internal migratory increase ratios. The model we have just used does not do more, in the final analysis, than present them from a different point of view. However, it also provides new and very interesting insight into the evolution of distribution of the Canadian population between Quebec and the rest of Canada. If we assume, for example, that propensities to migrate do not vary with mother tongue, the pattern observed over the last two five-year periods would cause the Quebec proportion to decrease, at the limit, to around 18% (as opposed to 27% in 1976). When we allow for the gaps between the propensities to migrate of various language groups, the demographic strength of Quebec declines much less at the limit (23–24%). This is because the groups whose migration pattern is most favourable to the rest of Canada would, in the long run, see their share of the Quebec population decline, which, by reaction, would cause the level of balance between Quebec and the rest of Canada to rise. Although the migration patterns observed between 1966 and 1971, and between 1971 and 1976 for each language group were unfavourable to Quebec, they are much less unfavourable for the French group than for the English and third-language groups. This causes both upward pressure on the proportion of French mother-tongue persons in Quebec and a slackening of redistribution of the Canadian population to the benefit of the rest of Canada.

A disadvantage of the above model is that it envisages only limit situations and assumes that the migration patterns considered will not vary over time. We can, however, approach more concrete situations and attempt to find differential fertility rates that would counterbalance the demolinguistic effects of internal migration rather than seeking distributions or limit compositions. To do this, we must again state a few simplifying hypotheses. We will thus assume that there are no migratory exchanges with other countries, that the probability for survival of the populations present at the beginning of the period will not vary with mother tongue during the period under study and, finally, that age compositions of the various language groups are much the same. Based on this, if the mother-tongue composition within a given region is not to vary between the beginning and the end of the period studied, language groups must counterbalance by their fertility (which acts on the size and mother-tongue composition of the population under 5 years old) the effects of internal migration on the linguistic composition of the population aged 5 years and over.

We will use the expression *fertility ratio* to designate the ratio of the population under 5 to that 5 and over. Based on the internal migratory increase ratios estimated for the periods 1966−1971 and 1971−1976 (Table 6.9), and the fertility ratios observed in the total population of Quebec and the rest of Canada in 1971 and in 1976, we can easily calculate the fertility ratios for each language group that would enable them to counterbalance the demolinguistic effects of internal migration[14] in each region. The results are as follows:

	Quebec		Canada Less Quebec	
	1971	**1976**	**1971**	**1976**
English	0.1526	0.1436	0.0948	0.0832
French	0.0748	0.0657	0.0826	0.0826
Other	0.1092	0.0843	0.0948	0.0849
All mother tongues	0.0866	0.0764	0.0940	0.0834

In Quebec, the fertility ratio of the third-language group, and especially of the English group, must be much higher than that of the French group, both in 1971 and 1976, to cancel out the demolinguistic effects of internal migration, which are clearly favourable to the French group. The fertility of the English group would have had to be double that of the French group in 1971 (2.04 = 0.1526/0.0748) and slightly more even than that in 1976 (2.19 = 0.1436/0.0657). In the rest of Canada, the demolinguistic effects of internal migration may be counterbalanced by much smaller differences in fertility, especially in 1976, when they are in any case negligible. It should be noted that in 1971 the excess fertility of the English and third-language groups compared to the French group would have had to be about 15%.

Let us look now at the actual fertility ratios observed in 1971 and 1976.[15]

	Quebec		Canada Less Quebec	
	1971	**1976**	**1971**	**1976**
English	0.0814	0.0707	0.1018	0.0910
French	0.0873	0.0777	0.0782	0.0657
Other	0.0889	0.0714	0.0622	0.0504
All mother tongues	0.0866	0.0764	0.0940	0.0834

Obviously, these ratios do not only vary with differential fertility by mother tongue, they also depend on differences in composition by age as well as accumulated language transfers, since, as we saw in the last chapter, young children have as their mother tongue the home language of their mother. This is why the third-language group often has fertility ratios lower than those of the English and French groups, even though its total fertility indices were much higher than those of the rest of the population during the periods 1966−1971 and 1971−1976 (Table 4.8).

We can also compare the observed fertility ratios with the ratios that would have been necessary to counterbalance the demolinguistic effects of internal migration. We will use as a comparative index the ratio of the second ratios to the first (multiplied by 100):

	Quebec		Canada Less Quebec	
	1971	**1976**	**1971**	**1976**
English	187	203	93	91
French	86	85	106	126
Other	123	118	152	168
All mother tongues	100	100	100	100

The advantage of these indices is that they almost only express differences in fertility for each geolinguistic group, since they implicitly control the effects of composition by age and of linguistic mobility, these two factors appearing both in the numerator and denominator of the ratios. They do however have the disadvantage of rendering the interpretation of the ratio of the two indices rather complicated. We will therefore avoid this operation in future.

In order to counterbalance the demolinguistic effects of internal migration, the English group fertility in Quebec would have to have been 87% greater than it was during the period 1966−1971, while that of the French group could have been 14% lower than it was. The third-language group, like the English group, would have had to achieve a fertility rate about 23% greater. The situation is little different in the following five-year period. In the rest of Canada, the English group could have been content with lower fertility, by 7% in 1966−1971 and by 9% in 1971−1976, while the French group and, above all, the third-language group should have had an even higher fertility; in the case of the French group, this would have compensated not for the effects of internal migration, since these are in their favour, but for the indirect impact of language transfers on fertility ratios.

These developments may appear somewhat complicated. They are nonetheless all based on simplifying hypotheses. We were thus able to develop coherent and generally unambiguous models; in spite of their apparent complexity, these models are very schematic compared to the richness and complexity of demographic reality. Any coherent discourse tends to reduce and impoverish reality, and this is the sacrifice that must be made if we are to apply rigorous reasoning and communicate the results obtained with as little ambiguity as possible.

One question immediately comes to mind after the examination of, first, the effects of linguistic mobility (preceding chapter) and then those of internal migration on the linguistic composition of Quebec. Do the favourable effects of linguistic mobility on the anglophone group outweigh the unfavourable effects of internal migration? Strictly speaking, the data we have available do not enable us to give a clear and precise answer to this question, since migration is measured over well-defined periods, five years in this case, while linguistic mobility is estimated over the whole lifetime of those questioned in censuses. We are not, however, completely without resources. We can, if we are willing to accept some simplifying hypotheses, carry out simulations that yield estimates of the effects of linguistic mobility over five-year periods. The results[16] lead us to believe that for the English group in Quebec, the unfavourable effects of internal migration no doubt clearly outweighed the favourable effects of linguistic mobility between 1966 and 1976. This conclusion would also appear to be valid if we compare the combined effects of internal migration and of international migration (Table 6.6) with the effects of linguistic mobility.

We should repeat that the foregoing results are only for the two periods 1966−1971 and 1971−1976. As we saw, these two periods were not representative of the situation that prevailed over the past twenty-five years, since Quebec lost more heavily in its migratory exchanges with the rest of Canada between 1966 and 1976 than between 1951 and 1966. This remark certainly in no way invalidates the description we have made of migration over the past ten years. It does, however, raise some doubts about any generalizations that we might be tempted to draw.

2. From 1956−1961 to 1966−1971

With the help of unpublished tables from the 1961 census, we were able to estimate the migrant streams, by ethnic origin, between Quebec and the rest of Canada for the period 1956−1961. Although it appears quite likely that these data understate the number of migrants (Lachapelle and Gervais, 1982), we may no doubt consider, at least at the outset, that they provide almost satisfactory estimates of the ethnic composition of the streams of migrants. We will content ourselves with this in comparing the period 1956−1961 to the period 1966−1971, for which these data are also available.

It can be seen from Table 6.10 that the ethnic composition of migrant streams between Quebec and the rest of Canada remained quite stable

Table 6.10
MIGRATORY EXCHANGES BETWEEN QUEBEC AND THE REST OF CANADA, BY ETHNIC ORIGIN, FOR THE POPULATION 5 YEARS OF AGE AND OVER AT THE END OF THE PERIOD, 1956−1961 AND 1966−1971

MIGRATION STREAM	ETHNIC ORIGIN			
	All Origins	British	French	Other
1956−1961[a]				
Quebec to Rest of Canada	68,800	33,100	23,800	11,900
	(100.0)	*(48.1)*	*(34.6)*	*(17.3)*
Rest of Canada to Quebec	62,900	30,500	23,700	8,700
	(100.0)	*(48.5)*	*(37.7)*	*(13.8)*
Balance for Quebec	−5,900	−2,600	−100	−3,200
	(100.0)	*(44.1)*	*(1.7)*	*(54.2)*
1966−1971[b]				
Quebec to Rest of Canada	160,200	78,200	51,400	30,600
	(100.0)	*(48.8)*	*(32.1)*	*(19.1)*
Rest of Canada to Quebec	84,600	34,700	36,900	13,000
	(100.0)	*(41.0)*	*(43.6)*	*(15.4)*
Balance for Quebec	−75,600	−43,500	−14,500	−17,600
	(100.0)	*(57.5)*	*(19.2)*	*(23.3)*

Sources: Census of Canada, 1961 and 1971, unpublished and special tables.
Note: [a] These figures most likely understate migratory movements. We were unable to correct them due to lack of precise data.
　　　[b] Migrants who did not state their place of residence in Canada in 1966 were distributed proportionately between intraprovincial and interprovincial migrants.

between 1956—1961 and 1966—1971. There were nevertheless a few slight changes from one period to the other: the percentage of British-origin persons among migrants leaving Quebec for the rest of Canada increased very slightly, while the proportion of French-origin persons in this migration stream declined; conversely, among migrants coming to Quebec from the rest of Canada, the strength of French-origin persons increased very appreciably between 1956—1961 (37.7%) and 1966—1971 (43.6%), while the proportion of British-origin persons dropped from 48.5% to 41.0%. These trends appear to continue, for mother tongue this time, from 1966—1971 to 1971—1976 (Table 6.8). Some part of these changes in composition by ethnic origin or by mother tongue in the migrant streams may be due to changes in the ethnolinguistic compositions of the population likely to migrate. This factor may play a considerable role in the evolution of the composition of migrant streams going from Quebec to the rest of Canada, although there is an element of doubt here, since the fraction of French-origin or mother-tongue persons decreased at more or less the same rate in Quebec as that of British-origin persons and the English group, between 1951 and 1971. Moreover, in the very clear evolution of the ethnolinguistic composition of migrant streams from the rest of Canada into Quebec, the above factor no doubt had a considerable effect, but in the opposite direction, since the percentage of British-origin persons and the English group increased between 1961 and 1971 in the rest of Canada, while the proportion of French-origin and French mother-tongue persons declined.

3. General Remarks

Relatively speaking it would appear that, since the period 1956—1961, Quebec has attracted increasing numbers of francophones, while the other provinces have drawn more and more members from the anglophone group in Quebec. There is no evidence that these trends will continue through the coming years. Considering the very strong language legislation enacted in Quebec in 1974 and 1977, which is aimed at safeguarding and improving the position of French as a language of work and education, we may nevertheless expect that these trends will persist and perhaps even become more pronounced during the next two or three five-year periods.

The effects of internal migration on the evolution of the linguistic composition of Quebec will also depend on the job situation and, more generally, on the socio-economic situation of Quebec in comparison with that of the rest of Canada. Although it is not easy to dissociate socio-economic factors from factors that are specifically demolinguistic, we may no doubt assume, at the outset, that these two sets of factors are to a great extent independent of one another. To put it more specifically, this means that we assume that the linguistic composition of migrant streams between Quebec and the rest of Canada is fairly independent of the overall balance of migratory exchanges between these two regions. This, of course, is only a hypothesis, but this hypothesis will be considered axiomatic in our method and we will therefore not attempt to test it (Boudon, 1971*b*). This hypothesis in any case will not be used to describe and analyse, but to explore the plausible demolinguistic effects of changes in the overall balance of exchanges between Quebec and the rest of Canada.

Let us first calculate the internal migratory balance for Quebec, by mother tongue, in 1966−1971 and in 1971−1976, using the hypothesis that these balances for all mother tongues combined would have been nil. To do this, we assume that the total number of migrants between Quebec and the rest of Canada, as well as the linguistic compositions of streams, correspond to those actually observed (Table 6.8). These hypotheses yield the following results, by mother tongue:

	1966−1971		1971−1976	
English	−8 100	(−10.9)	−16 800	(−22.2)
French	12 400	(2.8)	18 500	(4.1)
Other	−4 300	(−14.9)	−1 700	(− 5.4)
Total	0		0	

We have shown in parenthesis the net internal migration ratio for the Quebec population (per thousand). In these hypothetical conditions of migratory equilibrium between Quebec and the rest of Canada, the French group in Quebec would nonetheless have benefited, or so it would seem, from internal migration, not only in relative terms, but also in terms of numbers. As for the English group, it could have balanced the favourable effects of this phenomenon on the French group, by having an excess fertility, compared to the latter group, of 20% in 1966−1971 and 40% in 1971−1976. We have already seen, however, that the English group would have had to achieve an excess fertility of 104% in 1966−1971 and 119% in 1971−1976 in order to counterbalance the *observed* demolinguistic effects of internal migration. This leads us to believe that in Quebec the relative effects of internal migration would become increasingly favourable to the French group as the migratory losses of Quebec rise.

C. SOME FACTORS OF MIGRATION BETWEEN QUEBEC AND THE REST OF CANADA

We saw previouly that we could derive the linguistic composition of the migrant streams between Quebec and the rest of Canada by considering the linguistic compositions of the regions of origin and of destination together. While there appears to be a rather close relation between, on the one hand, propensities to move from Quebec to the rest of Canada and from the rest of

Canada to Quebec, by mother tongue and, on the other hand, the linguistic compositions of the regions of destination, this still does not mean that linguistic composition itself acts on differential migration. It is rather that the linguistic composition of a region constitutes an approximation of the costs of acquiring information regarding migration opportunities, as well as the costs of cultural and linguistic adaptation and integration for potential immigrants. The relative size of these costs, by mother tongue, determines the gaps between the propensities to migrate of the various language groups. If there is a basis for this explanation, it should also explain the sizeable variations that appear in propensities to migrate when we consider other variables together with mother tongue.

For each language group, we will first describe variations by age and then by level of schooling in propensities to migrate from Quebec to the rest of Canada and from the rest of Canada to Quebec. These two variables, age and level of schooling, are mainly of documentary interest. The same is not true of the next group of variables we will examine: place of birth, ethnic origin, and home language. These variables complement and give more depth to the explanatory framework of which, up to now, we have given only a rough outline.

1. Age

It can be seen from Tables 6.11 and 6.12 that propensities to migrate from Quebec to the rest of Canada or from the rest of Canada to Quebec, between 1966 and 1971,[17] tended always to be arranged in the same manner, by mother tongue, no matter what age group was considered. This was not entirely unexpected, since the differential structuring of the costs associated with migration is no doubt the same, with a few minor adjustments, at all ages.

Propensities to migrate are highest among persons who were between 25 and 29 at the end of the period. There is one exception, however: this maximum comes a little earlier in the French group in Quebec, or rather there is practically no difference between the propensities to migrate of persons 20−24 years old (2.1%) and those 25−29 years old (2.0%) at the end of the period. The propensity to migrate is at its maximum among young adults in all areas of the world (United Nations, 1973). This is due to the fact that at these ages individuals seek to enter the labour force, marry and, consequently, change their place of residence frequently.

No matter which geolinguistic group we consider, the propensity to migrate decreases regularly from the 25−29 age group to the older years. There is occasionally a slight upswing among people between 65 and 69 at the end of the period, when retired persons return to their place of origin or move to milder climates. The propensities of children to migrate obviously reflect those of their parents.

Table 6.11

OUT-MIGRATION (AND *NET INTERNAL MIGRATION*) RATIOS,[a] BY MOTHER TONGUE AND AGE GROUP, QUEBEC, 1966–1971

(percentage)

AGE GROUP IN 1971	MOTHER TONGUE			
	All Mother Tongues	English	French	Other
5–9	3.1 (−1.3)	16.8 (−8.2)	1.0 (−0.2)	2.9 (−2.1)
10–14	2.4 (−1.2)	13.9 (−7.6)	0.6 (−0.2)	3.5 (−2.8)
15–19	2.2 (−1.2)	11.4 (−6.9)	0.7 (−0.4)	3.3 (−2.6)
20–24	4.1 (−2.0)	16.5 (−7.7)	2.1 (−1.1)	6.2 (−3.9)
25–29	4.5 (−1.6)	20.6 (−8.1)	2.0 (−0.5)	8.9 (−5.5)
30–34	4.0 (−1.5)	19.3 (−9.0)	1.5 (−0.2)	7.6 (−4.9)
35–39	3.3 (−1.6)	15.8 (−8.3)	1.1 (−0.2)	6.4 (−4.5)
40–44	2.7 (−1.5)	13.1 (−8.0)	0.8 (−0.2)	5.3 (−3.5)
45–49	2.4 (−1.4)	10.9 (−7.1)	0.6 (−0.2)	4.6 (−3.4)
50–54	1.8 (−1.1)	7.7 (−5.2)	0.5 (−0.1)	3.4 (−2.4)
55–59	1.4 (−0.7)	5.6 (−3.6)	0.3 (0.0)	3.2 (−2.5)
60–64	1.3 (−0.7)	5.5 (−4.0)	0.3 (−0.1)	2.4 (−1.7)
65–69	1.4 (−0.8)	5.6 (−4.3)	0.4 (0.0)	2.3 (−1.7)
70+	1.1 (−0.6)	4.0 (−2.7)	0.3 (0.0)	1.9 (−1.4)
5+	2.8 (−1.3)	12.7 (−6.8)	1.0 (−0.3)	4.6 (−3.2)

Source: Census of Canada, 1971, special tables.
Note: [a] In calculating these ratios (see Note *a*, Table 6.9), we used only those census respondents who stated their place of residence in 1966.

Table 6.12
OUT-MIGRATION (AND *NET INTERNAL MIGRATION*) RATIOS,[a] BY MOTHER TONGUE AND AGE GROUP, CANADA LESS QUEBEC, 1966–1971
(percentage)

AGE GROUP IN 1971	MOTHER TONGUE			
	All Mother Tongues	English	French	Other
5–9	0.7 (0.5)	0.5 (0.5)	4.8 (1.0)	0.2 (0.5)
10–14	0.5 (0.5)	0.4 (0.5)	2.8 (1.0)	0.1 (0.5)
15–19	0.4 (0.4)	0.3 (0.4)	2.2 (2.1)	0.1 (0.4)
20–24	0.9 (0.9)	0.6 (0.5)	6.1 (6.3)	0.4 (0.6)
25–29	1.4 (0.8)	0.9 (0.6)	8.7 (2.9)	0.5 (0.9)
30–34	1.1 (0.7)	0.7 (0.6)	6.8 (0.8)	0.4 (0.8)
35–39	0.8 (0.7)	0.6 (0.6)	4.3 (1.2)	0.3 (0.7)
40–44	0.5 (0.6)	0.4 (0.6)	3.1 (0.9)	0.2 (0.5)
45–49	0.4 (0.6)	0.3 (0.6)	2.3 (0.9)	0.2 (0.5)
50–54	0.3 (0.4)	0.2 (0.4)	1.7 (0.7)	0.1 (0.3)
55–59	0.2 (0.3)	0.2 (0.3)	1.6 (0.1)	0.1 (0.3)
60–64	0.2 (0.3)	0.1 (0.3)	1.7 (−0.4)	0.1 (0.2)
65–69	0.2 (0.3)	0.1 (0.4)	2.0 (−0.3)	0.1 (0.2)
70+	0.2 (0.2)	0.1 (0.2)	1.3 (−0.1)	0.1 (0.1)
5+	0.6 (0.5)	0.4 (0.5)	3.8 (1.5)	0.2 (0.5)

Source: Census of Canada, 1971, special tables.
Note: [a] See Note a, Table 6.11.

2. Level of Schooling

Tables 6.13 and 6.14 show the out-migration ratios (and the net internal migration ratios) for Quebec and the rest of Canada between 1966 and 1971, both by mother tongue and by level of schooling. These figures were calculated for the adult population (20−59 years old in 1971). It should be noted that, in this case, out-migration ratios do not necessarily constitute a good approximation of propensities to migrate: the former use level of schooling at the end of the period, while in estimating the latter it would be better to consider level of schooling at the beginning of the period or, more exactly, prior to migration. We may nevertheless assume, bearing this in mind, that variations in the ratios approximately reflect variations in propensities, at least when the relative variance between the ratios is large.

Like mother tongue, level of schooling causes great variations in propensities to migrate from Quebec to the rest of Canada and, to a lesser extent, in propensities to migrate from the rest of Canada into Quebec. These two variables, mother tongue and level of schooling, are almost independent of each other. In any given language group, propensities to migrate increase with the level of schooling:[18] they are generally three to six times higher among persons with university education than among those with primary education. By the same token, whatever the level of schooling, propensities to migrate are organized in the same way by mother tongue. In fact, the propensities to leave Quebec shown in Table 6.13 almost constitute a

Table 6.13
OUT-MIGRATION (AND *NET INTERNAL MIGRATION*) RATIOS,[a] BY MOTHER TONGUE AND LEVEL OF SCHOOLING, IN POPULATION AGED 20−59 IN 1971, QUEBEC, 1966−1971
(percentage)

LEVEL OF SCHOOLING	MOTHER TONGUE			
	English	French	Other	All Languages
Primary	4.1 (− 2.3)	0.6 (−0.3)	2.2 (−1.6)	1.0 (−0.5)
Secondary with no further training	12.0 (− 6.0)	1.4 (−0.4)	6.1 (−4.3)	3.1 (−1.4)
Secondary with professional or post-secondary non-university training	18.0 (− 8.7)	1.8 (−0.5)	9.9 (−6.0)	4.7 (−2.0)
University	20.4 (−11.0)	2.5 (−0.8)	12.3 (−8.1)	8.1 (−4.1)
All levels	14.0 (− 7.2)	1.3 (−0.4)	5.8 (−3.9)	3.2 (−1.5)

Source: Census of Canada, 1971, special tables.
Note: [a] See Note *a*, Table 6.11.

Table 6.14
OUT-MIGRATION (AND *NET INTERNAL MIGRATION*) RATIOS,[a]
BY MOTHER TONGUE AND LEVEL OF SCHOOLING, IN
POPULATION AGED 20–59 IN 1971, CANADA LESS QUEBEC,
1966–1971
(percentage)

LEVEL OF SCHOOLING	MOTHER TONGUE			
	English	French	Other	All Languages
Primary	0.2 (+0.3)	2.9 (+1.9)	0.1 (+0.4)	0.6 (+0.6)
Secondary with no further training	0.3 (+0.3)	3.9 (+1.4)	0.2 (+0.4)	0.5 (+0.4)
Secondary with professional or post-secondary non-university training	0.6 (+0.6)	7.4 (+2.7)	0.4 (+0.7)	0.9 (+0.7)
University	1.2 (+1.4)	9.6 (+4.3)	0.9 (+1.8)	1.5 (+1.6)
All levels	0.5 (+0.5)	4.6 (+2.0)	0.3 (+0.6)	0.7 (+0.6)

Source: Census of Canada, 1971, special tables.
Note: [a] See Note *a*, Table 6.11.

textbook example. To demonstrate this, let us compare the propensities of each language group, by level of schooling, to that observed among persons having elementary education, this level being fixed at 100. The following indices are obtained:

	English	**French**	**Other**
Primary	100	100	100
Secondary with no further training	293	233	277
Secondary with further training . . .	439	300	450
University	498	417	559

The impact of schooling is much the same from one language group to another; allowing for errors in estimation, we can no doubt say that it is almost identical.

Let us now compare the ratios of propensities by mother tongue for each level of schooling to those of the French group, which are given the base value of 100:

	English	**French**	**Other**
Primary	683	100	367
Secondary with no further training	857	100	436
Secondary with further training . . .	1 000	100	550
University	816	100	492

Here again, it appears that, roughly speaking, the impact of the mother-tongue variable does not vary greatly with level of schooling. This leads us to believe that the mother-tongue and level-of-schooling variables act independently of each other on internal migration, and that their effects combine in a multiplying manner.

We have seen that the demolinguistic consequences of internal migration can be estimated using a net internal migration ratio. These are given (in parenthesis) by mother tongue and by level of schooling in Tables 6.13 and 6.14. It can be seen that in Quebec as in the rest of Canada, internal migration always favours the French group, no matter what level of schooling is considered, and works to the disadvantage of the English and third-language groups. In addition, judging from the variances between net internal migration ratios,[19] it would seem that the higher the level of schooling, the more favourable the effects of internal migration are to the French group, and the more unfavourable they are to the English and third-language group. This statement is especially valid for Quebec.

3. Place of Birth

In Section *B*, we suggested an explanation for the great variations by mother-tongue in propensities to leave Quebec for the rest of Canada and the rest of Canada for Quebec. This explanation is derived from two factors: first, the ability to acquire information regarding migration opportunities and, second, the costs of linguistic and cultural adaptation and integration. If we assume that these are determining factors in migratory exchanges between Quebec and the rest of Canada, we would expect that propensities to migrate would be organized in the same manner, by mother tongue, whether the individuals considered are born in Quebec, the rest of Canada, or in another country. We would also predict that propensities to migrate from one region to another would be much higher, for any given language group, among persons born in the region of destination than for those born in the region of origin, since the former would have a much better-developed information network at their disposal and would also be faced with lower costs of linguistic and cultural adaptation and integration than the latter. In so far as the propensities of foreign-born persons are concerned, we would expect them to occupy an intermediate position, since these persons would, on the one hand, be less well integrated in the region of origin than those born there, but, on the other hand, they have neither the information network nor the capacity to adapt and integrate of persons born in the region of destination.

We have shown in Tables 6.15 and 6.16 the ratios of out-migration (and of internal migratory increase) observed during the period 1966—1971 for the population of Quebec and that of the rest of Canada. These ratios are given by mother tongue and by place of birth. They correspond perfectly to the propositions we have just advanced, assuming of course that we can make

Table 6.15
OUT-MIGRATION (AND *NET INTERNAL MIGRATION*) RATIOS,[a]
BY MOTHER TONGUE AND PLACE OF BIRTH, IN POPULATION
AGED 20−59 IN 1971, QUEBEC, 1966−1971
(percentage)

PLACE OF BIRTH	MOTHER TONGUE			
	English	French	Other	All Languages
Outside Canada	14.7 (−8.8)	2.1 (−0.7)	6.3 (−4.4)	7.7 (−4.9)
Canada				
Quebec	8.4 (−6.6)	1.0 (−0.5)	2.0 (−1.4)	1.7 (−1.1)
Elsewhere in Canada	29.2 (−7.8)	9.4 (+3.7)	21.4 (−4.7)	20.8 (−3.0)
Total	13.9 (−6.9)	1.3 (−0.4)	3.6 (−1.7)	2.8 (−1.1)
All Places of Birth	14.0 (−7.2)	1.3 (−0.4)	5.8 (−3.9)	3.2 (−1.5)

Source: Census of Canada, 1971, special tables.
Note: [a] See Note *a*, Table 6.11.

Table 6.16
OUT-MIGRATION (AND *NET INTERNAL MIGRATION*) RATIOS,[a]
BY MOTHER TONGUE AND PLACE OF BIRTH, IN POPULATION
AGED 20−59 IN 1971, CANADA LESS QUEBEC, 1966−1971
(percentage)

PLACE OF BIRTH	MOTHER TONGUE			
	English	French	Other	All Languages
Outside Canada	0.7 (+ 1.0)	4.5 (+ 2.3)	0.4 (+ 0.8)	0.5 (+ 0.9)
Canada				
Quebec	4.9 (+18.2)	15.2 (+14.2)	4.4 (+10.7)	9.7 (+16.2)
Elsewhere in Canada	0.4 (+ 0.1)	2.4 (− 0.7)	0.1 (+ 0.0)	0.5 (+ 0.1)
Total	0.5 (+ 0.5)	4.6 (+ 2.0)	0.2 (+ 0.1)	0.8 (+ 0.6)
All Places of Birth	0.5 (+ 0.5)	4.6 (+ 2.0)	0.3 (+ 0.6)	0.7 (+ 0.6)

Source: Census of Canada, 1971, special tables.
Note: [a] See Note *a*, Table 6.11.

approximate estimates of the propensities to migrate using out-migration ratios.

These results enable us to give a simple interpretation to the decrease in emigration ratios from Quebec to the rest of Canada observed in all language groups between 1966−1971 and 1971−1976 (Table 6.9). Given the great losses experienced by Quebec in its migratory exchanges with the rest of Canada between 1966 and 1971, it is likely that the proportion of persons born in Canada less Quebec was lower for every language group in 1971 than in 1966. This composition effect alone can probably account for a large part of the reduction in out-migration ratios. By the same token, in the rest of Canada, we would rather expect that the composition effect would cause an increase in out-migration ratios between 1966–1971 and 1971–1976. The increase, however, only occurred in the French group (Table 6.9). The decline in the out-migration ratios of the English and third-language groups can no doubt be interpreted as a sign of a reduction in the drawing power of Quebec for these language groups.

4. Ethnic Origin

Traditionally, ethnic origin was often used in differentiating characteristics and behaviour patterns within the Canadian population. As we saw in Chapter Two, however, ethnic origin, which in census terms is the ethnic or cultural group of the male ancestor when he arrived in America, does not necessarily reflect the present ethnic identity of the Canadian population. This led us to assume that the mother-tongue variable causes much greater variations in propensities to migrate than does the ethnic-origin variable, since the latter variable is often an ancestral characteristic having relatively little influence on the present behaviour of Canadians. To see this more clearly, it would be wise to examine propensities to migrate both by ethnic origin and by mother tongue.

In Tables 6.17 and 6.18, we have shown the internal emigration ratios (and net internal migration ratios), by ethnic origin and mother tongue, for the population of Quebec and the rest of Canada between 1966 and 1971. Bearing in mind the small numbers on which some of these ratios are based, the hypotheses we have just proposed appear to be well founded. Propensities to migrate are basically determined by mother tongue, with ethnic origin adding only variations that may, in any case, be partly due to statistical deficiencies.

On the whole, variations in the propensities to migrate from Quebec to the rest of Canada and from the rest of Canada to Quebec are to a much greater extent due to linguistic factors than to ethnic factors, at least in the sense that the word "ethnic" is used in Canadian censuses. But mother tongue, like ethnic origin, although to a lesser degree, does not reflect the present linguistic situation. It corresponds rather to the predominant home language in the families of origin of persons counted by censuses during their childhood. Home language, that is, the language most often spoken at the present time in the home, is a much better reflection than mother tongue of the current linguistic situation of Canadians in 1971.

Table 6.17
OUT-MIGRATION (AND *NET INTERNAL MIGRATION*) RATIOS,[a]
BY MOTHER TONGUE AND ETHNIC ORIGIN, IN POPULATION
AGED 20−59 IN 1971, QUEBEC, 1966−1971
(percentage)

ETHNIC ORIGIN	MOTHER TONGUE			
	English	French	Other	All Languages
British	15.7 (−8.4)	2.3 (−0.7)	8.2 (−4.0)	13.2 (−7.0)
French	9.8 (−3.9)	1.2 (−0.4)	2.9 (−1.3)	1.4 (−0.4)
Other	10.3 (−4.8)	1.9 (−0.7)	5.8 (−3.9)	6.4 (−3.7)
Amerindian	8.1 (−2.5)	1.5 (−0.2)	1.2 (−0.1)	2.0 (−0.3)
German	22.9 (−6.4)	1.8 (−0.3)	12.9 (−7.5)	12.1 (−5.2)
Italian	6.1 (−2.7)	0.9 (−0.5)	1.9 (−1.2)	2.1 (−1.2)
Ukranian	13.5 (−1.2)	2.8 (−0.6)	7.7 (−4.2)	9.2 (−3.0)
Other	9.2 (−5.2)	2.7 (−1.3)	7.9 (−5.8)	7.8 (−5.0)
All origins	14.0 (−7.2)	1.3 (−0.4)	5.8 (−3.9)	3.2 (−1.5)

Source: Census of Canada, 1971, special tables.
Note: [a] See Note *a*, Table 6.11.

Table 6.18
OUT-MIGRATION (AND *NET INTERNAL MIGRATION*) RATIOS,[a]
BY MOTHER TONGUE AND ETHNIC ORIGIN, IN POPULATION
AGED 20−59 IN 1971, CANADA LESS QUEBEC, 1966−1971
(percentage)

ETHNIC ORIGIN	MOTHER TONGUE			
	English	French	Other	All Languages
British	0.5 (+0.6)	4.5 (+2.0)	0.4 (+0.4)	0.5 (+0.6)
French	1.0 (+0.7)	4.7 (+2.0)	1.5 (+1.2)	3.4 (+1.5)
Other	0.4 (+0.3)	3.9 (+2.5)	0.3 (+0.6)	0.3 (+0.5)
Amerindian	0.2 (+0.1)	7.2 (+1.3)	0.2 (0.0)	0.3 (+0.1)
German	0.3 (+0.1)	4.4 (+1.0)	0.3 (+0.4)	0.3 (+0.3)
Italian	0.4 (+0.3)	2.9 (+4.7)	0.2 (+0.4)	0.3 (+0.4)
Ukranian	0.4 (0.0)	2.4 (+0.6)	0.1 (+0.2)	0.3 (+0.1)
Other	0.5 (+0.6)	3.6 (+3.2)	0.3 (+0.9)	0.4 (+0.7)
All origins	0.5 (+0.5)	4.6 (+2.0)	0.3 (+0.6)	0.7 (+0.6)

Source: Census of Canada, 1971, special tables.
Note: [a] See Note *a*, Table 6.11.

5. Home Language

In Tables 6.19 and 6.20, we have estimated the out-migration (and net internal migration) ratios for the populations of Quebec and the rest of Canada, by mother tongue and by home language, during the period 1966–1971. As a first step, let us assume that out-migration ratios can be assimilated to propensities to migrate, which is the same as assuming that during the five-year period under study, migrants are subject to the linguistic

Table 6.19
OUT-MIGRATION (AND *NET INTERNAL MIGRATION*) RATIOS,[a]
BY MOTHER TONGUE AND HOME LANGUAGE, IN
POPULATION AGED 20–59 IN 1971, QUEBEC, 1966–1971
(percentage)

HOME LANGUAGE	MOTHER TONGUE			
	English	French	Other	All Languages
English	15.0(−7.8)	14.3(−7.5)	11.5(−7.3)	14.6(−7.7)
French	2.5(−0.1)	1.0(−0.2)	1.5(−0.3)	1.0(−0.2)
Other	8.2(−5.7)	2.8(−1.6)	3.9(−3.0)	4.0(−3.0)
All languages	14.0(−7.2)	1.3(−0.4)	5.8(−3.9)	3.2(−1.5)

Source: Census of Canada, 1971, special tables.
Note: [a] See Note *a*, Table 6.11.

Table 6.20
OUT-MIGRATION (AND *NET INTERNAL MIGRATION*) RATIOS,[a]
BY MOTHER TONGUE AND HOME LANGUAGE, IN
POPULATION AGED 20–59 IN 1971, CANADA LESS QUEBEC,
1966–1971
(percentage)

HOME LANGUAGE	MOTHER TONGUE			
	English	French	Other	All Languages
English	0.5(+0.5)	2.0(+2.2)	0.3(+0.5)	0.5(+0.6)
French	7.3(+0.4)	6.3(+1.9)	8.9(+2.6)	6.3(+1.8)
Other	0.4(+0.9)	2.7(+3.7)	0.2(+0.7)	0.2(+0.7)
All languages	0.5(+0.5)	4.6(+2.0)	0.3(+0.6)	0.7(+0.6)

Source: Census of Canada, 1971, special tables.
Note: [a] See Note *a*, Table 6.11.

mobility of their region of origin or, in other words, that language transfers always precede migrations.

It can be seen that variations in propensities to migrate are due more to home language than to mother tongue.[20] This is not very surprising, since we might expect that the ability to obtain information regarding migration opportunities, and above all the costs of linguistic and cultural adaptation and integration (the home language of an individual often being that which predominates in his family) depends more on home language than on mother tongue, except of course when these two variables are the same. These results reinforce the explanatory framework we have been describing up to now.

We can therefore postulate that linguistic mobility towards English is not an entirely cumulative phenomenon in Quebec, since persons who adopt or retain English as their home language are more likely to migrate to the rest of Canada than are those who retain or take French as their home language. We might also state a corresponding conclusion for the rest of Canada, but here language transfers to French are quite rare, or in fact almost non-existent, as we saw in the last chapter.

D. INTERREGIONAL MIGRATORY EXCHANGES BY MOTHER TONGUE

Even if we deal with only two regions, Quebec and the rest of Canada, it is not always easy to describe the characteristics and evolution of internal migration, nor to make precise and coherent statements about the demolinguistic effects of this phenomenon. This is indicative of the difficulties encountered and the precautions that must be taken when we consider a larger number of regions. Strictly speaking, since we are dealing with the effects of internal migration, the presentation is no more difficult whether we analyse ten or twenty regions instead of two: it is only more cumbersome. The study of the factors of internal migration does, however, become increasingly difficult as the number of regions increases, not necessarily on the theoretical level, since an appropriate territorial breakdown will enable us to better grasp and extract the factors involved, but certainly from a technical standpoint, since there are more data to be handled. The best approach is generally to make use of more sophisticated statistical methods. These will only give interesting and relevant results if we first make them fit the requirements of a clear and well-developed theory. This involves intellectual and technical operations that are not only long, but difficult and costly. They cannot all be performed at the outset, and this is why we should first undertake some preliminary study.

In the pages that follow, we will examine migratory exchanges, by mother tongue, among thirteen regions. These are the same regions we have often used in the foregoing chapters. We will be mainly interested here in the demographic effects of internal migration, but we will also look at the distribution of out-migrants from each region among the possible regions of destination, while seeking to integrate the results of our analysis into the explanatory framework described and illustrated in the preceding sections.

1. Demo-Regional and Demolinguistic Effects of Internal Migration

Table 6.21 shows the net internal migration ratios, by mother tongue, for the thirteen regions during the periods 1966–1971 and 1971–1976.

Table 6.21
NET INTERNAL MIGRATION RATIO,[a] BY MOTHER TONGUE, IN POPULATION 5 YEARS AND OVER AT THE END OF THE PERIOD, FOR THIRTEEN REGIONS, 1966–1971 AND 1971–1976
(percentage)

REGION[b]	PERIOD	MOTHER TONGUE			
		Total	English	French	Other
Other Atlantic	1966–1971	−2.0	−2.0	−0.2	−1.6
Provinces	1971–1976	+0.1	+0.1	−0.1	+0.3
North-and-East	1966–1971	−1.9	−3.4	−1.0	−3.9
New Brunswick	1971–1976	−0.3	−2.2	+1.1	+1.3
South of New Brunswick	1966–1971	−0.8	−1.1	+6.0	−3.9
	1971–1976	+4.0	+3.7	+11.5	+0.4
Outaouais	1966–1971	+2.5	−1.9	+3.6	+3.1
	1971–1976	+5.4	+6.4	+5.0	+16.1
Eastern Townships	1966–1971	−1.1	−5.7	−0.3	+3.5
	1971–1976	−0.9	−1.2	−0.9	+3.6
Montreal	1966–1971	−0.1	−5.8	+2.1	−3.0
	1971–1976	−0.5	−5.7	+1.3	−1.6
Interior of Quebec	1966–1971	−1.0	−11.4	−0.6	−9.5
	1971–1976	−1.5	−27.5	−0.7	−24.2
Periphery of Quebec	1966–1971	−6.9	−25.0	−5.8	−8.6
	1971–1976	−4.0	−20.1	−3.2	−3.6
Northeast of Ontario	1966–1971	−0.2	−1.0	+1.8	−3.0
	1971–1976	−5.6	−6.5	−4.0	−5.9
Southeast of Ontario	1966–1971	+4.8	+6.5	+0.9	+5.8
	1971–1976	+2.2	+2.7	+0.8	+4.0
Northwest of Ontario	1966–1971	−2.3	−2.6	+1.9	−2.5
	1971–1976	−2.6	−2.8	−0.5	−2.2
Interior of Ontario	1966–1971	+0.8	+0.7	+5.1	+0.8
	1971–1976	−0.6	−0.7	−0.5	−0.1
West-and-North of Canada	1966–1971	+1.0	+1.1	+2.4	+0.5
	1971–1976	+2.0	+2.1	+3.9	+0.9

Sources: Estimates made by authors using results obtained by Leroy O. Stone based on special tables from 1971 and 1976 census of Canada.

Note: [a] See Table 6.9.
   [b] See Appendix *A*.

These ratios may be described from two points of view, that of the *demo-regional effects* of internal migration and that of the *demolinguistic effects* of this phenomenon in each of our regions. We know that migratory exchanges between a group of regions can be compared to zero-sum games, with the losses of one region constituting the gains of the other regions. This means that a region having a positive ratio of net internal migration would benefit from migratory exchanges or, in other words, that internal migration would redistribute the population in its favour, while, conversely, a negative net internal migration ratio indicates that internal migration works against the region in question. The value taken by the ratio shows the extent of the redistributing or demo-regional effect. The demo-regional effects of internal migration may just as well be studied for the total population as for each language group. Internal migration does not, however, only cause a redistribution of the population among regions, it also acts on the composition of each of the regions, in this case on the regional linguistic composition. This is what we have called the demolinguistic effect of internal migration. In relative terms, internal migration is favourable or unfavourable to a language group in a given region depending on whether its net internal migration ratio is greater or less than that of the total regional population. The variance between the ratio of one linguistic group and that of the total regional population under study is an approximate measurement of the intensity of the demolinguistic effect.

We will first describe the demo-regional effects of internal migration. Three regions benefited from population redistribution caused by internal migration during the periods 1966−1971 and 1971−1976 (Table 6.21): these were the Southeast of Ontario, the Outaouais, and the West-and-North of Canada (western provinces and northern territories), with the first region gaining less in 1971−1976 than in 1966−1971, while the two other regions improved their position between 1966−1971 and 1971−1976. Conversely, a number of regions suffered during both five-year periods: the Periphery of Quebec, the Eastern Townships, the North-and-East of New Brunswick, the Northwest and Northeast of Ontario, the Interior of Quebec, and Montreal, with the first three regions losing less ground in the second period than in the first, while the last four regions had heavier losses in 1971−1976 than in 1966−1971. In three regions, demo-regional effects were reversed in 1966−1971 compared to 1971−1976: in the South of New Brunswick as well as in the "Other Atlantic Provinces" (Newfoundland, Prince Edward Island, and Nova Scotia), they went from unfavourable to favourable, while the opposite was observed in the Interior region of Ontario.

During the last two five-year periods, the English mother-tongue population in two regions benefited from the redistributive effects of internal migration: the Southeast of Ontario, and the West-and-North of Canada. The Interior region of Ontario also showed gains for this group between 1966 and 1971, but losses during the following period. Changes in the opposite direction were observed in the South of New Brunswick, in the "Other Atlantic Provinces," and in the Outaouais. The very recent attraction of the Outaouais for the English mother-tongue population is very likely due, at least in part, to the creation of the National Capital Region and the federal government's development strategy in that area. Elsewhere in Quebec, internal migration has always had clearly unfavourable demo-regional effects on the English group.

Between 1966—1971 and 1971—1976, the demo-regional effects of internal migration also showed a certain variability in the French mother-tongue population. Five regions clearly benefited during both periods: the South of New Brunswick, Montreal, the Outaouais, the Southeast of Ontario, and the West-and-North of Canada. In three Ontario regions (Interior, Northwest, and Northeast), the effects of migration were favourable in 1966—1971, but changed to unfavourable during the following period, while in the North-and-East of New Brunswick, the contrary was observed.

On the whole, the English and French groups appear to react in a similar, if not identical, way to the socio-economic changes reflected by migration streams during the past two five-year periods. Between 1966—1971 and 1971—1976, we saw an increased orientation of migration towards the West of Canada and a fairly sizeable improvement in the migratory situation of the Atlantic regions (Canada, Statistics Canada, 1977; Termote and Fréchette, 1979). It is likely that the smaller losses or recent gains in regions located east of Quebec are the result of strong return migrations, with "natives" of the Atlantic provinces returning to their region of origin after a more or less prolonged stay in Ontario or Quebec. We may note that two central regions have resisted this movement towards the East and, to an even greater degree, towards the West: they face each other across the Ottawa River, one being located in Quebec (Outaouais) and the other in Ontario (Southeast). While the Southeast region of Ontario still showed a positive balance in migratory exchanges between 1971 and 1976, this region attracted less migrants during this period than during the preceding period. It was a completely different story in the Outaouais: its drawing power increased between 1966—1971 and 1971—1976, especially for the English group, but also for the French group. The Montreal region also made gains during the last two periods, although only for the French group. There was, however, an appreciable reduction in the internal migratory increase ratio for the French mother-tongue group between 1966—1971 (2.1%) and 1971—1976 (1.3%).

The demolinguistic effects of internal migration are much simpler to describe than are demo-regional effects, since, in almost all regions, internal migration clearly favours the French group and works against the English group, in relative terms. There were a few exceptions: only one in 1966—1971, in the Southeast of Ontario, to which should be added, in 1971—1976, the "Other Atlantic Provinces" and, above all, the Outaouais. The overall picture remains very clear and not a little surprising. To see this, we should take a closer look at the structure of migratory exchanges between regions, that is, the distribution of migrant streams among possible regions of destination.

2. Breakdown of Migrants by Region of Destination

Due both to the efforts required to obtain information on migration opportunities, and to the differential costs of linguistic and cultural adaptation and integration, we might expect that for any given region of origin, French mother-tongue migrants would head mainly for regions with francophone majorities, and that, similarly, those of English mother tongue would move instead into regions with anglophone majorities. To test this proposition, we have shown in Table 6.22 the percentage of out-migrants from each language group winding up in predominantly francophone regions of destination.[21] It will be recalled that there are six regions that satisfy this condition: the five regions of Quebec and the North-and-East of New Brunswick, with all other regions having anglophone majorities.

The facts generally bear out the above proposition. For all regions of origin, both in 1966–1971 and in 1971–1976, French mother-tongue migrants moved to regions with francophone majorities in much higher proportions than did English-group migrants. We should also emphasize that these proportions varied little from one period to the other, which is hardly surprising. If we assume that the attraction of regions of destination for migrants from the various groups depends essentially on their linguistic composition, we would expect that the breakdown of migrants by region of destination would change relatively little over the short term, since the linguistic composition of regions evolves quite slowly. For almost all regions of origin, we nevertheless observed a slight increase in the fraction of migrants moving to regions with francophone majorities between 1966–1971 and 1971–1976. For the French group, this increase is seen in all regions of origin. There would thus appear to have been an increase in the drawing power of regions with francophone majorities during the past two periods, with this increased attraction acting mainly on the French group.

It can also be seen from Table 6.22 that the migratory behaviour of the third-language group, at least with respect to its regions of destination, is much more like that of the English group than of the French group for most regions of origin. This is no doubt due to the fact that, in almost all regions, persons of other mother-tongue adopt English more often than French as their home language.

Migratory exchanges between regions appear to be organized more as a function of the demolinguistic situation of possible regions of destination than as a function of geographical proximity or even socio-economic conditions. Wherever they come from, French mother-tongue out-migrants move, in the great majority of cases, to regions where the French group

Table 6.22
PERCENTAGE OF OUT-MIGRANTS SETTLING IN REGIONS OF
DESTINATION WITH FRANCOPHONE MAJORITIES, BY MOTHER
TONGUE, FOR THIRTEEN REGIONS OF ORIGIN,
1966–1971 AND 1971–1976
(percentage)

REGION[a] OF ORIGIN	PERIOD	MOTHER TONGUE			
		Total	English	French	Other
Other Atlantic	1966–1971	13.3	11.8	56.9	18.7
Provinces	1971–1976	15.1	12.0	64.3	17.3
North-and-East	1966–1971	20.2	7.2	45.1	36.1
New Brunswick	1971–1976	18.0	5.6	47.5	16.0
South of New Brunswick	1966–1971	26.0	22.0	72.3	25.6
	1971–1976	28.8	24.0	78.6	27.6
Outaouais	1966–1971	41.2	10.9	59.1	24.3
	1971–1976	44.8	11.7	62.3	17.0
Eastern Townships	1966–1971	79.8	46.5	91.9	48.9
	1971–1976	85.0	48.0	93.5	63.8
Montreal	1966–1971	43.0	9.1	80.5	9.5
	1971–1976	49.2	10.3	84.4	12.3
Interior of Quebec	1966–1971	87.4	49.9	92.2	65.6
	1971–1976	86.9	54.2	92.3	77.0
Periphery of Quebec	1966–1971	74.8	31.2	84.8	36.0
	1971–1976	82.3	43.2	89.7	62.5
Northeast of Ontario	1966–1971	5.2	2.8	27.0	2.4
	1971–1976	4.5	2.6	30.0	2.1
Southeast of Ontario	1966–1971	28.9	15.4	73.3	20.7
	1971–1976	26.9	13.4	75.8	21.5
Northwest of Ontario	1966–1971	10.3	5.0	29.0	3.4
	1971–1976	11.8	4.4	37.5	3.2
Interior of Ontario	1966–1971	15.7	12.3	51.3	4.0
	1971–1976	13.4	9.8	54.5	13.9
West-and-North of Canada	1966–1971	15.6	12.0	54.8	10.4
	1971–1976	13.4	10.8	61.5	13.4

Sources: As for Table 6.21.
Note: [a] See Appendix A.

dominates, mainly the regions of Quebec, while those from the English and third-language groups mainly move, whatever their region of origin, to regions with anglophone majorities. There are necessarily some exceptions to this general trend. In fact, strictly speaking, these are not exceptions, since the same tendency is seen in all areas. It would be better to speak of variations, of nuances. These can be explained mainly by the geographical location of regions of origin, or more exactly by the linguistic composition of the potential regions of destination adjacent to them.

3. Exchanges and Migratory Balances of Transition Regions

While it is clear that there are two quite distinct migratory systems in Canada, one for the French group, the other for the English and third-language groups, these systems are not completely isolated from one another. In regions that are heterogeneous from a demolinguistic viewpoint and not too distant from either predominantly French or predominantly English regions, the two systems meet or, more precisely, are superimposed without mixing to any great extent. Depending on the language group considered, these transition regions form part of one system or the other. It is therefore of interest to describe and analyse the migratory situation of these regions. We will examine them in the following order: the North-and-East of New Brunswick, the Outaouais, the Southeast and Northeast of Ontario and, finally, the Montreal region.

During the period 1971–1976,[22] out-migrants from the North-and-East of New Brunswick settled in Quebec in 5.6% of cases if their mother tongue was English and in 47.5% of cases if they belonged to the French group. These movements into Quebec are to a great extent counterbalanced by movements in the other direction, since the North-and-East of New Brunswick gained from migratory exchanges with Quebec in 1966–1971 and even more in 1971–1976 (Table 6.23). It should be noted that after losing 3,000 persons from 1966 to 1971 in its exchanges with Ontario, it gained

Table 6.23
MIGRATORY BALANCE OF THE NORTH-AND-EAST REGION OF NEW BRUNSWICK WITH THE VARIOUS REGIONS OF CANADA, BY MOTHER TONGUE, 1966–1971 AND 1971–1976

PERIOD AND MOTHER TONGUE	MIGRATORY BALANCE OF THE NORTH-AND-EAST REGION OF NEW BRUNSWICK WITH					
	All Other Regions of Canada	South of New Brunswick	Other Atlantic Provinces	Quebec	Ontario	Rest of Canada
1966–1971						
English	−4,200	−1,700	0	+700	−2,000	−1,200
French	−1,800	−600	−100	0	−900	−200
Other	−100	0	0	0	−100	0
Total	−6,100	−2,300	−100	+700	−3,000	−1,400
1971–1976						
English	−3,000	−3,600	0	+600	+1,700	−1,700
French	+2,100	−800	+200	+1,100	+1,900	−300
Other	+100	+100	0	0	+100	−100
Total	−800	−4,300	+200	+1,700	+3,700	−2,100

Sources: As for Table 6.21.

3,700 between 1971 and 1976. This change is most likely the result of a heavy stream of return migration. In addition, a sizeable fraction of migrants leaving the North-and-East of New Brunswick did not leave that province but moved to the South: 38.3% for the English group and 24.2% for the French group in 1971–1976. In the same way, still in 1971–1976, out-migrants from the South moved to the North-and-East in 19.4% of cases if English was their mother tongue and in 58.6% of cases if their mother tongue was French. This indicates that there are many migratory exchanges between these two regions. A great deal of this movement is probably to and fro, the streams of one period contributing to the flows in the other direction in the following period. On the whole, these exchanges are clearly to the disadvantage of the North-and-East, particularly the English group in that region, both in 1966–1971 and even more in 1971–1976.

Migrants leaving the Outaouais during the period 1971–1976 moved to other regions of Quebec in 11.5% of cases if they were in the English group (9.0% to Montreal) and in 62.0% of cases if French was their mother tongue (32.9% to Montreal). The Southeast region of Ontario, of course, also received a sizeable proportion: 53.5% of English-group out-migrants and 27.7% of those from the French group. The reverse movement mainly involved the French group: 41.9% of out-migrants from the Southeast of Ontario whose mother tongue was French moved to the Outaouais (32.8% to other regions of Quebec, of whom 22.1% to Montreal), as opposed to only 7.1% of those in the English group (5.5% to other regions of Quebec, of whom 4.8% to Montreal). The English and French groups in the Southeast of Ontario thus have diametrically opposed migratory orientations: migrants from the English group move mainly towards the Interior of Ontario (48.3%) and the West-and-North of Canada (25.7%), while those from the French group mainly choose the Outaouais (41.9%) and the Montreal region (22.1%).

The Outaouais had a positive internal migratory balance with most regions in the country over the last two five-year periods (Table 6.24). Except for exchanges with the West-and-North of Canada, this region greatly improved its performance from one period to the next, not only with the other regions of Quebec but also with the Southeast of Ontario and even with the other regions of Ontario, where its migratory balance went from −200 in 1966–1971 to +1,800 in 1971–1976. The French group in the Outaouais received a net input of 5,400 persons from other regions in the country in 1966–1971, while the English group had net losses totalling approximately 700 persons. Both groups made appreciable gains during the following period: 8,300 persons for the French group and 2,500 for the English group. In relative terms, this development was to the benefit of the English group and to the detriment of the French group, in spite of the noteworthy increase in the drawing power of the French group in the Outaouais between 1966–1971 and 1971–1976 (Table 6.21). Let us examine this a little more closely.

Table 6.24

MIGRATORY BALANCE OF THE OUTAOUAIS WITH VARIOUS REGIONS OF CANADA, BY MOTHER TONGUE, 1966–1971 AND 1971–1976

PERIOD AND MOTHER TONGUE	MIGRATORY BALANCE OF THE OUTAOUAIS WITH					
	All Other Regions of Canada	Other Regions of Quebec	Southeast of Ontario	Other Regions of Ontario	Atlantic Provinces	Rest of Canada
1966–1971						
English	−700	+300	−600	−500	+100	0
French	+5,400	+2,100	+2,700	+300	+100	+200
Other	+100	0	+100	0	0	0
Total	+4,800	+2,400	+2,200	−200	+200	+200
1971–1976						
English	+2,500	+800	+700	+900	+200	−100
French	+8,300	+4,000	+3,400	+800	+200	−100
Other	+500	+200	+200	+100	0	0
Total	+11,300	+5,000	+4,300	+1,800	+400	−200

Sources: As for Table 6.21.

We saw in Chapter Two that in the Outaouais, the proportion of persons of French mother tongue decreased from 79.3% in 1971 to 78.5% in 1976 (following a rising trend lasting over a century), while that of the English group increased very slightly, from 18.8% to 18.9%, and the third-language group saw its strength rise from 1.9% to 2.6%. What part did internal migration play in this development? We can get a fairly good idea by estimating what would have been the linguistic composition of the Outaouais in 1976 if, during the preceding five years, the balance of internal migratory exchanges had been identical to that observed between 1966 and 1971. Having made these calculations, we obtain the following hypothetical composition: English, 18.1%; French, 79.4%; and other, 2.5%. This clearly shows that compared to the migratory situation that prevailed from 1966 to 1971, that observed between 1971 and 1976 was favourable to the English group and unfavourable to the French group. The increase in the strength of the third-language group, still quite small in 1976, can no doubt be attributed to international migration.

The Southeast region of Ontario also shows a positive internal migration balance (Table 6.25). It should be noted, however, that the balances decreased between 1966–1971 and 1971–1976, especially for the English group. This is due to the fact that the migratory exchanges of the Southeast region were, from one period to the next, both more unfavourable with the Outaouais and less favourable with all the Atlantic provinces, while going from favourable to unfavourable with the West-and-North of Canada. We

Table 6.25

MIGRATORY BALANCE OF THE SOUTHEAST REGION OF ONTARIO WITH VARIOUS REGIONS OF CANADA, BY MOTHER TONGUE, 1966–1971 AND 1971–1976

PERIOD AND MOTHER TONGUE	MIGRATORY BALANCE OF THE SOUTHEAST REGION OF ONTARIO WITH						
	All Other Regions of Canada	Northeast of Ontario	Other Regions of Ontario	Outaouais	Other Regions of Quebec	Atlantic Provinces	Rest of Canada
1966–1971							
English	+20,700	+1,000	+4,600	+600	+8,600	+4,200	+1,700
French	+1,300	+500	+100	−2,700	+3,100	+100	+200
Other	+1,800	+100	+400	−100	+1,200	+100	+100
Total	+23,800	+1,600	+5,100	−2,200	+12,900	+4,400	+2,000
1971–1976							
English	+10,100	+1,300	+3,500	−700	+8,700	+1,600	−4,300
French	+1,200	+1,200	+900	−3,400	+2,700	+100	−300
Other	+1,400	+100	+500	−200	+1,000	+100	−100
Total	+12,700	+2,600	+4,900	−4,300	+12,400	+1,800	−4,700

Sources: As for Table 6.21.

should also mention that exchanges by the Southeast of Ontario have always shown positive balances with the Northeast as well as with the other regions of that province, for all language groups and during both periods under study. The Southeast region of Ontario also made quite sizeable gains from Quebec regions other than the Outaouais: 12,900 persons in 1966−1971 and 12,400 in 1971−1976, with two thirds of these persons belonging to the English group.

Let us now look at the migratory situation of the other Ontario region where francophones represent a sizeable fraction of the population. During the period 1971−1976, migrants leaving the Northeast region of Ontario moved to Quebec in proportions of 2.0% and 27.5% respectively, depending on whether they were from the English group or the French group. In fact, migrants from both groups were more likely to move to the Southeast of Ontario: 12.0% among those of English mother tongue and 30.8% of those of French mother tongue. Migrants from the Northeast belonging to the French group thus appear to act as if the Southeast of their province was one of the predominantly francophone regions.

In 1966−1971, the Northeast of Ontario showed a slight negative balance in its migratory exchanges with other regions of the country (Table 6.26). This is the result of compensation between language groups: the French group gained 2,400 persons, while the English group and the third-language group lost 2,000 and 1,100 persons respectively. In 1971−1976, all groups showed substantial losses.

Table 6.26
MIGRATORY BALANCE OF THE NORTHEAST REGION OF ONTARIO WITH VARIOUS REGIONS OF CANADA, BY MOTHER TONGUE, 1966−1971 AND 1971−1976

PERIOD AND MOTHER TONGUE	MIGRATORY BALANCE OF THE NORTHEAST REGION OF ONTARIO WITH					
	All Other Regions of Canada	Southeast of Ontario	Other Regions of Ontario	Atlantic Provinces	Quebec	Rest of Canada
1966−1971						
English	−2,000	−1,000	−1,700	+1,200	+1,400	−1,900
French	+2,400	−500	−1,100	+200	+4,200	−400
Other	−1,100	−100	−1,100	0	+300	−200
Total	−700	−1,600	−3,900	+1,400	+5,900	−2,500
1971−1976						
English	−14,900	−1,300	−8,000	−1,400	+300	−4,500
French	−5,500	−1,200	−1,600	−200	−1,800	−700
Other	−1,800	−100	−1,300	0	0	−400
Total	−22,200	−2,600	−10,900	−1,600	−1,500	−5,600

Sources: As for Table 6.21.

The Montreal region was a centre of attraction for French mother-tongue out-migrants from almost all regions of the country. In 1971—1976, 20.7% of those leaving the "Other Atlantic Provinces" moved to Montreal, 7.9% and 21.1% respectively of those from the South and the North-and-East of New Brunswick, 48.2% of those from the Eastern Townships, 41.1% and 60.2% respectively of those from the Periphery and the Interior of Quebec, 32.9% of those from the Outaouais, 22.1%, 6.7%, 9.1%, and 19.5% respectively of those from the Southeast, Northeast, Northwest, and Interior of Ontario, and finally 27.7% of those from the West-and-North of Canada. This region also attracts a substantial fraction of English mother-tongue out-migrants from three Quebec regions: the Interior (46.3%), the Eastern Townships (38.2%), and the Periphery (29.6%). English-group migrants leaving the Montreal region, however, moved in 89.7% of cases to regions with anglophone majorities, mainly the Interior of Ontario (42.9%), the West-and-North of Canada (24.1%), and also the Southeast of Ontario (12.5%), while 84.4% of French mother-tongue migrants moved to regions with francophone majorities, mainly the Interior of Quebec (47.5%), but also the Periphery (18.5%), the Eastern Townships (9.6%), and the Outaouais (5.5%).

In both 1966—1971 and 1971—1976, the Montreal region showed negative balances in its migratory exchanges with Ontario, the West-and-North of Canada and also the Atlantic provinces (Table 6.27). While all

Table 6.27
MIGRATORY BALANCE OF THE MONTREAL REGION WITH VARIOUS REGIONS OF CANADA, BY MOTHER TONGUE, 1966—1971 AND 1971—1976

PERIOD AND MOTHER TONGUE	MIGRATORY BALANCE OF THE MONTREAL REGION WITH				
	All Other Regions of Canada	Other Regions of Quebec	Atlantic Provinces	Ontario	West-and-North of Canada
1966—1971					
English	−33,600	+4,700	−1,600	−27,700	−9,000
French	+39,000	+43,500	−200	−2,700	−1,600
Other	−7,700	+700	−100	−5,800	−2,500
Total	−2,300	+48,900	−1,900	−36,200	−13,100
1971—1976					
English	−35,100	+6,800	−3,300	−26,500	−12,100
French	+25,500	+29,000	−1,400	−700	−1,400
Other	−4,000	+1,400	−200	−3,500	−1,700
Total	−13,600	+37,200	−4,900	−30,700	−15,200

Sources: As for Table 6.21.

groups experienced losses, those of the English group were much higher than those of the French group. The Montreal region did, however, make appreciable gains from the other regions of Quebec; these gains were observed for all language groups,[23] and may be broken down by mother tongue as follows:

	1966–1971	1971–1976
English	9.6	18.3
French	89.0	77.9
Other	1.4	3.8
Total	100.0	100.0

These proportions, of course, also correspond to the breakdown of losses in the region Quebec less Montreal in its migratory exchanges with the Montreal region. To better appreciate the effects of these migratory exchanges, here again are the mother-tongue compositions of these two regions in 1961 and in 1971:

	Montreal		Quebec less Montreal	
	1961	**1971**	**1961**	**1971**
English	21.4	20.3	5.8	5.5
French	68.4	68.9	92.9	93.2
Other	10.2	10.8	1.3	1.3
Total	100.0	100.0	100.0	100.0

A comparison of these compositions to the above breakdowns of net balances clearly indicates that migratory exchanges between the Montreal region and the rest of Quebec have had, over the past two five-year periods, favourable effects on the French group and unfavourable effects on the English group in both regions, since, in Montreal, the fraction of migratory gains going to the French group exceeds the proportion it already represents, while in the rest of Quebec, the fraction it represents exceeds its proportion of the losses incurred. The reader will no doubt recall that quite a similar point was introduced and discussed in Chapter Two.

On the whole, the Montreal region shows a slight negative migratory balance in 1966–1971 (−2,300). This becomes somewhat more pronounced during the following period (−13,600), mainly due to the drop in net gains from other regions of Quebec between 1966–1971 (+48,900) and 1971–1976 (+37,200), since net losses to the benefit of Canada less Quebec varied little between 1966–1971 (−51,200) and 1971–1976 (−50,800). The French group nevertheless made appreciable gains during both periods, although these were smaller in 1971–1976 (+25,500) than in 1966–1971 (+39,000);[24] the English group experienced slightly greater losses in 1971–1976 (−35,100) than in 1966–1971 (−33,600).

4. An Attempt to Explain the Demolinguistic Effects of Internal Migration

Three statements will briefly describe the observations we have presented concerning interregional migratory exchanges by mother tongue over the past two five-year periods. First, whatever their point of origin, French-group out-migrants most often move to regions with francophone majorities, while out-migrants from the English group and the third-language group, no matter which region they leave, generally move towards regions with anglophone majorities. Second, almost all regions with francophone majorities had negative internal balances, while positive balances were observed in certain anglophone-majority regions; in more precise terms, the proportion of the Canadian population with French as its mother tongue living in regions with positive migratory balances is much smaller than the corresponding proportion in the English mother-tongue population.[25] Third, in almost all regions, the demolinguistic effects of internal migration favoured the French group and worked against the English group. From a purely empirical point of view, these three statements have an identical status: they summarize the migratory situation observed in Canada during the periods 1966–1971 and 1971–1976. Their theoretical status is, however, quite different. The first statement is, in effect, both theoretical and descriptive, as opposed to the other two statements, which are purely descriptive. Since it is derived from a simple but explicit explanatory framework, the first statement has the value of a theoretical proposition[26] that we may claim to be universal; its descriptive element is, in the final analysis, only a test of the proposition that was carried out using Canadian data on internal migration. The second statement, on the other hand, is solely descriptive. It is certainly possible that it will hold true over fairly long periods, and we might then speak of an empirical generalization valid for a specific geographical area. Nothing, at least for the moment, allows us to postulate that the regions where a given language group is concentrated will always either most often have positive balances or most often have negative balances. As for the third statement, we will attempt to demonstrate that it derives from the other two.

One would not expect this to be a demonstration in due form, since our statements deal with the direction in which relations develop rather than with their exact values. They are of the model "if . . . then . . . greater than (or smaller than) . . . ," which is, in any event, most often the case in the social sciences. Statements of this type cannot, however, be associated according to the rules of traditional logic (Boudon, 1974). To apply any rigorous reasoning to them, we would first have to develop complex mathematical models, establish the variation interval of a large number of parameters and, finally, carry out a great many simulation operations. Such a feat clearly falls outside the limits we have laid down for our study. We will therefore confine ourselves to a simple justification based on approximate reasoning.

Let us assume that the first statement has a basis in fact, that is, that wherever French mother-tongue out-migrants come from, they most often move to regions with francophone majorities, while those from the English group generally move to regions with anglophone majorities. Let us further assume that the French mother-tongue population lives, in much greater proportions than the English mother-tongue population, in regions with negative migration balances. Then, because of the costs of information as well as those of linguistic and cultural adaptation and integration, we may expect that in predominantly francophone regions, members of the English group will encounter relatively heavier net losses than those of the French group, who circulate mainly between regions with francophone majorities. In looking at regions with anglophone majorities, we must distinguish those with positive balances from those with negative balances. In regions with positive balances, it is likely that all language groups will make gains. When the French group represents a small proportion of the population of the region in question (West-and-North of Canada, South of New Brunswick, Interior of Ontario), we may expect internal migratory exchanges to work in its favour, but only in relative terms. When it forms a sizeable proportion of the regional population (Southeast of Ontario), it is more difficult to make predictions: in relative terms, it could just as well benefit as lose. In regions with negative balances, it is likely that the English mother-tongue population will experience heavier losses than the French mother-tongue population, since members of the English group may profit from many migratory opportunities in other regions with anglophone majorities, which is less the case for members of the French group, since regions with francophone majorities have negative balances.

As might have been expected, the above reasoning is not completely convincing. It nevertheless appears plausible that the third statement is to a great extent derived from the first two. For the time being, it is difficult to go much farther than this rather vague and equivocal formulation. The entire question should eventually be examined in a much more rigorous manner.

E. LINGUISTIC COMPOSITION OF INTERNATIONAL IMMIGRATION

As we saw above, while we have at our disposal sufficiently varied information on international immigration, we have neither a clear idea of the number of international emigrants nor any information on the linguistic composition of international emigration. Unless we construct hypotheses and make guestimates of the number and mother-tongue composition of international emigrants,[27] we cannot measure and describe either the demo-regional or the demolinguistic effects of international migration, since these effects are dependent on international migration balances and, to calculate a balance, we must obviously know the inflow as well as the outflow. It can thus be seen that it is quite difficult to undertake a rigorous study of the demographic effects of international migration in Canada. Although we are unable to analyse gains and losses together, we can nevertheless attempt to make clearer the characteristics of international immigration—the gains—provided we bear in mind that we will obtain only part of the overall picture of international migratory exchanges.

In the remarks that follow, we will confine ourselves to census statistics on the international immigrants remaining in the periods 1966–1971 and 1971–1976, that is, those persons (5 years old and over) still in Canada at the end of the period, but who stated that they lived in another country five years before. We should note that these immigrants fall into two categories: immigrants as defined in the immigration laws and Canadians returning home after a relatively long stay abroad.

Our analysis will be very brief. We will simply link up observations regarding international immigration with the evolution of internal migration already described, and show that the explanatory model used to examine the demolinguistic pattern of internal migration can also be used to account for the linguistic composition of international immigration.

We have shown that between 1966–1971 and 1971–1976, the migratory situation of the Atlantic provinces and, to an even greater extent, of the West-and-North of Canada improved at the expense of the central provinces, especially Ontario. If these changes indicate a displacement of migratory opportunities, we must then expect more international immigrants to settle in the Atlantic provinces and in the West-and-North of Canada in 1971–1976 than in 1966–1971. This is exactly what was observed to happen. Shown below is the territorial distribution of international immigrants remaining in the past two periods.

	1966–1971	1971–1976
Atlantic	3.4	4.4
Quebec	16.7	15.0
Ontario	53.2	50.5
West-and-North	26.7	30.1
Total Canada	100.0	100.0

It has also been noted that the Montreal region gained less in 1971–1976 than in 1966–1971 in its migratory exchanges with the other regions of Quebec. The same decline can be seen for international immigrants. Among those moving to Quebec, 85.7% settled in the Montreal region during the period 1966–1971, compared to 82.0% during the following period.

It is likely that because of the differential costs associated with, on the one hand, obtaining information about migration opportunities and, on the other, linguistic and cultural adaptation and integration, French mother-tongue out-migrants from any given region of Canada are seen to move most often into regions with francophone majorities, while those from the English and third-language groups generally prefer regions with anglophone majorities. If we assume that the same factors influence international immigrants, we should expect that international immigrants of French mother tongue would move mainly to Quebec, while those of English mother tongue would rather settle in the rest of Canada. To put it another way, we would expect the proportion of French mother-tongue immigrants to be higher in Quebec than elsewhere in Canada and the reverse to be true for immigrants belonging to the English group. This is in fact what has been observed (Table 6.28). If we follow this line of reasoning, the proportion of French mother-tongue immigrants should then be lower in the Montreal region than elsewhere in Quebec, since francophones represent a smaller fraction of the population of the Montreal region than that of the rest of Quebec. The reverse should be true for the proportion of English and third-language immigrants. The facts support this assumption, both in 1966–1971 and in 1971–1976 (Table 6.29).

All this appears to indicate that the same factors determine the orientation and demolinguistic structure of both internal migration and international migration. These two phenomena are nevertheless different in one important respect. In the case of international migration, political authorities have, and often use, fairly extensive regulatory and selection powers, while in many countries including Canada, internal migration is rarely subject to direct government control. This particular characteristic of international migration might perhaps account for changes in the linguistic composition of international immigrants between 1966–1971 and 1971–1976.

Table 6.28
COMPOSITION BY MOTHER TONGUE OF INTERNATIONAL IMMIGRANTS REMAINING AT THE END OF THE PERIOD, CANADA, QUEBEC, AND CANADA LESS QUEBEC, 1966–1971 AND 1971–1976[a]
(percentage)

MOTHER TONGUE	CANADA		QUEBEC		CANADA LESS QUEBEC	
	1966–1971	1971–1976	1966–1971	1971–1976	1966–1971	1971–1976
English	50.2	55.3	26.8	30.4	54.9	59.7
French	6.2	7.4	28.0	36.6	1.9	2.3
Other	43.6	37.3	45.2	33.0	43.2	38.0
All languages	100.0	100.0	100.0	100.0	100.0	100.0
Total numbers	*823,600*	*719,700*	*137,600*	*108,200*	*686,000*	*611,500*

Sources: Census of Canada, 1971 and 1976, special tables.
Note: [a] Mother-tongue compositions observed in the 1976 census have been adjusted to render them approximately comparable with those observed in the preceding census (Lachapelle, 1982a).

Table 6.29
COMPOSITION BY MOTHER TONGUE OF INTERNATIONAL
IMMIGRANTS REMAINING AT THE END OF THE PERIOD,
MONTREAL AND QUEBEC LESS MONTREAL,
1966–1971 AND 1971–1976[a]
(percentage)

MOTHER TONGUE	MONTREAL		QUEBEC LESS MONTREAL	
	1966–1971	1971–1976	1966–1971	1971–1976
English	27.7	33.0	21.9	18.6
French	22.4	30.0	61.1	66.5
Other	49.9	37.0	17.0	14.9
All languages	100.0	100.0	100.0	100.0
Total numbers	*118,000*	*88,700*	*19,600*	*19,500*

Sources: Census of Canada, 1971 and 1976, special tables.
Note: [a] Mother-tongue compositions observed in the 1976 census have been adjusted to render them approximately comparable with those observed in the preceding census (Lachapelle, 1982b).

Let us assume that, outside Canada, there are three pools of potential immigrants, the first being made up of French mother-tongue persons, the second of English mother-tongue persons, and the third of persons belonging to the third-language group. It is safe to assume that the first pool is considerably smaller than the second, which in turn is much smaller than the third. We will consider one region where these immigrants may settle, for instance, Quebec. When the "demand" for immigrants increases, it may reasonably be assumed, all other things being equal, that the supply of immigrants will also rise in each language group. If we further assume that the elasticity of the supply of immigrants varies directly with the size of pools of potential immigrants, we would expect that the proportion of immigrants from the third-language group would vary in direct proportion to the total number of immigrants, and that the proportion of the French group would vary in the opposite direction. In other words, when the total number of immigrants increases, we should observe an increase in the proportion of those coming from the third-language group and a reduction in the fraction of French mother-tongue immigrants. The proportion held by immigrants of English mother-tongue should either increase to a lesser extent than that of the third-language group or decrease less than that of the French group.

For the whole of Canada as for many of its regions, variations in the linguistic composition of international immigrants between 1966–1971 and 1971–1976 (it might be preferable to say between 1971–1976 and

1966−1971, since the total number of immigrants was higher in 1966−1971 than in 1971−1976) corresponds in most cases to the propositions we have just stated (Tables 6.28 and 6.29). There may be, of course, a number of other theoretical frameworks[28] that might explain these observations. The one we have presented and tested nevertheless has the advantage of already existing and being relatively simple. It also enables us to better distinguish two plans of action that might cause the linguistic composition of international immigration to vary. The first would be to act only on the total number of international immigrants, doing little to change the other elements of immigration policy, while in the second strategy, an attempt would be made instead to modify the immigrant supply curve of the various language groups. In order to expand and develop these two strategies, we would first have to describe and analyse immigration policies, and this falls outside the range of our study.

F. SUMMARY

In this study of migration, we have been careful to distinguish the measurement of the phenomenon and the analysis of its factors from the description of its demographic effects. In the first case, we considered migration in itself, that is, we first attempted to estimate the propensities to emigrate and to determine the regions of destination of migrants, then we tried to pinpoint those factors that might account for the variances observed. In the second case, we were interested instead in the redistributive effects of migration: demo-regional effects, or redistribution of the population among regions, and demolinguistic effects, or redistribution of the population of each region among the various language groups. In both cases, our descriptions and analyses dealt mainly with the last two five-year periods, for which a wealth of varied statistical information is available.

A fairly simple theoretical framework was found adequate to account for most of the variances in internal migration—and also in international migration—observed between language groups. It is based on two hypotheses that are quite plausible, at least in societies where migration is done mainly on an individual or family basis. As a reminder, let us again consider two regions: region E having an anglophone majority and region F, a francophone majority. The first hypothesis deals with the costs of obtaining information on migration opportunities. We have assumed that francophones living in region E would, on the average, incur lower costs than would anglophones living in the same region in inquiring about migration opportunities offered in region F, and vice versa. The second hypothesis deals with the costs of linguistic and cultural adaptation and integration in the region of destination. We have postulated that these are lower for in-migrants who belong to the majority language group. The effects of both these hypotheses act in the same direction and thus increase the differential costs of migration. In either region

(E or F), it follows that the minority group's propensity to migrate should be much higher than that of the majority group. This proposition corresponds quite well to the observations we have been able to make on migratory exchanges between Quebec and the rest of Canada, by mother tongue, during the periods 1966–1971 and 1971–1976. The minority group's propensity to migrate is always ten to fifteen times greater than that of the majority group in the same region. We were also able to verify a number of other assumptions derived from the theoretical framework we have just described. One of these dealt with the structuring of migratory exchanges among the thirteen regions and deserves special attention.

No matter what region they come from, in Canada or abroad, we have seen that French mother-tongue emigrants most often (or at least more often than those from other groups) move to regions with francophone majorities, while English mother-tongue emigrants generally head for regions with anglophone majorities. There are thus two quite distinct migratory systems in Canada, one centred on regions with francophone majorities, the other on anglophone-majority regions. They are obviously not clearly distinct one from the other. In certain regions, we might speak of a second-degree relation to one system or the other. Thus, French mother-tongue out-migrants leaving the Northeast region of Ontario are a little more likely to move to the Southeast region of that province than to one of the Quebec regions, but from the Southeast of Ontario, French-group out-migrants have a very high tendency to move to Quebec. By the same token, English mother-tongue out-migrants from three Quebec regions (the Eastern Townships, the Interior, and the Periphery) settle mainly in the Montreal region; however, English-group out-migrants leaving Montreal almost all move to regions with anglophone majorities. The Southeast of Ontario and the Montreal region act as a sort of marshalling yard.

In conclusion, let us briefly review the demolinguistic effects of migration.

As we saw, international migration clearly favours the third-language group, at least between 1966 and 1976, and most often works to the detriment of the English and French groups, both in Quebec and in the rest of Canada. We should specify that for Canada as a whole, international migration is more to the disadvantage of the French group than to that of the English group. While it appears likely that in the past the demolinguistic effects of international migration underwent large variations, we can nevertheless assume that in most of the periods characterized by high net immigration, these demolinguistic effects must have followed much the same pattern as those observed during the last two five-year periods.

The demolinguistic effects of internal migration are also quite easy to summarize. In almost all regions, the French group benefits from this phenomenon, at least in relative terms, while the English group is at a disadvantage. This situation is no doubt in some way related to the fact that the French mother-tongue population has a much greater tendency than does the English mother-tongue population to live in regions having negative internal migration balances. This regional imbalance probably slows down internal migration by persons from the French group somewhat, since these persons circulate between regions with francophone majorities. There are several plans of action that might eventually favour a better distribution of migration opportunities between the English and French groups. One of these would consist in promoting rapid economic growth in more francophone-majority regions, with the consequence that internal migratory balances would become positive.

NOTES

[1] Apparently inspired by the method we have just described, Caldwell (1974) nevertheless attempted to estimate the external migratory balance of Quebec by mother tongue for the period 1961−1971. To do this, he developed a number of hypotheses, some of which are somewhat difficult to grasp, and applied them in a rather complex fashion.

[2] This is more exactly the balance of migrants that remain and is very close to net migration (Lachapelle and Gervais, 1982). We can therefore consider that, in practice, they are the same thing.

[3] These inconsistencies are not found in the French-origin or mother-tongue groups, nor in the group of third ethnic origin or mother tongue, nor for that matter in the total population, where international emigration has been estimated at approximately 230,000 persons (Lachapelle and Gervais, 1982). For the period 1951−1961, however, this method of estimating yields a total number of international emigrants slightly less than 0. This is no doubt due to the fact that under-enumeration was much greater in the 1951 census than in the 1961 census (McInnis, 1974).

[4] For Quebec as for the rest of Canada, we obtained positive estimates of the number of international emigrants in the French group and the third-language group, as well as for all groups combined.

[5] There are very little data on differential under-enumeration by ethnic origin or by mother tongue (Blackstone and Gosselin, 1974; Demers, 1979; Théroux and Gosselin, 1978). Moreover, the method of estimation used, the reverse record check, sometimes yields rather surprising evolutions in the rate of under-enumeration. For example, the estimated rates of under-enumeration for the total Quebec population in the last four censuses were 2.10% in 1961; 2.95% in 1966; 2.10% in 1971; and 2.95% in 1976 (Théroux and Gosselin, 1978). It is hard to know what to think of these see-saw variations. While the studies mentioned are most interesting and great care appears to have been taken in calculating the rates of under-enumeration, it would perhaps be wise to consider their results as assessments of orders of magnitude rather than unbiased estimates.

[6] The statistical data presently available do not lend themselves to exact measurements of these substitutions, much less of their changes over time. It would be helpful, for example, to estimate the proportion of substitutions due to changes in census practices. This would enable us to distinguish artificial substitutions from "real" substitutions. Since we cannot isolate the second type, nor can we measure their evolution from one intercensal period to the next, it is difficult to propose explanations having any degree of precision.

[7] More specifically, the external balance here is that of migrants remaining who were 5 years of age or over at the end of the period.

[8] Natural increase by mother tongue obviously includes the indirect effects of linguistic mobility, the mother tongue of new-borns being the home language of their mothers.

[9] According to estimates based on changes in address in family allowance records, Quebec appears to have had a consistent negative balance, during the last five five-year periods, in its migratory exchanges with the rest of Canada (Canada, Statistics Canada, 1975, 1977). Losses were, however, higher between 1971 and 1976 (78,000) and, above all, between 1966 and 1971 (123,000) than from 1961 to 1966 (20,000), from 1956 to 1961 (28,000), and also from 1951 to 1956 (68,000).

[10] Strictly speaking, it is not possible, with the data we have available to us, to calculate propensities to migrate. We may nevertheless assume, without too much risk of error, that out-migration ratios constitute approximations of the unknown propensities.

[11] If we base our calculations on mother-tongue compositions for Quebec and the rest of Canada as shown in the 1976 census, we will obtain the following expected composition: English, 66%; French, 28%; and other, 6%. If we take instead the mother-tongue compositions observed in the 1961 census, we would have English, 62%; French, 33%; and other, 5%.

[12] These balances are given by mother tongue. We might also consider the balances of migratory exchanges between Quebec and the rest of Canada (in the population 5 years of age and over at the end of the period) by home language. Of course, we can only make these estimates for the period 1966−1971. The balances obtained for Quebec using data from the 1971 census were English, −61,000; French, −9,000; and other, −5,400.

[13] This method is often called markovian, because of the use made of stationary markovian processes. A variation of this method was used in estimating the effects of linguistic mobility (Lachapelle, 1982c).

[14] The method used is fairly simple. Assume a region made up of two language groups whose numbers total p_e^t and p_f^t respectively, at a given moment t. According to our hypotheses, the population of mother tongue e aged 5 and older at $t + 5$ equals $_{(5+)}p_e^{t+5} = p_e^t s \, (1 + m_e)$, where s is a coefficient of survival, identical for each language group, and where m_e corresponds to the internal migratory increase ratio of group e during the five-year period under study. The fertility ratio of group e at $t + 5$ (b_e) is obviously equal to $_{(-5)}p_e^{t+5} / _{(5+)}p_e^{t+5}$. We can then easily calculate the total size of group e at $t + 5$, that is, $p_e^{t+5} = p_e^t s \, (1 + m_e)(1 + b_e)$. The proportion this group represents in the total population is also easy to establish:

$$p_e^{t+5} = p_e^t \, \frac{(1 + m_e)(1 + b_e)}{(1 + m)(1 + b)} \, ,$$

where m and b are respectively the internal migratory increase ratio and the fertility ratio of the regional population considered. In order for the proportion held by group e not to change between t and $t + 5$, the following must apply:

$$1 + b_e = \frac{(1 + m)(1 + b)}{(1 + m_e)} \, .$$

When the internal migratory increase ratios are known, we need only fix the value of b to determine that of b_e.

[15] The population has been broken down by mother tongue using a method of rectification described in Lachapelle (1982*a*).

[16] Interested readers may obtain additional information by communicating with the authors. It is, in any case, our intention to publish in a future work the methods used as well as the results obtained.

[17] We do not show here the figures we obtained for the period 1971–1976, since they showed a pattern quite similar to those observed for the preceding five-year period.

[18] This relation has often been noted for the total population in Canada (Stone, 1974, 1976) as well as in other countries (United Nations, 1973).

[19] This is an approximate method. We also considered a much more rigorous method but we have preferred not to present it here, as it would only add to the complexity of our presentation. Suffice it to say that, in this case, it yields the same conclusion as the approximate method.

[20] We reach the same conclusion when we assume that during the five-year period considered, migrants are subject to the linguistic mobility of the region of destination. If we apply this hypothesis (and to do this we must make an approximate estimate of the propensities to make a language transfer that characterized the period 1966–1971), we of course see that certain propensities to migrate are manifestly lower than the corresponding out-migration ratios shown in Tables 6.19 and 6.20 (for a Quebecker with French mother tongue and English home language, for example), and that other propensities are clearly higher (for a Quebecker with English mother tongue and French home language, for example). The patterns shown in Tables 6.19 and 6.20 nevertheless hold true, apart from some slight modifications, with home language dominating mother tongue.

[21] The remainder out of 100 would obviously correspond to the percentage of out-migrants moving to regions with anglophone majorities.

[22] In order not to make our presentation too cumbersome, we will henceforth give only the proportions for 1971–1976. These are not, in any case, greatly different from the corresponding proportions observed for the preceding period.

[23] We were also able to calculate, for 1966–1971 alone, the net gains, by home language, made by the Montreal region from the rest of Quebec. Our results were English, 5,500; French 43,000; and other, 400.

[24] Here, for 1966–1971, is the balance of migratory exchanges for the Montreal region with the other regions of Canada, by home language: English, −38,700; French, +40,600; and other, −4,200.

[25] It will be recalled that during the period 1971–1976, five regions had positive internal migration balances: the "Other Atlantic Provinces," the South of New Brunswick, the Outaouais, the Southeast of Ontario, and the West-and-North of Canada. In these regions lived 50.1% of the English mother-tongue population of Canada in 1971, but only 10.0% of the French mother-tongue population. The gap is even more pronounced if we look at the regions with positive migratory balances during the preceding period: 76.7% of those persons belonging to the English group lived there in 1971, compared to 11.4% of persons of French mother tongue. A finer regional breakdown could obviously modify these proportions somewhat, but it appears unlikely that it could change the nature of the variances.

[26] It is well known that the concept of theory is a complex one. It has been examined in very fine detail by Merton (1957) and by Boudon (1971*a*). Some very precise viewpoints, although less useful in practice, will be found in Popper (1972*a*, 1972*b*).

[27] This is what we did in Section *A*, but only for very large regions, that is, the whole of Quebec and the rest of Canada.

[28] We prefer the expressions ''theoretical framework'' or ''explanatory framework'' because, strictly speaking, there are almost no exact scientific theories in the field of social sciences.

Part Three

Future Prospects

Chapter Seven

Projection Model and Hypotheses

We have had to be content up to now with presenting observed developments in linguistic composition (Chapters One and Two) and describing each of the demolinguistic phenomena (Chapters Three to Six). It has not been possible, however, to establish the fact that the combined effects of all these phenomena correspond exactly to actual changes in linguistic composition, because of deficiencies and gaps in data concerning mother tongue, and also because statistics on home language are only available for the 1971 census. In other words, we have described successively the whole and its parts, but we have not been able to make a systematic study of the means by which the parts generate the whole, in short, to achieve a synthesis. Such a delicate and complex operation would involve, in this case, the use of demographic simulations or projections. These devices may be used not only in studying the past, but also in exploring the future.

Population projections obey very simple laws of logic (Tabah, 1968): they are hypothetico-deductive operations destined to permit the emergence of new structures based on ''mobility'' hypotheses applied to the last known structure or, more generally, to an initial structure, whether observed or chosen arbitrarily. Population projections are therefore done in four distinct stages (Lachapelle, 1976 and 1977b): (1) choice of the initial structure; (2) development of a projection model, that is, defining the *form* the operations will take; (3) fixing the variation range of hypotheses concerning ''demographic mobility'' (mortality, fertility, linguistic mobility, migration), that is, determining the *content* of the operations; and (4) organization of hypotheses, and calculation and presentation of results. Each stage obviously raises a number of problems, and the solutions to these determine the subsequent stages and limit the possibilities of choice. This is why the objectives we have set—which will only be attained in the fourth stage—must always guide our decisions and direct our choices if we are to avoid taking the means for the end. Although we do not deal with the fourth stage here, since this is the subject of the next chapter, we will nevertheless present, in the first section, the frame of reference underlying this exercise in demographic forecasting. We will then go on to describe the initial structure, the projection model we have developed and, lastly, the hypotheses we have adopted.

243

A. PROJECTIONS AND FUTURE PROSPECTS

Two types of inquiry direct and structure the implementation of population projections: on the one hand, scientific inquiry, and on the other, prospective inquiry. If we wish to understand the interrelations between demographic phenomena, or if we seek to clarify the processes by which population structures develop and are transformed, population projections represent an exploratory method that has often proved worthwhile. These projections of course do not pretend to predict, but they do enable us to better understand situations and developments. Once we know more about the mechanisms that govern observed demographic evolution, in particular the inertia of structures, we are then in a better position to pinpoint what, in the past, binds and limits the future; this is what, for the sake of brevity, we will call the *predetermined future*. As opposed to these scientifically oriented projections that deal with the *demographic past*, *prospectively oriented* projections are more concerned with the *political present*, that is, the time of decision. Demographic forecasting obviously takes in the results of the scientific analyses generated by population projections, but it is not limited to them.

We may roughly distinguish four types of demographic forecasting based, on the one hand, on the socio-political ability to modify demographic evolution and, on the other, on the degree of uncertainty of future developments.[1] These are predictions,[2] forecasts, scenarios,[3] and futuribles (Table 7.1). Let us examine each of these in turn.

1. *Predictions*. The future evolution of a given population may be estimated reliably, and the political ability to modify it is judged negligible. This enables us to estimate the number of students in all the secondary

Table 7.1
FOUR TYPES OF DEMOGRAPHIC FORECASTING

NATURE OF THE CAPACITY FOR SOCIO-POLITICAL INTERVENTION	DEGREE OF UNCERTAINTY OF FUTURE DEVELOPMENT	
	Low	High
Adapting to future developments	Predictions	Forecasts
Modifying future developments (and adapting to them if necessary)	Scenarios	Futuribles

schools in Canada between now and 1985 or 1990 with a very small margin of error, since the persons involved—the 12−17 age group—were already born in 1979. This statement is based on the fact that the mortality rate for this age group is very low and on the assumption that migration, however variable it might be, has little effect on numbers for Canada as a whole. Predictions thus deal with what we have called predetermined futures. They show what constraints exist. We can adapt to them, but we cannot change them.

2. *Forecasts*. The future evolution of any given population bears a fairly high margin of uncertainty, and we rightly or wrongly make the implicit judgement that these developments cannot be modified by planned political intervention. To return to our example, it is thus difficult to make precise estimates of the total number of students in all secondary schools in Canada between 1990 and 2010, since the evolution of the school population depends on variations in the number of births over the next twenty years, and these are difficult to forecast. It should be noted, however, that the distinction between predictions and forecasts does not correspond exactly to the distinction between short term and long term. For small regions, the evolution of the secondary-school population between now and 1985 or 1990 is on the average just as uncertain, if not more so, than the Canada-wide evolution of the secondary-school population between 1990 and 2010, because of the significant and fairly unpredictable effects of migration at the regional level.

3. *Scenarios*. We postulate that it is possible to modify the future evolution of a given population by planned political intervention and that we can make approximate estimates of the effects. The evolution of the secondary-school population of Canada or Quebec between now and 1985 can be forecast, as we have seen, with a fairly low margin of uncertainty. This proposition is valid for the entire school system, public and private schools combined. If we had to estimate the proportion of students who would be attending a private school in 1985, we would then have to make assumptions about possible government intervention and its effects. We could, for example, consider five types of measures: (*a*) complete government control of secondary schools (private schools prohibited); (*b*) private schools authorized, but with no government financing; (*c*) public financing of private schools equal to 50% of the cost per student in public schools; (*d*) 80% financing; and (*e*) 100% financing. If we feel we can make fairly reliable estimates of the effects of these types of political intervention, we then only have to implement five scenarios, which would each provide a conditional forecast of the fraction of students going to private schools in 1985.

4. *Futuribles*. We accept that the future evolution of the populations studied is quite uncertain, but we do assume, however, that it is possible to modify its course, to various degrees, by planned political intervention. Suppose, for example, that we wished to have an idea of the proportion of

secondary-school students who would be taught in English by the end of the century in Quebec. This proportion would obviously depend in part on the nature of legislative and regulatory intervention, with respect to admission requirements for English schools, undertaken during the next twenty years. In addition, for each possible type of intervention, we would also have to take into account two types of uncertainty: first, uncertainty about the effects of intervention and, second, uncertainty about all the other factors that might influence changes in the various demolinguistic phenomena. This means that the implementation of futuribles is highly delicate and complex. They provide indications, but rarely firm and non-equivocal conclusions.

The future would then be the product of a *predetermined future*, resulting from the inertia of the past, of a *planned future*, oriented by socio-political intervention, and of an *indeterminable future*, reflecting the present limits of scientific knowledge. This is obviously a heuristic framework and not a philosophical position about the future. In fact, only futuribles draw upon the distinction between the three types of future: predetermined, planned, and indeterminable. Predictions assume that the future is finally predetermined; forecasts implicitly admit that we cannot isolate the planned future and that it is included in the indeterminable future; while scenarios assume that the future is generated by the combined action of the predetermined future and a planned future, with the effect of the predetermined future being judged negligible.

Strictly speaking, the demographer as a researcher is not interested in the future, since there are no observations of the future. Assuming that we have sufficient knowledge of the laws governing demographic evolution, we could obviously make predictions, or at least forecasts. In fact, experience shows that as soon as demographers exceed the boundaries of what we have called the predetermined future, they frequently fall into error (Dorn, 1950; Hajnal, 1955; Keyfitz, 1972; Lachapelle, 1976, 1977*b*; Siegel, 1972). If we had to stick to purely scientific criteria, we would surely judge prospective studies futile and highly unprofitable. We would enjoin demographers to try to better understand the past before exploring the ever-elusive future. This attitude goes against another type of logic, the logic of action. When the prevailing ideology consists in believing (and it is not our intention either to condone or to condemn this) that society is the product of its acts and that it has full power over itself, as suggested by Alain Touraine (1977), it is easily understandable that the government should intervene when ''spontaneous'' trends do not correspond to those goals that are judged desirable. The social sciences, particularly demography, are more and more frequently called upon to clarify objectives, pinpoint the required action, and ensure that this action produces the desired effects. However meagre and shaky our demographic knowledge may be, we would be ill-advised not to draw upon it rather than run the risk of making errors that might have been avoided. The point of all this is that, except perhaps with respect to coherence, prospective studies should not be judged in the same way as purely scientific studies. In the final analysis, the quality of prospective research can perhaps best be appreciated by the contribution it brings to a collective debate and, occasionally, to the decision-making process.

Having said this, is it possible to ensure that a prospective examination of the Canadian demolinguistic situation will be both relevant and enlightening? What sort of prospective techniques should be used to do this? The foregoing chapters have shown, fairly convincingly we hope, that the future evolution of linguistic composition is rather uncertain. We are thus obliged to choose between forecasts and futuribles. In addition, it seems quite likely that federal and provincial governments have at their disposal a number of ways by which they can accentuate, reorientate, and even reverse certain "spontaneous" changes in the socio-economic field (notably in the area of job creation), as well as the socio-linguistic field (in particular with respect to the language of work and of teaching). We can also assume, and this is quite plausible, that the socio-economic conditions in the various regions have some influence on their migratory balances, and also that the socio-linguistic conditions prevailing in these regions act both on linguistic mobility and on the linguistic composition of migrant streams. All this leads us to think that linguistic composition projections are the equivalent of futuribles.

B. INITIAL STRUCTURE

The choice of the initial structure is a very important operation that is charged with consequences, since it is this structure that will then be projected into time. The decision taken is thus obviously the result of a delicate and complex weighing of a number of elements: first, data available on the recent past; next, the ability to construct hypotheses with respect to future variations in the demographic phenomena involved; then the analyses we intend to carry out on the results; and finally the socio-political relevance of the variables contained in the structure. The problem of constructing a satisfactory projection model must, of course, also be considered.

We will first describe, then justify, the initial structure we have chosen.

The demographic structure we have decided to project includes four variables: age, region, mother tongue, and home language. The age variable is broken down into fifteen categories or age groups: 0−4 years, 5−9 years, . . . 65−69 years, and 70 and over. For mother tongue and home language, we have kept in each case to the three language groups often mentioned in examining the past: English, French, and other. Three regions were used: Montreal, Quebec less Montreal, and Canada less Quebec. We can thus easily obtain (by simple addition) the demographic structure of Canada as a whole, as well as of Quebec as a whole. The demographic structure we have just described, simple and rather basic though it may be, is only available for the 1971 census. This observation forms our starting point.

It may be found surprising that our projections begin in 1971. We could obviously have estimated, using a large number of hypotheses, the demolinguistic structure for 1976 or even 1979, but this would have represented a very costly and, in addition, not particularly profitable task, bearing in mind our objectives. Demographic structures in any case evolve very slowly, and it is fairly safe to assume that the structure observed in 1971 is not very different from that of 1976 or 1979. This being the case, when we give results for the year 2001, it should be understood that this result should be read as what happened after thirty years (2001 − 1971) and not as the specific situation of the year 2001.

In view of the problems involved in constructing satisfactory hypotheses on internal migration, we decided to limit our study to three regions. It will be recalled that these regions showed very different home-language compositions in 1971. In Canada less Quebec, anglophones made up 87% of the population and francophones, 4%, while francophones formed 93% of the population of Quebec less Montreal and anglophones, 6%. The demolinguistic situation in Montreal was more balanced, with anglophones and francophones accounting for 23% and 69% respectively of the population. Taken as a whole, the populations of Canada less Quebec and of Quebec less Montreal are linguistically quite homogeneous; when we break them down, however, we often find large variations, with francophones being concentrated in three regions of Canada less Quebec (North-and-East New Brunswick, and Southeast and Northeast Ontario), and anglophones, in two regions of Quebec less Montreal (the Outaouais and the Eastern Townships). This is to say that the results of our projections concerning the populations of Canada less Quebec and of Quebec less Montreal reflect average situations, and a great deal of care should be exercised in interpreting them. Our prospective study is then valid mainly at three levels: Montreal, Quebec as a whole, and Canada as a whole. Some details of the demolinguistic situation of other regions will be given in the last chapter.

It should be noted that, in our calculations, we have not distinguished males from females. The only really important consequence of this simplification is that we were obliged to define fertility "rates" in a rather unusual manner.

Finally, we should mention that our results are only valid for anglophones, francophones, and all other language groups combined, that is, the group we normally call allophones. In the last group, we have not sought to distinguish endophones from exophones.[4] Such a distinction would, of course, have been useful if we had isolated regions where endophones represent a sizeable fraction of the population, but their demographic importance in the three large regions we have used is quite limited.

C. DESCRIPTION OF THE PROJECTION MODEL

Constructing a projection model of a demolinguistic structure is much like inventing reality. We have to admit a number of hypotheses, and these will never be completely satisfactory in the observable reality. They do, however, enable us to apply a fairly strict reasoning. The results obtained and the properties demonstrated on this constructed reality are thus not a mirror image of the reality we can perceive. We must first try to appreciate the degree to which they coincide. Notwithstanding this, it will be admitted that the results obtained on our constructed reality can at least be observed as tendencies in the perceivable reality.

Two concepts form the basis for demolinguistic reality, that of mother tongue and that of home language. The home language of an individual is the language he most often uses in the family milieu. His mother tongue is the language most often used in his family during his early childhood (Lachapelle, 1977*a* and 1982*c*). In the pages that follow, we will assume that the mother tongue of an individual is an invariable characteristic, like his place of birth. We will further assume that the mother tongue of a child corresponds to his mother's home language.

The projection model we have used causes the demolinguistic structure to evolve in jumps of five years. Each jump actually includes five stages: the first four yield the population aged 5 and over at the end of the period and the fifth provides the population under 5. We will describe each of these stages in turn. In order to make our presentation less cumbersome, we will assume that the hypotheses made about each demographic phenomenon do not vary over time.

1. Mortality (*M*)

The first stage consists in aging the population by five years. We proceeded as follows:

$$_{x+5}^{k}P_{ij(t+5)}^{\mid} = {_{x}^{k}P_{ij(t)}} \cdot {_{x}^{k}s_{i}} \qquad \text{(for every } x, i, j, \text{ and } k) \qquad (1)$$

where $_{x}^{k}P_{ij(t)}$ is the population in age group x (x varies from 0 to 70 by five-year intervals), living in region k at the moment t and having i as their mother tongue and j as their home language, and where $_{x}^{k}s_{i}$ corresponds to a coefficient of survival. It will be noted that we have assumed that mortality (or survival) varies with region and mother tongue, but not with home language. Equation (1) provides the expected population at the end of the period, if there are no language transfers or migrations.

2. Linguistic Mobility *(L)*

The second stage takes into account language transfers in the population surviving in $t+5$:

$$_{x+5}^{k}P_{ij(t+5)}^{\prime\prime} = {}_{x+5}^{k}P_{ij(t+5)}^{\prime} + [^{k}b_{ij} \cdot {}_{x+5}^{k}a_i \cdot {}_{x+5}^{k}P_{ii(t+5)}^{\prime}] \qquad (2)$$

(for every $x+5$, i, j, and k)

where

$_{x+5}^{k}a_i$ corresponds, for persons of i mother tongue in age group $x+5$ in $t+5$ having i as their home language in t, to the propensity to adopt a different home language during the period $(t, t+5)$;

$^{k}b_{ij}$ designates, if j is different from i, the fraction of persons who adopt home language j among those who made a language transfer from home language i, during the period $(t, t+5)$; we have assumed that this fraction does not vary with age.

As for $^{k}b_{ii}$, it is always equal to -1.

3. Regional Migration (R)

The third stage introduces interregional migratory exchanges:

$$_{x+5}^{k}P_{ij(t+5)}^{\prime\prime\prime} = \sum_{l} {}_{x+5}^{l}P_{ij(t+5)}^{\prime\prime} \cdot {}_{x+5}^{lk}e_{ij} -$$
$$_{x+5}^{k}P_{ij(t+5)}^{\prime\prime} \cdot \sum_{l}{}_{x+5}^{kl}e_{ij} \qquad \text{(for every } x+5, i, j, \text{ and } k) \qquad (3)$$
$$(k \neq l)$$

where

$_{x+5}^{lk}e_{ij}$ designates, if l is different from k, the propensity to leave region l for region k during the period $(t, t+5)$, for persons of i mother tongue in the age group $x+5$ having j as their home language in $t+5$;

$_{x+5}^{kk}e_{ij}$ corresponds to the probability of remaining in region k during the period $(t, t+5)$.

4. International Migration (N)

The fourth stage completes the calculation of the population aged 5 and over at the end of the period. This stage deals with international migratory balances:

$$_{x+5}^{k}P_{ij(t+5)} = {}_{x+5}^{k}P_{ij(t+5)}^{\prime\prime\prime} + {}_{x+5}^{k}S_{ij} \qquad \text{(for every } x+5, i, j, \text{ and } k) \qquad (4)$$

where $_{x+5}^{k}S_{ij}$ corresponds to the international migratory balance, for the period $(t, t+5)$, in the population of i mother tongue living in region k, belonging to the age group $x+5$ and having j as their home language in $t+5$.

5. Fertility (F)

The fifth stage is devoted to calculating the population under 5. We first assumed that, in this age group, the mother tongue and home language groups to be identical in numbers, which is the same as assuming that very young children make no language transfers. Thus, for every j, we have $_{0}^{k}P_{j.(t+5)} = {}_{0}^{k}P_{.j(t+5)}$. If we further assume that the mother tongue of children is the dominant home language of their parents, we may proceed as follows:

$$^{k}_{0}P_{.j(t+5)} = \sum_{x} {^{k}_{x}P_{.j(t+5)}} \cdot {^{k}_{x}F_{j}} \qquad \text{(for every } k \text{ and } j) \qquad (5)$$

where $^{k}_{x}F_{j}$ corresponds *approximately*, for each home language j, to the differences between, on the one hand, cumulative fertility in $t+5$ for women of age x and, on the other, cumulative fertility in t for women of age $x-5$. It will be noted that the values $\sum_{x} {^{k}_{x}F_{j}}$ may be interpreted as gross reproduction rates of that point in time.

6. Advantages and Limits of the Projection Model

Application in sequence of equations (1) to (5) enables us to project, by jumps of five years, the distribution of the population by age, mother tongue, home language, and region. These five equations unequivocally define a projection model of the demolinguistic and demo-regional structure. In developing this model, we took our inspiration both from prospective studies already carried out on language groups (Baillargeon and Benjamin, 1978; Benjamin and Baillargeon, 1977; Charbonneau and Maheu, 1973) and from multiregional demographic studies (Rogers, 1975). It is, of course, not the only projection model possible, and we did experiment with others.

The projection model we have just presented may be described symbolically as follows: Pr (M, L, R, N, F). This notation shows the order in which the phenomena are introduced. In this model, we have assumed that interregional migrants are subject to the linguistic mobility of their region of origin. If it were judged preferable to apply to interregional migrants the linguistic mobility of their region of destination, we would only have to adopt the following projection model: Pr (M, R, L, N, F), which comes down to inverting equations (2) and (3). It is rather difficult to give a rational basis for choosing one projection model or the other. In fact, we could choose either one: we have verified that, all other things being equal, the two models yield almost identical results. We have therefore decided to stay with the first.

The projection model was constructed, and this should be emphasized, in such a way that we can isolate, for each five-year period, the effects of each phenomenon on the evolution of linguistic composition. This enables us, in particular, to make a systematic comparison of the effects of the various demolinguistic phenomena. We have preferred not to discuss this any further here, as it would only make our presentation unnecessarily long.

Because it is also destined to give a model of the interrelations between migration and linguistic mobility, the projection model includes a great many equations and entails a large number of parameters. It is nevertheless very simple when compared to the complexity of reality. It assumes, for example, that the propensities to migrate of one period are not dependent upon migration events that occurred during previous periods, and also that if age is constant, linguistic mobility does not vary with duration of presence within any given region. This type of simplification is inevitable, as a model will not accept an infinity of complications. Beyond a certain size, a model becomes so heavy and unwieldy that it threatens to hide reality rather than contribute to revealing it. We must accordingly seek a balance between the size of the model and its capacity for analysis.

D. PRESENTATION OF HYPOTHESES

To satisfactorily delimit the future development of demographic phenomena, we could adopt one of two extreme strategies: either take in all that is not impossible, or else limit ourselves to what appears probable. We are almost never wrong if we choose the first, but we can rarely draw conclusions; conversely, the second often allows us to make conclusions, but with a risk of error that is sometimes quite high. There is no way out of such a dilemma. It is, in fact, an integral part of any attempt to explore the future. While the prospective approach does not eliminate this dilemma, it does enable us to better delimit the sources of uncertainty. This is why, in constructing our hypotheses, we have tried to bear in mind three factors: (1) socio-linguistic conditions, which are partly the result of federal and provincial government intervention with respect to language; (2) socio-economic conditions; and (3) uncertainty related either to the difficulty of estimating the effects of the above factors or to the action of all factors not explicitly considered, or else to our only partial knowledge of past variations in this phenomenon. For the purposes of our analysis, we have assumed that socio-economic conditions only have significant consequences for inter-regional and international migration. We have further assumed that socio-linguistic conditions would have noticeable effects not only on linguistic mobility but also on the linguistic composition of interregional and international migration streams.

The specific hypotheses with respect to each phenomenon will be presented from two points of view. We will first describe the parameters that characterize each hypothesis; for the sake of brevity, we will keep to the essential, and interested readers may of course obtain further information from the authors. In order to better show the effects each phenomenon may have, we have also calculated the linguistic compositions that would be generated by each of the hypotheses adopted—or at least a certain number of them—in 2001 and in 2031. These simulations were carried out using null hypotheses—that is, neutral from a demolinguistic standpoint—for the other phenomena. This allows us to compare the hypotheses that are relative to the same phenomenon. It should be noted, however, that even when all phenomena are perfectly neutral from a demolinguistic point of view, linguistic compositions may nevertheless vary, to a certain extent, due to the momentum contained in the initial structure. This problem will be dealt with at the outset, after which we will describe in turn the hypotheses of mortality, fertility, linguistic mobility, interregional migration, and international migration. At the end, we will attempt to compare the uncertainty inherent in each phenomenon.

1. Demolinguistic Effects of the Initial Structure

We suggested above that the strict neutrality of all demolinguistic phenomena is not a guarantee that linguistic composition will not vary over time. To demonstrate this, let us assume that mortality and fertility are the same for all and, further, that from 1971 on there were neither language transfers, interregional migration, nor international migration.[5] We have shown in Table 7.2 the home-language compositions in 2001 and 2031 that would result from the implementation of all these hypotheses.

The neutrality of demolinguistic phenomena is to the advantage of francophones in all areas, and the reverse would be true for allophones. Anglophones would be at a disadvantage in Quebec as in its regions, but they would benefit elsewhere in Canada, as well as in Canada as a whole in the very long term. We should mention, in this connection, that we have been able to verify the fact that there would be no more variations in linguistic composition after sixty years. This means that the compositions calculated for 2031 are close to a limit situation. We should further mention that at the limit—and already in 2031—home-language compositions are identical to mother-tongue compositions, since we have assumed that there were no language transfers.

Table 7.2
EVOLUTION OF HOME LANGUAGE COMPOSITION UNDER THE HYPOTHESIS THAT MORTALITY AND FERTILITY ARE EQUAL FOR ALL, AND WHERE THERE ARE NO LANGUAGE TRANSFERS, INTERNAL MIGRATION, OR INTERNATIONAL MIGRATION,[a] CANADA, CANADA LESS QUEBEC, QUEBEC, MONTREAL, AND QUEBEC LESS MONTREAL, 1971 TO 2031
(percentage)

YEAR AND HOME LANGUAGE	CANADA	CANADA LESS QUEBEC	QUEBEC	MONTREAL	QUEBEC LESS MONTREAL
1971					
English	67.0	87.2	14.7	23.3	5.8
French	25.7	4.4	80.8	68.8	93.3
Other	7.3	8.4	4.5	7.9	0.9
2001					
English	66.9	88.3	13.7	22.2	5.3
French	26.8	4.5	82.3	70.5	93.8
Other	6.3	7.2	4.1	7.3	0.9
2031					
English	67.2	88.7	13.4	22.0	5.2
French	27.0	4.7	82.8	71.1	93.8
Other	5.8	6.6	3.8	6.9	1.0

Note: The sum of percentages may not equal 100 due to rounding.
[a] This is the simulation S (M_0, L_0, R_0, N_0, F_0): the constituent hypotheses are described later.

254 / Future Prospects

If the evolution of linguistic composition cannot be attributed to one or another of the five demolinguistic phenomena, to what factor should we impute it? The answer is simple: it is entirely due to the differences in age composition in the initial structure, that is, in 1971. The younger the age composition of a group, the more this group will see its relative strength increase over time, since only those persons under age 45 are able to contribute to replacement of generations. This means that, in the very long term, the linguistic composition of the population as a whole will be quite near the composition observed among children and young adults in 1971. We were also able to verify the fact that the limit linguistic compositions of the three base regions (Montreal, Quebec less Montreal, and Canada less Quebec) are almost identical to those observed in 1971 in the population under age 20.

As we know, variations in age composition are essentially due to differences in fertility observed in the past (United Nations, 1957). Francophones for many years had an excess fertility, both in Quebec and in the rest of Canada, and although this almost completely disappeared during the 1960s, the age composition of francophones still shows traces of their past prolificity. Thus, in Quebec in 1971, persons under age 20 formed 41% of the francophone group, 36% of the anglophone group, and 34% of the allophone group. In Quebec as in the rest of Canada, the low proportion of young people in the allophone population is not the result of low fertility, since their fertility was above average during the last two periods, but rather of their linguistic mobility as well as high international immigration in this group, the immigrants being mainly adults.

On the whole, francophones started with a slight advantage in 1971. Since that time, bearing in mind recent changes in fertility, this advantage appears to have disappeared in Canada as a whole, although it no doubt persists in Quebec and perhaps elsewhere in Canada. Whatever the case may be, the demolinguistic effects of differences in age composition are unquestionably much weaker than those that may be generated by certain demographic phenomena.

2. Mortality

Two life tables were used in our calculations: (a) that for the total Canadian population (both sexes combined) in 1970—1972 and (b) that for the female population in Canada less Quebec,[6] still in 1970—1972. The first corresponds to a life expectancy at birth of 72.8 years, while the second shows an average lifespan of 76.8 years, for a difference of four years between the two. As we saw in the chapter on mortality, the excess mortality of francophones in Quebec is reflected in a life expectancy at birth that is clearly lower than that of the rest of the population. The variance is at least two years and at most four years. We therefore adopted two extreme hypotheses to translate differential survival by mother tongue.

- M_0 The coefficients of survival are the same for all: they correspond to those in table *a* mentioned above.
- M_1 The coefficients of survival for the French mother-tongue population are equal to those in table *a*, while those in table *b* are used for the English or other mother-tongue population.

It will be recalled that these hypotheses were applied to the combined population of both sexes. In comparison to the differential mortality rates that have been estimated, hypothesis M_0 is favourable to francophones while hypothesis M_1 is unfavourable to them.

Let us now see what effects these two mortality hypotheses have on the evolution of home-language composition in the various regions. To do this, we have compared two simulations.

- $S(M_0) = S(M_0, L_0, R_0, N_0, F_0)$
- $S(M_1) = S(M_1, L_0, R_0, N_0, F_0)$

It will be noted that the first corresponds to the bench-mark projection we have just discussed. In the second, we simply replaced hypothesis M_0 by hypothesis M_1.

The results of the two simulations appear in Table 7.3. It will be seen that the effect of the French group excess mortality is negligible after 30 years and still remains quite weak after 60 years. This is not particularly surprising, since it has already been demonstrated by another method in Chapter Three.

3. Fertility

Apart from the neutral hypothesis (F_0), which corresponds to identical fertility for all, we considered three other hypotheses in order to show differential fertility by home language. Hypothesis F_1 is unfavourable to francophones in all regions; conversely, hypothesis F_3 is favourable to them everywhere, and corresponds more or less to the situation that prevailed during the 1950s. Hypothesis F_2 approximately reflects the situation observed in the early 1970s. This is to say that only hypothesis F_1 has never yet been observed.

Under hypothesis F_0, we assumed that fertility would be much the same as the generation-replacement level. Within our unisexual projection model and bearing in mind the mortality hypotheses adopted, this would correspond to a completed fertility of about 1.02 children per adult or, which is approximately the same thing, 2.1 children per woman. Taking as our base the completed fertility per adult (1.0223) used for each geolinguistic group under hypothesis F_0, we constructed the other fertility hypotheses with the help of the indices shown in Table 7.4. For example, in Montreal, we have assumed under hypothesis F_2 that the completed fertility of anglophones would be 0.767 (1.0223 × 0.75) children per adult and that of francophones,

Table 7.3

EVOLUTION OF COMPOSITION BY HOME LANGUAGE, UNDER TWO MORTALITY HYPOTHESES, CANADA, CANADA LESS QUEBEC, QUEBEC, MONTREAL, AND QUEBEC LESS MONTREAL, 1971 TO 2031

(percentage)

YEAR AND MORTALITY HYPOTHESIS[a]	CANADA			CANADA LESS QUEBEC			QUEBEC		
	English	French	Other	English	French	Other	English	French	Other
1971	67.0	25.7	7.3	87.2	4.4	8.4	14.7	80.8	4.5
2001									
M_0	66.9	26.8	6.3	88.3	4.5	7.2	13.7	82.3	4.1
M_1	67.5	26.2	6.4	88.3	4.4	7.3	14.0	81.8	4.2
2031									
M_0	67.2	27.0	5.8	88.7	4.7	6.6	13.4	82.8	3.8
M_1	68.1	25.9	5.9	88.9	4.4	6.7	14.0	82.0	4.0

YEAR AND MORTALITY HYPOTHESIS[a]	MONTREAL			QUEBEC LESS MONTREAL		
	English	French	Other	English	French	Other
1971	23.3	68.8	7.9	5.8	93.3	0.9
2001						
M_0	22.2	70.5	7.3	5.3	93.8	0.9
M_1	22.7	69.8	7.5	5.4	93.6	0.9
2031						
M_0	22.0	71.1	6.9	5.2	93.8	1.0
M_1	22.9	69.9	7.2	5.4	93.6	1.0

Note: [a] Other hypotheses used: linguistic mobility $-L_0$; regional migration $-R_0$; international migration $-N_0$; and fertility $-F_0$.

Table 7.4
RELATIVE FERTILITY INDEX BY HOME LANGUAGE AND BY REGION, USING THREE DIFFERENT HYPOTHESES
(Average Number of Children per Adult Under Hypothesis $F_0 = 100$)

HYPOTHESIS AND HOME LANGUAGE	REGION				
	Canada	Canada Less Quebec	Quebec	Montreal	Quebec Less Montreal
F_1					
English	104	*105*	94	*90*	*110*
French	85	*102*	83	*80*	*85*
Other	119	*120*	117	*115*	*130*
Total	100	106	86	85	87
F_2					
English	103	*104*	81	*75*	*105*
French	90	*112*	87	*83*	*90*
Other	116	*120*	98	*95*	*125*
Total	100	105	87	82	91
F_3					
English	96	*96*	88	*85*	*100*
French	109	*110*	109	*100*	*115*
Other	99	*110*	98	*95*	*125*
Total	100	98	105	96	114

Note: Hypothesis F_1 is unfavourable to francophones while hypothesis F_3 is favourable to them. Hypothesis F_2 is close to the situation observed during the past two five-year periods. Only the indices in italics were used in the projections; these do not vary over time. The other indices represent weighted averages, which, by their nature, are subject to slight variations from one period to another as linguistic and regional compositions evolve. The figures given here were calculated from the results obtained for the first period (1971−1976) in the projections described in Table 7.5

0.849 (1.0223 × 0.83). Under all hypotheses, we have tried to ensure that, for the Canadian population as a whole, completed fertility would be little different than that required for replacement of generations. This means that we have only caused the relative level of fertility of geolinguistic groups to vary from one hypothesis to another.

To determine the value of the parameters effectively used in the projection model described above, we also had to break down the chosen completed fertility rates by the age of parents. We used the same breakdown in each case. In other words, we assumed, to use demographic jargon, that all geolinguistic groups had an identical fertility timetable.

Let us now examine the differences caused by the fertility hypotheses alone on the evolution of linguistic composition (Table 7.5). The variances are of course much greater than those we just showed for mortality, but they nevertheless appear relatively low. In Montreal in 2001, for example, anglophones and francophones would represent 22.8% and 68.8% respectively of the population under hypothesis F_1 (unfavourable to francophones),

Table 7.5
EVOLUTION OF THE COMPOSITION BY HOME LANGUAGE, UNDER FOUR FERTILITY HYPOTHESES, CANADA, CANADA LESS QUEBEC, QUEBEC, MONTREAL, AND QUEBEC LESS MONTREAL, 1971 TO 2031
(percentage)

YEAR AND FERTILITY HYPOTHESIS[a]	CANADA			CANADA LESS QUEBEC			QUEBEC		
	English	French	Other	English	French	Other	English	French	Other
1971	67.0	25.7	7.3	87.2	4.4	8.4	14.7	80.8	4.5
2001									
F_0	66.9	26.8	6.3	88.3	4.5	7.2	13.7	82.3	4.1
F_1	68.4	24.8	6.9	87.9	4.5	7.6	14.3	81.0	4.7
F_2	67.8	25.4	6.8	87.7	4.7	7.6	13.3	82.4	4.3
F_3	65.5	28.0	6.5	87.6	4.8	7.6	12.5	83.6	3.9
2031									
F_0	67.2	27.0	5.8	88.7	4.7	6.6	13.4	82.8	3.8
F_1	70.7	21.9	7.4	87.6	4.4	7.9	15.0	79.2	5.8
F_2	69.3	23.5	7.2	87.0	5.0	8.0	12.4	83.0	4.6
F_3	63.1	30.4	6.5	86.7	5.5	7.8	10.5	86.0	3.5

YEAR AND FERTILITY HYPOTHESIS[a]	MONTREAL			QUEBEC LESS MONTREAL		
	English	French	Other	English	French	Other
1971	23.3	68.8	7.9	5.8	93.3	0.9
2001						
F_0	22.2	70.5	7.3	5.3	93.8	0.9
F_1	22.8	68.8	8.4	5.9	92.9	1.1
F_2	21.4	70.8	7.8	5.7	93.2	1.1
F_3	21.0	71.8	7.2	4.9	94.1	1.0
2031						
F_0	22.0	71.1	6.9	5.2	93.8	1.0
F_1	23.6	66.1	10.3	7.1	91.2	1.7
F_2	19.8	71.9	8.3	6.3	92.3	1.5
F_3	18.7	74.5	6.8	4.3	94.6	1.1

Note: [a] Other hypotheses used: mortality — M_0; linguistic mobility — L_0; regional migration — R_0; and international migration — N_0.

while they would form 21.0% and 71.8% respectively of the population under hypothesis F_3 (favourable to francophones). While they are not negligible, these variances between extreme hypotheses do appear quite small, at least if we recall that these linguistic compositions have had thirty years in which to vary. It should be mentioned, however, that the variances are higher in Canada as a whole. This is due to the combined effect of differences in fertility between the extreme hypotheses and of the territorial distribution of language groups.

We would no doubt have diagnosed this quite differently if we had examined the linguistic compositions of 2031. In the case of fertility, as well as in that of mortality, we felt it was quite risky to consider the linguistic compositions reached in the very long term, since, in a given region, the relative strength of the language group with the highest fertility rate tends asymptotically towards 100%.

4. Linguistic Mobility

In Chapter Five, we saw that linguistic mobility had evolved quite regularly in the past, and typically, for certain groups, it has varied hardly at all in recent generations. This is, of course, no proof that these trends will continue in the future. Depending on the region, language group, and circumstances, they can either become more pronounced or slacken off, or even reverse. This will no doubt depend to a great extent on the evolution of socio-linguistic conditions both in the schools and at work, and in neighbourhoods and families. There are obviously limits not only to the possible, but to the plausible, and it is not our intention here to establish the degree of plausibility of the various socio-linguistic conditions, since this question will be dealt with in the next chapter. We will limit ourselves here to outlining the range of possible conditions, or rather of those that do not appear impossible.

Taking francophones as the reference group, we have considered three possibilities: a deterioration in their socio-linguistic situation, a slight improvement, and a great improvement. To translate the uncertainty with respect to the effects of socio-linguistic conditions, we moreover envisaged three contrasting situations for each socio-linguistic condition. We ended up with a table having nine divisions which we decided to fill using seven linguistic mobility hypotheses (Table 7.6).

As we go from hypothesis L_1 to hypothesis L_7, linguistic mobility is increasingly to the benefit of the French group or, more exactly, less to its detriment. The reverse is obviously true for the English group. To simplify the construction of hypotheses, we assumed that the linguistic mobility of the third-language group varies in the same direction as that of the French group. This conjecture is obviously debatable, but it is not without some basis. We may effectively assume that, outside Quebec, acceptance by anglophones of

Table 7.6
BREAKDOWN OF LINGUISTIC MOBILITY HYPOTHESES BY SOCIO-LINGUISTIC CONDITION OF FRENCH AND THE MEANS OF RESOLVING UNCERTAINTY WITH RESPECT TO THE ACTION OF OTHER FACTORS

SOCIO-LINGUISTIC CONDITION OF FRENCH	UNCERTAINTY IS RESOLVED IN A WAY		
	More Favourable to English	Neither Less nor More Favourable to English	Less Favourable to English
Deterioration	L_1	L_2	L_3
Slight improvement	L_3	L_4	L_5
Great improvement	L_5	L_6	L_7

a significant improvement in the socio-linguistic conditions of the French group would favour linguistic pluralism, which might have the effect of reducing somewhat the very high linguistic mobility of the third-language group. Moreover, in Quebec, it seems likely that an increase in the drawing power of the French group would not completely counterbalance the reduction in that of the English group. This situation would bring about a rise in language maintenance in the third-language group.

Before giving a more detailed description of the linguistic mobility hypotheses, it would be well to mention that, from all appearances, socio-linguistic conditions do not depend exclusively on government intervention with respect to language. Other policies may also have incidental effects on these conditions, as may factors over which governments have little control. The fact remains that the scope for direct action on the part of governments seems to be considerable. To avoid any misunderstanding, we should also mention the fact that the relation we have established between socio-linguistic conditions and the linguistic mobility hypotheses is obviously somewhat arbitrary. It nevertheless emphasizes— and we feel there is little doubt about this—that the intensity of the linguistic mobility of a given group varies directly with its socio-linguistic conditions.

In all our linguistic mobility hypotheses, we have assumed that language transfers can take place only once during the lifetime of any individual (Lachapelle, 1982c). We have further assumed that there were no further language transfers after the ages 40–44. In addition, whatever the language group, region, or hypothesis considered, we have always adopted the same age breakdown—the same timetable—for language transfers. We then only have to choose the rates of final language maintenance and the breakdown of the transfers among the target home languages to characterize these as linguistic mobility hypotheses. The rates we have chosen appear in Tables 7.7 and 7.8. We should also mention that we have always assumed that transfers from the French group are towards English and vice versa for those from the English group.

There are a number of ways of comparing the hypotheses chosen with the situation observed for recent birth cohorts. We have chosen to present the continuity indices we would have obtained in 1971 for persons born in Canada and belonging to the 35−44 age group if the observed rates had been those shown in Tables 7.7 and 7.8. The results of our calculations are given in Table 7.9. We have also added the continuity indices calculated using 1971 census data. It will be seen that, on the whole, hypotheses L_3 and L_5 come fairly close to the figures observed among recent cohorts, although our hypotheses will perhaps appear to be a little too unfavourable to the French group living outside Quebec. This is not impossible. It should nevertheless be recalled that their linguistic mobility was on the upswing in recent cohorts and that it is moreover possible that their continuity index is at least slightly overestimated in 1971, as certain persons no longer state their mother tongue as French after having adopted English as their home language. It will also be noted that the continuity index for the third-language group is much higher in the region Quebec less Montreal than in the other two regions. This is because, in this region, the third-language group includes a large proportion of Amerindians. As we saw in Chapter Five, the endogenous-language group displays much lower linguistic mobility than the exogenous-language group.

In Table 7.10, we can see the effects of some of the hypotheses we have just described on the evolution of linguistic composition. In all the situations envisaged, linguistic mobility is unfavourable to allophones, as well as always being unfavourable to francophones in Canada less Quebec. As a result, under all hypotheses, the anglophones of Canada less Quebec benefit from linguistic mobility. The Quebec situation is obviously more complex, especially in Montreal. Here we have introduced, and we feel we were right to do so, a dissymmetry in favour of the anglophone group. Judging from the linguistic compositions calculated after thirty years (2001), the anglophone group in Montreal benefits from linguistic mobility under most of the hypotheses, with one exception: it experiences slight losses under hypothesis L_7, the one that is favourable to the French group. The francophone group, for its part, benefits from linguistic mobility under all hypotheses numbered higher than 3 or 4, and always experiences losses under hypotheses 1 and 2.

5. Interregional Migration

It is obviously not easy to develop coherent sets of relations between the rates of interregional out-migration by mother tongue, home language, and

Table 7.7
COMPLETED LANGUAGE MAINTENANCE, BY MOTHER TONGUE AND BY REGION, THAT CHARACTERIZES THE SEVEN LINGUISTIC MOBILITY HYPOTHESES
(percentage)

HYPOTHESIS AND MOTHER TONGUE	REGION		
	Canada Less Quebec	Montreal	Quebec Less Montreal
L_1			
English	100.0	96.0	90.0
French	35.0	95.0	98.0
Other	10.0	10.0	25.0
L_2			
English	100.0	94.5	87.5
French	40.0	95.5	98.25
Other	15.0	15.0	32.5
L_3			
English	100.0	93.0	85.0
French	45.0	96.0	98.5
Other	20.0	20.0	40.0
L_4			
English	99.95	91.5	80.0
French	50.0	96.5	98.75
Other	27.5	27.5	50.0
L_5			
English	99.9	90.0	75.0
French	55.0	97.0	99.0
Other	35.0	35,0	60.0
L_6			
English	99.8	87.5	70.0
French	60.0	97.5	99.25
Other	40.0	40.0	65.0
L_7			
English	99.7	85.0	65.0
French	65.0	98.0	99.5
Other	45.0	45.0	70.0

Note: By completed language maintenance, we mean the proportion of persons who keep their mother tongue as their home language throughout their lives.

Table 7.8

BREAKDOWN OF THIRD-LANGUAGE GROUP LANGUAGE TRANSFERS BETWEEN ENGLISH AND FRENCH, BY REGION AND UNDER VARIOUS LINGUISTIC MOBILITY HYPOTHESES

(percentage)

HYPOTHESIS AND HOME LANGUAGE ADOPTED	REGION		
	Canada Less Quebec	Montreal	Quebec Less Montreal
L_1			
English	100	85	65
French	0	15	35
L_2			
English	100	80	57.5
French	0	20	42.5
L_3			
English	100	75	50
French	0	25	50
L_4			
English	100	70	40
French	0	30	60
L_5			
English	100	65	30
French	0	35	70
L_6			
English	100	52.5	22.5
French	0	47.5	77.5
L_7			
English	100	40	15
French	0	60	85

age group. To achieve this, we first assumed, in line with the results obtained in Chapter Six, that interregional migration is essentially the result of two sets of factors: socio-economic factors and socio-linguistic factors. We then considered two constrasting situations as regards the socio-economic conditions of Quebec compared to those of the rest of Canada: on the one hand, similar or only slightly unfavourable conditions and, on the other, unfavourable conditions. We might say that the first correspond approximately to the migratory situation that characterized the period 1956–1966, while the second are closer to the migratory situation observed over the last ten years (1966–1976). As for the socio-linguistic conditions, we have envisaged three situations, as we did for linguistic mobility. By combining the various socio-economic and socio-linguistic conditions, we get a total of

Table 7.9
LINGUISTIC CONTINUITY INDEX FOR THE CANADIAN-BORN POPULATION AGED 35–44, UNDER VARIOUS LINGUISTIC MOBILITY HYPOTHESES, CANADA LESS QUEBEC, MONTREAL, AND QUEBEC LESS MONTREAL
(percentage)

LINGUISTIC MOBILITY HYPOTHESIS	CANADA LESS QUEBEC			MONTREAL			QUEBEC LESS MONTREAL		
	English	French	Other	English	French	Other	English	French	Other
Situation observed in 1971	114	61	21	114	99	23	106	100	73
L_1	118	35	10	128	96	10	137	99	25
L_3	115	45	20	119	98	20	119	99	40
L_4	114	51	28	114	99	28	107	100	50
L_5	113	56	35	109	100	35	96	100	60
L_7	110	68	45	97	102	45	75	101	70

Sources: Census of Canada, 1971, special tables; also Tables 7.7 and 7.8.
Note: The continuity index is the ratio between the number of persons of a given home language to the number of persons having the corresponding mother tongue.

Table 7.10
EVOLUTION OF THE COMPOSITION BY HOME LANGUAGE, UNDER FIVE LINGUISTIC MOBILITY HYPOTHESES, CANADA, CANADA LESS QUEBEC, QUEBEC, MONTREAL, AND QUEBEC LESS MONTREAL, 1971 TO 2031
(percentage)

YEAR AND LINGUISTIC MOBILITY HYPOTHESIS[a]	CANADA			CANADA LESS QUEBEC			QUEBEC		
	English	French	Other	English	French	Other	English	French	Other
1971	67.0	25.7	7.3	87.2	4.4	8.4	14.7	80.8	4.5
2001									
L_0	66.9	26.8	6.3	88.3	4.5	7.2	13.7	82.3	4.1
L_1	72.6	25.0	2.4	94.8	2.4	2.8	17.1	81.3	1.6
L_3	71.5	25.5	3.0	93.8	2.7	3.4	15.9	82.2	1.9
L_5	70.3	26.0	3.7	92.6	3.1	4.3	14.6	83.0	2.4
L_7	69.2	26.6	4.2	91.7	3.6	4.7	13.2	84.1	2.7
2031									
L_0	67.2	27.0	5.8	88.7	4.7	6.6	13.4	82.8	3.8
L_1	75.7	23.8	0.6	98.3	1.1	0.6	19.2	80.5	0.4
L_3	74.5	24.6	0.9	97.5	1.5	1.0	17.0	82.3	0.5
L_5	72.9	25.5	1.6	96.2	2.1	1.7	14.7	84.2	1.1
L_7	71.2	26.7	2.1	94.9	2.8	2.3	12.1	86.5	1.4

YEAR AND LINGUISTIC MOBILITY HYPOTHESIS[a]	MONTREAL			QUEBEC LESS MONTREAL		
	English	French	Other	English	French	Other
1971	23.3	68.8	7.9	5.8	93.3	0.9
2001						
L_0	22.2	70.5	7.3	5.3	93.8	0.9
L_1	27.9	69.4	2.7	6.6	93.0	0.4
L_3	26.0	70.6	3.4	5.9	93.5	0.5
L_5	24.2	71.6	4.2	5.1	94.2	0.7
L_7	22.1	73.2	4.7	4.4	94.9	0.7
2031						
L_0	22.0	71.1	6.9	5.2	93.8	1.0
L_1	31.3	68.1	0.6	7.7	92.1	0.2
L_3	28.3	70.7	1.0	6.5	93.3	0.3
L_5	25.2	73.0	1.8	4.9	94.7	0.5
L_7	21.1	76.5	2.4	3.5	95.9	0.6

Note: [a] Other hypotheses used: mortality $-M_0$; regional migration $-R_0$; international migration $-N_0$; and fertility $-F_0$.

six possibilities. To take into account the uncertainty with regard to the impact of all these factors together, it appeared necessary to propose, in each case, two sets of interregional out-migration rates. This gives us a total of twelve possibilities. They do not all correspond to a different hypothesis, since we have considered only eight sets of interregional out-migration rates (Table 7.11). We felt this was quite sufficient to cover the range of possible situations.

We should again mention that the reader should not try to read too much into the relation we have just shown between the interregional migration hypotheses, and socio-economic and socio-linguistic conditions. The relationship here is obviously a little vague. It is nevertheless useful to us in developing futuribles. In addition, it has considerable value as a mnemonic device.

Our eight interregional migration hypotheses were developed in four stages:

a. Using data from the 1971 census, we estimated, for the period 1966−1971, the propensities to migrate between the three regions considered, by mother tongue, home language, and age group. This set of rates will be designated by the symbol J_1.

b. With the help of the results of the preceding stage and guided by the overall migratory exchanges between our regions during the period 1956−1961 (data from the 1961 census), we estimated, by a rather complex

Table 7.11
BREAKDOWN OF INTERREGIONAL MIGRATION HYPOTHESES ACCORDING TO THE SOCIO-ECONOMIC CONDITIONS OF QUEBEC COMPARED TO THE REST OF CANADA, THE SOCIO-LINGUISTIC CONDITIONS OF FRENCH, AND THE MEANS IN WHICH UNCERTAINTY WITH RESPECT TO THE ACTION OF OTHER FACTORS IS RESOLVED

SOCIO-ECONOMIC CONDITIONS OF QUEBEC COMPARED TO THOSE OF THE REST OF CANADA	SOCIO-LINGUISTIC CONDITIONS OF FRENCH	UNCERTAINTY RESOLVED IN A WAY	
		Less Unfavourable to Quebec Anglophones	More Unfavourable to Quebec Anglophones
Similar	Deterioration	R_8	R_7
	Slight improvement	R_7	R_6
	Great improvement	R_6	R_5
Unfavourable	Deterioration	R_4	R_3
	Slight improvement	R_3	R_2
	Great improvement	R_2	R_1

method, what might have been, between 1956 and 1961, the propensities to migrate according to mother tongue, home language, and age group.[7] We have adopted the symbol K to designate this second set of rates.

c. In calculating all these rates, we had to assume that language transfers always precede migrations. Using simulations, we were able to make approximate estimates of the coefficients that would allow us to establish sets of rates based on the reverse hypothesis, which consists in assuming that migrations always precede language transfers.[8] These coefficients are shown in Table 7.12. They have been applied only to the set K. The new set of rates thus obtained will be designated J_2.

d. We now have two sets (J_1 and J_2) for contrasting socio-economic situations. The next step is to vary them depending on possible variations in socio-linguistic conditions. To do this, we adopted four sets of coefficients (A, B, C, and D). These are shown in Table 7.13. We applied them (for all age groups) to the two base sets. This enabled us to derive the eight interregional migration hypotheses.

$$R_1 = J_1 \times A \qquad\qquad R_5 = J_2 \times A$$
$$R_2 = J_1 \times B \qquad\qquad R_6 = J_2 \times B$$
$$R_3 = J_1 \times C \qquad\qquad R_7 = J_2 \times C$$
$$R_4 = J_1 \times D \qquad\qquad R_8 = J_2 \times D$$

Table 7.12
COEFFICIENTS APPLIED TO SET K IN ORDER TO FORM SET J_2

MOTHER TONGUE AND HOME LANGUAGE	CANADA LESS QUEBEC TOWARDS		MONTREAL TOWARDS		QUEBEC LESS MONTREAL TOWARDS	
	Montreal	Quebec Less Montreal	Canada Less Quebec	Quebec Less Montreal	Canada Less Quebec	Montreal
English						
English	1.01	1.01	1.00	1.00	1.00	1.00
French	0.60	0.60	1.10	1.00	1.10	1.00
Other	1.04	1.04	1.15	1.00	1.15	1.00
French						
English	1.01	1.01	0.60	1.00	0.60	1.00
French	1.00	1.00	1.10	1.00	1.10	1.00
Other	1.04	1.04	1.15	1.00	1.15	1.00
Other						
English	1.01	1.01	0.85	1.00	0.85	1.00
French	0.70	0.70	1.10	1.00	1.10	1.00
Other	1.04	1.04	1.15	1.00	1.15	1.00

Table 7.13
COEFFICIENTS USED IN DEVELOPING THE EIGHT
INTERREGIONAL MIGRATION HYPOTHESES

SETS OF COEFFICIENTS AND HOME LANGUAGE	CANADA LESS QUEBEC TOWARDS		MONTREAL TOWARDS		QUEBEC LESS MONTREAL TOWARDS	
	Montreal	Quebec Less Montreal	Canada Less Quebec	Quebec Less Montreal	Canada Less Quebec	Montreal
A						
English	0.50	0.50	1.05	0.85	1.05	0.85
French	1.30	1.30	0.95	1.00	0.95	1.00
Other	0.85	0.85	1.05	0.90	1.05	0.90
B						
English	0.80	0.80	1.00	1.00	1.00	1.00
French	1.10	1.10	1.00	1.00	1.00	1.00
Other	0.95	0.95	1.00	1.00	1.00	1.00
C						
English	1.00	1.00	1.00	1.00	1.00	1.00
French	1.00	1.00	1.00	1.00	1.00	1.00
Other	1.00	1.00	1.00	1.00	1.00	1.00
D						
English	1.05	1.05	0.85	1.10	0.85	1.10
French	0.90	0.90	1.05	1.00	1.05	1.00
Other	1.10	1.10	0.85	1.00	0.85	1.10

It will be noted that hypothesis R_3 is identical to J_1 and that R_7 corresponds to J_2, since the coefficients of set C are all equal to 1.

We henceforth always assume that the interregional migration hypotheses, and thus the propensities to migrate, do not vary over time. There may be, however, quite sizeable variations in the migration balances from one period to another, due to the differential evolution of the populations to which the propensities to migrate apply. Whatever the case may be, we have shown in Table 7.14, for the first projection period, the internal migratory balances by mother tongue that are produced by the implementation of the six interregional migration hypotheses. As might have been expected, we can see that hypothesis R_3 leads to migratory balances very close to those observed during the period 1966–1971.

Interregional migration appears to have a very great impact on the evolution of linguistic composition (Table 7.15). In Quebec, it is most often to the advantage of the francophone group and to the detriment of the allophone and, especially, the anglophone groups. These effects are much more pronounced when socio-economic conditions are much worse in

Table 7.14
INTERNAL MIGRATORY BALANCE FOR THE FIRST FIVE-YEAR PROJECTION PERIOD, BY MOTHER TONGUE, UNDER VARIOUS INTERNAL MIGRATION HYPOTHESES, CANADA LESS QUEBEC, MONTREAL, AND QUEBEC LESS MONTREAL

REGION AND HYPOTHESIS	MOTHER TONGUE			
	Total	English	French	Other
Canada Less Quebec				
R_1	95,000	79,200	2,100	13,700
R_2	79,800	59,000	8,900	11,900
R_3	71,300	48,700	11,300	11,300
R_6	14,200	22,700	−14,500	6,000
R_7	4,800	11,400	−11,900	5,300
R_8	−6,100	−1,600	−7,900	3,400
Montreal				
R_1	−21,300	−56,300	46,400	−11,400
R_2	−6,800	−40,800	44,000	−9,900
R_3	300	−33,300	43,100	−9,500
R_6	68,000	−6,700	78,800	−4,100
R_7	75,600	1,400	77,800	−3,600
R_8	86,100	11,500	76,500	−1,900
Quebec Less Montreal				
R_1	−73,700	−22,900	−48,500	−2,300
R_2	−73,000	−18,200	−52,800	−2,000
R_3	−71,600	−15,400	−54,400	−1,800
R_6	−82,200	−16,000	−64,300	−1,900
R_7	−80,400	−12,800	−65,900	−1,700
R_8	−80,000	−9,900	−68,600	−1,500

Note: These results are from simulations in which null hypotheses were used for the other phenomena.

Quebec than in the rest of Canada. Studies of past developments show this to be true. The hypotheses we have adopted do nothing more than reflect the mechanisms we have already described. The contrary would have been rather embarrassing.

While we will most often confine ourselves to the eight sets of rates described above, we have occasionally used another group of eight sets as well. These were obtained by applying the coefficients shown in Table 7.16 to hypotheses R_1 to R_8. We thus developed interregional migration hypotheses that reflected a deterioration in socio-economic conditions in Montreal compared to those in the rest of Quebec. This conjecture was not without some basis, since we saw in Chapter Six that migratory gains made by Montreal at the expense of the rest of Quebec decreased appreciably between 1966−1971 and 1971−1976. It is not impossible that these trends will continue for some years to come.

Table 7.15
EVOLUTION OF COMPOSITION BY HOME LANGUAGE, UNDER FIVE INTERREGIONAL MIGRATION HYPOTHESES, CANADA, CANADA LESS QUEBEC, QUEBEC, MONTREAL, AND QUEBEC LESS MONTREAL, 1971 TO 2031
(percentage)

YEAR AND INTERREGIONAL MIGRATION HYPOTHESIS[a]	CANADA			CANADA LESS QUEBEC			QUEBEC			MONTREAL			QUEBEC LESS MONTREAL		
	English	French	Other	English	French	Other	English	French	Other	English	French	Other	English	French	Other
1971	67.0	25.7	7.3	87.2	4.4	8.4	14.7	80.8	4.5	23.3	68.8	7.9	5.8	93.3	0.9
2001															
R_0	66.9	26.8	6.3	88.3	4.5	7.2	13.7	82.3	4.1	22.2	70.5	7.3	5.3	93.8	0.9
R_8	66.9	26.8	6.3	88.4	4.3	7.3	14.1	82.2	3.8	21.0	73.1	5.9	4.7	94.5	0.8
R_6	66.9	26.8	6.3	88.8	3.9	7.3	12.0	84.3	3.7	18.3	75.9	5.9	3.7	95.5	0.8
R_3	66.9	26.8	6.3	88.1	4.7	7.3	10.3	86.1	3.6	16.1	77.8	6.1	3.6	95.6	0.8
R_1	66.9	26.8	6.3	88.6	4.2	7.3	7.7	88.7	3.6	12.5	81.3	6.2	2.4	96.9	0.8
2031															
R_0	67.2	27.0	5.8	88.7	4.7	6.6	13.4	82.8	3.8	22.0	71.1	6.9	5.2	93.8	1.0
R_8	67.2	27.0	5.8	89.0	4.2	6.9	13.9	82.8	3.3	19.7	75.4	4.9	4.6	94.5	0.8
R_6	67.2	27.0	5.8	89.5	3.6	6.8	10.6	86.2	3.2	15.4	79.8	4.8	3.4	95.9	0.7
R_3	67.2	27.0	5.8	88.3	4.8	6.9	8.6	88.4	3.0	13.0	82.1	4.9	3.2	96.1	0.7
R_1	67.2	27.0	5.8	89.1	4.0	6.9	5.1	92.0	3.0	8.0	87.1	4.9	1.7	97.6	0.7

Note: [a] Other hypotheses used: mortality $-M_0$; linguistic mobility $-L_0$; international migration $-N_0$; and fertility $-F_0$.

Table 7.16
COEFFICIENTS USED IN CONSTRUCTING HYPOTHESES REFLECTING A DETERIORATION IN SOCIO-ECONOMIC CONDITIONS IN MONTREAL COMPARED TO THOSE OF THE REST OF QUEBEC

REGION OF ORIGIN AND HOME LANGUAGE	REGION OF DESTINATION		
	Canada Less Quebec	Montreal	Quebec Less Montreal
Canada Less Quebec	—	0.70	1.05
English	—	0.90	1.07
French	—	0.80	1.10
Other			
Montreal	1.05	—	1.20
English	0.90	—	1.20
French	1.00	—	1.20
Other			
Quebec Less Montreal	0.90	0.70	—
English	0.90	0.70	—
French	0.90	0.70	—
Other			

6. International Migration

Our mortality, fertility, linguistic mobility, and interregional migration hypotheses are all composed of rates or propensities. In the case of international migration, we had instead to establish balances (in absolute numbers) by region, mother tongue, home language, and age group. In constructing our hypotheses, we took into account three groups of factors: (1) socio-economic conditions of Canada as a whole, (2) socio-economic conditions in Quebec compared to those in the rest of Canada, and (3) socio-linguistic conditions. By combining these three factors, we obtained twelve hypotheses (Table 7.17).

In Table 7.18, we have shown the international migration balances, by mother tongue, that we have adopted for each of the twelve hypotheses. All these balances were, of course, also broken down, for each mother tongue, by age and home language. In this connection, we should mention that the age breakdown of migrant balances was made using the same standard distribution.

It will no doubt be noted that the international migration hypotheses show, from one extreme to the other (N_1 to N_{12}), much more pronounced contrasts than those envisaged for the other phenomena. Since international migration is a phenomenon that was measured only imprecisely in the past, it is hard to see by what device we might have succeeded in making future variations fit between very narrow limits. We were obliged to make the range

Table 7.17

BREAKDOWN OF INTERNATIONAL MIGRATION HYPOTHESES ACCORDING TO THE SOCIO-ECONOMIC CONDITIONS OF CANADA AS A WHOLE, THOSE OF QUEBEC COMPARED TO THOSE OF THE REST OF CANADA, AS WELL AS THE SOCIO-LINGUISTIC CONDITIONS OF FRENCH

SOCIO-ECONOMIC CONDITIONS OF CANADA AS A WHOLE	SOCIO-ECONOMIC CONDITIONS OF QUEBEC COMPARED TO THOSE OF THE REST OF CANADA	SOCIO-LINGUISTIC CONDITIONS OF FRENCH	INTERNATIONAL MIGRATION HYPOTHESIS
Favourable	Similar	Deterioration	N_1
		Slight improvement	N_2
		Great improvement	N_3
	Unfavourable	Deterioration	N_4
		Slight improvement	N_5
		Great improvement	N_6
Unfavourable	Similar	Deterioration	N_7
		Slight improvement	N_8
		Great improvement	N_9
	Unfavourable	Deterioration	N_{10}
		Slight improvement	N_{11}
		Great improvement	N_{12}

a little broader. We would nevertheless point out that hypotheses N_5 and N_8 are in the approximate area of the estimates we were able to make for Quebec during the period 1971−1976.

In Canada less Quebec, judging from the hypotheses we have adopted, international migration appears detrimental to the anglophone group as well as to the francophone group (Table 7.19). The proportion of anglophones would vary in reverse proportion to the migration balance. By the same token, in Quebec, the fraction of francophones would vary in reverse proportion to the migration balance. As for the fraction of anglophones in the Quebec population, it would instead vary in direct proportion to the migration balance, as would the proportion of allophones, both in Quebec and elsewhere in Canada. None of this is very unexpected. These propositions, although debatable, are still plausible and served as our guide in the construction of our hypotheses. We should not be surprised to find them in our results.

Table 7.18

INTERNATIONAL MIGRATION BALANCE BY FIVE-YEAR PERIOD, ACCORDING TO MOTHER TONGUE, UNDER TWELVE HYPOTHESES, CANADA, CANADA LESS QUEBEC, QUEBEC, MONTREAL, AND QUEBEC LESS MONTREAL

REGION AND HYPOTHESIS	MOTHER TONGUE			
	Total	English	French	Other
Canada				
N_1	600,000	262,000	9,000	329,000
N_2	600,000	244,500	18,000	337,500
N_3	600,000	227,000	27,000	346,000
Canada Less Quebec				
N_1	480,000	221,000	8,000	251,000
N_2	480,000	221,000	8,000	251,000
N_3	480,000	221,000	8,000	251,000
Quebec				
N_1	120,000	41,000	1,000	78,000
N_2	120,000	23,500	10,000	86,500
N_3	120,000	6,000	19,000	95,000
Montreal				
N_1	118,800	38,100	5,700	75,000
N_2	105,350	20,800	10,350	74,200
N_3	91,900	3,500	15,000	73,400
Quebec Less Montreal				
N_1	1,200	2,900	−4,700	3,000
N_2	14,650	2,700	−350	12,300
N_3	28,100	2,500	4,000	21,600

7. Comparison of the Uncertainty Inherent to Each Phenomenon

If we knew exactly what the future development of a phenomenon would be, there would be no uncertainty attached to its effects on the evolution of linguistic composition. This, however, is not the case. Each phenomenon varies in a fashion that is partly unpredictable. To take this into account, we have adopted a number of hypotheses. The divergence between the linguistic compositions generated by the various hypotheses about a single phenomenon, after thirty or sixty years, is an approximate reflection of the uncertainty inherent to this phenomenon. There are, of course, many ways of measuring the divergence between two linguistic compositions. For the sake of convenience, we have adopted the sum (divided by two) of the absolute

REGION AND HYPOTHESIS	MOTHER TONGUE			
	Total	English	French	Other
Canada				
N_4	600,000	254,000	4,500	341,500
N_5	600,000	238,500	13,500	348,000
N_6	600,000	223,000	22,500	354,500
Canada Less Quebec				
N_4	530,000	226,000	8,500	295,500
N_5	530,000	226,000	8,500	295,500
N_6	530,000	226,000	8,500	295,500
Quebec				
N_4	70,000	28,000	−4,000	46,000
N_5	70,000	12,500	5,000	52,500
N_6	70,000	−3,000	14,000	59,000
Montreal				
N_4	72,500	26,200	2,000	44,300
N_5	63,250	11,350	6,950	44,950
N_6	54,000	−3,500	11,900	45,600
Quebec Less Montreal				
N_4	−2,500	1,800	−6,000	1,700
N_5	6,750	1,150	−1,950	7,550
N_6	16,000	500	2,100	13,400

Table 7.18 *(cont'd.)*

values of the differences between the corresponding proportions. This is what is often called the dissimilarity index. It varies between 0 and 1.

For each region and each phenomenon, we have calculated, in 2001 and 2031, two divergences (except for mortality): (1) the divergence between the linguistic compositions resulting from the intermediate hypotheses, and (2) the divergence between the linguistic compositions generated by the extreme hypotheses. All these figures are shown in Table 7.20.

It would appear that for most of the phenomena, uncertainty is greater in the demolinguistically heterogeneous region (Montreal) than in the two homogeneous regions. This property may be indicative of the strong inertia of homogeneous populations. Whether it is a normal property or one dependent on the hypotheses we have adopted is a very delicate question, and we cannot examine all aspects of it here. We will confine ourselves to briefly examining one immediate consequence of linguistic homogeneity.

To keep the explanation simple, let us consider a set of regions made up of two language groups, e and f. We can imagine a number of methods to measure the linguistic homogeneity of a region. When there are only two

Table 7.18 *(cont'd.)*				
REGION AND HYPOTHESIS	**MOTHER TONGUE**			
	Total	English	French	Other
Canada				
N_7	100,000	54,000	−6,000	41,000
N_8	100,000	52,000	3,500	44,500
N_9	100,000	39,000	13,000	48,000
Canada Less Quebec				
N_7	80,000	51,000	3,000	26,000
N_8	80,000	51,000	3,000	26,000
N_9	80,000	51,000	3,000	26,000
Quebec				
N_7	20,000	14,000	−9,000	15,000
N_8	20,000	1,000	500	18,500
N_9	20,000	−12,000	10,000	22,000
Montreal				
N_7	26,500	13,500	−1,600	14,600
N_8	20,900	1,450	3,900	15,550
N_9	15,300	−10,600	9,400	16,500
Quebec Less Montreal				
N_7	−6,500	500	−7,400	400
N_8	−900	−450	−3,400	2,950
N_9	4,700	−1,400	600	5,500

language groups, we can safely adopt as our index of homogeneity the absolute value of the difference between the proportions of groups e and f, that is, $|p_e - p_f|$. Let us assume that three regions have the following linguistic compositions:

	Group e	Group f
V_1	0.9	0.1
V_2	0.7	0.3
V_3	0.5	0.5

The homogeneity indices are 0.8, 0.4, and 0 respectively. Region V_1 is very homogeneous, region V_3 is perfectly heterogeneous (non-homogeneous), and region V_2 is intermediate. As an aid to understanding, let us assume that we have been led to envisage two hypotheses that are identical and opposite in each of the regions. Each hypothesis is characterized by two growth rates, one for each language group. The numerical values of these rates (r) are as follows:

REGION AND HYPOTHESIS	MOTHER TONGUE			
	Total	English	French	Other
Canada				
N_{10}	100,000	74,000	−17,000	43,000
N_{11}	100,000	65,000	−8,500	43,500
N_{12}	100,000	56,000	0	44,000
Canada Less Quebec				
N_{10}	130,000	78,000	4,000	48,000
N_{11}	130,000	78,000	4,000	48,000
N_{12}	130,000	78,000	4,000	48,000
Quebec				
N_{10}	−30,000	−4,000	−21,000	−5,000
N_{11}	−30,000	−13,000	−12,500	−4,500
N_{12}	−30,000	−22,000	−4,000	−4,000
Montreal				
N_{10}	−17,500	−2,800	−10,200	−4,500
N_{11}	−19,550	−10,700	−4,650	−4,200
N_{12}	−21,600	−18,600	−900	−3,900
Quebec Less Montreal				
N_{10}	−12,500	−1,200	−10,800	−1,000
N_{11}	−10,450	−2,300	−7,850	−300
N_{12}	−8,400	−3,400	−4,900	−100

Table 7.18 (cont'd.)

	r_e	r_f
Hypothesis I	0.4	0.1
Hypothesis II	0.1	0.4

It will be noted that these hypotheses are perfectly symmetrical. At the end of the period under study, there would then be two possible linguistic compositions for each region.

		Group *e*	Group *f*
V_1	I	0.920	0.080
	II	0.876	0.124
V_2	I	0.748	0.252
	II	0.647	0.353
V_3	I	0.560	0.440
	II	0.440	0.560

Table 7.19
EVOLUTION OF COMPOSITION BY HOME LANGUAGE, UNDER FIVE INTERNATIONAL MIGRATION HYPOTHESES, CANADA, CANADA LESS QUEBEC, MONTREAL, AND QUEBEC LESS MONTREAL, 1971 TO 2031
(percentage)

YEAR AND INTERNATIONAL MIGRATION HYPOTHESIS	CANADA			CANADA LESS QUEBEC			QUEBEC		
	English	French	Other	English	French	Other	English	French	Other
1971	67.0	25.7	7.3	87.2	4.4	8.4	14.7	80.8	4.5
2001									
N_0	66.9	26.8	6.3	88.3	4.5	7.2	13.7	82.3	4.1
N_1	64.5	23.0	12.5	82.5	3.9	13.5	16.5	73.6	9.9
N_5	63.9	23.1	13.0	81.5	3.9	14.6	14.0	77.7	8.3
N_8	66.3	26.1	7.6	87.3	4.5	8.3	13.4	80.8	5.8
N_{12}	66.5	26.0	7.5	86.8	4.4	8.8	11.5	84.5	4.0
2031									
N_0	67.2	27.0	5.8	88.7	4.7	6.6	13.4	82.8	3.8
N_1	62.8	20.2	17.0	78.6	3.6	17.8	18.6	66.9	14.5
N_5	61.8	20.4	17.8	76.9	3.5	19.6	14.0	74.0	12.1
N_8	66.0	25.6	8.4	86.7	4.5	8.8	12.8	79.8	7.4
N_{12}	66.3	25.4	8.3	85.7	4.4	9.9	8.9	87.4	3.7

YEAR AND INTERNATIONAL MIGRATION HYPOTHESIS	MONTREAL			QUEBEC LESS MONTREAL		
	English	French	Other	English	French	Other
1971	23.3	68.8	7.9	5.8	93.3	0.9
2001						
N_0	22.2	70.5	7.3	5.3	93.8	0.9
N_1	25.1	58.1	16.9	6.0	92.7	1.3
N_5	21.7	64.2	14.0	5.4	92.5	2.1
N_8	21.4	68.5	10.1	5.2	93.4	1.4
N_{12}	18.7	74.1	7.2	4.5	94.5	1.0
2031						
N_0	22.0	71.1	6.9	5.2	93.8	1.0
N_1	27.0	49.5	23.5	6.7	91.6	1.7
N_5	21.2	59.3	19.5	5.5	91.2	3.3
N_8	20.4	67.0	12.6	5.0	93.0	2.0
N_{12}	14.7	78.6	6.7	3.8	95.2	1.0

Note: [a] Other hypotheses used: mortality $-M_0$, linguistic mobility $-L_0$, interregional migration $-R_0$; and fertility $-F_0$.

Table 7.20
DIVERGENCES BETWEEN THE LINGUISTIC COMPOSITIONS GENERATED BY THE HYPOTHESES SPECIFIC TO EACH PHENOMENON, CANADA, CANADA LESS QUEBEC, QUEBEC, MONTREAL, AND QUEBEC LESS MONTREAL, 2001 AND 2031
(percentage)

YEAR AND REGION	MORTALITY	FERTILITY		LINGUISTIC MOBILITY		INTERNAL MIGRATION		INTERNATIONAL MIGRATION	
	$D(0,1)$	$D(0,2)$	$D(1,3)$	$D(3,5)$	$D(1,7)$	$D(3,6)$	$D(1,8)$	$D(5,8)$	$D(1,12)$
2001									
Canada	0.65	1.40	3.25	1.20	3.40	0	0	5.40	5.00
Canada less Quebec	0.10	0.60	0.30	1.25	3.10	0.75	0.15	6.35	4.75
Quebec	0.45	0.35	2.60	1.30	3.90	1.80	6.55	3.10	10.90
Montreal	0.70	0.80	3.00	1.80	5.80	2.15	8.50	4.25	16.05
Quebec less Montreal	0.15	0.30	1.15	0.85	2.20	0.10	2.35	0.90	1.80
2031									
Canada	1.05	3.50	8.50	1.60	4.45	0	0	9.40	8.70
Canada less Quebec	0.30	1.70	1.05	1.30	3.40	1.25	0.15	10.80	7.90
Quebec	0.80	1.00	6.80	2.35	7.05	2.20	9.15	5.85	20.50
Montreal	1.20	2.20	8.40	1.80	10.20	2.30	11.70	7.70	29.10
Quebec less Montreal	0.20	1.55	3.40	0.85	4.20	0.10	3.05	1.80	3.60

Sources: Tables 7.3, 7.5, 7.10, 7.15, and 7.19.

Note: $D(k, j)$ is the divergence between the linguistic compositions generated by hypotheses k and j of the phenomenon in question. If p_i^k and p_i^j respectively correspond to the proportion of persons of i home language at a given moment, under hypotheses k and j, we have:[1]

$$D(k, j) = \tfrac{1}{2} \sum_i \mid p_i^k - p_i^j \mid.$$ We can easily show that this measurement has all the properties of a divergence.

We can then calculate the divergence (dissimilarity index) between each pair of linguistic compositions. This would be 0.044 for V_1, 0.101 for V_2, and 0.120 for V_3. Note that the smaller the divergence, the greater the demolinguistic inertia of the region. This would lead us to think that, all other things being equal, there is a direct relation between the linguistic homogeneity of a region and the inertia of its linguistic composition. This relation is, of course, only valid if the clause "all other things being equal" is satisfied, and it would perhaps be wise to examine these other things, or at least some of them. We may nevertheless assume that heterogeneous regions generally put up less resistance than homogeneous regions to variations in their linguistic composition.

To go on to another point, it can be seen in Table 7.20 that in the Montreal region as in the whole of Quebec, the phenomena line up, in increasing order of uncertainty, in the following way: mortality, fertility, linguistic mobility, interregional migration, and international migration. This order is not unexpected. We would effectively expect uncertainty to rise in direct proportion to the number of factors of variation *explicitly* taken into consideration. We considered three for international migration (Table 7.17), two for interregional migration (Table 7.11), one for linguistic mobility (Table 7.6), and none for fertility and mortality. This means that, in our projections, the linguistic composition of the Montreal region will be more sensitive to variations in the migration hypotheses than to changes in hypotheses on linguistic mobility, fertility, and mortality. We should emphasize here that we did not deliberately seek to plan things this way when constructing our hypotheses. We have simply taken notice of the order we have implicitly generated among the phenomena and have attempted to understand it. We feel that, on the whole, it is a fairly good reflection of the respective importance of the demolinguistic effects of each of the phenomena over the past few periods.

E. SUMMARY

We have presented, in turn, the frame of reference underlying our exploration of the future, as well as the first three stages in this prospective exercise, that is, description of the initial structure, construction of the projection model, and presentation of the hypotheses. Counting null or neutral hypotheses, we have developed 2 mortality hypotheses, 4 for fertility, 8 for linguistic mobility, 9 for interregional migration (17 if we add the sets destined to reflect a deterioration in socio-economic conditions in Montreal compared to those of the rest of Quebec), and 13 for international migration. If we had to consider all possible combinations of these hypotheses, we would have to analyse 7,488 simulations ($2 \times 4 \times 8 \times 9 \times 13$), or even 14,144 ($2 \times 4 \times 8 \times 17 \times 13$). Such a strategy would obviously be absurd. By wanting to take in everything, it would discover nothing. What is needed is the most significant combination of hypotheses, and choosing these is not an easy task.

NOTES

[1] These two variables are closely related to the distinctions between event and act, on the one hand, and between certain and uncertain, on the other; these were proposed by Schumacher (1973):

> The distinction between acts and events is as basic as that between active and passive or between 'within my control' or 'outside my control'. To apply the word 'planning' to matters outside the planner's control is absurd. Events, as far as the planner is concerned, simply happen. He may be able to forecast them and this may well influence his plan; but they cannot possibly be part of the plan (p. 211).

[2] The expressions *demographic* (or population) *projections* and *forecasts* are frequently used in demography. Here is how the *Multilingual Demographic Dictionary* (United Nations, 1958, p. 45) describes them:

> *Population projections* are calculations which show the future development of a population when certain assumptions are made about the future course of fertility, mortality and migration. They are in general purely formal calculations, developing the implications of the assumptions that are made. *A population forecast* is a projection in which the assumptions are considered to yield a realistic picture of the probable future development of a population.

It will be seen that we have attempted to draw a further distinction within the expression *forecast*, where *prediction* describes a relatively shorter-term forecast based on the examination of facts, while the term *forecast* is reserved for more far-reaching exercises based on the arrangement and examination of possibilities and probabilities.

[3] The expressions *scenarios* and *futuribles* are not often used in demography, particularly the second. They do, however, occur fairly often in social and technological prospective studies (Hetman, 1969).

[4] It will be recalled that by *endophones* we mean the group of persons whose home language is one or another of the many Amerindian languages, *including* Inuktitut. The exophone group includes all allophones who are not in the endophone group.

[5] This is obviously not the only way to implement the hypothesis of neutrality of demolinguistic phenomena. We can easily imagine a number of others. Our method nevertheless has the twofold merit of being simple and forming, at least in this case, a useful point of reference.

[6] This life table was calculated by Jean Dumas, professor of demography at the University of Moncton.

[7] A more detailed description of the first two stages is given in Stone (1978*b*).

[8] We of course did this in such a way as to make sure that the coefficients cause almost no change in the propensities to migrate according to mother tongue. In each language group, however, they do cause quite considerable variations in the propensities by home language. In the case of migration by the French group of Montreal to Canada less Quebec, we therefore decreased by 40%, for all ages, the propensity with respect to English home language. This reduction is intended to take into account the fact that certain persons migrated first and then

adopted English as their home language, which artificially swells the number of migrants having English as their home language. A similar reasoning was used in the other cases. We should also mention that we assumed differences in linguistic mobility between Montreal and the rest of Quebec to be negligible. This assumption made it simpler to estimate the coefficients.

Chapter Eight

From the Possible to the Plausible

We should start by stating clearly what sort of results we will be reporting in this chapter. One should not look for predictions, since, based on the criteria in the previous chapter, making predictions is, from a scientific standpoint, a fairly risky enterprise. Politicians, no doubt, are obliged, when making decisions, to take a chance on the future, but this is not our case. Conversely, it should not be imagined that we can act as simple robots, collecting great quantities of data and applying to them some magic formula taken from the treasure trove of science in order to conjure up a picture of the future, hard and bright as a diamond. Throughout this study, we have had to make choices, and they have all been at least partly arbitrary. For example, we adopted a regional breakdown, but there were others we could have picked. We chose, except in certain cases, to analyse only three language groups, but we could also have made a further breakdown of the group whose mother tongue is neither French nor English. As for the phenomena we have considered (mortality, fertility, linguistic mobility, international and inter-regional migration), it is hard to imagine what other choices might be made, except that of completely changing the framework of the study. Past trends with respect to these phenomena might, of course, have been analysed in many ways, but we did have to bear in mind the limits imposed by availability of data. Finally, we have made hypotheses about the possible future evolution of each of these phenomena, and it is most likely here that there is the greatest uncertainty, in particular as regards migration, fertility, and linguistic mobility.

Prospective exercises are, of course, worth no more than the hypotheses on which they are based. In this connection, our strategy is clear and relatively simple: we have first attempted to delimit the possible, giving this term what we think is a fairly broad interpretation, that is, we feel it is practically impossible that future reality would be situated outside these limits; second, we have narrowed the range by trying to take in only what we felt was plausible, that is, what had a more than negligible chance of happening.

Our hypotheses might be characterized by the fact that they are either more or less favourable to French or more or less favourable to English, while other languages never play a very important role, except indirectly. In our simulation models, there are four phenomena for which our hypotheses show substantial variations: fertility, linguistic mobility, international migration, and interregional migration. Let us assume that for each phenomenon considered, the limit probable (or possible) hypothesis has a 5% chance of happening, and that each phenomenon is independent of the others. Under these conditions, the probability that, for all four phenomena, the limit hypotheses favourable to English (or French) will come about is only six millionths. In fact, things are not quite that simple: the probability that one hypothesis about a given phenomenon will come about—note that we cannot measure this probability—is not independent of the probability that a hypothesis concerning another phenomenon will be realized. To illustrate this by an example, if economic conditions became particularly favourable in Quebec, interregional net migration would become less negative and perhaps even positive; at the same time, international net immigration would become more positive. These two eventualities are favourable to the growth of the anglophone population of Quebec and are interrelated. We could give another example: if the conditions of access to English-language schools in Quebec were very strict, this would favour the linguistic mobility of allophones towards French while no doubt causing the proportion of anglophones among immigrants to decline.

To take into account the possible relations between phenomena, we have assumed that two overall factors determine the realization of the various hypotheses: the socio-economic situation and socio-linguistic conditions. These two factors are neither described nor measured; they are rather contextual variables connected with situations that, while necessarily concrete, are for us a means of identifying sets of hypotheses that are more likely than others, since, as we have seen, these hypotheses are not independent from one another, and certain sets of hypotheses are more realistic than others. The four combinations of overall factors shown below were judged plausible.

Socio-economic situation	Socio-linguistic conditions with respect to French	
	Slight improvement	Great improvement
Good	GS	GG
Mediocre	MS	MG

To each of these combinations, we have associated a set of hypotheses. We have also considered two sets of hypotheses that reflect the limits of the possible, one combining all the most extreme hypotheses in favour of English, the other taking in the opposite hypotheses.

One last remark should be added concerning our strategy. This is a rule that we have adopted and that deals with what we might call the "argumentative" or polemic aspect of forecasting. When an expert undertakes to demonstrate that the presence of an element in a given situation has practically no chance of causing unfavourable effects, he takes care, if he wishes to be convincing, to stack the deck against himself, so to speak; that is, he will give that element all possible chances to come into play, even slightly overstating the extent to which the element penetrates into the milieu, as well as its effects. If, in spite of this unfavourable bias towards his thesis, he succeeds in demonstrating that the element in question is inoffensive, his demonstration will be all the more convincing. In the present case, we did not strictly speaking have a thesis to prove, but we knew that the most feared eventuality was that of a reduction in the proportion of francophones, first in Quebec, in particular in Montreal, and also in other regions of Canada. In a certain sense, our "thesis" became: there is little chance that the proportion of francophones in Quebec and in Montreal will decline. Based on this, every time an arbitrary choice came up, we decided to systematically act in such a way that our decisions went against our "thesis." In practice, this means that the choice of hypotheses has been deliberately slanted in favour of the anglophone group. For example, in the future we judged plausible, the migratory streams most unfavourable to anglophones are close to those observed between 1966 and 1971. Conversely, we have been "generous" with respect to the hypotheses destined to reflect situations that were favourable to anglophones and thus unfavourable to francophones. In other words, we have deliberately made things easy for anglophones and difficult for francophones (at least in Quebec). If, in spite of this bias, francophones come out unscathed, there would be good reason to feel confident in their collective destiny. There is one drawback to this strategy: from the anglophone point of view, a conclusion favourable to them is less reliable, since it would be partly due to the fact that we were more generous with them.

The impact of this bias should not be exaggerated. To a certain extent, it compensates for a distortion in our data that works against the anglophone group. It would effectively appear that, in the past, many people stated their mother tongue as English, when in fact this language had become their home language but was not, strictly speaking, their mother tongue. These persons would then not be included in measurements of linguistic mobility towards English. We were unable either to measure or to correct this error, which has the effect of causing a phenomenon favourable to the members of the English home-language group to be underestimated. The deliberate bias we have adopted in favour of English is, however, probably larger than would have been necessary to offset this deficiency in the data.

Such a strategy might shock those who are unaware that in the social sciences, and to an even greater extent in forecasting, we are more often faced with uncertainty than with certainty, and with relative inexactitude more often than with absolute precision. They may also be unaware that this type of strategy is used to test not only the effects of medical remedies but also the strength of parachute cables. It is also true that when dealing with social phenomena, scholars are often less careful and even less conscious of their lack of prudence. This is to be regretted.

In Section *A*, we will look at the results given by the extreme hypotheses, those that lead us to the frontiers of the impossible, although this latter term should not be taken too literally, since completely unforeseeable but important events could always occur. In Section *B*, we will spend more time on the sets of plausible hypotheses, those that are more likely and, in our opinion, have a higher probability of delimiting future reality, at least up to the year 2000. In Section *C*, we will depart somewhat from the precautions and rigorous method observed so far, to reduce the plausible to what appears most probable and make some remarks that are not far removed from considerations of a political nature.

One last caution: our simulations on the future have as their point of departure the observations of the 1971 census, the last to have data on home language. They then progress by bounds of five years up until 2031. It should be clear that the farther we move into the future, the lower our chances to give a clear picture of the reality of that period, and we should avoid attaching too much credit to what happens after the year 2001, at least from the point of view of exploring plausible futures. It was certainly interesting to extend our simulations over sixty years, in order to allow the phenomena sufficient time to produce their effects, but except for some rare exceptions, we will only report here the results obtained after thirty years.

Another point is that we have paid no attention to the *actual* evolution of our phenomena after 1971, which might have been possible, at least to a certain extent, for fertility and migration. From 1971 on, it is the hypotheses that govern the system, and some of them have obviously already been refuted by the facts. This is of relatively little importance if we agree to adopt the following point of view: our results for 2001 reflect situations brought about by our various sets of hypotheses, at the end of thirty years of application. Since the demolinguistic structure in 1979 is not very different from that of 1971, our results for the year 2001 can be interpreted as being those that would be obtained after thirty years of application of the various sets of hypotheses starting in 1979, that is, in 2009 rather than in 2001.

What we are basically looking for is less to predict how things will look in 2001 or in 2009 than to estimate where one set of plausible hypotheses or another will lead in thirty years' time.

A. THE FRONTIERS OF THE POSSIBLE

As the heading of this section indicates, we place ourselves here at the limit of what can be imagined as still being even remotely possible, in light of observation of the past and what we can foresee for the future. It should also be noted that this likelihood limit is characteristic of each hypothesis, so that a group of equally unlikely hypotheses all going in the same direction (either in favour of French or in favour of English) becomes even more unlikely. This is why we do not hesitate to speak of the frontiers of the possible, because we are not very far from the impossible.

1. Extreme Hypotheses

The limit or extreme hypotheses discussed here are defined according to whether they give the greatest advantage to anglophones or francophones in Quebec as a whole. They thus do not always have the same effect in each region, and in particular in the rest of Canada. Here is a brief description of each limit set in the case of Quebec.

a. Hypotheses favourable to francophones

Mortality: The same for all (M_0).

Fertility: In Quebec, the fertility of francophones is 24% greater than that of anglophones and 11% greater than that of allophones (F_3).

Linguistic mobility: In Montreal, 15% of English mother-tongue individuals adopt French as their home language during the course of their lives (35% in the rest of Quebec); still in Montreal, 33% of individuals from the third-language group adopt French and 22%, English; only 2% of French mother-tongue individuals adopt English in Montreal and 0.5% in the rest of Quebec (L_7).

International migration: Five-year net emigration is 30,000 for all groups in Quebec: 22,000 for English mother-tongue individuals, 4,000 for those of French mother tongue as well as for those from the third-language group (N_{12}).

Interregional migration: Quebec experiences a net loss of 95,000 during the first five-year projection period (1971−1976); 76,000 are of English mother tongue, 5,000 are French, and 14,000 of other mother tongues (R_1). These figures will decrease over time, except for French mother tongue.

b. Hypotheses favourable to anglophones

Mortality: Persons in the French group have the Canadian mortality rate for both sexes combined in 1970−1972; members of the English and third-language groups have the female mortality rate for Canada less Quebec in 1970−1972 (M_1).

Fertility: In Quebec, the fertility of anglophones is 13% greater than that of francophones, but remains about 20% less than that of allophones (F_1).

Linguistic mobility: In Montreal, 4% of English mother-tongue individuals adopt French during the course of their lives (10% in the rest of the province); still in Montreal, 76% of persons of other mother tongues adopt English and 14% adopt French; 5% of French mother-tongue persons adopt English in Montreal and 2% in the rest of Quebec (L_1).

International migration: Net immigration per five-year period is 120,000 for all groups in Quebec: 41,000 for the English mother-tongue group, 1,000 for the French mother-tongue group, and 78,000 for the third-language group (N_1).

Interregional migration: Quebec has a net gain of 2,000 during the first five-year projection period (1971−1976); this is the result of a net gain of 2,000 for English mother-tongue persons and 4,000 for French mother-tongue persons, and a net loss of 4,000 for other languages (R_8). These figures vary greatly over time, with net migration finally becoming negative for all groups.

It will be noted that for the hypotheses related to linguistic mobility, we have adopted relative variances that are more or less symmetrical compared to the 1971 observation, in spite of the fact that we feel that the position of French is more likely to improve than to deteriorate.

It is difficult to assess the international migration hypotheses, since we must bear in mind their effects on the three language groups, and little dependable information is available for even the recent past. Compared to the estimates made for the past two five-year periods (see Chapter Six), which indicate that international migration by language probably does not have a very marked influence on the relative strength of the two dominant groups, our hypothesis favourable to French is slightly in favour of French, while the hypothesis favourable to English gives that language a very large comparative advantage. The hypothesis favourable to English has the effect, compared to a neutral hypothesis (N_0), of increasing the fraction of anglophones in Quebec by 2.8 percentage points in 2001 and reducing the francophone fraction by 8.7 points.[1] The hypothesis favourable to French has a more limited effect: it causes 2.2% of the Quebec population to pass from English to French, compared to the neutral hypothesis.

Finally, the extreme hypotheses regarding interregional migration depart from the situation recently observed by about the same amount, in one direction or the other depending on the case, but slightly more in the case of the hypothesis favourable to English. Thus, if recent trends were continued (R_3), they would have the effect, compared to the null hypothesis (R_0), of reducing the anglophone fraction by 3.4 percentage points after thirty years. The extreme hypothesis favourable to English would cause this fraction to increase by 0.4 point, while the hypothesis favourable to French would reduce the anglophone fraction by 6.0 points after thirty years, which represents a smaller variance, compared to recent observations, than the opposite hypothesis.

In short, as regards these extreme hypotheses, it can be seen that we have respected our overall strategy, which consists in being systematically a little more generous in the case of English than in that of French. Some of these hypotheses, taken individually, are highly improbable; however, the combination of all the hypotheses tending in the same direction (favourable to French or to English) is even more so, and the probability of occurrence of the results they should generate is thus probably so small that it would not exceed one in a hundred thousand. As we will see in the following section, these results delimit a fairly large range of possibilities.

2. Results

In Table 8.1, we show the results for two timespans: thirty years and sixty years, that is, according to the convention described above, for the years 2001 and 2031. We will not comment on them in detail, since, due to their scope and their low probability, they do not merit prolonged discussion. It is not very interesting to learn that in Quebec the proportion of anglophones could be between 3% and 32% in 2031, nor that the fraction of francophones in the rest of Canada might be between 1.1% and 3.3%. The results shown in Table 8.1 do enable us, however, to discard certain eventualities as being practically impossible sixty years from now. Here are the main ones:
— That the fraction of anglophones would decrease in Canada as a whole or in Canada less Quebec.
— That the fraction of anglophones would exceed 32% in Quebec as a whole or 40% in the Montreal region.
— That the fraction of francophones would exceed 27% in Canada as a whole or succeed in maintaining its percentage outside Quebec (4.4% in 1971).
— That the fraction of francophones would fall below 62% in Quebec as a whole, 51% in the Montreal region, and 87% in Quebec less Montreal.
— That the anglophone fraction would fall below 3% in Quebec as a whole, 5% in the Montreal region, and 1% in the rest of Quebec.
We should add one caution, however: the results in Table 8.1 are only extremes, as we have already explained, for the anglophones and francophones of Quebec, and strictly speaking, the frontiers of the possible only concern these groups. It might nevertheless be thought that the extremes for the other geolinguistic groups are not too far removed from those shown in the table.

Once again, it should be recalled that these linguistic compositions come extremely close to being impossible, and we would do well to consider some more plausible eventualities.

Table 8.1
COMPOSITION BY HOME LANGUAGE IN 1971 AND FOR TWO
EXTREME FUTURIBLES[a] IN 2001 AND 2031, CANADA,
CANADA LESS QUEBEC, QUEBEC, MONTREAL,
AND QUEBEC LESS MONTREAL
(percentage)

YEAR AND REGION	HYPOTHESES FAVOURABLE TO ANGLOPHONES			HYPOTHESES FAVOURABLE TO FRANCOPHONES		
	English	French	Other	English	French	Other
Canada						
1971	67.0	25.7	7.3	67.0	25.7	7.3
2001	73.8	19.3	6.9	67.9	26.7	5.4
2031	80.7	13.7	5.6	68.7	27.3	4.1
Canada Less Quebec						
1971	87.2	4.4	8.4	87.2	4.4	8.4
2001	90.7	2.1	7.2	89.9	3.6	6.5
2031	93.4	1.1	5.5	91.5	3.3	5.1
Quebec						
1971	14.7	80.8	4.5	14.7	80.8	4.5
2001	22.8	71.5	5.8	5.8	91.9	2.3
2031	31.6	62.4	6.0	2.9	96.2	0.9
Montreal						
1971	23.3	68.8	7.9	23.3	68.8	7.9
2001	31.9	59.3	8.8	9.7	86.4	3.9
2031	40.4	51.4	8.2	4.6	94.0	1.4
Quebec Less Montreal						
1971	5.8	93.3	0.9	5.8	93.3	0.9
2001	7.7	91.4	0.8	1.8	97.6	0.6
2031	11.5	87.6	0.9	1.2	98.4	0.4

Note: [a] These two futuribles express the limits of the possible for Quebec anglophones and francophones, but not necessarily for other geolinguistic groups.

B. PLAUSIBLE FUTURES

What we wish to designate by the term "plausible" is that which has a reasonable chance of occurring. But what is a reasonable probability? We could not place a numerical value on this, but, to give some idea, we might say that they are eventualities that policy makers, for example, could not ignore. The whole problem resides in separating what is plausible from what is not. There is no hard and fast rule for this, and we must be guided by a number of elements: the past evolution of the phenomena and the circumstances that accompanied it; the estimation of the future evolution of these circumstances; and what form we think government intervention might take. We can illustrate this by two examples. The circumstances that influenced the excess fertility of francophones in Canada up to the last world war are not likely to reappear, and we fail to see what other combination of circumstances could produce the same type of results. On the other hand, in spite of possible government changes in Quebec, it is hard to imagine that, thirty years from now, Quebec could return to *laissez-faire* with respect to language, unless the relative strength of English became so weak that the domination of French was completely ensured in all fields of community life.

Several eventualities are obviously plausible. This will lead us to construct several sets of hypotheses, bearing in mind two contradictory objectives: (1) to pick out the essential of what is plausible, (2) to avoid handling such a large number of sets of hypotheses that we can no longer find our way through them. Regarding the latter objective, we decided to spare the reader and limit ourselves, for the most part, to only four sets.

1. Sets of Plausible Hypotheses

Our sets of hypotheses are based on two contextual variables: first, socio-economic conditions in Canada and particularly in Quebec; second, socio-linguistic conditions, or to give a better idea of what this means, the extent of government intervention in favour of French. At the beginning of this chapter, we described the four futuribles generated by the combination of these variables. In the remarks that follow, they will be designated by letters, as shown below:

GS   Good socio-economic conditions and slight improvement in the situation with respect to French

GG   Good socio-economic conditions and great improvement in the situation with respect to French

MS   Mediocre socio-economic conditions and slight improvement in the situation with respect to French

MG   Mediocre socio-economic conditions and great improvement in the situation with respect to French

As mentioned earlier, the contextual variables are not described in detail; this would in any case be a complex task. We can, however, evoke some historical situations that correspond to them, or in relation to which their properties may be shown. For socio-economic conditions, we might think of the 1950s as representative of good conditions and recent years as corresponding to mediocre conditions. With respect to socio-linguistic conditions and, more precisely, the extent of intervention in favour of French, we have known only two historical situations in Quebec: the *laissez-faire*, which prevailed until the early 1960s, and the present system, laid down by the Charter of the French Language (Bill 101) in 1977, but preceded by the Official Languages Act (Bill 22) in 1974, as well as various manifestations of impatience on the part of a number of francophone movements during the preceding decade, ranging from the planting of bombs right up to the creation of a political party dedicated to Quebec sovereignty. These last elements are obviously not the equivalent of a policy in the full sense of the word, but they are related to policy through certain of their effects. In order to represent a slight increase in the position of French, we simply carried forward into the future the linguistic mobility estimated for recent periods.

We should make it clear on which phenomena the contextual variables act. We have assumed that neither the socio-economic situation nor the socio-linguistic conditions of French would have any effect on mortality. In fact, we have kept only one hypothesis for this phenomenon: francophone mortality will be that of the total Canadian population in 1970−1972 (both sexes combined), while that of the rest of the population will correspond to female mortality in Canada less Quebec in 1970−1972 (M_1). Mortality thus does not vary from one set of hypotheses to another, and no further mention will be made of this.

Four other phenomena govern the future evolution of geolinguistic groups: fertility (F), linguistic mobility (L), interregional migration (R), and international migration (N). We have assumed that the socio-economic situation has a direct or indirect influence on these four phenomena, as do the socio-linguistic conditions, except on fertility. Let us first describe the four sets of hypotheses, in terms of symbols, after which we will comment on their internal logic:

Overall Situation	Hypotheses Chosen
GS	L_3, R_6, N_5, F_0
GG	L_5, R_5, N_6, F_0
MS	L_4, R_3, N_8, F_2
MG	L_6, R_2, N_9, F_2

The subscripts that identify each hypothesis (below and to the right of each letter) are those used in the preceding chapter, where these hypotheses were precisely and quantitatively described. We will limit ourselves here to giving the main direction, by showing their relation with the four futuribles in the left-hand column.

A. FERTILITY

Let us look first at the case of fertility, which has only two variants. We have assumed that if socio-economic conditions are good, all geolinguistic groups will have the same fertility and that this will just ensure the replacement of generations. If conditions are mediocre, however, we would have variances between groups and regions quite similar to those observed recently. It will be recalled that these variances generally favour franco-phones over anglophones, in Quebec as in the rest of Canada, but give each language group in Quebec a lower fertility rate than the rest of Canada. This link that we have established between socio-economic conditions and relative fertility variances might be debatable. The shift from F_0 to F_2 in any case has only a slight effect on the proportions of the various language groups. It favours francophones in Quebec and in the rest of Canada, but works against them in the country as a whole. Note also that hypothesis F_0 gives anglophones a fertility rate equal to that of the rest of the population, which has never occurred in Quebec as a whole or in Montreal, or even in the whole of Canada.

B. LINGUISTIC MOBILITY

This factor is mainly sensitive to the relative position of French, particularly in Quebec; however, we have also caused it to vary with socio-economic conditions, assuming that good economic conditions would encourage language transfers towards English and work against transfers towards French. The reason for this connection is perhaps not obvious: if socio-economic conditions are good, the anglophones in Quebec benefit from migratory streams (or rather they are less at a disadvantage). Their relative strength is consequently greater and their drawing power would probably be reinforced, as would their resistance to the attraction of French.

When we pass from L_3 to L_6, linguistic mobility becomes less and less favourable to English, although it never becomes unfavourable. The situation observed in 1971 is close to L_4, an hypothesis that corresponds to mediocre socio-economic conditions and a slight improvement in the position of French. As a matter of fact, the situation observed in 1971 was more the result of *laissez-faire*, and we favour English here (while penalizing French) by assuming that an improvement in the position of French would not make things more favourable to francophones than what was observed in 1971. To give some idea of the effect of passing from a system that corresponds to a slight improvement to one that would allow a great improvement in the socio-linguistic conditions of French, we may take the case of the Montreal region. We have calculated what would be the limit linguistic composition of the Montreal population, if only linguistic mobility varied: under hypothesis L_3, there would be 64% francophones and 36% anglophones; under hypothesis L_5, there would be 77% and 23% respectively. In the rest of Quebec, linguistic mobility varies little, but in the rest of Canada, it is the most important factor for the French group, and the second most important factor for anglophones and allophones.

C. INTERREGIONAL MIGRATION

This is one of the most important factors in the future evolution of linguistic composition in Quebec, at least for anglophones and francophones, and in particular in Montreal. It is almost as important as international migration. It is mainly affected by socio-economic conditions, but also by the

294 / Future Prospects

situation of French, although we have deliberately allowed interventions and changes favourable to French to have only little influence, in order not to put the anglophone group at a disadvantage. In truth, there is very little difference between R_6 and R_5, or between R_3 and R_2, the two variances that reflect the effect of a great improvement compared to a slight improvement in the socio-linguistic conditions of French. The first two hypotheses roughly translate what was observed during the 1950s and the other two, what was observed during the period 1966–1976. The latter are more unfavourable to Quebec anglophones than the former.

It should be noted that all the interregional migration hypotheses used here are unfavourable to Quebec anglophones, with hypothesis R_2 being the most unfavourable. But even if this last hypothesis is meant to represent socio-linguistic conditions particularly favourable to French, the migration streams to which it corresponds are not much different from those observed during the last ten years. It is possible that we could have imagined hypotheses that were even more unfavourable to the English group, while still remaining in the realm of the plausible, but we have again chosen to keep our bias in favour of the English language.

D. INTERNATIONAL MIGRATION

According to our hypotheses, international migration is affected only by socio-economic conditions, when no distinction is made between languages: five-year net international migration for Quebec would be 70,000 if conditions were good and 20,000 if they were poor. In 1971–1976, we can estimate that the total was between 35,000 and 50,000. We have assumed, however, that the linguistic composition of these migrations was affected by the extent of improvement in the socio-linguistic conditions of French. As we pass from hypothesis N_5 to N_6 and from hypothesis N_8 to N_9, we move towards balances that are less favourable or more unfavourable to anglophones and less unfavourable to francophones.

Contrary to current belief, international migration streams are probably unfavourable to anglophones both in Quebec and in the rest of Canada, at least from the point of view of their relative strength; they are also unfavourable to francophones, and any benefit is in favour of allophones. In general, international migration is the factor that has the most effect on linguistic composition. This is the case in all areas with respect to the relative strength of allophones, which is easily understandable. It is also the case for anglophones in Canada less Quebec (within Quebec, they are more affected by interregional migration), as well as for francophones in Quebec as a whole and in Montreal (in the rest of Canada, the proportion of francophones is mainly affected by linguistic mobility).

This completes the description of our hypotheses and the way in which we have linked them to four typical futuribles. Of course, none of them will be realized exactly as described. The only claims we make for them are, first, that for each phenomenon they cover the whole range of the plausible and, second, that these four sets of hypotheses have a strong probability of delimiting the future thirty years from now in so far as concerns the linguistic composition of the regions for which they have been constructed.

We should also mention that we have introduced a slightly different variant of certain of these hypotheses in order to account for the fact that the Montreal region seems to be losing some of its drawing power compared to the rest of Quebec. We did not want to further complicate the description of our hypotheses by introducing this rather unimportant element, but we will mention it where necessary in presenting our results.

Before going on to the results, we should add that, in addition to the factors we have just dealt with, there is one other factor that has an influence on the future demolinguistic composition of the population: the composition by age of each group at the point of departure in 1971. Even if fertility and mortality were identical for all, and there was neither linguistic mobility nor migration, the demolinguistic composition would nevertheless change over time, due to the momentum provided by the age composition. This momentum works mainly to the benefit of Quebec francophones, particularly in Montreal, but also to the benefit of anglophones in the rest of Canada. This factor alone has the effect of increasing the fraction of francophones by 1.5 percentage points in Quebec as a whole and by 1.7 percentage points in Montreal (in thirty years); it also increases the fraction of anglophones in the rest of Canada by 1.1 points and reduces it by the same amount in Montreal. This factor is almost always unfavourable to allophones.[2]

2. Results

It will be recalled that we envisaged four typical contexts; these are defined by the fact that socio-economic conditions in Canada and in Quebec are good (*G*) or mediocre (*M*). In addition, we have assumed that, for each of these two conditions, the position of French was either slightly (*S*) or greatly (*G*) improved. We will give results only for the year 2001, or more exactly for the end of the thirty-year period during which the hypotheses chosen acted on an initial situation similar to that observed in 1971. Calculations were made for a sixty-year period, but we felt that past thirty years, we ran the risk of no longer covering the range of plausible developments, since unforeseen circumstances could arise.

Certain trends are independent of the hypotheses chosen, in the sense that in relation to the situation observed in 1971, evolution is always in the same direction for all four futuribles (Table 8.2):
— In Canada as a whole and in Canada less Quebec, the fraction of anglophones always increases (by a maximum of 5 percentage points), while it always decreases in the Montreal region and the rest of Quebec,

Table 8.2
COMPOSITION OF THE POPULATION BY HOME LANGUAGE IN 1971 AND FOR FOUR FUTURIBLES IN 2001, CANADA, CANADA LESS QUEBEC, QUEBEC, MONTREAL, AND QUEBEC LESS MONTREAL
(percentage)

REGION AND HOME LANGUAGE	1971	FUTURIBLES 2001			
		GS	GG	MS	MG
Canada					
English	67.0	70.5	68.4	72.2	70.6
French	25.7	21.6	22.3	23.1	23.9
Other	7.3	8.0	9.3	4.7	5.5
Canada Less Quebec					
English	87.2	88.8	87.3	91.7	90.6
French	4.4	2.2	2.3	3.2	3.5
Other	8.4	9.0	10.4	5.1	5.8
Quebec					
English	14.7	15.8	11.2	12.1	9.1
French	80.8	79.3	82.6	84.3	86.5
Other	4.5	5.0	6.2	3.7	4.4
Montreal					
English	23.3	23.1	16.8	18.6	14.2
French	68.8	69.5	74.2	75.5	78.9
Other	7.9	7.4	9.0	5.9	6.9
Quebec Less Montreal					
English	5.8	5.0	3.4	4.4	3.3
French	93.3	93.6	94.2	94.5	95.1
Other	0.9	1.4	2.4	1.0	1.5

although not always for Quebec as a whole. We will come back to this rather paradoxical result, which is related to certain past developments.
— The fraction of francophones always increases in the Montreal region (by a maximum of 10 percentage points) and in the rest of Quebec (by a maximum of 2 points), but not always in the *whole* of Quebec. In Canada as a whole, however, it is always lower (by a maximum of 4 points), as well as in Canada less Quebec (by a maximum of 2 points).
— The allophone fraction always increases, if only slightly, in Quebec less Montreal, where they are not very numerous. In all other areas, this fraction varies in either direction, depending on the hypothesis applied.

The paradoxical result noted above, for Quebec anglophones and francophones, occurs only in the case of the futurible GS, which incidentally is the one that gives rise to the least modifications in the linguistic composition of Quebec. In this futurible, immigration makes a large contribution to the population of the Montreal region; anglophones are highly concentrated in this region, and even if they lose a little of their relative strength (23.3% to 23.1%), the increased importance of Montreal compensates for the relative losses they experience in the two Quebec regions. This factor is not powerful enough, however, to withstand the effect of a great improvement in the position of French. Developments for francophones are the opposite of those described above.

Good socio-economic conditions favour allophones in all regions, but the effects from one region to another are not the same for the two other groups. Good conditions work against anglophones in Canada less Quebec, but in their favour in the two Quebec regions, while the contrary occurs for francophones.

It should not come as a surprise to anyone that a great improvement in the relative situation of French would favour francophones and work against anglophones in Quebec. As we had assumed, it also works to the benefit of the allophones of that province. The effect is particularly strong for the anglophones of Montreal: going from a slight improvement in the socio-linguistic conditions of French to a great improvement brings about a 4.4 percentage point decrease in their percentage under mediocre socio-economic conditions or a 6.3 point loss under good conditions in 2001. The effect on Montreal francophones is not quite as strong, but remains significant: increases of 3.4 and 4.7 points respectively. Socio-linguistic conditions also have some effect in the rest of Canada, but never to any great extent.

We mentioned above, in describing our hypotheses, that we had introduced a variant to take into account the fact that the Montreal region could lose some of its drawing power, and thus some of its strength, to the benefit of the rest of Quebec. This makes no significant change to the results for Canada as a whole or Canada less Quebec. In Quebec, this variant has the effect of slightly reducing the fractions of anglophones and allophones to the benefit of francophones, as can be seen in Table 8.3. The effects of this development are, however, not the same in Montreal and in the rest of Quebec: francophones gain little in Montreal and lose a little strength elsewhere in Quebec to the benefit of anglophones. It should also be pointed out that this variant shows no futurible for which the anglophone fraction would increase in Quebec as a whole. Futurible GS', which is the most favourable to them, indicates that they would maintain their strength.

No reference has been made so far to the future size of the various geolinguistic groups. It was not our objective to make such conjectures, and our projections are not entirely appropriate for doing this, particularly because of the way we have dealt with fertility. In connection with this phenomenon, we have only been interested in the relative differences between geolinguistic groups, since we had assumed, for the whole of Canada, that fertility would remain almost exactly at the level that would just ensure replacement of generations. This was sufficient to enable us to estimate the demolinguistic composition, but not to estimate absolute numbers, since these are greatly affected by the *level* of fertility. It appears

Table 8.3

COMPOSITION OF THE POPULATION BY HOME LANGUAGE IN 1971 AND FOR FOUR FUTURIBLES IN 2001, UNDER THE HYPOTHESIS THAT MONTREAL HAS LESS DRAWING POWER THAN THE REST OF THE PROVINCE, QUEBEC, MONTREAL, AND QUEBEC LESS MONTREAL

(percentage)

REGION AND HOME LANGUAGE	1971	FUTURIBLES 2001			
		GS'	GG'	MS'	MG'
Quebec					
English	14.7	14.7 (15.8)	10.5 (11.2)	11.0 (12.1)	8.2 (9.1)
French	80.8	80.3 (79.3)	83.3 (82.6)	85.4 (84.3)	87.4 (86.5)
Other	4.5	5.0 (5.0)	6.2 (6.2)	3.7 (3.7)	4.4 (4.4)
Montreal					
English	23.3	22.5 (23.1)	16.4 (16.8)	17.6 (18.6)	13.2 (14.2)
French	68.8	69.4 (69.5)	73.9 (74.2)	75.9 (75.5)	79.1 (78.9)
Other	7.9	8.0 (7.4)	9.7 (9.0)	6.6 (5.9)	7.7 (6.9)
Quebec Less Montreal					
English	5.8	5.5 (5.0)	3.8 (3.4)	4.8 (4.4)	3.6 (3.3)
French	93.3	93.1 (93.6)	93.9 (94.2)	94.2 (94.5)	94.9 (95.1)
Other	0.9	1.4 (1.4)	2.3 (2.4)	1.0 (1.0)	1.5 (1.5)

Note: Results from Table 8.2 shown in brackets.

evident that if in Canada as a whole fertility remained well below the replacement level, absolute numbers would be lower, and vice versa.

Having said this, we will limit ourselves to those groups for which absolute numbers as such are likely to have particular significance from the viewpoint of the future of language groups; these are the anglophones of Quebec, the francophones of the rest of Canada, and the allophones in both regions. Table 8.4 shows the size of each home-language group in 1971 and in 2001 for the four plausible futuribles. Quebec anglophones would see their numbers increase if socio-economic conditions were good and decrease if these conditions were mediocre, but this decrease would only be sizeable if, in addition, there were a great improvement in the position of French. In any case, we are a long way from the near disappearance of Quebec anglophones, even though the reduction may be significant: around 25% or even more if they emigrated from Quebec in greater numbers than we had assumed.

The number of francophones in the rest of Canada would not necessarily decrease. This would appear to be the case if socio-economic conditions were particularly good in Quebec, while if a relatively poor economic situation existed in Quebec, many Quebec francophones might move to other provinces.

As for allophones, their numbers would increase greatly, both in Quebec and in the rest of Canada, if socio-economic conditions were good. If they were poor, their numbers would decrease slightly or remain almost stable.

These futuribles concerning absolute numbers should not be given as much credit as those dealing with the percentages represented by each group. However, they do provide a certain illustration of the inertia of demographic phenomena: even minorities whose survival sometimes appears precarious show a remarkable resistance to disappearance.

Table 8.4
POPULATION OF CERTAIN GEOLINGUISTIC GROUPS (HOME LANGUAGE) IN 1971 AND FOR FOUR FUTURIBLES IN 2001
(in thousands)

GEOLINGUISTIC GROUPS	1971	FUTURIBLES 2001			
		GS	GG	MS	MG
Quebec-English	888	1,312	923	856	650
Canada Less Quebec-French	676	555	573	710	770
Quebec-Other	270	413	514	260	315
Canada Less Quebec-Other	1,306	2,231	2,582	1,109	1,276

C. FROM THE PLAUSIBLE TO THE CRYSTAL BALL

We have just explored what appeared to us to be the range of the plausible thirty years from now. It is fairly wide. For Quebec alone, the fraction of anglophones should be between 8.2% and 15.8% shortly after the year 2000, while that of francophones would be between 79.3% and 87.4%, and that of allophones, between 3.7% and 6.2%. In Montreal in particular, the fraction of francophones would be in practically no danger of decreasing, and could even become almost as high as the proportion they hold today in Quebec as a whole, while the strength of anglophones could either remain the same or decrease by two fifths and fall to 13%. It should be recalled that in the case of Montreal, we are dealing with a region slightly larger than the census metropolitan area.

Within the limits we have traced, what might happen? Just about anything! If we were asked to be more explicit, if our backs were really to the wall, we would then have to become slightly less circumspect than we hope we have been up until now. Basically, we would have to make conjectures about what socio-economic conditions would be in Quebec and in Canada thirty years from now and predict not only attitudes and behaviour with respect to socio-linguistic matters, but also the extent of government intervention in favour of French, to which might be added various trends of opinion that might either support or work against them. We are decidedly no longer in the realm of what can be perceived precisely, objectively, or cool-headedly. In fact, we have to fall back on what must be called a sort of intuition. This is nothing to be ashamed of, but it must be clear that we would then be performing operations of a quite different nature. Armed with these reservations, let us then venture a few steps along this perilous trail.

We will begin by mentioning again the bias we deliberately introduced in our methods in favour of English and to the detriment of French in Quebec. It might then be imagined—if we have not gone too far out of line in choosing our hypotheses—that things would probably be a little more favourable to francophones and a little less to anglophones than the results we have just described would indicate. It is clear that none of these results presents what might be called a danger to the preponderance of French in Quebec, and in Montreal in particular. It would appear that, barring unforeseen events or situations, the fraction of francophones would increase in Montreal and that it would remain the same in almost all of Quebec, this under the hypothesis the least favourable to francophones, which would only occur if socio-economic conditions were good throughout the thirty-year period, and this is without historical precedent. We have of course rejected the possibility of a deterioration in the socio-linguistic conditions of French following on a return to *laissez-faire* with respect to language; if this occurred, the present predominance of French could be significantly reduced. We have made calculations that would correspond to *laissez-faire*: the proportion of francophones could decline, by the year 2000, to 76% in Quebec as a whole and to 65% in Montreal. Once again, however, this return to *laissez-faire* appears rather implausible.

In Canada less Quebec, at least taking this region as a whole, anglophones have already acquired a fairly comfortable majority; this will most likely be strengthened whatever happens, and it is hard to imagine why governments should have any cause for concern. The reverse is true in the case of francophones: in 1971, they formed only 4.4% of the population of that region, and this fraction will no doubt decline by anywhere from a fifth to almost a half within thirty years, not to mention the fact that their absolute numbers might also decrease. The dominant factor here is linguistic mobility, and even if we could slow it down, we could probably not curb it enough to change the prospects in view. The case of the Acadians is no doubt a special one, but it is too specific to be dealt with here, and we will come to it in the next chapter.

Outside Quebec, allophones are almost twice as numerous as francophones. Their future proportion and numbers depend essentially on international immigration. We have shown that their languages have a very small probability of survival in Canada, due to their very high linguistic mobility. If we exclude Amerindians, in two generations, allophones lose more than 90% of their potential strength to the benefit of English in Canada less Quebec. High immigration could nevertheless cause their relative strength to increase (by about a fifth), at least during the next thirty years. However, it is unlikely that immigration policy would be directed to this objective, except indirectly by the desire to allow immigrants to be reunited with the family members already established here. We should mention in passing that allophones benefit from an improvement in the socio-linguistic conditions of French. This is not surprising, since we have assumed that their rate of language maintenance would vary directly with that of the French group (see Chapter Seven).

In Quebec, choices are a little more tricky, since the three language groups could see their relative strength increase or decrease depending on the intensity of the various factors involved. Good economic and social conditions would be necessary, as would a very slight improvement in the socio-linguistic conditions of French, for the proportion of anglophones to increase; this increase would be very small, it is true, but it is not impossible. Strange as it may seem, anglophones could see their relative strength increase in Quebec as a whole, but not in Montreal. It should be added that this probability of an increase in their relative strength in Quebec as a whole is rather small if we bear in mind the "favours" we granted them in developing our hypotheses. If proponents of French predominance wanted to guard against all danger from that quarter, we could not accuse them of going too far if they recommended rather forceful language policies. In fact, we are in no position to judge, since no one would be able to calculate the demolinguistic effects of present policy due to lack of information on what has happened since they came into effect.

On the other hand, if anglophones for their part wanted to ensure the maintenance of their relative strength in Quebec, they could only count on unfailingly good economic conditions, which would increase their immigration (from the rest of Canada and from other countries) and reduce their emigration. They must also be able to attract, as they do now, a majority of persons of other mother tongues who would adopt English as their home language. If the overall economic situation is somewhat mediocre, they have almost no chance of maintaining their relative strength in Quebec as a whole. In any case, whatever the economic situation, the best they could do would be to maintain their relative strength in the Montreal region, and there is a strong probability that this relative importance will decline, as we know it has been doing for at least the past forty years.

D. CONCLUSION

We should once again caution that the results we have described in this chapter should not be taken as predictions. Our primary goal was to see the effect of the various phenomena involved on the evolution of the linguistic composition of the Canadian population and that of three regions that have, from this point of view, particular significance: Montreal, the rest of Quebec, and the rest of Canada. While doing this, we found it interesting to construct hypotheses on the future evolution of these phenomena, in order to trace the limits first of the possible, then of the plausible. These expressions should not be taken too literally: we cannot foresee all that is possible, and as for the plausible, we cannot deny that the arbitrary comes into play.

We nevertheless feel that we have given some insight into the future and very briefly outlined the field of political intervention in this respect. It is not our place to propose objectives; that is a task for policy makers and, through them, for all citizens. Each of them can at least appreciate what might happen if a given phenomenon took on certain values and, if necessary, suggest interventions that might modify its course. However precise our hypotheses and calculations might be, a great deal of uncertainty still remains. This is due first to the impossibility of predicting the socio-economic situation of Quebec and of Canada as a whole; these conditions will be largely responsible for determining migration streams, and these have a great effect on demolinguistic composition. Relative fertility levels could also be affected. Another element of uncertainty is the reaction to government intervention in favour of French, as well as pressure by various groups for and against. If it is already difficult to measure the linguistic mobility of recent years, we can only imagine how it might vary due to measures taken recently; in any case, we cannot know now whether these measures will be maintained or whether they will be strictly or flexibly applied.

In spite of this uncertainty, it appears almost impossible that the fraction of francophones can be maintained outside Quebec and in Canada as a whole. As for Quebec, it is not impossible that the anglophone fraction will increase, but this eventuality appears much less probable than the contrary, and we may very well see a fairly sizeable reduction in anglophone strength, particularly in the Montreal region.

We will wind up this chapter by going back to the remarks we made at the beginning of our conclusion regarding the meaning of our futuribles. Some people will want at all costs to see them as predictions. If we hold to this term, it must be taken in the same sense as it would in the case of a meteorologist who would try, on December 1, to predict the weather for the month to come. He might say "Not much probability of thunderstorms, slight probability of rain; but strong probability of snow." Our task was a little more difficult, since social events do not have the same regularity as natural events; on the other hand, the inertia of many demographic phenomena is greater than that of atmospheric currents. Our meteorologist could not, however, predict to the millimetre the amount of snow that would fall. From this point of view, we are not much better off than he is, and the reader should not be misled by the apparent preciseness of our results.

NOTES

[1] These estimates do not have an absolute meaning. In actual fact, the effect of the variation of a phenomenon on the fraction represented by a given language group depends on the values we give to other phenomena. When we make this type of estimation, we always assume that fertility and mortality are the same for all geolinguistic groups and that, except for the phenomenon considered, all others have a null value. These are the hypotheses we have marked 0. It will be recalled that simulations of this kind were presented in the preceding chapter.

[2] In this connection, see also Table 7.2.

Chapter Nine

Past Developments and Future Prospects: A Brief Review

Once we have briefly sketched the demographic history of Canada, then described and analysed the main demolinguistic phenomena, and finally projected the evolution of linguistic compositions, we reach the limits of our undertaking and can thus better appreciate its limitations and weaknesses. In order to encompass and grasp demolinguistic events, to give them a certain coherence, and to show their interdependent nature, we had to confine ourselves to examining only certain aspects of them, to occasionally curtail them or at least to make them fit into a framework developed before the fact, and then to study them from a certain point of view, in this instance the viewpoint of demography. Without going so far as to try to embrace the whole of reality, which is the province of mysticism rather than that of science, we might nevertheless, in many cases, have made use of other viewpoints to complement our demographic approach, notably by emphasizing and analysing the relations between demolinguistic events and economic, social, and cultural situations and events. Such an ambitious project was certainly tempting, but we quickly realized that it was beyond both our competence and our capacities. Our own small demolinguistic garden needed constant attention and care, and we thought it preferable to exploit it thoroughly, to fertilize the ground, to vary the crop, in short, to increase its productivity rather than leaving it lie fallow while we romped about the flower-beds of others at the risk of trampling them. If we confined our study to the demographic aspects, it was not a question of doctrine, but simply one of efficiency. In any case, with respect to the study of groups, demographic aspects are certainly not negligible.

The primary goal of a group is neither to grow richer nor to spread out over space, but rather to overcome time, to live on, in short, to ensure its survival. This goal conditions all others. If it cannot be attained, there is, strictly speaking, no group as such, but only a collection of individuals. Of course, groups, like individuals, are mortal, but on an entirely different time-scale. This is no doubt why they tend to be highly resistant to being reduced to the short timespan that is that of the individual. Thus emerges the first challenge that must be met by any group: that of ensuring the replacement of its generations or, at least, avoiding an excess of deaths over births for long periods. This is an internal goal, specific to each group, and its attainment allows the group to survive, although it does not always ensure this survival. Thus, when a number of language groups coexist on the same territory, it does not suffice for each of them to have a fertility rate that compensates for its mortality rate; this fertility must also balance the losses that result from linguistic exchanges (transfers) between the groups involved. This is only a minimum condition, and a group that slips below it would put its integrity in jeopardy. Once this is ensured, another goal looms, less fundamental perhaps, but often pursued: each group aims at maintaining and increasing its strength in comparison with its competitors, whether the groups live on neighbouring territories or occupy the same territory. We often view with concern the decline of the *relative* strength of the population of a region, even though its numbers may be increasing. A similar observation may be made with respect to language groups: they all want to increase their relative strength. This is obviously impossible. If there is a winner, there must be a loser. This explains the very unpleasant and somewhat monstrous nature of zero-sum games. There is, of course, one way of avoiding this non-egalitarian logic, and that is not to play. Groups do not have this option, and this is an inevitable source of stress. A number of strategies might be imagined to minimize this. One would be to organize several games, some of which favour one group, while others work against it. In this way, all groups could both gain and lose, depending on their "table." Thus, in Quebec, the new rules of the game (Bills 22 and 101) favour francophones and work against anglophones; elsewhere in Canada, the dice are loaded in favour of anglophones and clearly work against francophones. However, we should not allow this symmetry to hide the imbalance reflected by the grand total of gains and losses at all "tables." If francophones are the winners at the "Quebec table," they nevertheless suffer losses on an all-Canada scale. Is this inevitable? We might also ask ourselves if it is inevitable that anglophone strength should decline in Quebec, while that of francophones should decrease in the rest of Canada.

As an almost invariable rule, the demographic future is largely uncertain and unpredictable. The image we have of it at a given moment is inspired to a great extent by the theories that prevail at that time, and this image is most often nothing more than a magnified reflection of the recent past. Let us look at one example (Lachapelle, 1977*b*). During the decades 1930 and 1940, demographers were quick to assume that in Western countries, fertility would continue to decline and that in almost all areas, the number of births would soon not exceed the number of deaths; it was even feared that natural increase would become negative during the 1950s and 1960s. The great migratory movements towards the New World were explained at that time by the new opportunities offered by the settlement of rich and unoccupied territories.

This settlement phase was at an end, or almost, in the interwar years. High net immigration was thus not foreseen for Canada or the United States during the 1950s and 1960s. Most demographers, aware of the high excess fertility of Quebeckers, and more specifically of francophones, and having little reason to predict its early disappearance, were inevitably led to predict, for the coming decades, an increase in the demographic weight of Quebec within Canada and a rise in the relative strength of francophones. As we have seen, and as we will see again further on, the facts have completely contradicted these assumptions. It would be too easy to make fun of the claims made by our predecessors. We will not yield to this, since we are well aware that we, like them, could quite easily be wrong, and to do so would only leave us open to ridicule by our successors who, thirty years from now, will perhaps examine our futuribles with some amusement.

This is to say that even the results we esteem highly probable may very well never be observed. The goal of our futuribles is not, in any case, to predict the future, since this would be doomed to failure, but they may well contribute to guiding and directing those who seek to shape it. If this is the case, and we obviously hope it is, we run into another problem. Suppose we deemed a situation to be probable that many actors judged very desirable. It is then possible that our forecast would have the consequence of demobilizing a large fraction of them, which might jeopardize the implementation of the minimum measures necessary for the fulfilment of our prediction. Conversely, if we predicted a situation held to be undesirable, it might be imagined that governments would act in such a way that the future would contradict what we foresaw.[1] This second possibility might upset the demographer, but it would delight the citizen. As for the first eventuality, it is a matter of concern to both of them. It is the biggest stumbling-block in forecasting, and we must never lose sight of it.

In the prospective considerations that follow, we will confine ourselves, in almost all cases, to future situations that we *now* feel are plausible. We will begin by going over the results presented in the last chapter with respect to Quebec, the rest of Canada, and the country as a whole. We will then risk a few prospective views of the linguistic regions that have often been used in studying the past demolinguistic situation.

A. CANADA, QUEBEC, AND THE REST OF CANADA

For Canada as a whole, our futuribles are, in the final analysis, nothing more than the extension of a trend that is already twenty-five years old. Between 1951 and 1976, the proportion held by the French group declined from 29.0% to 26.0%, while that of the English group increased from 59.1% to 61.5%. These proportions are for composition by mother tongue, but the development observed probably also holds true for home-language composition. We only have figures on the latter for 1971, however, when

anglophones represented 67.0% of the Canadian population and francophones, 25.7%. After thirty years, at the beginning of the next century, the
relative strength of francophones could be between 21.0% and 24.0%, and
that of anglophones between 68.0% and 72.0%. These ranges correspond
approximately, as we saw in the last chapter, to developments that appear
plausible, at least at present. Why is this so?

The evolution of the home-language composition of the Canadian
population depends on four phenomena: mortality, fertility, linguistic
mobility, and international migration. Mortality has probably always worked
against francophones and to the benefit of anglophones, and this situation
persists. The demolinguistic effects of mortality are now quite small,
however, and in fact negligible. Linguistic mobility works against the
francophone group and to the advantage of the anglophone group. Not only
does the latter receive almost all transfers from the allophone group, but it
also comes out the winner in its linguistic exchanges with the francophone
group. We do not feel it is likely that this situation could be reversed during
the coming decades. At the most, it might ease somewhat. As for
international migration, it appears that this phenomenon is essentially to the
advantage of allophones, especially when the migratory balance is strongly
positive. It works to the disadvantage of both the anglophone and
francophone groups, but to a greater extent for the latter than the former. We
felt it was best to maintain these positions in the futuribles that reflect
plausible developments. It is, of course, not impossible that the future will
bear no resemblance to this conjecture. However, we do not see what other
conjecture we might have made while still remaining in the realm of the
plausible. The last factor is fertility. Francophones have long been able to
compensate for the unfavourable effects of the other phenomena thanks to
their legendary fertility. This enabled them to maintain their relative strength
in the Canadian population between 1851 and 1951. Already much less
marked in the early 1950s, francophone excess fertility melted away during
the years that followed, to the point where it was transformed into
under-fertility from the mid-1960s on. Some recovery might be imagined,
but it is hard to see how francophones could return to significant excess
fertility.

All in all, barring unforeseen circumstances, we should expect the
coming decades to bring a sizeable reduction in the francophone fraction and
an increase in the proportion of anglophones in the Canadian population as a
whole. Governments might, through appropriate action, cause some slackening in these trends, but it is difficult to imagine what policies could guarantee
maintenance of francophone strength. These trends obviously cause great
stress on the Canadian political system, and it might be wise to modify
institutions in such a way that they can lessen the principal undesirable
effects that might result from these trends.

Francophones, as we know, are to a very great extent concentrated in Quebec (87.8% in 1971), while anglophones live mainly in the rest of Canada (93.8% in 1971). This situation has become even more pronounced over the past twenty-five years. The proportion of French mother-tongue persons living in Quebec rose from 82.3% in 1951 to 84.8% in 1976, while the proportion of English mother-tongue persons declined from 7.1% in 1951 to 5.6% in 1976. These trends are likely to continue over the coming decades (Table 9.1). The reduction in the anglophone fraction of the Quebec population is essentially due to internal migration, with more anglophones leaving Quebec than moving in, while the increase in the francophone concentration in Quebec is a consequence of the high linguistic mobility of the francophone group in the rest of Canada. Although more recent and perhaps less well established, another trend emerges from our prospective exercises: the demographic weight of Quebec in the whole of Canada is likely to decrease over the next few decades.[2] Although this trend only began around 1966, it is hard now to see what might reverse it, since it seems unlikely that Quebec will return in the near future to a situation of appreciable excess fertility compared to the rest of Canada. There is, of course, another component that influences regional distribution, and this is migratory increase, but it has almost always worked against Quebec during the past hundred years. It would have been quite risky to go against such a century-old trend.

Let us look once again at the evolution of the linguistic composition of Quebec, as well as that of the rest of Canada. Outside Quebec, the trends have been very clear for over twenty-five years, and there is every indication

Table 9.1
PERCENTAGE OF THE CANADIAN POPULATION LIVING IN QUEBEC, BY HOME LANGUAGE IN 1971 AND FOR FOUR FUTURIBLES IN 2001

YEAR AND FUTURIBLE	HOME LANGUAGE			
	All Languages	English	French	Other
1971	27.9	6.1	87.8	17.1
2001				
GS	25.1	5.6	92.2	15.6
GG	24.9	4.1	92.2	16.6
MS	24.5	4.1	89.4	19.0
MG	24.6	3.2	88.9	19.8

Sources: Census of Canada, 1971, and projections made by the authors.

that they will continue over the coming decades. The proportion held by the French group declined from 7.5% in 1951 to 6.0% in 1971, then to 5.4% in 1976. As for the English group, it first decreased from 77.8% to 76.8% between 1951 and 1961, because of high international immigration that caused the proportion of the third-language group to rise from 15.2% to 16.6%. The English group then increased to 79.7% in 1976, while the strength of the third mother-tongue group decreased (14.9% in 1976). Future evolution of the proportion of allophones will depend mainly on the amount of international immigration and thus on future socio-economic conditions. If the latter are good, we will no doubt see an increase in their share, while this would decline if socio-economic conditions were mediocre, since international immigration then could not compensate for massive transfers by allophones to English. Whatever the socio-economic conditions or the socio-linguistic conditions of French, we will no doubt see, in the decades to come, a significant reduction in the relative strength of francophones. The proportion of anglophones will increase at least slightly in all the situations we have judged plausible. This means that if we confined ourselves to purely demographic considerations, the majority group could face even the strongest intervention in favour of French without concern.

In Quebec, the demolinguistic scene is more complex, since, although in the minority, anglophones hold a privileged socio-economic position. Their demographic weight has nevertheless been declining slowly and steadily for about a century. Looking only at statistics related to mother tongue, we have seen that their share dropped from 14.9% in 1931 to 13.8% in 1951, then to 13.1% in 1971, and finally to 12.8% in 1976. The fraction held by the French group varied in reverse proportion to that of the third-language group, whose development was dependent on the level of international immigration. Between 1931 and 1951, the French group increased from 79.8% to 82.5%, while the third-language group declined from 5.3% to 3.7%; the latter group increased from 3.7% in 1951 to 6.2% in 1971, while the French group decreased from 82.5% to 80.7%; and, finally, the French group rose to 81.1% in 1976 while the third mother-tongue group suffered a slight decline (6.1% in 1976).

In forecasting the future evolution of Quebec's linguistic composition, we considered, as explained in the last chapter, four eventualities: socio-economic conditions could be good (*G*) or mediocre (*M*), and the relative position of French could either improve slightly (*S*) or greatly (*G*). We did not think it was plausible that the position of French compared to English could deteriorate. On the one hand, it seemed likely to assume that francophones would continue to gain ground socially and economically over the coming decades, and this trend would no doubt have the effect of enhancing the relative position of French, especially as a language of work. On the other hand, above and beyond the debate generated by language laws (Official Language Act in 1974 and Charter of the French Language in 1977), there would appear to exist a considerable amount of agreement on the principle of intervention by the Quebec government in the socio-linguistic area. Disagreement of course subsists, especially with respect to regulations governing access to English schools. It nevertheless seems that all the major political parties would like to limit access to English schools to children from the anglophone group only. There is, however, no agreement on the definition of this group. All in all, we felt it was reasonable to assume that language policy would back up gains made by francophones in the socio-economic field, and that the end result would be at least a slight improvement in the relative position of French.

In Quebec as elsewhere in Canada, the proportion of allophones will no doubt increase in the future if socio-economic conditions are good, that is, if international immigration remains at a high level; if the reverse is true, we will probably see a reduction in their relative strength. In three of the four futuribles considered, the anglophone fraction would decrease during the coming decades, while that of francophones would increase; this would be true especially if socio-economic conditions were mediocre! One futurible (GS) gave the opposite results, that is, a slight improvement in the proportion of anglophones and a slight decrease in the francophone fraction. Are these trends really plausible? They are the result, and this should be emphasized, of a futurible that assumes both good socio-economic conditions and a slight improvement in the position of French. We will first present the arguments that would lead us to believe that this futurible is somewhat unlikely. Following this, we will show that if it is no doubt not the most probable, it would nevertheless be foolhardy to consider it unlikely.

The above futurible assumes that the Montreal region will show very high gains in its migratory exchanges with the rest of Quebec; in other words, that the next few decades will be similar from this point of view to the situation observed during the 1950s. During the last two five-year periods, however, gains by the Montreal region were much lower than during the preceding periods and, in addition, these gains decreased between 1966−1971 and 1971−1976. If we take this into account, there would no longer be, as we saw in the last chapter, any increase in the proportion of anglophones, who would remain at the level they reached in 1971 (14.7%), while the proportion of francophones would decrease very slightly. Similarly, we should mention that in all the futuribles considered, the proportion of anglophones decreased in the Montreal region as in the rest of Quebec, and the fraction of francophones increased in both regions. If these very clear trends are not always found for Quebec as a whole, this is because the Quebec population is becoming more and more concentrated in the Montreal region, and this region has a high percentage of anglophones. In the final analysis, what is significant and of bearing for the future is much more the evolution of linguistic composition where the position of francophones is less solid, that is, in Montreal. On the scale of Quebec as a whole, a number of very diverse situations are combined. The question of whether the hypotheses that enable us to generate the futurible GS are very realistic may also be raised. Let us examine this more closely.

We have assumed that for thirty years Quebec will benefit from fairly high net international migration and that it will lose little in its migratory exchanges with the rest of Canada. This situation has certainly already been observed between 1951 and 1966, but in a context much more favourable to Quebec anglophones than that which the future may hold. In addition, it appears somewhat surprising that such hypotheses would be implemented between 1971 and 1979, when we know that, during this period, Quebec experienced great losses in its migratory exchanges with the rest of Canada and that these losses were no doubt heavier for the anglophone group. We may, of course, accept the fact that these projections began in 1979 and not in 1971. Apart from the fact that this artifice does not take into account the probable decrease in the anglophone fraction between 1971 and 1979, it makes it even more difficult to justify the hypotheses adopted for linguistic mobility. It is, in fact, hard to see by what combination of circumstances the English group of Quebec might benefit more from linguistic mobility between 1979 and 2009 than it did in the past, yet this is what the futurible GS assumes. All this leads us to think that it is unlikely that we will not see a sizeable reduction in the anglophone fraction, even in Quebec as a whole, over the next few decades.

This argument could appear quite convincing, but we must hear from the defence before judging. Of course, we implicitly assumed that the English group in Quebec would have a linguistic continuity index slightly higher than that calculated in the 1971 census. As we saw, this index enables us to calculate the intensity of the effect of linguistic mobility. We should emphasize, however, that the continuity index of the English group was probably somewhat underestimated in the past, as certain persons claimed English as their mother tongue even though it was not the first language they had spoken. In calculating our forecasts, we did not explicitly take into consideration this mother-tongue substitution factor. To compensate for this bias that works against the anglophone group, we have had to reinforce the linguistic mobility hypotheses in their favour. It is true that for certain of their aspects, the international migration and internal migration hypotheses were inspired more by the situation that prevailed during the 1950s than by the situation observed during the past decade. It is not unlikely, however, that socio-economic conditions in Quebec might improve considerably and that we might once again observe more balanced migratory exchanges between Quebec and the rest of Canada. All in all, although the futurible GS is certainly not the most probable, it does not, in our opinion, fall outside the range of the plausible.

We could easily add arguments to one side and the other, and embark on an endless discussion of the merits and weaknesses of the futurible in question, and there is no reason why we could not call upon other futuribles, but this could turn into an exercise in futility. We should not find this surprising, when we think that the future, which is open and uncertain, can accommodate without resistance all points of view, if they are expressed in a sufficiently equivocal manner. Each of us can, of course, imagine a future that corresponds to his dreams, but dreams are rarely a helpful guide for someone who wants to shape the future in such a way that it comes close to fulfilling the wishes of all citizens.

To sum up, it is probable that, barring circumstances that are at present unforeseeable, the proportion of anglophones in Quebec will decrease during the coming decades, while the percentage of francophones will remain stable or increase. Conversely, there will be a reduction of the fraction of francophones elsewhere in Canada and an increase in anglophone strength and, in all probability, the same will be true for Canada as a whole. In addition, it would appear that francophones will be increasingly concentrated in Quebec and anglophones in the rest of Canada.

Is Canada then heading towards a regional concentration of its two major language groups similar to that which can be seen in Switzerland, a country having highly differentiated linguistic regions? Let us look more closely at this. The 1970 Swiss census enables us to establish the mother-tongue composition of four linguistic regions: German, French, Italian, and Romansh (Mayer, 1977). If we confine our examination to those language groups that hold a majority in any region, we find that 13.5% of the inhabitants live in minority situations, that is, in regions where the majority group has a mother tongue different from theirs. We can make the same calculation for Canada, considering Quebec as a French region and the rest of Canada as an English region, and confining ourselves to persons of French or English mother tongue. The proportion of members of the two major language groups who were in minority situations was 9.1% in 1971 and 8.5% in 1976. Does this mean that the regional concentration of language groups is greater in Canada than in Switzerland? Before making a judgement, it should be noted that the proportion we calculated for Switzerland is distorted by the significant regional dispersion of the two numerically smallest language groups: the Italian and Romansh groups. To make a fairer comparison, let us confine ourselves to the German and French regions, and to these two language groups. In this more limited framework, we see that 4.4% of the population considered is in a minority situation, which is less than in Canada. Let us nevertheless compare the linguistic composition of these regions to that of Quebec and of the rest of Canada, limiting ourselves in each case to the population made up of the two main language groups. In the French region of Switzerland, the German group forms 12.0% of the population and the French group, 88.0%; in Quebec, the English group represents 13.6% and the French group, 86.4%, the last figures being for 1976. In the German region of Switzerland, the German group makes up 97.8% of the population and the French group, 2.2%, while outside Quebec, the English group represented 93.6% of the population in 1976, and the French group, 6.4%. We cannot help but be struck by these similarities. This does not mean, of course, that the institutions and language policies of Switzerland could or should be imported to Canada or vice versa.

B. LINGUISTIC REGIONS

Throughout this study, we felt it was useful to go beyond the polarization Quebec/rest of Canada and to consider a larger number of regions.[3] These regions may be divided into six categories, based on their linguistic composition.

a. Homogeneous French regions (the Interior and the Periphery of Quebec)

b. Heterogeneous regions with large francophone majorities (the Eastern Townships, Montreal, and the Outaouais)

c. Heterogeneous regions with small francophone majorities (North-and-East New Brunswick)

d. Heterogeneous regions with small anglophone majorities (none of the regions considered here belongs in this category)

e. Heterogeneous regions with large anglophone majorities (Southeast and Northeast Ontario)

f. Homogeneous English regions (all the other regions of Canada).

To decide in which category a region belonged, we simply calculated the difference between the proportion of francophones and anglophones in 1971. Depending on whether the difference was positive or negative, we knew we had a francophone-majority region (the first three categories) or an anglophone-majority region (the last three categories). All we had to do then was to examine the absolute value of the difference to place the region in the appropriate category. A region is homogeneous if this figure is greater than 0.75 or 0.80; if it is less than 0.20, we have instead a heterogeneous region with a small majority. In the other cases, we would speak of a heterogeneous region with a large majority.

This classification shows clearly the contrast between the Quebec regions (first and second category) and those of the rest of Canada. One region, however, reflects an ambiguous situation: North-and-East New Brunswick is located outside Quebec and yet has a small francophone majority (third category). This unusual situation is reinforced by the fact that there is no region with a small anglophone majority (fourth category). In this connection, we cannot help but remark the small representation in the two middle categories, those made up of very heterogeneous regions. Before attempting to determine if this is a general trend, let us briefly examine the distribution of the Canadian population among the six categories of regions.

In 1971, approximately 11.0% of Canadians lived in homogeneous French regions, as opposed to 66.0% in homogeneous English regions (Table

9.2). These latter regions contained 88.0% of the anglophones in Canada. To arrive at a similar concentration of francophones, we would have to combine the homogeneous French regions and the heterogeneous regions with large francophone majorities. It can also be seen from Table 9.2 that the distribution of allophones in the various categories is more like that of anglophones than that of francophones. It should be mentioned, however, that in the heterogeneous regions with large francophone majorities, the proportion of allophones is almost as high as that observed in Canada as a whole (Table 9.3). Finally, we should emphasize that only 1.6% of the Canadian population falls into either of the two middle categories. As we have seen, these are the persons living in the North-and-East region of New Brunswick.

Although certain of the regions considered changed from one category to another in the nineteenth or early twentieth century, the overall situation has been much more stable since the Second World War. There were, of course, some noticeable changes between 1951 and 1976, but these were not great enough to bring about changes of category. What will happen during the next thirty years?

It does not appear plausible that the homogeneous regions, whether French or English, will lose this characteristic. One region, however, may move into the homogeneous French category: the Eastern Townships. In this region, the proportion represented by the English group has declined steadily for the past century. It was only 14.2% in 1976, compared to 84.5% for the

Table 9.2
BREAKDOWN OF THE CANADIAN POPULATION AMONG SIX CATEGORIES OF LINGUISTIC REGIONS, BY HOME LANGUAGE, 1971
(percentage)

LINGUISTIC REGION	HOME LANGUAGE			
	All Languages	English	French	Other
Homogeneous—French	11.2	0.5	41.8	1.4
Heterogeneous—large francophone majority	16.7	5.6	46.0	15.7
Heterogeneous—small francophone majority	1.6	1.1	3.4	0.2
Heterogeneous—small anglophone majority	0.0	0.0	0.0	0.0
Heterogeneous—large anglophone majority	4.7	4.8	4.9	3.0
Homogeneous—English	65.8	88.0	3.9	79.7
All regions	100.0	100.0	100.0	100.0

Sources: Tables *B*.9 and *B*.28.

Table 9.3
HOME-LANGUAGE COMPOSITION OF THE POPULATION IN SIX CATEGORIES OF LINGUISTIC REGIONS, 1971
(percentage)

LINGUISTIC REGION	HOME LANGUAGE			
	All Languages	English	French	Other
Homogeneous—French	100.0	3.2	95.9	0.9
Heterogeneous—large francophone majority	100.0	22.5	70.7	6.8
Heterogeneous—small francophone majority	100.0	43.7	55.4	0.9
Heterogeneous—small anglophone majority	—[a]	—[a]	—[a]	—[a]
Heterogeneous—large anglophone majority	100.0	68.8	26.6	4.6
Homogeneous—English	100.0	89.6	1.5	8.9
All regions	100.0	67.0	25.7	7.3

Sources: Tables *B*.9 and *B*.28.
Note: [a] Not applicable.

French group. Many factors indicate that the proportion of anglophones will continue to decrease during the coming decades. They will no doubt practically cease to benefit from language transfers, and migration will have, as in the past, unfavourable effects for them, but the dominating factor will most likely be the great degree of aging of the population. In 1971, persons aged 60 and over made up 21.9% of the English group in the Eastern Townships, as opposed to 9.6% in the French group. In short, between 1830 and the beginning of the twenty-first century, the Eastern Townships will have gone progressively from the sixth category (homogeneous English regions) to the first (homogeneous French regions).

This development in the Eastern Townships raises an interesting problem. As we showed in Chapter Seven, all other things being equal, the linguistic composition of a homogeneous region displays a greater resistance to change than that of a heterogeneous region, or, in other words, homogeneous regions are more stable than heterogeneous regions. The example of the Eastern Townships is a good reminder of the danger of hasty generalizations. Homogeneous regions are not always very stable, especially in the initial phase of their settlement.

Let us turn now to the other heterogeneous regions with large anglophone or francophone majorities. There are four of these: Montreal, the Outaouais, and Southeast and Northeast Ontario. They are likely to remain in the same category during the next three decades, with the position of francophones no doubt improving in the first two and that of anglophones improving in the two Ontario regions. This symmetry in evolution is the result of factors that are often quite different.

We have seen that in the Montreal region, bearing in mind changes in territory, the proportion of anglophones most probably declined continually over the past century. The economic metropolis of Canada in the nineteenth and early twentieth century, Montreal saw its relative position deteriorate to the benefit of Toronto, then to that of the large agglomerations of the Prairies and British Columbia. These changes appear to be associated with a westward movement of the Canadian population. Montreal is no longer the economic metropolis of Canada, but it remains, and will no doubt become increasingly so, that of Quebec (Martin, 1979). This development can only reinforce the upward movement of the proportion of francophones.

English will nevertheless continue to hold a very enviable position in the Montreal region, mainly because of the power this language has in the world, and above all in North America. It is precisely this situation, however, that renders the demographic position of anglophones somewhat fragile. On the one hand, because of its integration in the larger anglophone community of North America and its concentration in the higher ranks of the socio-occupational hierarchy, the anglophone group of Montreal exercises a strong attraction on the other language groups, in particular the third-language group. This is why language transfers have always favoured the anglophone group in the past and why they will continue to do so in the future, although to a lesser degree. On the other hand, precisely because of the predominance of English in the United States and in the Canadian provinces other than Quebec, Montreal anglophones are very sensitive to migration opportunities opening up outside Quebec, and this has the indirect effect of reducing their representation in the Montreal region. The same factor—the strength of English in North America—thus produces, relatively speaking, both favourable and unfavourable effects on the anglophone group of Montreal. It might be imagined that policies destined to improve the relative position of French as a working and teaching language would lessen the first and strengthen the second, thus leading to a probable reduction in the anglophone fraction in the Montreal region (see in this connection Chapter Eight).

These remarks also hold true, although to a lesser degree, for the Outaouais. In this region, it will be recalled, linguistic mobility definitely favours the English group and works against the French group. This is no doubt partly due to the numerous contacts between residents of the Outaouais and those of the Southeast region of Ontario. In spite of linguistic mobility, the proportion held by the French group increased continually for almost a century, up until 1971, while that of the English group decreased steadily. This century-old trend is due both to the traditional excess fertility of francophones and to the unfavourable effects of migration on the anglophone group. Since internal migration was, relatively speaking, unfavourable to the French group and favourable to the English group between 1971 and 1976, this period saw a sizeable decrease in the proportion of the French group and a very slight increase in that of the English group. This is most likely a temporary change related to the policy of developing the National Capital Region. Principally because of the language policies adopted by the Quebec government, we feel it is probable that, in the long term, the relative strength of francophones should again rise slightly in the Outaouais, and that of anglophones decrease somewhat. This will depend above all on internal migration, however, and this is largely unpredictable. This means that the evolution of the demolinguistic situation in this region will have to be followed closely.

In the Southeast and Northeast regions of Ontario, the proportion of French mother-tongue persons has decreased constantly over the past twenty-five years. This decline would no doubt have been even more pronounced if we had been able to study the evolution of the proportion of francophones, that is, persons of French home language, because of the heavy losses they experience from language transfers. We can certainly look forward to and hope for a considerable improvement in the relative position of French in the future, but it is hard to see through what combination of plausible circumstances linguistic mobility could cease to be so clearly unfavourable to francophones. This means that we should expect a sizeable reduction in the fraction of francophones during the next few decades, unless of course, in relative terms, internal migration should be overwhelmingly in their favour. This last eventuality does not appear plausible, however, except for short periods.

Lastly, we must look at the demolinguistic situation in the North-and-East region of New Brunswick. As we have seen, this is the region in which are concentrated the Acadians. In 1871, the English group formed the majority. At that time, it was a heterogeneous region with a small anglophone majority. In the years that followed, the French group reversed the situation and consolidated its position up until 1951. In that year, the French group formed 59.6% of the population, and the English group, 39.6%. This trend did not continue, however, since the English-group proportion increased slowly between 1951 (39.6%) and 1971 (40.8%) and even rose slightly up until 1976 (41.0%), while that of the French group decreased between 1951 (59.6%) and 1971 (58.0%), and then remained stationary until 1976 (58.0%). At first glance, these recent developments would appear to indicate that this region is close to an equilibrium situation. There is, however, no guarantee that this equilibrium will be stable. On the one hand, linguistic mobility benefits the English group and works against the French group. On the other, internal migration is, relatively speaking, to the advantage of the French group and to the disadvantage of the English group. On the whole, the effects of these two phenomena seem to offset one another, or practically. What will the future bring? We can envisage two futuribles. In both of them, we may assume that the French group will suffer losses from language transfers. It is, of course, possible that, as we might conclude from the comparison of the 1976 and 1971 censuses made in Chapter Five, these losses will be smaller than in the past but, in all probability, they will nevertheless be appreciable. We must next try to predict internal migration. If we assume that socio-economic conditions in the North-and-East region will be somewhat mediocre compared to those that prevail in the South of New Brunswick, it is probable that anglophones will leave the North-and-East in greater numbers than will francophones, in which case internal migration will, relatively speaking, clearly favour francophones. We might then see both a depopulation of the region, both of francophones and, above all, of anglophones, and a stabilization or even an increase in the proportion of francophones. Conversely, if socio-economic conditions improve greatly in the North-and-East region, it is more than likely that, except in the short term, internal migration will cease to favour francophones, in relative terms. Their numbers will no doubt increase, but their relative strength will probably decline quite rapidly.

In either case, the future of the Acadians is problematic. This little people has faced up in the past to much more difficult situations, however, and due to lack of time, we were unable to consider all the plausible situations. To get a better understanding of this, it would be best to examine separately the demolinguistic evolution presently taking place in the various subregions that make up the North-and-East region and to study in greater detail the interrelation between these trends and socio-economic factors.

C. CONCLUSION

Throughout this chapter and the preceding one, we have been engaged in a very risky venture, that of forecasting. In this field, experience shows that set-backs are much more numerous than successes, and this is why we have been generous in posting warnings. But too many reservations and too many nuances might lead us to think that almost anything is possible. This would no doubt be a rathcr comfortable position. It has the advantage of safeguarding the tranquillity of the researcher, but it leaves little room for the concerns and questions of political agents. In addition, those who criticize forecasting without making any attempt to improve it often make forecasts without knowing or admitting it. For our part, we have preferred to lay all our cards on the table, that is, to attempt to select, among all the developments that did not appear impossible, those that we felt were the most probable or, at the very least, the most plausible. Notwithstanding all the precautions we have taken, the future will almost certainly contradict some of our forecasts. We have accepted this risk. It is only at this price that forecasting can be of some use.

NOTES

[1] This is what Merton (1957, pp. 128–30) calls a suicidal (or self-defeating) prediction. See also Henshel (1976).

[2] In its most recent population projections, Statistics Canada (1979) predicts that the demographic weight of Quebec could vary between 23.2% and 24.6% in 2001. Our calculations yield slightly higher percentages (Table 9.1). This is due to a great extent to the fact that we have assumed that internal migratory exchanges would be less unfavourable to Quebec than did Statistics Canada.

[3] The regional breakdown we have used is described in Appendix *A*. It will be recalled that this breakdown is based essentially on the territorial distribution of the anglophone and francophone groups. It should again be emphasized that it does not reflect the large concentration of Amerindians in the northern areas of the country.

Appendices
and
Bibliography

Appendix A

Description of Linguistic Regions

Demographic, economic, or social studies are often limited to describing, comparing, or analysing changes in various indicators at the provincial level. This is not surprising, since statistical data are often only available for these geopolitical units. In the period following the Second World War, however, the need was felt for a regional breakdown that would be more representative of the structural and functional charteristics of economic activity throughout Canada. Such a regional breakdown, it was thought, would not only provide the opportunity to study and better understand demographic, economic, and social structures and processes, but also would enable government action to be more meaningfully oriented and organized. Based on this thinking, Camu, Weeks, and Sametz (1964) developed a system of sixty-eight regions. This territorial breakdown, destined mainly to facilitate studies on regional economy, is not particularly useful to the researcher interested in the demography of language groups.

There is no such thing as a "natural" territorial breakdown (Brewis, 1969). Depending on one's objectives and the subjects one wishes to describe and analyse, some very different regional systems may be considered. A territorial breakdown has no value in itself; its interest and relevance can only be appreciated in retrospect, through the insight and clarification it brings, as well as by the phenomena it reveals. This is why researchers must develop a regional breakdown that appears best suited to the objectives that they pursue, bearing in mind any material and intellectual constraints that they themselves have adopted or that have been imposed upon them.

In the demolinguistic field, Joy (1967) was the first to propose and use a system of seven linguistic regions: three unilingual English regions, one unilingual French region, and three bilingual regions, the latter forming a "bilingual belt" around the French region located in the heartland of Quebec. He demonstrated that demolinguistic situations could not be properly described and analysed at the provincial level, especially in the case of New Brunswick, Quebec, and Ontario. The territorial breakdown proposed by Joy constituted an important reference point for studies and projects carried out subsequently (Cartwright, 1976; Castonguay and Marion, 1974; Canada, Bilingual Districts Advisory Board, 1975; Joy, 1978, Vallee and Dufour, 1974). For us as well, he was a source of inspiration and valuable guidance. It could even be said that the territorial breakdown that follows is, in the final analysis, only an updating of that proposed by Joy.

The following three parameters were used in working out our regional breakdown:

1. Each region must have had a population of at least 100,000 in 1971.
2. Each region must be made up of complete census divisions.
3. No region may straddle a provincial boundary.

These parameters are in part arbitrary. They are derived at once from considerations of analytical efficiency (to avoid multiplying the number of regions), from material considerations (availability of statistical data), and from considerations of socio-political relevance. In practice, we found them in any case more a help than a hindrance. Let us now look briefly at the criteria that enabled us to delimit these linguistic regions.

The 1971 census provides a great deal of demolinguistic data on each of the census divisions. We used mainly the breakdowns by home language, that is, the language most often spoken at home. We considered above all the proportion of anglophones in the Quebec census divisions and the proportion of francophones in those of the other provinces. We have sought to combine into regions the census divisions where these proportions were equal to or greater than 10%. In addition, when this appeared useful or worthwhile, we have distinguished those regions that while similar from a demolinguistic point of view, have contrasting economic functions and structures.

Let us now see how we used the foregoing parameters and criteria to divide the provinces into linguistic regions.

1. ATLANTIC PROVINCES

The Province of Newfoundland had 522,095 inhabitants at the time of the 1971 census, 517,210 whose home language was English (99.1%) and 2,295 whose home language was French (0.4%). Almost 55% of these francophones lived in only one of the ten census divisions of Newfoundland, that being No. 10—Labrador; however, there they formed only 4.5% of the population. This means that it is impossible to form a region where francophones constitute an appreciable fraction of the population.

Prince Edward Island had 111,640 inhabitants in 1971, with 106,795 anglophones (95.7%) and 4,405 francophones (3.9%). A little over 90% of the francophones live in the division of Prince, where they represent 9.5% of the population. Here again, it did not seem essential to separate linguistic regions.

In 1971, Nova Scotia had a population of 788,960, of which 753,725 were anglophones (95.5%) and 27,220 were francophones (3.5%). Almost 80% of the latter lived in four census divisions: Digby, Inverness, Richmond, and Yarmouth, where they represented 35.9%, 17.3%, 32.4%, and 26.3% respectively of the population. Two of the divisions, Digby and Yarmouth, are adjacent; however, their combined population is only 45,000. It did not seem advisable to combine these two census divisions into a linguistic region.

New Brunswick had 634,560 inhabitants in 1971, with 430,720 anglophones (67.9%) and 199,085 francophones (31.4%). Over 96% of the francophones lived in seven of the fifteen census divisions. All of these divisions had sizeable percentages of francophones: Gloucester, 81.0%; Kent, 80.2%; Madawaska, 94.8%; Northumberland, 23.1%; Restigouche, 56.7%; Victoria, 36.1%; and Westmorland, 36.1%. We combined these census divisions to form the region of North-and-East New Brunswick (Table *A*.1 and Map *A*.1).[1] This region had a population of 345,935 in 1971, including 151,180 anglophones (43.7%) and 191,760 francophones (55.4%). The region of Southern New Brunswick was made up of the eight other census divisions, which had a combined population of 288,625 in 1971, with 279,540 anglophones (96.9%) and 7,325 francophones (2.5%).

We thus divided the Atlantic provinces into three regions, one anglophone-francophone contact region, North-and-East New Brunswick; and two predominantly English regions, Southern New Brunswick and the Atlantic provinces less New Brunswick.

2. QUEBEC

Quebec had a population of 6,027,765 in 1971, which included 4,870,100 francophones (80.8%) and 887,875 anglophones (14.7%). Anglophones accounted for over 10% of the population in twenty-two census divisions out of seventy-four. In two of them, moreover, anglophones formed the majority of the population: Brome, in the Eastern Townships (54.0%), and Pontiac (61.1%), in the Outaouais. Of the twenty-two census divisions where anglophones formed a sizeable fraction of the population, nineteen are located in southwestern Quebec. Of the remaining three divisions, one is located to the north of the Outaouais (Témiscamingue), while the two others are at the extreme tip of the Gaspé Peninsula (Bonaventure and Gaspé-Est.) Anglophones represent 10.6%, 15.5%, and 15.0% respectively of the population.

We distinguished three anglophone-francophone contact regions in southwestern Quebec: the Eastern Townships, Montreal, and the Outaouais (Table *A*.1 and Map *A*.1). The Montreal region, as we have defined it, had a population of 3,080,930 in 1971. This region contains the census metropolitan area, which had a population of 2,743,235 in 1971, but is itself included in the census region proposed by the Quebec Planning and Development Bureau (O.P.D.Q., 1976), which had 3,414,655 inhabitants in 1971.[2] Our region is also included in the region integrated into the Montreal urban system; this latter region was used by the Economic Council of Canada (1977, p. 135) and showed a population of 4,105,125 in 1971.

Table A.1
CENSUS DIVISIONS MAKING UP THE LINGUISTIC REGIONS OF NEW BRUNSWICK, QUEBEC, AND ONTARIO

REGION	CENSUS DIVISIONS MAKING UP EACH REGION *(with division numbers assigned in 1971 census)*
New Brunswick	
North-and-East	Gloucester *(4)*, Kent *(5)*, Madawaska *(7)*, Northumberland *(8)*, Restigouche *(10)*, Victoria *(13)*, Westmorland *(14)*
South	Albert *(1)*, Carleton *(2)*, Charlotte *(3)*, Kings *(6)*, Queens *(9)*, St. John *(11)*, Sunbury *(12)*, York *(15)*
Quebec	
Outaouais	Gatineau *(24)*, Hull *(25)*, Papineau *(51)*, Pontiac *(52)*
Montreal	Argenteuil *(2)*, Beauharnois *(6)*, Chambly *(11)*, Châteauguay *(15)*, Deux-Montagnes *(18)*, Huntingdon *(26)*, Iberville *(27)*, Île-de-Montréall et Île-Jésus *(28)*, Laprairie *(35)1*, *L'Assomption (36)*, Napierville *(49)*, Rouville *(59)*, Saint-Jean *(62)*, Soulanges *(66)*, Terrebonne *(70)*, Vaudreuil *(71)*, Verchères *(72)*
Eastern Townships	Brome *(10)*, Compton *(17)*, Missisquoi *(44)*, Richmond *(56)*, Shefford *(64)*, Sherbrooke *(65)*, Stanstead *(67)*
Interior	Arthabaska *(3)*, Bagot *(4)*, Beauce *(5)*, Bellechasse *(7)*, Berthier *(8)*, Champlain *(12)*, Dorchester *(19)*, Drummond *(20)*, Frontenac *(21)*, Joliette *(30)*, Labelle *(32)*, Lévis *(37)*, Lotbinière *(39)*, Masinongé *(40)*, Mégantic *(43)*, Montcalm *(45)*, Montmagny *(46)*, Montmorency No. 1 *(47)*, Montmorency No. 2 *(48)*, Nicolet *(50)*, Portneuf *(53)*, Québec *(54)*, Richelieu *(55)*, Saint-Hyacinthe *(61)*, Saint-Maurice *(63)*, Wolfe *(73)*, Yamaska *(74)*

The three contact regions contained, in 1971, 91% of Quebec anglophones, 52% of the francophones, and 92% of the allophones. The rest of the Quebec population has been divided into three regions: the Interior region and two periphery regions (or resource regions), the North and the Gaspé (or Eastern Quebec). It might be noted here that the contact regions and the Interior region form what is sometimes called Southern Quebec (Biays, 1967) or Central Quebec (Yeates, 1975).

3. ONTARIO

In 1971, Ontario had 7,703,105 inhabitants, of whom 6,558,065 (85.1%) were anglophones, and 352,460 (4.6%) were francophones. The latter represented more than 10% of the population in nine census divisions

Table A.1 *(cont'd.)*	
REGION	**CENSUS DIVISIONS MAKING UP EACH REGION** *(with division numbers assigned in 1971 census)*
Quebec (cont'd.) Gaspé	Bonaventure *(9)*, Gaspé-Est *(22)*, Gaspé-Ouest *(23)*, Île-de-la-Madeleine *(29)*, Kamouraska *(31)*, L'Islet *(38)*, Matane *(41)*, Matapédia *(42)*, Rimouski *(57)*, Rivière-du-Loup *(58)*, Témiscouata *(69)*
North	Abitibi *(1)*, Charlevoix-Est *(13)*, Charlevoix-Ouest *(14)*, Chicoutimi *(16)*, Lac-Saint-Jean-Est *(33)*, Lac-Saint-Jean-Ouest *(34)*, Saguenay *(60)*, Témiscamingue *(68)*
Ontario Northeast	Cochrane *(4)*, Nipissing *(29)*, Sudbury *(46)*, Timiskaming (48)
Southeast	Glengarry *(11)*, Ottawa-Carleton *(33)*, Prescott *(39)*, Russell *(43)*, Stormont *(45)*
Northwest	Algoma *(1)*, Kenora *(19)*, Manitoulin *(25)*, Parry Sound *(35)*, Rainy River *(41)*, Thunder Bay *(47)*
Interior	Brant *(2)*, Bruce *(3)*, Dufferin *(5)*, Dundas *(6)*, Durham *(7)*, Elgin *(8)*, Essex *(9)*, Frontenac *(10)*, Grenville *(12)*, Grey *(13)*, Haldimand *(14)*, Haliburton *(15)*, Halton *(16)*, Hastings *(17)*, Huron *(18)*, Kent *(20)*, Lambton *(21)*, Lanark *(22)*, Leeds *(23)*, Lennox & Addington *(24)*, Middlesex *(26)*, Muskoka *(27)*, Niagara *(28)*, Norfolk *(30)*, Northumberland *(31)*, Ontario *(32)*, Oxford *(34)*, Peel *(36)*, Perth *(37)*, Peterborough *(38)*, Prince Edward *(40)*, Renfrew *(42)*, Simcoe *(44)*, Toronto *(49)*, Victoria *(50)*, Waterloo *(51)*, Wellington *(52)*, Wentworth *(53)*, York *(54)*

out of fifty-four: Cochrane, 44.7%; Glengarry, 39.5%; Nipissing, 27.2%; Ottawa-Carleton, 17.5%; Prescott, 80.7%; Russell, 83.0%; Stormont, 27.5%; Sudbury 26.3%; and Timiskaming, 23.0%. All of these census divisions can be grouped into two regions, the Southeast and the Northeast (Table *A*.1 and Map *A*.1). The Southeast had 595,830 inhabitants in 1971, 142,870 (24.0%) of them francophones. The Northeast region had a population of 419,265, including 127,125 francophones (30.3%). These two regions together account for 77% of the francophones in Ontario.

We divided the rest of Ontario into two regions, the Interior and the Northwest. The Interior region and the Southeast region form what might be called Central Ontario (Yeates, 1975).

Map A.1

LINGUISTIC REGIONS OF NEW BRUNSWICK, QUEBEC, AND ONTARIO

GASPÉ
(ÎLE DE LA MADELEINE)

NORTH

GASPÉ

N & E

NEW BRUNSWICK

SOUTH

LABRADOR
(NEWFOUNDLAND)

INTERIOR

EASTERN
TOWNSHIPS

MONTREAL

S.E.

INTERIOR

NORTH

QUEBEC

OUTAOUAIS

INTERIOR

NORTH
WEST

N.W.

N.W.

NORTHEAST

ONTARIO

NORTHWEST

4. WESTERN PROVINCES AND NORTHERN TERRITORIES

This vast region had a population of 5,780,170 in 1971, with 5,191,845 anglophones (89.8%) and 90,460 francophones (1.6%). We were unsuccessful in isolating a region having more than 100,000 inhabitants where francophones represented at least 10% of the population. The four western provinces (Manitoba, Saskatchewan, Alberta, and British Columbia) and the northern territories (Yukon and Northwest Territories) form one predominantly anglophone region.[3]

NOTES

[1] This is the procedure followed by the Société des Acadiens du Nouveau-Brunswick (Fédération des Francophones hors Québec, 1977, p. 27).

[2] This corresponds approximately to the administrative region of Montreal.

[3] The northern parts of the Prairie provinces as well as the Northwest Territories could be considered as a contact region between anglophones and endophones, that is, persons whose home language is one of the many Amerindian languages. It should also be mentioned that large concentrations of endophones live in the northern parts of Quebec and Ontario.

Appendix B

Statistical Tables

	\multicolumn{5}{c}{Table B.1 \ POPULATION BY ETHNIC ORIGIN, CANADA, 1871–1971}

YEAR	ETHNIC ORIGIN				
	ALL ORIGINS	BRITISH	FRENCH	AMERINDIAN[d]	OTHER[e]
1871[a]	3,485,761	2,110,502	1,082,940	23,037	269,282
1901[a]	4,622,539	2,618,901	1,605,926	37,910	359,802
1901[b]	5,371,315	3,063,195	1,649,371	127,941	530,808
1911[b]	7,206,643	3,999,081	2,061,719	105,611	1,040,232
1921[b]	8,787,949	4,868,738	2,452,743	113,724	1,352,744
1931[b]	10,376,786	5,381,071	2,927,990	128,890	1,938,835
1941[b]	11,506,655	5,715,904	3,483,038	125,521	2,182,192
1951[b]	13,648,013	6,371,905	4,309,326	164,480	2,802,302
1951[c]	14,009,429	6,709,685	4,319,167	165,607	2,814,970
1961[c]	18,238,247	7,996,669	5,540,346	220,121	4,481,111
1971[c]	21,568,310	9,624,115	6,180,120	312,760	5,451,315

Sources: Canada, Royal Commission (1970), p. 247; Census of Canada, 1951 and 1971.

Note: [a] Nova Scotia, New Brunswick, Quebec, and Ontario only.

[b] Not including Newfoundland.

[c] Including Newfoundland.

[d] Erratic changes in the numbers of Indian and Inuit origin are mainly due to changes in census-taking practices, particularly as concerns Métis. Although since 1951 Amerindian origin is determined through the paternal line, in the same way as the rest of the Canadian population, previous censuses used special criteria for counting them. From 1911 to 1931, this was done through the maternal line; in 1941, all Métis were counted separately, while before 1911 they seem to have most often been included in the Amerindian population. Camu, Sametz, and Weeks (1964, p. 35) have attempted to make some corrections in order to make the census counts going back to 1871 approximately comparable to those of 1961.

[e] This residual category also includes non-responses when these have not been imputed. There do not appear to be a significant number of these, and they probably do not change the *general* pattern of evolution of the numbers and relative strength of this category.

Table B.2

POPULATION BY MOTHER TONGUE (M.T.) AND BY HOME LANGUAGE (H.L.), CANADA, 1931–1976

YEAR	LANGUAGE			
	ALL LANGUAGES	ENGLISH	FRENCH	OTHER
1931[a]				
M.T.	10,376,786	5,914,402	2,832,298	1,630,086
1941[a]				
M.T.	11,506,655	6,488,190	3,354,753	1,663,712
1951[a]				
M.T.	13,648,013	7,923,481	4,066,529	1,658,003
1951[b]				
M.T.	14,009,429	8,280,809	4,068,850	1,659,770
1961[b]				
M.T.	18,238,247	10,660,534	5,123,151	2,454,562
1971[b]				
M.T.	21,568,310	12,973,810	5,793,650	2,800,850
H.L.	21,568,310	14,446,235	5,546,025	1,576,050
1976[b,c]				
M.T.	22,992,625	14,149,520	5,966,700	2,876,405

Sources: Census of Canada, 1931, 1941, 1951, 1961, and 1971; Lachapelle (1982a).

Note: [a] Not including Newfoundland.

[b] Including Newfoundland.

[c] These figures are approximately comparable to the corresponding figures in the 1971 census (Lachapelle, 1982a). Cases of multiple replies to the question on mother tongue have been handled in the same way as in the 1971 census. Cases of non-response have been prorated to the distribution of respondents; this distribution was done on the provincial level, except for New Brunswick, Quebec, and Ontario, where it was done by census division with one exception: in the Île-de-Montréal division in Quebec, distribution was by federal electoral riding.

Table B.3
POPULATION BY KNOWLEDGE OF OFFICIAL LANGUAGES, CANADA, 1931–1971

YEAR	TOTAL	KNOWLEDGE OF OFFICIAL LANGUAGES			
		ENGLISH ONLY	FRENCH ONLY	BOTH ENGLISH AND FRENCH	NEITHER ENGLISH NOR FRENCH
1931[a]	10,376,786	6,999,913	1,779,338	1,322,370	275,165
1941[a]	11,506,655	7,735,486	2,181,746	1,474,009	115,414
1951[a]	13,648,013	9,031,018	2,741,659	1,723,457	151,879
1951[b]	14,009,429	9,387,395	2,741,812	1,727,447	152,775
1961[b]	18,238,247	12,284,762	3,489,866	2,231,172	232,447
1971[b]	21,568,310	14,469,540	3,879,255	2,900,155	319,360

Sources: Census of Canada, 1931, 1941, 1951, 1961, and 1971.
Note: [a] Not including Newfoundland.
[b] Including Newfoundland.

Table B.4

POPULATION BY ETHNIC ORIGIN (E.O.), BY MOTHER TONGUE (M.T.), AND BY HOME LANGUAGE (H.L.), QUEBEC, 1871–1976

YEAR AND VARIABLE	ETHNIC ORIGIN OR LANGUAGE			
	TOTAL	BRITISH OR ENGLISH	FRENCH	OTHER[b]
1871				
E.O.	1,191,516	243,041	929,817	18,658
1901				
E.O.	1,648,898	290,169	1,322,115	36,614
1911				
E.O.	2,005,776	318,799	1,606,535	80,442
1921				
E.O.	2,360,510	356,943	1,889,269	114,298
1931				
E.O.	2,874,255	432,726	2,270,059	171,470
M.T.	2,874,255	429,613	2,292,193	152,449
1941				
E.O.	3,331,882	452,887	2,695,032	183,963
M.T.	3,331,882	468,996	2,717,287	145,599
1951				
E.O.	4,055,681	491,818	3,327,128	236,735
M.T.	4,055,681	558,256	3,347,030	150,395
1961				
E.O.	5,259,211	567,057	4,241,354	450,800
M.T.	5,259,211	697,402	4,269,689	292,120
1971				
E.O.	6,027,765	640,045	4,759,360	628,360
M.T.	6,027,765	789,185	4,867,250	371,330
H.L.	6,027,765	887,875	4,870,100	269,790
1976[a]				
M.T.	6,234,430	796,665	5,058,260	379,505

Sources: Canada, Royal Commission (1970), p. 255; Census of Canada, 1931, 1941, 1951, 1961, and 1971; Lachapelle (1982*a*).

Note: [a] See Note *c*, Table *B*.2.

   [b] See Notes *d* and *e*, Table *B*.1.

Table B.5

POPULATION BY KNOWLEDGE OF OFFICIAL LANGUAGES, QUEBEC, 1931–1971

YEAR	KNOWLEDGE OF OFFICIAL LANGUAGES				
	TOTAL	ENGLISH ONLY	FRENCH ONLY	BOTH ENGLISH AND FRENCH	NEITHER ENGLISH NOR FRENCH
1931	2,874,255	395,995	1,615,155	842,369	20,736
1941	3,331,882	410,721	2,016,089	892,984	12,088
1951	4,055,681	462,813	2,534,242	1,038,130	20,496
1961	5,259,211	608,635	3,254,850	1,338,878	56,848
1971	6,027,765	632,515	3,668,015	1,663,790	63,445

Sources: Census of Canada, 1931, 1941, 1951, 1961, and 1971.

Table B.6
POPULATION BY ETHNIC ORIGIN (E.O.), BY MOTHER TONGUE (M.T.), AND BY HOME LANGUAGE (H.L.), CANADA LESS QUEBEC, 1871–1976

YEAR AND VARIABLE	ETHNIC GROUP OR LANGUAGE			
	TOTAL	BRITISH OR ENGLISH	FRENCH	OTHER[d]
1871[a]				
E.O.	2,294,245	1,867,461	153,123	273,661
1901[a]				
E.O.	2,973,641	2,328,732	283,811	361,098
1901[b]				
E.O.	3,722,417	2,773,026	327,256	622,135
1911[b]				
E.O.	5,200,867	3,680,282	455,184	1,065,401
1921[b]				
E.O.	6,427,439	4,511,795	563,474	1,352,170
1931[b]				
E.O.	7,502,531	4,948,345	657,931	1,896,255
M.T.	7,502,531	5,484,789	540,105	1,477,637
1941[b]				
E.O.	8,174,773	5,263,017	788,006	2,123,750
M.T.	8,174,773	6,019,194	637,466	1,518,113
1951[b]				
E.O.	9,592,332	5,880,087	982,198	2,730,047
M.T.	9,592,332	7,365,225	719,499	1,507,608
1951				
E.O.	9,953,748	6,217,867	992,039	2,743,842
M.T.	9,953,748	7,722,553	721,820	1,509,375
1961				
E.O.	12,979,036	7,429,612	1,298,992	4,250,432
M.T.	12,979,036	9,963,132	853,462	2,162,442
1971				
E.O.	15,540,545	8,984,070	1,420,760	5,135,715
M.T.	15,540,545	12,184,625	926,400	2,429,520
H.L.	15,540,545	13,558,360	675,925	1,306,260
1976[c]				
M.T.	16,758,195	13,352,855	908,440	2,496,900

Sources: Canada, Royal Commission (1970); Census of Canada, 1931, 1941, 1951, 1961, and 1971; Lachapelle (1982*a*).

Note: [a] Nova Scotia, New Brunswick, and Ontario only.

[b] Not including Newfoundland.

[c] See Note *c*, Table *B*.2.

[d] See Notes *d* and *e*, Table *B*.1.

Table B.7

POPULATION BY KNOWLEDGE OF OFFICIAL LANGUAGES, CANADA LESS QUEBEC, 1931–1971

YEAR	KNOWLEDGE OF OFFICIAL LANGUAGES				
	TOTAL	ENGLISH ONLY	FRENCH ONLY	BOTH ENGLISH AND FRENCH	NEITHER ENGLISH NOR FRENCH
1931[a]	7,502,531	6,603,918	164,183	480,001	254,429
1941[a]	8,174,773	7,324,765	165,657	581,025	103,326
1951[a]	9,592,332	8,568,205	207,417	685,327	131,383
1951	9,953,748	8,924,582	207,570	689,317	132,279
1961	12,979,036	11,676,127	235,016	892,294	175,599
1971	15,540,545	13,837,025	211,240	1,236,365	255,915

Sources: Census of Canada, 1931, 1941, 1951, 1961, and 1971.
Note: [a] Canada less Quebec does not include Newfoundland.

Table B.8

POPULATION OF QUEBEC AND REGIONS, 1871–1976

REGION[a]	1871[b]	1901[c]	1931	1941	1951
Quebec Total	1,191,516	1,648,898	2,874,255	3,331,882	4,055,681
Contact Regions	524,928	809,076	1,564,346	1,748,185	2,156,756
Outaouais	54,205	89,678	114,357	118,591	142,659
Montreal	377,972	590,446	1,280,281	1,437,284	1,777,527
Montreal Island and Île-Jésus	153,516	371,086	1,020,018	1,138,431	1,358,075
Periphery	224,456	219,360	260,263	298,853	419,452
Eastern Townships	92,751	128,952	169,708	192,310	236,570
Predominantly French Regions	666,588	839,822	1,309,909	1,583,697	1,898,925
Interior	508,431	609,339	864,816	979,419	1,152,363
Gaspé	119,332	158,058	250,121	297,850	336,271
North	38,825	72,425	194,972	306,428	410,291

Sources: Census of Canada, 1871, 1901, 1931, 1941, 1951, 1956, 1961, 1966, 1971, and 1976.
Note: [a] See Appendix *A*.
[b] See Table *B*.10.
[c] See Table *B*.11.

REGION[a]	1956	1961	1966	1971	1976
Quebec Total	4,628,378	5,259,211	5,780,845	6,027,755	6,234,430
Contact Regions	2,513,345	2,976,542	3,389,313	3,609,750	3,747,870
Outaouais	161,003	181,755	198,459	217,035	243,545
Montreal	2,093,529	2,513,380	2,889,563	3,080,935	3,180,800
Montreal Island and Île-Jésus	1,577,063	1,872,437	2,119,266	2,187,155	2,115,885
Periphery	516,466	640,943	770,297	893,780	1,064,915
Eastern Townships	258,813	281,407	301,291	311,780	323,525
Predominantly French Regions	2,115,033	2,282,669	2,391,532	2,418,005	2,486,560
Interior	1,267,734	1,364,214	1,447,555	1,494,775	1,550,205
Gaspé	367,761	374,516	362,546	348,995	340,885
North	479,538	543,939	581,431	574,235	595,470

Table B.8 *(cont'd.)*

Table B.9
POPULATION BY HOME LANGUAGE, QUEBEC AND REGIONS, 1971

REGION[a]	ALL LANGUAGES	ENGLISH	FRENCH	OTHER
Quebec Total	6,027,765	887,875	4,870,100	269,790
Contact Regions	3,609,740	811,480	2,550,800	247,460
Outaouais	217,040	45,595	168,965	2,480
Montreal	3,080,930	716,895	2,120,785	243,250
Montreal Island and Île-Jésus	2,187,155	572,675	1,383,785	230,695
Periphery	893,775	144,220	737,000	12,555
Eastern Townships	311,770	48,990	261,050	1,730
Predominantly French Regions	2,418,025	76,425	2,319,290	22,310
Interior	1,494,785	33,905	1,456,225	4,655
Gaspé	348,995	15,580	332,495	920
North	574,245	26,940	530,570	16,735

Source: Census of Canada, 1971.
Note: Columns may not add due to rounding.
   [a] See Appendix *A*.

Table B.10

POPULATION BY ETHNIC ORIGIN, QUEBEC AND REGIONS, 1871[a]

REGION[b]	ALL ORIGINS	BRITISH	FRENCH	OTHER
Quebec Total	1,191,516	243,041	929,817	18,658
Contact Regions	524,928	171,428	340,864	12,636
Outaouais	54,205	26,921	24,947	2,337
Montreal	377,972	92,636	279,450	5,886
Montreal Island and Île-Jésus	153,516	54,958	96,171	2,387
Periphery	224,456	37,678	183,279	3,499
Eastern Townships	92,751	51,871	36,467	4,413
Predominantly French Regions	666,588	71,613	588,953	6,022
Interior	508,431	56,856	448,819	2,756
Gaspé	119,332	13,438	104,680	1,214
North	38,825	1,319	35,454	2,052

Source: Census of Canada, 1871.

Note: [a] In spite of boundary changes in many census divisions, it was relatively easy to calculate regional population by ethnic origin. Territorial transfers between census divisions generally took place within a given region. When transfers affected two adjacent regions, the census gave sufficiently detailed geographic information within census subdivisions to enable us to maintain our regional breakdown without risk of error. When territorial transfers involved parts of parishes or villages, we were unable to take this into account, but these changes affected a very limited number of people and were most often made inside the limits of the region.

[b] See Appendix *A*.

Table B.11
POPULATION BY ETHNIC ORIGIN, QUEBEC AND REGIONS, 1901[a]

REGION[b]	ALL ORIGINS	BRITISH	FRENCH	OTHER
Quebec Total	1,648,898	290,169	1,322,115	36,614
Contact Regions	809,076	233,433	549,680	25,963
Outaouais	89,678	32,758	54,290	2,630
Montreal	590,446	146,385	423,646	20,415
Montreal Island and Île-Jésus	371,086	114,293	240,523	16,270
Periphery	219,360	32,092	183,123	4,145
Eastern Townships	128,952	54,290	71,744	2,918
Predominantly French Regions	839,822	56,736	772,435	10,651
Interior	609,339	37,446	566,062	5,831
Gaspé	158,058	16,681	140,051	1,326
North	72,425	2,609	66,322	3,494

Source: Census of Canada, 1901.
Note: [a] See Table *B*.10, Note *a*.
[b] See Appendix *A*.

Table B.12
POPULATION BY ETHNIC ORIGIN, QUEBEC AND REGIONS, 1931

REGION[a]	ALL ORIGINS	BRITISH	FRENCH	OTHER
Quebec Total	2,874,255	432,726	2,270,059	171,470
Contact Regions	1,564,346	374,483	1,037,896	151,967
Outaouais	114,357	27,648	82,311	4,398
Montreal	1,280,281	301,020	834,413	144,848
Montreal Island and Île-Jésus	1,020,018	264,548	619,783	135,687
Periphery	260,263	36,472	214,630	9,161
Eastern Townships	169,708	45,815	121,172	2,721
Predominantly French Regions	1,309,909	58,243	1,232,163	19,503
Interior	864,816	30,551	827,482	6,783
Gaspé	250,121	18,854	229,634	1,633
North	194,972	8,838	175,047	11,087

Source: Census of Canada, 1931.
Note: [a] See Appendix *A*.

Table B.13
POPULATION BY ETHNIC ORIGIN, QUEBEC AND REGIONS, 1941

REGION[a]	ALL ORIGINS	BRITISH	FRENCH	OTHER
Quebec Total	3,331,882	452,887	2,695,032	183,963
Contact Regions	1,748,185	385,788	1,203,376	159,021
Outaouais	118,591	25,763	89,351	3,477
Montreal	1,437,284	315,070	969,660	152,554
Montreal Island and Île-Jésus	1,138,431	274,760	719,240	144,431
Periphery	298,853	40,310	250,420	8,123
Eastern Townships	192,310	44,955	144,365	2,990
Predominantly French Regions	1,583,697	67,099	1,491,656	24,942
Interior	979,419	32,379	939,922	7,118
Gaspé	297,850	19,739	276,177	1,934
North	306,428	14,981	275,557	15,890

Source: Census of Canada, 1941.
Note: [a] See Appendix A.

Table B.14
POPULATION BY ETHNIC ORIGIN, QUEBEC AND REGIONS, 1951

REGION[a]	ALL ORIGINS	BRITISH	FRENCH	OTHER
Quebec Total	4,055,681	491,818	3,327,128	236,735
Contact Regions	2,156,756	422,530	1,527,570	206,656
Outaouais	142,659	28,129	110,303	4,227
Montreal	1,777,527	350,035	1,228,777	198,715
Montreal Island and Île-Jésus	1,358,075	295,980	876,174	185,921
Periphery	419,452	54,055	352,603	12,794
Eastern Townships	236,570	44,366	188,490	3,714
Predominantly French Regions	1,898,925	69,288	1,799,558	30,079
Interior	1,152,363	32,475	1,111,844	8,044
Gaspé	336,271	17,803	315,094	3,374
North	410,291	19,010	372,620	18,661

Source: Census of Canada, 1951.
Note: [a] See Appendix A.

Table B.15
POPULATION BY ETHNIC ORIGIN, QUEBEC AND REGIONS, 1961

REGION[a]	ALL ORIGINS	BRITISH	FRENCH	OTHER
Quebec Total	5,259,211	567,057	4,241,354	450,800
Contact Regions	2,976,542	490,263	2,079,994	406,285
Outaouais	181,755	30,409	144,265	7,081
Montreal	2,513,380	416,346	1,705,375	391,659
Montreal Island and Île-Jésus	1,872,437	328,448	1,183,629	360,360
Periphery	640,943	87,898	521,746	31,299
Eastern Townships	281,407	43,508	230,354	7,545
Predominantly French Regions	2,282,669	76,794	2,161,360	44,515
Interior	1,364,214	35,626	1,312,226	16,362
Gaspé	374,516	17,155	354,142	3,219
North	543,939	24,013	494,992	24,934

Source: Census of Canada, 1961.
Note: [a] See Appendix *A*.

Table B.16
POPULATION BY ETHNIC ORIGIN, QUEBEC AND REGIONS, 1971

REGION[a]	ALL ORIGINS	BRITISH	FRENCH	OTHER
Quebec Total	6,027,765	640,045	4,759,360	628,360
Contact Regions	3,609,735	548,350	2,490,060	571,325
Outaouais	217,035	35,280	171,960	9,795
Montreal	3,080,925	468,405	2,059,595	552,925
Montreal Island and Île-Jésus	2,187,150	351,465	1,333,150	502,535
Periphery	893,775	116,940	726,445	50,390
Eastern Townships	311,775	44,665	258,505	8,605
Predominantly French Regions	2,418,030	91,695	2,269,300	57,035
Interior	1,494,795	45,600	1,424,070	25,125
Gaspé	348,985	19,150	325,760	4,075
North	574,250	26,945	519,470	27,835

Source: Census of Canada, 1971.
Note: [a] See Appendix *A*.

Table B.17
POPULATION BY MOTHER TONGUE, QUEBEC AND REGIONS, 1941

REGION[a]	ALL LANGUAGES	BRITISH	FRENCH	OTHER
Quebec Total	3,331,882	468,996	2,717,287	145,599
Contact Regions	1,748,185	409,753	1,211,906	126,526
Outaouais	118,591	27,390	89,073	2,128
Montreal	1,437,284	336,121	978,674	122,489
Montreal Island and Île-Jésus	1,138,431	296,036	726,807	115,588
Periphery	298,853	40,085	251,867	6,901
Eastern Townships	192,310	46,242	144,159	1,909
Predominantly French Regions	1,583,697	59,243	1,505,381	19,073
Interior	979,419	27,639	947,814	3,966
Gaspé	297,850	16,800	279,941	1,109
North	306,428	14,804	277,626	13,998

Source: Census of Canada, 1941.
Note: [a] See Appendix *A*.

Table B.18
POPULATION BY MOTHER TONGUE, QUEBEC AND REGIONS, 1951

REGION[a]	ALL LANGUAGES	BRITISH	FRENCH	OTHER
Quebec Total	4,055,681	558,256	3,347,030	150,395
Contact Regions	2,156,756	493,204	1,531,913	131,639
Outaouais	142,659	31,525	109,068	2,066
Montreal	1,777,527	414,220	1,235,695	127,612
Montreal Island and Île-Jésus	1,358,075	357,068	881,234	119,773
Periphery	419,452	57,152	354,461	7,839
Eastern Townships	236,570	47,459	187,150	1,961
Predominantly French Regions	1,898,925	65,052	1,815,117	18,756
Interior	1,152,363	29,548	1,119,211	3,604
Gaspé	336,271	15,954	319,199	1,118
North	410,291	19,550	376,707	14,034

Source: Census of Canada, 1951.
Note: [a] See Appendix *A*.

Table B.19

POPULATION BY MOTHER TONGUE, QUEBEC AND REGIONS, 1961

REGION[a]	ALL LANGUAGES	BRITISH	FRENCH	OTHER
Quebec Total	5,259,211	697,402	4,269,689	292,120
Contact Regions	2,976,542	621,943	2,091,755	262,844
Outaouais	181,755	36,048	142,536	3,171
Montreal	2,513,380	537,546	1,719,775	256,059
Montreal Island and Île-Jésus	1,872,437	436,606	1,196,510	239,321
Periphery	640,943	100,940	523,265	16,738
Eastern Townships	281,407	48,349	229,444	3,614
Predominantly French Regions	2,282,669	75,459	2,177,934	29,276
Interior	1,364,214	34,444	1,321,620	8,150
Gaspé	374,516	15,721	356,860	1,935
North	543,939	25,294	499,454	19,191

Source: Census of Canada, 1961.
Note: [a] See Appendix A.

Table B.20

POPULATION BY MOTHER TONGUE, QUEBEC AND REGIONS, 1971

REGION[a]	ALL LANGUAGES	BRITISH	FRENCH	OTHER
Quebec Total	6,027,765	789,185	4,867,250	371,330
Contact Regions	3,609,740	713,695	2,554,745	341,300
Outaouais	217,040	40,830	172,050	4,160
Montreal	3,080,930	625,885	2,121,405	333,640
Montreal Island and Île-Jésus	2,187,150	494,950	1,382,325	209,875
Periphery	893,780	130,935	739,080	23,765
Eastern Townships	311,770	46,980	261,290	3,500
Predominantly French Regions	2,418,025	75,505	2,312,500	30,020
Interior	1,494,785	35,190	1,450,705	8,890
Gaspé	348,995	15,240	332,280	1,475
North	574,245	25,075	529,515	19,655

Source: Census of Canada, 1971.
Note: [a] See Appendix A.

Table B.21
POPULATION BY MOTHER TONGUE,[a] QUEBEC AND REGIONS, 1976

REGION[b]	ALL LANGUAGES	BRITISH	FRENCH	OTHER
Quebec Total	6,234,430	796,665	5,058,260	379,505
Contact Regions	3,747,870	729,120	2,670,580	348,170
Outaouais	243,545	46,080	191,135	6,330
Montreal	3,180,800	637,240	2,206,035	337,525
Montreal Island and Île-Jésus	2,115,885	490,930	1,317,195	307,760
Periphery	1,064,915	146,310	888,840	29,765
Eastern Townships	323,525	45,800	273,410	4,315
Predominantly French Regions	2,486,560	67,545	2,387,680	31,335
Interior	1,550,205	31,090	1,509,145	9,970
Gaspé	340,885	15,155	324,540	1,190
North	595,470	21,300	553,995	20,175

Source: Census of Canada, 1976; and Lachapelle (1982*a*).
Note: [a] See Table *B*.2, Note *c*.
       [b] See Appendix *A*.

Table B.22

POPULATION BY KNOWLEDGE OF OFFICIAL LANGUAGES, QUEBEC AND REGIONS, 1931

REGION[a]	TOTAL	ENGLISH ONLY	FRENCH ONLY	BOTH ENGLISH AND FRENCH	NEITHER ENGLISH NOR FRENCH
Quebec Total	2,874,255	395,995	1,615,155	842,369	20,736
Contact Regions	1,564,346	362,644	575,895	611,490	14,317
Outaouais	114,357	25,341	48,257	40,311	448
Montreal	1,280,281	298,020	454,854	513,659	13,748
Montreal Island and Île-Jésus	1,020,018	267,830	296,283	443,586	12,319
Periphery	260,263	30,190	158,571	70,073	1,429
Eastern Townships	169,708	39,283	72,784	57,520	121
Predominantly French Regions	1,309,909	33,351	1,039,260	230,879	6,419
Interior	864,813	12,967	680,612	170,694	540
Gaspé	250,124	12,458	201,188	36,250	228
North	194,972	7,926	157,460	23,935	5,651

Source: Census of Canada, 1931.
Note: [a] See Appendix *A*.

Table B.23
POPULATION BY KNOWLEDGE OF OFFICIAL LANGUAGES, QUEBEC AND REGIONS, 1941

REGION[a]	TOTAL	ENGLISH ONLY	FRENCH ONLY	BOTH ENGLISH AND FRENCH	NEITHER ENGLISH NOR FRENCH
Quebec Total	3,331,882	410,721	2,016,089	892,984	12,088
Contact Regions	1,748,185	369,422	721,468	652,489	4,806
Outaouais	118,591	23,245	53,235	41,977	134
Montreal	1,437,284	311,064	578,303	543,320	4,597
Montreal Island and Île-Jésus	1,138,431	278,310	390,051	465,923	4,147
Periphery	298,853	32,754	188,252	77,397	450
Eastern Townships	192,310	35,113	89,930	67,192	75
Predominantly French Regions	1,583,697	41,299	1,294,621	240,495	7,282
Interior	979,419	12,079	802,145	164,629	566
Gaspé	297,850	12,969	248,900	35,814	167
North	306,428	16,251	243,576	40,052	6,549

Source: Census of Canada, 1941.
Note: [a] See Appendix *A*.

Table B.24
POPULATION BY KNOWLEDGE OF OFFICIAL LANGUAGES, QUEBEC AND REGIONS, 1951

REGION[a]	TOTAL	ENGLISH ONLY	FRENCH ONLY	BOTH ENGLISH AND FRENCH	NEITHER ENGLISH NOR FRENCH
Quebec Total	4,055,681	462,813	2,534,242	1,038,130	20,496
Contact Regions	2,156,756	421,071	946,144	776,648	12,893
Outaouais	142,659	26,290	65,014	51,023	332
Montreal	1,777,527	360,139	749,663	655,316	12,409
Montreal Island and Île-Jésus	1,358,075	315,875	487,552	542,953	11,695
Periphery	419,452	44,264	262,111	112,363	714
Eastern Townships	236,570	34,642	131,467	70,309	152
Predominantly French Regions	1,898,925	41,742	1,588,098	261,482	7,603
Interior	1,152,363	12,350	961,696	177,818	499
Gaspé	336,271	12,095	291,031	32,932	213
North	410,291	17,297	335,371	50,732	6,891

Source: Census of Canada, 1951.
Note: [a] See Appendix A.

Table B.25

POPULATION BY KNOWLEDGE OF OFFICIAL LANGUAGES, QUEBEC AND REGIONS, 1961

REGION[a]	TOTAL	ENGLISH ONLY	FRENCH ONLY	BOTH ENGLISH AND FRENCH	NEITHER ENGLISH NOR FRENCH
Quebec Total	5,259,211	608,635	3,254,850	1,338,878	56,848
Contact Regions	2,976,542	559,057	1,347,159	1,023,962	46,364
Outaouais	181,755	29,365	83,127	68,532	731
Montreal	2,513,380	494,831	1,097,475	875,918	45,156
Montreal Island and Île-Jésus	1,872,437	414,222	714,756	699,980	43,479
Periphery	640,943	80,609	382,719	175,938	1,677
Eastern Townships	281,407	34,861	166,557	79,512	477
Predominantly French Regions	2,282,669	49,578	1,907,691	314,916	10,484
Interior	1,364,214	16,041	1,137,880	208,713	1,580
Gaspé	374,516	11,685	327,782	34,441	608
North	543,939	21,852	442,029	71,762	8,296

Source: Census of Canada, 1961.
Note: [a] See Appendix *A*.

Table B.26

POPULATION BY KNOWLEDGE OF OFFICIAL LANGUAGES, QUEBEC AND REGIONS, 1971

REGION[a]	TOTAL	ENGLISH ONLY	FRENCH ONLY	BOTH ENGLISH AND FRENCH	NEITHER ENGLISH NOR FRENCH
Quebec Total	6,027,755	632,525	3,667,990	1,663,775	63,440
Contact Regions	3,609,750	589,990	1,677,105	1,287,350	55,280
Outaouais	217,035	30,730	93,530	92,100	670
Montreal	3,080,935	528,545	1,393,470	1,104,470	54,435
Montreal Island and Île-Jésus	2,187,155	433,445	866,380	834,325	52,995
Periphery	893,780	95,100	527,090	270,145	1,440
Eastern Townships	311,780	30,715	180,105	90,780	175
Predominantly French Regions	2,418,005	42,535	1,990,885	376,425	8,160
Interior	1,494,775	11,745	1,231,855	250,145	1,050
Gaspé	348,995	10,835	299,315	38,795	35
North	574,235	19,955	459,715	87,485	7,075

Source: Census of Canada, 1971.
Note: [a] See Appendix *A*.

Table B.27
POPULATION OF CANADA LESS QUEBEC AND REGIONS, 1871–1976

REGION[a]	1871[b]	1901[b]	1931	1941	1951
CANADA LESS QUEBEC	2,294,245[c]	3,722,417[d] (2,973,641)[c]	7,502,531[d]	8,174,773[d]	9,953,748 (9,592,332)[d]
Newfoundland	—	—	—	—	361,416
Prince Edward Island	—	103,259	88,038	95,047	98,429
Nova Scotia	387,800	459,574	512,846	577,962	642,584
New Brunswick	285,594	331,120	408,219	457,401	515,697
North-and-East	104,578	154,219	226,315	256,623	296,344
South	181,016	176,901	181,904	200,778	219,353
Ontario	1,620,851	2,182,947	3,431,683	3,787,655	4,597,542
Southeast	118,786	195,638	264,313	304,866	351,649
Northeast	1,791	35,060	194,534	255,464	293,973
Interior	1,491,697	1,862,816	2,785,335	2,996,695	3,682,128
Northwest	8,577	89,433	187,501	230,630	269,792
Manitoba	—	255,211	700,139	729,744	776,541
Saskatchewan	—	91,279	921,785	895,992	831,728
Alberta	—	73,022	731,605	796,169	939,501
British Columbia	—	178,657	694,263	817,861	1,165,210
Northern Territories	—	47,348	13,953	16,942	25,100

Sources: Census of Canada, 1871, 1901, 1931, 1941, 1951, 1956, 1961, 1966, 1971, and 1976.

Note: [a] See Appendix *A*.

[b] See Tables *B*.10 and *B*.11.

[c] New Brunswick, Nova Scotia, and Ontario only.

[d] Newfoundland not included.

Table B.27 *(cont'd.)*					
REGION[a]	1956	1961	1966	1971	1976
CANADA LESS QUEBEC	11,452,413	12,979,036	14,234,035	15,540,545	16,758,195
Newfoundland	415,074	457,853	493,396	522,100	557,725
Prince Edward Island	99,285	104,629	108,535	111,640	118,230
Nova Scotia	694,717	737,007	756,039	788,960	828,570
New Brunswick	554,616	597,936	616,788	634,560	677,260
North-and-East	319,976	336,392	340,050	345,935	366,080
South	234,640	261,544	276,738	288,625	311,180
Ontario	5,404,933	6,236,092	6,960,870	7,703,105	8,264,475
Southeast	403,060	478,134	533,456	595,830	649,815
Northeast	339,459	383,067	392,123	419,265	417,315
Interior	4,345,671	5,006,152	5,659,367	6,300,535	6,797,530
Northwest	316,743	368,739	375,924	387,475	399,815
Manitoba	850,040	921,686	963,066	988,245	1,021,510
Saskatchewan	880,665	925,181	955,344	926,240	921,325
Alberta	1,123,116	1,331,944	1,463,203	1,627,870	1,838,040
British Columbia	1,398,464	1,629,082	1,873,674	2,184,620	2,466,610
Northern Territories	31,503	37,626	43,120	53,195	64,450

Table B.28
POPULATION BY HOME LANGUAGE,
CANADA LESS QUEBEC AND REGIONS, 1971

REGION[a]	HOME LANGUAGE			
	TOTAL	ENGLISH	FRENCH	OTHER
CANADA LESS QUEBEC	15,540,545	13,558,360	675,920	1,306,265
Newfoundland	522,100	517,210	2,295	2,595
Prince Edward Island	111,640	106,795	4,405	440
Nova Scotia	788,960	753,725	27,220	8,015
New Brunswick	634,560	430,720	199,080	4,760
North-and-East	345,935	151,180	191,760	2,995
South	288,625	279,540	7,325	1,760
Ontario	7,703,105	6,558,060	352,465	792,580
Southeast	595,830	428,355	142,870	24,605
Northeast	419,265	270,075	127,125	22,065
Interior	6,300,535	5,530,345	69,015	701,175
Northwest	387,475	329,290	13,455	44,730
Manitoba	988,245	816,560	39,600	132,085
Saskatchewan	926,240	832,515	15,930	77,795
Alberta	1,627,870	1,477,960	22,700	127,210
British Columbia	2,184,620	2,027,120	11,505	145,995
Northern Territories	53,195	37,690	725	14,780

Source: Census of Canada, 1971.
Note: Columns may not add due to rounding.
   [a] See Appendix *A*.

Table B.29
POPULATION BY ETHNIC ORIGIN,
CANADA LESS QUEBEC AND REGIONS, 1871[a]

REGION[b]	ETHNIC ORIGIN			
	TOTAL	BRITISH	FRENCH	OTHER
CANADA LESS QUEBEC	5,294,245	1,867,461	153,123	273,661
Nova Scotia	387,800	308,224	32,833	46,743
New Brunswick	285,594	226,195	44,907	14,492
North-and-East	104,578	59,170	42,441	2,967
South	181,016	167,025	2,466	11,525
Ontario	1,620,851	1,333,042	75,383	212,426
Southeast	118,786	84,517	28,074	6,195
Northeast	1,791	731	358	702
Interior	1,491,697	1,244,508	45,787	201,402
Northwest	8,577	3,286	1,164	4,127

Source: Census of Canada, 1871.
Note: [a] See Table *B*.10.
 [b] See Appendix *A*.

Table B.30
POPULATION BY ETHNIC ORIGIN, CANADA LESS QUEBEC AND REGIONS, 1901[a]

REGION[b]	ETHNIC ORIGIN			
	TOTAL	BRITISH	FRENCH	OTHER
CANADA LESS QUEBEC	3,722,417	2,773,026	327,256	622,135
Prince Edward Island	103,259	87,883	13,866	1,510
Nova Scotia	459,574	359,064	45,161	55,349
New Brunswick	331,120	237,524	79,979	13,617
North-and-East	154,219	72,739	77,265	4,215
South	176,901	164,785	2,714	9,402
Ontario	2,182,947	1,732,144	158,671	292,132
Southeast	195,638	109,648	72,544	13,446
Northeast	35,060	15,024	14,921	5,115
Interior	1,862,816	1,545,003	64,525	253,288
Northwest	89,433	62,469	6,681	20,283
Manitoba	255,211	164,239	16,021	74,951
Territories[c]	158,940	74,870	7,040	77,030
British Columbia	178,657	106,403	4,600	67,654
Unorganized Northern Territories	52,709	10,899	1,918	39,892

Source: Census of Canada, 1901.
Note: [a] See Table *B*.11.
   [b] See Appendix *A*.
   [c] Includes Alberta, Assiniboia East and West, and Saskatchewan.

Table B.31
POPULATION BY ETHNIC ORIGIN,
CANADA LESS QUEBEC AND REGIONS, 1931

REGION^a	ETHNIC ORIGIN			
	TOTAL	BRITISH	FRENCH	OTHER
CANADA LESS QUEBEC^b	7,502,531	4,948,345	657,931	1,896,255
Prince Edward Island	88,038	73,758	12,962	1,318
Nova Scotia	512,846	391,878	56,629	64,339
New Brunswick	408,219	255,567	136,999	15,653
North-and-East	226,315	89,766	130,627	5,922
South	181,904	165,801	6,372	9,731
Ontario	3,431,683	2,539,771	299,732	592,180
Southeast	264,313	141,595	104,501	18,217
Northeast	194,534	76,816	73,899	43,819
Interior	2,785,335	2,216,802	105,332	463,201
Northwest	187,501	104,558	16,000	66,943
Manitoba	700,139	368,010	47,039	285,090
Saskatchewan	921,785	437,836	50,700	433,249
Alberta	731,605	389,238	38,377	303,990
British Columbia	694,263	489,923	15,028	189,312
Northern Territories	13,953	2,364	465	11,124

Source: Census of Canada, 1931.
Note: ^a See Appendix *A*.
  ^b Not including Newfoundland.

Table B.32
POPULATION BY ETHNIC ORIGIN,
CANADA LESS QUEBEC AND REGIONS, 1941

REGION[a]	ETHNIC ORIGIN			
	TOTAL	BRITISH	FRENCH	OTHER
CANADA LESS QUEBEC[b]	8,174,773	5,263,017	788,005	2,123,751
Prince Edward Island	95,047	78,714	14,799	1,534
Nova Scotia	577,962	445,178	66,260	66,524
New Brunswick	457,401	276,758	163,933	16,710
North-and-East	256,623	97,780	153,000	5,843
South	200,778	178,978	10,933	10,867
Ontario	3,787,655	2,729,830	373,990	683,835
Southeast	304,866	160,201	124,184	20,481
Northeast	255,464	104,314	97,360	53,790
Interior	2,996,695	2,343,169	127,265	526,261
Northwest	230,630	122,146	25,181	83,303
Manitoba	729,744	360,560	52,996	316,188
Saskatchewan	895,992	397,905	50,530	447,557
Alberta	796,169	399,432	42,979	353,758
British Columbia	817,861	571,336	21,876	224,649
Northern Territories	16,942	3,304	642	12,996

Source: Census of Canada, 1941.
Note: [a] See Appendix *A*.
  [b] Not including Newfoundland.

Table B.33
POPULATION BY ETHNIC ORIGIN, CANADA LESS QUEBEC AND REGIONS, 1951

REGION*a*	ETHNIC ORIGIN			
	TOTAL	BRITISH	FRENCH	OTHER
CANADA LESS QUEBEC	9,953,748	6,220,365	990,969	2,742,414
Newfoundland	361,416	337,780	9,481	14,155
Prince Edward Island	98,429	80,669	15,477	2,283
Nova Scotia	642,584	482,571	73,760	86,253
New Brunswick	515,697	294,694	197,631	23,372
North-and-East	296,344	106,272	181,968	8,104
South	219,353	188,422	15,663	15,268
Ontario	4,597,542	3,081,919	477,677	1,037,946
Southeast	351,649	180,015	140,336	31,298
Northeast	293,973	112,909	122,160	58,904
Interior	3,682,128	2,651,948	186,810	843,370
Northwest	269,792	137,047	28,371	104,374
Manitoba	776,541	362,550	66,020	347,971
Saskatchewan	831,728	351,862	51,930	427,936
Alberta	939,501	451,709	56,185	431,607
British Columbia	1,165,210	766,189	41,919	357,102
Northern Territories	25,100	10,422	889	13,789

Source: Census of Canada, 1951.
Note: *a* See Appendix *A*.

Table B.34
POPULATION BY ETHNIC ORIGIN,
CANADA LESS QUEBEC AND REGIONS, 1961

REGION[a]	ETHNIC ORIGIN			
	TOTAL	BRITISH	FRENCH	OTHER
CANADA LESS QUEBEC	12,979,036	7,429,612	1,298,992	4,250,432
Newfoundland	457,853	428,899	17,171	11,783
Prince Edward Island	104,629	83,501	17,418	3,710
Nova Scotia	737,007	525,448	87,883	123,676
New Brunswick	597,936	329,940	232,127	35,869
North-and-East	336,392	115,591	207,974	12,827
South	261,544	214,349	24,153	23,042
Ontario	6,236,092	3,711,536	647,941	1,876,615
Southeast	478,134	231,262	171,769	75,103
Northeast	383,067	135,645	159,098	88,324
Interior	5,006,152	3,176,890	271,727	1,557,535
Northwest	368,739	167,739	45,347	155,653
Manitoba	921,686	396,445	83,936	441,305
Saskatchewan	925,181	373,482	59,824	491,875
Alberta	1,331,944	601,755	83,319	646,870
British Columbia	1,629,082	966,881	66,970	595,231
Northern Territories	37,626	11,725	2,403	23,498

Source: Census of Canada, 1961.
Note: [a] See Appendix *A*.

Table B.35
POPULATION BY ETHNIC ORIGIN,
CANADA LESS QUEBEC AND REGIONS, 1971

REGION[a]	ETHNIC ORIGIN			
	TOTAL	BRITISH	FRENCH	OTHER
CANADA LESS QUEBEC	15,540,540	8,984,070	1,420,765	5,135,705
Newfoundland	522,100	489,565	15,410	17,125
Prince Edward Island	111,640	92,285	15,325	4,030
Nova Scotia	788,960	611,310	80,215	97,435
New Brunswick	634,555	365,735	235,025	33,795
North-and-East	345,940	124,760	208,480	12,700
South	288,620	240,975	26,545	21,100
Ontario	7,703,105	4,576,010	737,360	2,389,735
Southeast	595,845	307,030	190,695	98,120
Northeast	419,270	160,150	173,395	85,725
Interior	6,300,505	3,924,735	328,320	2,047,450
Northwest	387,485	184,095	44,950	158,440
Manitoba	988,250	414,125	86,510	487,615
Saskatchewan	926,245	390,190	56,200	479,855
Alberta	1,627,875	761,665	94,665	771,545
British Columbia	2,184,620	1,265,455	96,550	822,615
Northern Territories	53,190	17,730	3,505	31,955

Source: Census of Canada, 1971.
Note: [a] See Appendix *A*.

Table B.36
POPULATION BY MOTHER TONGUE,
CANADA LESS QUEBEC, 1931

REGION	MOTHER TONGUE			
	TOTAL	ENGLISH	FRENCH	OTHER
Canada Less Quebec	7,502,531	5,484,789	540,105	1,477,637
Prince Edward Island	88,038	76,326	10,137	1,575
Nova Scotia	512,846	436,498	39,018	37,330
New Brunswick	408,219	268,603	133,385	6,231
Ontario	3,431,683	2,796,821	236,386	398,476
Manitoba	700,139	399,009	42,499	258,631
Saskatchewan	921,785	516,842	42,283	362,660
Alberta	731,605	461,713	28,145	241,747
British Columbia	694,263	526,216	7,768	160,279
Northern Territories	13,953	2,761	484	10,708

Source: Census of Canada, 1931.

Note: Population statistics by mother tongue at the census division level were not available in 1931, and we were thus unable to establish distributions for regions within provinces.

Table B.37
POPULATION BY MOTHER TONGUE,
CANADA LESS QUEBEC AND REGIONS, 1941

REGION[a]	MOTHER TONGUE			
	TOTAL	ENGLISH	FRENCH	OTHER
CANADA LESS QUEBEC[b]	8,174,773	6,019,194	647,466	1,508,113
Prince Edward Island	95,047	83,242	10,678	1,127
Nova Scotia	577,962	514,043	41,350	22,569
New Brunswick	457,401	293,339	157,862	6,200
North-and-East	256,623	101,910	151,268	3,445
South	200,778	191,429	6,594	2,755
Ontario	3,787,655	3,073,320	289,146	425,189
Southeast	304,866	178,905	115,200	10,761
Northeast	255,464	120,790	92,666	42,008
Interior	2,996,695	2,625,130	67,577	303,988
Northwest	230,630	148,495	13,703	68,432
Manitoba	729,744	408,544	51,546	269,654
Saskatchewan	895,992	499,925	43,728	352,339
Alberta	796,169	500,926	41,451	253,792
British Columbia	817,861	641,419	11,058	165,384
Northern Territories	16,942	4,436	647	11,859

Source: Census of Canada, 1941.
Note: [a] See Appendix *A*.
   [b] Not including Newfoundland.

Table B.38
POPULATION BY MOTHER TONGUE,
CANADA LESS QUEBEC AND REGIONS, 1951

REGION[a]	MOTHER TONGUE			
	TOTAL	ENGLISH	FRENCH	OTHER
CANADA LESS QUEBEC	9,953,748	7,722,553	721,820	1,509,375
Newfoundland	361,416	357,328	2,321	1,767
Prince Edward Island	98,429	89,241	8,477	711
Nova Scotia	642,584	588,610	38,945	15,029
New Brunswick	515,697	325,412	185,110	5,175
North-and-East	296,344	116,674	176,624	3,046
South	219,353	208,738	8,486	2,129
Ontario	4,597,542	3,755,442	341,502	500,598
Southeast	351,649	215,548	125,567	10,534
Northeast	293,973	145,563	110,421	37,989
Interior	3,682,128	3,209,177	89,775	383,176
Northwest	269,792	185,154	15,739	68,899
Manitoba	776,541	467,892	54,199	254,450
Saskatchewan	831,728	515,873	36,815	279,040
Alberta	939,501	648,413	34,196	256,892
British Columbia	1,165,210	963,920	19,366	181,924
Northern Territories	25,100	10,422	889	13,789

Source: Census of Canada, 1951.
Note: [a] See Appendix *A*.

<table>
<tr><td colspan="5" align="center">Table B.39
POPULATION BY MOTHER TONGUE,
CANADA LESS QUEBEC AND REGIONS, 1961</td></tr>
</table>

REGION[a]	MOTHER TONGUE			
	TOTAL	ENGLISH	FRENCH	OTHER
CANADA LESS QUEBEC	12,979,036	9,963,132	853,462	2,162,442
Newfoundland	457,853	451,530	3,150	3,173
Prince Edward Island	104,629	95,564	7,958	1,107
Nova Scotia	737,007	680,233	39,568	17,206
New Brunswick	597,936	378,633	210,530	8,773
North-and-East	336,392	133,128	198,777	4,487
South	261,544	245,505	11,753	4,286
Ontario	6,236,092	4,834,623	425,302	976,167
Southeast	478,134	296,601	149,937	31,596
Northeast	383,067	193,212	138,112	51,743
Interior	5,006,152	4,090,910	113,469	801,773
Northwest	368,739	253,900	23,784	91,055
Manitoba	921,686	584,526	60,899	276,261
Saskatchewan	925,181	638,156	36,163	250,862
Alberta	1,331,944	962,319	42,276	327,349
British Columbia	1,629,082	1,318,498	26,179	284,405
Northern Territories	37,626	19,050	1,437	17,139

Source: Census of Canada, 1961.
Note: [a] See Appendix *A*.

Table B.40
POPULATION BY MOTHER TONGUE,
CANADA LESS QUEBEC AND REGIONS, 1971

REGION[a]	MOTHER TONGUE			
	TOTAL	ENGLISH	FRENCH	OTHER
CANADA LESS QUEBEC	15,540,545	12,184,625	926,400	2,429,520
Newfoundland	522,100	514,520	3,640	3,940
Prince Edward Island	111,645	103,105	7,360	1,180
Nova Scotia	788,960	733,555	39,335	16,070
New Brunswick	634,560	410,400	215,725	8,435
North-and-East	345,940	141,140	200,625	4,175
South	288,620	269,260	15,100	4,260
Ontario	7,703,105	5,971,570	482,045	1,249,490
Southeast	595,830	389,705	162,980	43,145
Northeast	419,275	227,425	149,850	42,000
Interior	6,300,520	5,067,705	146,360	1,086,455
Northwest	387,480	286,735	22,855	77,890
Manitoba	988,250	662,720	60,545	264,985
Saskatchewan	926,240	685,920	31,605	208,715
Alberta	1,627,875	1,263,935	46,500	317,440
British Columbia	2,184,620	1,807,255	38,035	339,330
Northern Territories	53,195	31,655	1,615	19,925

Source: Census of Canada, 1971.
Note: [a] See Appendix *A*.

Table B.41
POPULATION BY MOTHER TONGUE,
CANADA LESS QUEBEC AND REGIONS, 1976 [a]

REGION[b]	MOTHER TONGUE			
	TOTAL	ENGLISH	FRENCH	OTHER
CANADA LESS QUEBEC	16,758,195	13,352,855	908,440	2,496,900
Newfoundland	557,725	550,710	2,730	4,285
Prince Edward Island	118,230	110,535	6,590	1,105
Nova Scotia	828,570	775,285	37,300	15,985
New Brunswick	677,260	442,245	226,695	8,320
North-and-East	366,080	150,135	212,255	3,690
South	311,180	292,110	14,440	4,630
Ontario	8,264,475	6,467,830	467,540	1,329,105
Southeast	649,815	430,085	166,785	52,945
Northeast	417,315	238,470	143,850	34,995
Interior	6,797,530	5,490,605	135,940	1,170,985
Northwest	399,815	308,670	20,965	70,180
Manitoba	1,021,510	719,880	55,605	246,025
Saskatchewan	921,325	706,640	26,890	187,795
Alberta	1,838,040	1,484,060	44,810	309,170
British Columbia	2,466,610	2,053,475	38,635	374,500
Northern Territories	64,450	42,195	1,645	20,610

Sources: Census of Canada, 1976; and Lachapelle (1982*a*).
Notes: [a] See Note *c*, Table *B*.2.
    [b] See Appendix *A*.

Table B.42
POPULATION BY KNOWLEDGE OF OFFICIAL LANGUAGES,
CANADA LESS QUEBEC AND REGIONS, 1931

REGION[a]		KNOWLEDGE OF OFFICIAL LANGUAGES			
	TOTAL	ENGLISH ONLY	FRENCH ONLY	BOTH ENGLISH AND FRENCH	NEITHER ENGLISH NOR FRENCH
CANADA LESS QUEBEC[b]	7,502,531	6,603,918	164,183	480,001	254,429
Prince Edward Island	88,038	77,120	1,335	9,511	72
Nova Scotia	512,846	467,374	9,516	34,153	1,803
New Brunswick	408,219	267,371	66,255	74,080	513
North-and-East	226,315	90,456	65,794	69,752	313
South	181,904	176,915	461	4,328	200
Ontario	3,431,683	3,096,682	64,534	219,532	50,935
Southeast	264,313	154,834	33,610	75,160	709
Northeast	194,534	111,145	23,776	51,807	7,806
Interior	2,785,335	2,667,267	6,061	80,247	31,760
Northwest	187,501	163,436	1,087	12,318	10,660
Manitoba	700,139	600,139	9,280	43,397	47,323
Saskatchewan	921,785	808,100	7,059	44,463	62,163
Alberta	731,605	646,838	5,747	32,992	46,028
British Columbia	694,263	635,950	361	21,119	36,833
Northern Territories	13,953	4,344	96	754	8,759

Source: Census of Canada, 1931.
Note: [a] See Appendix *A*.
     [b] Not including Newfoundland.

Table B.43
POPULATION BY KNOWLEDGE OF OFFICIAL LANGUAGES,
CANADA LESS QUEBEC AND REGIONS, 1941

| REGION[a] | KNOWLEDGE OF OFFICIAL LANGUAGES | | | | |
	TOTAL	ENGLISH ONLY	FRENCH ONLY	BOTH ENGLISH AND FRENCH	NEITHER ENGLISH NOR FRENCH
CANADA LESS QUEBEC[b]	8,174,773	7,324,765	165,657	581,025	103,326
Prince Edward Island	95,047	83,814	955	10,262	16
Nova Scotia	577,962	530,467	6,800	40,253	442
New Brunswick	457,401	291,023	82,381	83,660	337
North-and-East	256,623	98,770	81,699	76,047	107
South	200,778	192,253	682	7,613	230
Ontario	3,787,655	3,425,266	61,533	283,195	17,661
Southeast	304,866	174,183	32,224	98,136	323
Northeast	255,464	153,907	25,620	73,711	2,226
Interior	2,996,695	2,891,601	3,195	95,331	6,568
Northwest	230,630	205,575	494	16,017	8,544
Manitoba	729,744	647,010	6,069	54,636	22,029
Saskatchewan	895,992	822,899	4,039	46,906	22,148
Alberta	796,169	738,582	3,322	37,057	17,208
British Columbia	817,861	777,860	254	23,525	16,222
Northern Territories	16,942	7,844	304	1,531	7,263

Source: Census of Canada, 1941.
Note: [a] See Appendix *A*.
[b] Not including Newfoundland.

Table B.44

POPULATION BY KNOWLEDGE OF OFFICIAL LANGUAGES, CANADA LESS QUEBEC AND REGIONS, 1951

REGION[a]		KNOWLEDGE OF OFFICIAL LANGUAGES			
	TOTAL	ENGLISH ONLY	FRENCH ONLY	BOTH ENGLISH AND FRENCH	NEITHER ENGLISH NOR FRENCH
CANADA LESS QUEBEC	9,953,748	8,924,582	207,570	689,317	132,279
Newfoundland	361,416	356,377	153	3,990	896
Prince Edward Island	98,429	88,743	914	8,745	27
Nova Scotia	642,584	595,257	7,462	39,524	341
New Brunswick	515,697	318,560	100,712	96,095	330
North-and-East	296,344	110,787	99,489	85,887	181
South	219,353	207,773	1,223	10,208	149
Ontario	4,597,542	4,115,584	78,974	359,965	43,019
Southeast	351,649	204,987	38,207	107,550	905
Northeast	293,973	169,305	30,676	90,595	3,397
Interior	3,682,128	3,500,741	8,041	143,713	29,633
Northwest	269,792	240,551	2,050	18,107	9,084
Manitoba	776,541	685,914	7,869	58,441	24,317
Saskatchewan	831,728	767,248	4,656	40,789	19,035
Alberta	939,501	868,696	5,922	40,785	24,098
British Columbia	1,165,210	1,112,937	727	39,433	12,113
Northern Territories	25,100	15,266	181	1,550	8,103

Source: Census of Canada, 1951.

Note: [a] See Appendix *A*.

Table B.45

POPULATION BY KNOWLEDGE OF OFFICIAL LANGUAGES, CANADA LESS QUEBEC AND REGIONS, 1961

REGION[a]	KNOWLEDGE OF OFFICIAL LANGUAGES				
	TOTAL	ENGLISH ONLY	FRENCH ONLY	BOTH ENGLISH AND FRENCH	NEITHER ENGLISH NOR FRENCH
CANADA LESS QUEBEC	12,979,036	11,676,127	235,016	892,294	175,599
Newfoundland	457,853	450,945	522	5,299	1,087
Prince Edward Island	104,629	95,296	1,219	7,938	176
Nova Scotia	737,007	684,805	5,938	44,987	1,277
New Brunswick	597,936	370,922	112,054	113,495	1,465
North-and-East	336,392	125,757	110,735	98,775	1,125
South	261,544	245,165	1,319	14,720	340
Ontario	6,236,092	5,548,766	95,236	493,270	98,820
Southeast	478,134	292,851	41,999	138,895	4,389
Northeast	383,067	224,655	36,703	116,013	5,696
Interior	5,006,152	4,706,054	12,573	211,428	76,097
Northwest	368,739	325,206	3,961	26,934	12,638
Manitoba	921,686	825,955	7,954	68,368	19,409
Saskatchewan	925,181	865,821	3,853	42,074	13,433
Alberta	1,331,944	1,253,824	5,534	56,920	15,666
British Columbia	1,629,082	1,552,560	2,559	57,504	16,459
Northern Territories	37,626	27,233	147	2,439	7,807

Source: Census of Canada, 1961.
Note: [a] See Appendix *A*.

Table B.46

POPULATION BY KNOWLEDGE OF OFFICIAL LANGUAGES, CANADA LESS QUEBEC AND REGIONS, 1971

REGION[a]	KNOWLEDGE OF OFFICIAL LANGUAGES				
	TOTAL	ENGLISH ONLY	FRENCH ONLY	BOTH ENGLISH AND FRENCH	NEITHER ENGLISH NOR FRENCH
CANADA LESS QUEBEC	15,540,535	13,837,020	211,240	1,236,360	255,910
Newfoundland	522,100	511,620	510	9,350	625
Prince Edward Island	111,640	101,820	680	9,110	30
Nova Scotia	788,960	730,700	4,185	53,035	1,035
New Brunswick	634,560	396,855	100,985	136,115	600
North-and-East	345,935	129,715	99,655	116,175	400
South	288,625	267,140	1,330	19,940	200
Ontario	7,703,105	6,724,100	92,845	716,065	170,090
Southeast	595,830	370,035	41,095	180,200	4,495
Northeast	419,265	239,850	35,295	140,390	3,720
Interior	6,300,535	5,773,020	12,925	363,110	151,480
Northwest	387,475	341,195	3,530	32,365	10,395
Manitoba	988,245	881,715	5,020	800,935	20,585
Saskatchewan	926,240	867,315	1,825	45,985	11,110
Alberta	1,627,870	1,525,575	3,310	81,000	17,990
British Columbia	2,184,620	2,054,690	1,775	101,435	26,725
Northern Territories	53,195	42,630	105	3,330	7,120

Source: Census of Canada, 1971.
Note: [a] See Appendix *A*.

Bibliography

Arès, Richard. 1975. *Les positions ethniques, linguistiques et religieuses des Canadiens français à la suite du recensement de 1971.* Montreal: Les Éditions Bellarmin.

Baillargeon, Mireille and Benjamin, Claire. 1978. *Les futurs linguistiques possibles de la région métropolitaine de Montréal en 2001.* Montreal: Ministère de l'Immigration, Direction de la recherche.

Beaujot, Roderic P. 1979. "A Demographic View on Canadian Language Policy." *Canadian Public Policy* 5 (Winter): 16–29.

Benjamin, Claire and Baillargeon, Mireille. 1977. "Les futurs linguistiques possibles de Montréal : aspects méthodologiques." *Cahiers québécois de démographie* 6, No. 3 (Special): 9–32

Bernard, Jean-Thomas. 1978. "La mobilité linguistique et l'attraction des langues au Québec." Quebec: Université Laval, Département d'économie (mimeo.).

Biays, Pierre. 1967. "Southern Quebec." In *Canada, a Geographical Interpretation,* edited by John Warkentin, pp. 281–333. Toronto: Methuen.

Billette, André. 1977. "Les inégalités sociales de mortalité au Québec." *Recherches sociographiques* 18 (September-December): 415–30.

Blackstone, G.J. and Gosselin, J.-F. 1974. "1971 Evaluation Project MP-1, 1971 Reverse Record Check." Results Memorandum CDN 71-E-3 (Part 1). Ottawa: Statistics Canada, Census Field (mimeo.).

Blau, Peter M. 1977. *Inequality and Heterogeneity: A Primitive Theory of Social Structure.* New York: Free Press.

Boudon, Raymond. 1971a. *La crise de la sociologie.* Geneva: Droz.

Boudon, Raymond. 1971b. *The Uses of Structuralism.* Translated by Michalina Vaughn. London: Heinemann.

Boudon, Raymond. 1974. *The Logic of Sociological Explanation.* Translated by Tom Burns. Harmondsworth: Penguin.

Brewis, T.N. 1969. *Regional Economic Policies in Canada.* Toronto: Macmillan.

Caldwell, Gary. 1974. *A Demographic Profile of the English-Speaking Population of Quebec, 1921–1971.* Quebec: International Centre for Research on Bilingualism.

Camu, Pierre; Weeks, E.P.; and Sametz, Z.M. 1964. *Economic Geography of Canada.* Toronto: Macmillan.

Canada, 1958. "Developments in Canadian Immigration." In *Canada Year Book, 1957–1958,* pp. 154–76. Ottawa: Queen's Printer.

Canada. Bilingual Districts Advisory Board. 1975. *Report of the Bilingual Districts Advisory Board.* Ottawa: Information Canada.

Canada. Department of Manpower and Immigration. 1975. *Internal Migration and Immigrant Settlement*. Ottawa: Information Canada.

Canada. Royal Commission on Bilingualism and Biculturalism. 1967. *The Official Languages* (Book I). Ottawa: Queen's Printer.

Canada. Royal Commission on Bilingualism and Biculturalism. 1969. *The Work World* (Book III). Ottawa: Queen's Printer.

Canada. Royal Commission on Bilingualism and Biculturalism. 1970. *The Cultural Contribution of the Other Ethnic Groups* (Book IV). Ottawa: Queen's Printer.

Canada. Statistics Canada. 1975. *Technical Report on Population Projections for Canada and the Provinces, 1972–2001*. Cat. No. 91–516. Ottawa: Information Canada.

Canada. Statistics Canada. 1977. *International and Interprovincial Migration in Canada, 1961–1962 to 1975–1976*. Cat. No. 91–208. Ottawa: Information Canada.

Canada. Statistics Canada. 1978. *Vital Statistics, 1975*. Vol. III—*Deaths*. Cat. No. 84–206. Ottawa: Minister of Supply and Services Canada.

Canada. Statistics Canada. 1979. *Population Projections for Canada and the Provinces, 1976–2001*. Cat. No. 91–520. Ottawa: Minister of Supply and Services Canada.

Cartwright, Donald G. 1976. *Language Zones in Canada*. A Reference Supplement to the Report of the Second Bilingual Districts Advisory Board. Ottawa.

Cartwright, Donald G. 1980. *Official Language Populations in Canada: Patterns and Contacts*. Montreal: The Institute for Research on Public Policy.

Castonguay, Charles. 1974. "Dimensions des transferts linguistiques entre groupes anglophone, francophone et autres d'après le recensement canadien de 1971." *Bulletin de l'Association des démographes du Québec* 3, No. 1 (Special): 110–24.

Castonguay, Charles. 1976*a*. "Quelques remarques sur les données du recensement de 1971 concernant la langue et l'origine ethnique." *Cahiers québécois de démographie* 5, No. 3 (Special): 211–41.

Castonguay, Charles. 1976*b*. "Les transferts linguistiques au foyer." *Recherches sociographiques* 17 (September-December): 341–51.

Castonguay, Charles. 1977. "La mobilité ethnique au Canada." *Recherches sociographiques* 18 (September-December): 431–50.

Castonguay, Charles. 1979*a*. "Why Hide the Facts? The Federalist Approach to the Language Crisis in Canada." *Canadian Public Policy* 5 (Winter): 4–15.

Castonguay, Charles. 1979*b*. "Exogamie et anglicisation chez les minorités canadiennes-françaises." *Canadian Review of Sociology and Anthropology* 16 (February): 21–31.

Castonguay, Charles and Marion, Jacques. 1974. "L'anglicisation du Canada." *Bulletin de l'Association des démographes du Québec* 3, No. 1: 19–40.

Charbonneau, Hubert and Maheu, Robert. 1973. *Les aspects démographiques de la question linguistique.* Synthesis S 3 prepared for the Commission of Inquiry into the Position of the French Language and Linguistic Rights in Quebec. Quebec: Éditeur officiel du Québec.

Charles, Enid. 1948. *The Changing Size of the Family in Canada.* Census Monograph No. 1. Ottawa: King's Printer.

Coale, Ansley J. 1959. "Increases in Expectation of Life and Population Growth." International Union for the Scientific Study of Population, *Proceedings* (Vienna), pp. 36–41.

Coale, Ansley J. 1972. *The Growth and Structure of Human Populations: A Mathematical Investigation.* Princeton, N.J.: Princeton University Press.

Coleman, James S. 1964. *Introduction to Mathematical Sociology.* New York: Free Press.

Courchene, Thomas J. 1974. *Migration, Income and Employment: Canada 1965–1968.* Montreal: C.D. Howe Research Institute.

Demers, Linda. 1979. "Évaluation de la qualité des informations ethniques et linguistiques fournies par les recensements canadiens, 1901 à 1976." Master's thesis, Université de Montréal, Départment de démographie.

Desrosiers, Denise; Gregory, Joël M.; and Piché, Victor. 1978. *La migration au Québec : synthèse et bilan bibliographique.* Quebec: Ministère de l'Immigration.

De Vries, John. 1974. "Net Effects of Language Shift in Finland, 1951–1960: A Demographic Analysis." *Acta Sociologica* 17, No. 2: 140–49.

De Vries, John. 1977a. "Explorations in the Demography of Language: Estimation of Net Language Shift in Finland, 1961–1970." *Acta Sociologica* 20, No. 2: 145–53.

De Vries, John. 1977b. "Languages in Contact: A Review of Canadian Research." In *The Individual, Language and Society in Canada*, edited by W.H. Coons, D.M. Taylor, and M.-A. Tremblay, pp. 15–43. Ottawa: The Canada Council.

De Vries, John and Vallee, Frank G. 1975. *Data Book on Aspects of Language Demography in Canada.* Study prepared for the Conference on the Individual, Language and Society. Ottawa: The Canada Council.

De Vries, John and Vallee, Frank G. 1980. *Language Use in Canada.* 1971 Census Analytical Study. Cat. No. 99–762. Ottawa: Minister of Supply and Services Canada.

Dorn, Harold F. 1950. "Pitfalls in Population Forecasts and Projections." *Journal of the American Statistical Association* 45 (September): 311–34.

Duchesne, Louis, 1977. "Analyse descriptive du bilinguisme au Québec selon la langue maternelle en 1951, 1961 et 1971." *Cahiers québécois de démographie* 6, No. 3 (Special): 33–65.

Economic Council of Canada. 1977. *Living Together: A Study of Regional Disparities*. Ottawa: Minister of Supply and Services Canada.

Fédération des Francophones hors Québec. 1977. *Les héritiers de Lord Durham*, Vol. 2. Ottawa.

Gosselin, J.-F. 1975. "Estimation of Intercensal Emigration Derived from the 1971 Reverse Record Check." Ottawa: Statistics Canada, Census Field (mimeo.).

Grant, E. Kenneth and Vanderkamp, John. 1976. *The Economic Causes and Effects of Migration: Canada, 1965—1971*. Study prepared for the Economic Council of Canada. Ottawa: Information Canada.

Great Britain. Central Statistical Office. 1974, 1977. *Social Trends*, Nos. 5 and 8. London: Her Majesty's Stationery Office.

Gryz, Zbigniew J. 1977. "A Modification of Lieberson's Technique for Estimating Intergenerational Language Shift." In *Language Maintenance and Language Shift in Canada: New Dimensions in the Use of Census Language Data*, edited by Paul Lamy, pp. 95—113. Ottawa: University of Ottawa Press.

Hajnal, John. 1955. "The Prospects for Population Forecasts." *Journal of the American Statistical Association* 50 (June): 309—22.

Henripin, Jacques. 1954. *La population canadienne au début du XVIIIe siècle*. Paris: Presses Universitaires de France.

Henripin, Jacques. 1961. "L'inégalité sociale devant la mort : la mortinalité et la mortalité infantile à Montréal." *Recherches sociographiques* 2, No. 1: 3—34.

Henripin, Jacques. 1972. *Trends and Factors of Fertility in Canada*. 1961 Census Monograph. Ottawa: Queen's Printer.

Henripin, Jacques. 1974. *Immigration and Language Imbalance*. Study commissioned for the Canadian Immigration and Population Study. Ottawa: Information Canada.

Henripin, Jacques; Charbonneau, Hubert; and Mertens, Walter. 1966. "Étude des aspects démographiques des problèmes ethniques et linguistiques au Canada." Unpublished report prepared for the Royal Commission on Bilingualism and Biculturalism.

Henripin, Jacques and Lachapelle, Réjean. 1982. "Mesure et description des différences de fécondité entre les groupes linguistiques." Montreal: The Institute for Research on Public Policy (forthcoming).

Henripin, Jacques and Peron, Yves. 1972. "The Demographic Transition of the Province of Quebec." In *Population and Social Change*, edited by D.V. Glass and Roger Revelle, pp. 213—31. London: Edward Arnold.

Henshel, Richard L. 1976. *On the Future of Social Prediction*. Indianapolis: Bobbs-Merrill.

Hetman, François. 1969. *Le langage de la prévision/The Language of Forecasting*. Paris: S.E.D.E.I.S. (coll. "futuribles").

I.N.E.D. 1977. "Sixième rapport sur la situation démographique de la France." *Population* 32 (March-April): 253−338.

Jacquard, Albert. 1970. *Structures génétiques des populations.* Paris: Masson.

Johnston, John. 1972. *Econometric Methods.* New York: McGraw-Hill.

Joy, Richard J. 1967. *Languages in Conflict: The Canadian Experience.* Ottawa: The Author.

Joy, Richard J. 1975. "Mesure des transferts linguistiques : faiblesse des données du recensement de 1971." *Cahiers québécois de démographie* 4, No. 1: 1−9.

Joy, Richard J. 1978. *Canada's Official Language Minorities.* Montreal: C.D. Howe Research Institute.

Kasahara, Y. 1963. "The Flow of Migration Among the Provinces in Canada, 1951−1961." *CPSA Conference on Statistics, 1961 Papers,* pp. 20−48. Toronto: University of Toronto Press.

Kelly, John J. 1977. "Alternative Estimates of the Volume of Emigration from Canada, 1961−71." *Canadian Review of Sociology and Anthropology* 14 (February): 57−67.

Keyfitz, Nathan. 1950. "The Growth of Canadian Population." *Population Studies* 4, No. 1: 47−63.

Keyfitz, Nathan. 1972. "On Future Population." *Journal of the American Statistical Association* 67 (June): 347−63.

Kralt, John M. 1976. *Language in Canada.* 1971 Census Profile Study. Cat. No. 99−707. Ottawa: Minister of Supply and Services Canada.

Kralt, John M. 1977. *Ethnic Origins of Canadians.* 1971 Census Profile Study. Cat. No. 99−709. Ottawa: Minister of Supply and Services Canada.

Lachapelle, Réjean. 1974. "La fécondité au Québec et en Ontario : quelques éléments de comparaison." *Canadian Studies in Population* 1: 13−28.

Lachapelle, Réjean. 1976. "Démographie et prospective." *Cahiers québécois de démographie* 5, No. 3 (Special): 347−83.

Lachapelle, Réjean. 1977a. "Quelques notes à propos de la comparabilité de la composition par langue maternelle aux recensements de 1971 et de 1976." *Cahiers québécois de démographie* 6, No. 3 (Special): 93−136.

Lachapelle, Réjean 1977b. "Prévisions démographiques et processus de décision." *Cahiers québécois de démographie* 6, No. 3 (Special): 267−79.

Lachapelle, Réjean. 1979. "Regard sur la population québécoise." *Annuaire du Québec, 1977−1978,* pp. 228−38. Quebec: Éditeur officielle du Québec.

Lachapelle, Réjean. 1980. "Evolution of Ethnic and Linguistic Composition." In *Cultural Boundaries and the Cohesion of Canada,* by Raymond Breton, Jeffrey G. Reitz, and Victor Valentine, pp. 17−36. Montreal: The Institute for Research on Public Policy.

Lachapelle, Réjean. 1982*a*. "Note à propos des problèmes que pose la comparaison des effectifs de la population selon la langue maternelle aux recensements de 1971 et de 1976." Montreal: The Institute for Research on Public Policy (forthcoming).

Lachapelle, Réjean. 1982*b*. "Quelques mesures de la mortalité différentielle entre les groupes linguistiques et estimation de son impact sur la croissance démographique." Montreal: The Institute for Research on Public Policy (forthcoming).

Lachapelle, Réjean. 1982*c*. "Définition, analyse et mesure de la mobilité linguistique." Montreal: The Institute for Research on Public Policy (forthcoming).

Lachapelle, Réjean and Gervais, Michèle. 1982. "Difficultés d'estimation de la migration nette par langue maternelle et par origine ethnique." Montreal: The Institute for Research on Public Policy (forthcoming).

Lavoie, Yolande. 1973. "Les mouvements migratoires des Canadiens entre leur pays et les États-Unis au XIXe et au XXe siècles." In *La population du Québec : études rétrospectives*, by Hubert Charbonneau, pp. 73–88. Montreal: Les Éditions du Boréal Express.

Lee, Everett S. 1966. "A Theory of Migration." *Demography* 3, No. 1: 47–57.

Lieberson, Stanley. 1970. *Language and Ethnic Relations in Canada*. New York: John Wiley.

Loslier, Luc. 1976. *La mortalité dans les aires sociales de la région métropolitaine de Montréal*. Quebec: Ministère des Affaires sociales, Service des études épidémiologiques.

Maheu, Robert. 1968. "Les francophones au Canada : 1941–1991." Master's thesis, Université de Montréal, Département de démographie.

Maheu, Robert. 1970. *Les francophones au Canada : 1941–1991*. Montreal: Parti Pris.

Martin, Fernand. 1979. *Montreal, an Economic Perspective*. Montreal: C.D. Howe Research Institute.

Mayer, K. B. 1977. "Groupes linguistiques en Suisse." *Recherches sociologiques* 8, No. 1: 75–94.

McInnis, R. Marvin. 1974. "Census Survival Ratio Estimates of Net Migration for Canadian Regions." *Canadian Studies in Population* 1: 93–116.

Merton, Robert K. 1957. *Social Theory and Social Structures*, rev. and enlarged ed. New York: Free Press.

Popper, Karl R. 1972*a*. *The Logic of Scientific Discovery*, 3d ed. rev. London: Hutchinson.

Popper, Karl R. 1972*b*. *Objective Knowledge: An Evolutionary Approach*. Oxford: Clarendon Press.

Porter, John. 1965. *The Vertical Mosaic: An Analysis of Social Power and Class in Canada*. Toronto: University of Toronto Press.

Preston, Samuel H. 1977. ''Mortality Trends.'' *Annual Review of Sociology* 3: 163–78.

Quebec. Commission of Inquiry into the Position of the French Language and Linguistic Rights in Quebec. 1973. *The Position of the French Language in Quebec*. Vol I: *The Language of Work*. Quebec: Éditeur officiel du Québec.

Quebec. Office de planification et de développement du Québec (O.P.D.Q.). 1976. *Les caractéristiques sectorielles interrégionales*, cahier 1, *Les indicateurs globaux*. Quebec: Éditeur officiel du Québec.

Richmond, Anthony H. and Kalbach, Warren E. 1980. *Factors in the Adjustment of Immigrants and Their Descendants*. 1971 Census Analytical Study. Cat. No. 99–761. Ottawa: Minister of Supply and Services Canada.

Rochon-Lesage, Madeleine and Maheu, Robert. 1975. ''Composition ethnique et linguistique de la population du Québec.'' *Annuaire du Québec, 1974*, pp. 206–12. Quebec: Éditeur officiel du Québec.

Rogers, Andrei. 1975. *Introduction to Multiregional Mathematical Demography*. New York: John Wiley.

Roy, Laurent. 1975*a*. ''La mortalité selon la cause de décès et l'origine ethnique au Québec, 1951–1961–1971.'' Master's thesis, Université de Montréal, Département de démographie.

Roy, Laurent. 1975*b*. ''La mortalité selon la cause de décès et l'origine ethnique au Québec, 1951, 1961, 1971. Quebec: Ministère des Affaires sociales, Registre de la population.

Ryder, N. B. 1955. ''The Interpretation of Origin Statistics.'' *Canadian Journal of Economic and Political Science* 21 (November): 466–79.

Sauvy, Alfred. 1949. ''Préface.'' In *Histoire de la population mondiale de 1700 à 1948*, by Marcel R. Reinhard. Paris: Domat-Montchrestien.

Sauvy, Alfred. 1969. *General Theory of Population*. Translated by Christophe Campos. New York: Basic Books.

Schumacher, E.F. 1973. *Small Is Beautiful: Economics as if People Mattered*. New York: Harper & Row.

Shryock, Henry S. and Siegel, Jacob S. and Associates. 1973. *The Methods and Materials of Demography*. Washington, D.C.: U.S. Government Printing Office.

Siegel, Jacob S. 1972. ''Development and Accuracy of Projections of Population and Households in the United States.'' *Demography* 9 (February): 51–68.

Stone, Leroy O. 1969. *Migration in Canada, Regional Aspects*. 1961 Census Monograph. Cat. No. 99–548. Ottawa: Queen's Printer.

Stone, Leroy O. 1974. ''What We Know About Migration Within Canada—A Selective Review and Agenda for Future Research.'' *International Migration Review* 8 (Summer): 267–81.

Stone, Leroy O. 1976. "Quelques nouveaux développements dans l'analyse de la migration interne au Canada." *Cahiers québécois de démographie* 5, No. 3 (Special): 125−45.

Stone, Leroy O. 1978a. *The Frequency of Geographic Mobility in the Population of Canada*. 1971 Census Analytical Study. Cat No. 99−751. Ottawa: Minister of Supply and Services Canada.

Stone, Leroy O. 1978b. "Out-Migration Rates Supplied for the Simulation Work." Research Notes. Montreal: The Institute for Research on Public Policy.

Stone, Leroy O. 1979. *Occupational Composition of Canadian Migration*. 1971 Census Analytical Study. Cat. No. 99−752. Ottawa: Minister of Supply and Services Canada.

Stone, Leroy O. and Fletcher, Susan. 1977. *Migration in Canada*. 1971 Census Profile Study. Cat. No 99−705. Ottawa: Minister of Supply and Services Canada.

Tabah, Léon. 1968. "Représentations matricielles de perspectives de population active." *Population* 23 (May-June): 437−76.

Termote, Marc and Fréchette, Raymonde. 1979. *Les variations du courant migratoire interprovincial*. Montreal: Institut national de la recherche scientifique, INRS urbanisation.

Theil, Henri. 1971. *Principles of Econometrics*. New York: John Wiley.

Théroux, G. 1976. "Sous-énumération des migrants et des non-migrants interprovinciaux (entre le recensement de 1966 et celui de 1971)." Memorandum addressed to R. Baby and dated 29 June. Ottawa: Statistics Canada (mimeo.).

Théroux, G. and Gosselin, J.-F. 1978. "1976 Census Parametrics Evaluation Reverse Check Record—Basic Results on Population and Household Undercoverage in the 1976 Census." Ottawa: Statistics Canada, Census Field (mimeo.).

Touraine, Alain. 1977. *The Self-Production of Society*. Translated by Derek Coltman. Chicago: University of Chicago Press.

United Nations. 1957. *The Aging of Population and Its Economic and Social Implications*. Population Studies No. 26. New York: United Nations.

United Nations. 1958. *Multilingual Demographic Dictionary, English Section*. Prepared by the International Union for the Scientific Study of Population. Population Studies No. 29. New York: United Nations.

United Nations. 1970. *Methods of Measuring Internal Migration*. (Manuals on Methods of Estimating Population, Manual VI). New York: United Nations.

United Nations. 1973. *The Determinants and Consequences of Population Trends*. New York: United Nations.

Vallee, Frank G. and De Vries, John, 1978. "Trends in Bilingualism in Canada." In *Advances in the Study of Societal Multilingualism*, edited by Joshua Fishman, pp. 761−92. The Hague: Mouton.

Vallee, Frank G. and Dufour, Albert. 1974. "The Bilingual Belt: A Garrotte for the French?" *Laurentian University Review* 6 (February): 19−44.

Vallee, Frank G. and Shulman, Norman. 1969. "The Viability of French Grouping Outside Quebec." In *Regionalism in the Canadian Community, 1867−1967*, edited by Mason Wade, pp. 83−99. Toronto: University of Toronto Press.

Vallin, Jacques and Chesnais, Jean-Claude. 1974. Évolution récente de la mortalité en Europe, dans les pays anglo-saxons et en Union Soviétique, 1960−1970." *Population* 29, No. 4-5: 861−98.

Vanasse, Diane. 1981. *L'évolution de la population scolaire du Québec*. Montreal: The Institute for Research on Public Policy.

Vanderkamp, John. 1973. *Mobility Patterns in the Labour Force*. Economic Council of Canada, Special Study No. 16. Ottawa: Queen's Printer.

Veltman, Calvin J. 1976. "Les incidences du revenu sur les transferts linguistiques dans la région métropolitaine de Montréal." *Recherches sociographiques* 17 (September-December): 323−39.

Veltman, Calvin J. 1979. "The Assimilation of American Language Minorities: Structure, Pace and Extent." Report prepared for the U.S. National Center for Education Statistics, Office of Education, Department of Health, Education and Welfare (mimeo.).

Yeates, Maurice. 1975. *Main Street: Windsor to Quebec City*. Toronto: Macmillan.

PUBLICATIONS AVAILABLE*
December 1981

BOOKS

Leroy O. Stone & Claude Marceau	*Canadian Population Trends and Public Policy Through the 1980s*. 1977 $4.00
Raymond Breton	*The Canadian Condition: A Guide to Research in Public Policy*. 1977 $2.95
Raymond Breton	*Une orientation de la recherche politique dans le contexte canadien*. 1978 $2.95
J.W. Rowley & W.T. Stanbury, eds.	*Competition Policy in Canada: Stage II, Bill C-13*. 1978 $12.95
C.F. Smart & W.T. Stanbury, eds.	*Studies on Crisis Management*. 1978 $9.95
W.T. Stanbury, ed.	*Studies on Regulation in Canada*. 1978 $9.95
Michael Hudson	*Canada in the New Monetary Order: Borrow? Devalue? Restructure!* 1978 $6.95
W.A.W. Neilson & J.C. MacPherson, eds.	*The Legislative Process in Canada: The Need for Reform*. 1978 $12.95
David K. Foot, ed.	*Public Employment and Compensation in Canada: Myths and Realities*. 1978 $10.95
W.E. Cundiff & Mado Reid, eds.	*Issues in Canadian/U.S. Transborder Computer Data Flows*. 1979 $6.50
David K. Foot	*Public Employment in Canada: Statistical Series*. 1979 $15.00
Meyer W. Bucovetsky, ed.	*Studies in Public Employment and Compensation in Canada*. 1979 $14.95
Richard French & André Béliveau	*The RCMP and the Management of National Security*. 1979 $6.95

---

* Order Address: The Institute for Research on Public Policy
P.O. Box 9300, Station A
TORONTO, Ontario
M5W 2C7

Richard French &
André Béliveau — *La GRC et la gestion de la sécurité nationale*. 1979 $6.95

Leroy O. Stone &
Michael J. MacLean — *Future Income Prospects for Canada's Senior Citizens*. 1979 $7.95

Richard Bird (in collaboration with Bucovetsky & Foot) — *The Growth of Public Employment in Canada*. 1979 $12.95

G. Bruce Doern &
Allan M. Maslove, eds. — *The Public Evaluation of Government Spending*. 1979 $10.95

Richard Price, ed. — *The Spirit of the Alberta Indian Treaties*. 1979 $8.95

Richard J. Schultz — *Federalism and the Regulatory Process*. 1979 $1.50

Richard J. Schultz — *Le fédéralisme et le processus de réglementation*. 1979 $1.50

Lionel D. Feldman &
Katherine A. Graham — *Bargaining for Cities. Municipalities and Intergovernmental Relations: An Assessment*. 1979 $10.95

Elliot J. Feldman &
Neil Nevitte, eds. — *The Future of North America: Canada, the United States, and Quebec Nationalism*. 1979 $7.95

Maximo Halty-Carrere — *Technological Development Strategies for Developing Countries*. 1979 $12.95

G.B. Reschenthaler — *Occupational Health and Safety in Canada: The Economics and Three Case Studies*. 1979 $5.00

David R. Protheroe — *Imports and Politics: Trade Decision-Making in Canada, 1968–1979*. 1980 $8.95

G. Bruce Doern — *Government Intervention in the Canadian Nuclear Industry*. 1980 $8.95

G. Bruce Doern &
Robert W. Morrison, eds. — *Canadian Nuclear Policies*. 1980 $14.95

W.T. Stanbury, ed. — *Government Regulation: Scope, Growth, Process*. 1980 $10.95

Yoshi Tsurumi with
Rebecca R. Tsurumi — *Sogoshosha: Engines of Export-Based Growth*. 1980 $8.95

Allan M. Maslove & Gene Swimmer	*Wage Controls in Canada, 1975 – 78: A Study of Public Decision Making.* 1980 $11.95
T. Gregory Kane	*Consumers and the Regulators: Intervention in the Federal Regulatory Process.* 1980 $10.95
Albert Breton & Anthony Scott	*The Design of Federations.* 1980 $6.95
A.R. Bailey & D.G. Hull	*The Way Out: A More Revenue-Dependent Public Sector and How It Might Revitalize the Process of Governing.* 1980 $6.95
Réjean Lachapelle & Jacques Henripin	*La situation démolinguistique au Canada: évolution passée et prospective.* 1980 $24.95
Raymond Breton, Jeffrey G. Reitz & Victor F. Valentine	*Cultural Boundaries and the Cohesion of Canada.* 1980 $18.95
David R. Harvey	*Christmas Turkey or Prairie Vulture? An Economic Analysis of the Crow's Nest Pass Grain Rates.* 1980 $10.95
Stuart McFadyen, Colin Hoskins & David Gillen	*Canadian Broadcasting: Market Structure and Economic Performance.* 1980 $15.95
Richard M. Bird	*Taxing Corporations.* 1980 $6.95
Albert Breton & Raymond Breton	*Why Disunity? An Analysis of Linguistic and Regional Cleavages in Canada.* 1980 $6.95
Leroy O. Stone & Susan Fletcher	*A Profile of Canada's Older Population.* 1980 $7.95
Peter N. Nemetz, ed.	*Resource Policy: International Perspectives.* 1980 $18.95
Keith A.J. Hay, ed.	*Canadian Perspectives on Economic Relations with Japan.* 1980 $18.95
Raymond Breton & Gail Grant	*La langue de travail au Québec : synthèse de la recherche sur la rencontre de deux langues.* 1981 $10.95
Diane Vanasse	*L'évolution de la population scolaire du Québec.* 1981 $12.95

Raymond Breton,
Jeffrey G. Reitz &
Victor F. Valentine

Les frontières culturelles et la cohésion du Canada.
1981 $18.95

H.V. Kroeker, ed.

Sovereign People or Sovereign Governments.
1981 $12.95

Peter Aucoin, ed.

*The Politics and Management of Restraint in
Government.* 1981 $17.95

David M. Cameron, ed.

*Regionalism and Supranationalism: Challenges and
Alternatives to the Nation-State in Canada and
Europe.* 1981 $9.95

Heather Menzies

Women and the Chip. 1981 $6.95

Nicole S. Morgan

*Nowhere to Go? Possible Consequences of the
Demographic Imbalance in Decision-Making
Groups of the Federal Public Service.* 1981 $8.95

Nicole S. Morgan

*Où aller? Les conséquences prévisibles des
déséquilibres démographiques chez les groupes de
décision de la fonction publique fédérale.*
1981 $8.95

Peter N. Nemetz, ed.

Energy Crisis: Policy Response. 1981 $10.95

Allan Tupper &
G. Bruce Doern, eds.

Public Corporations and Public Policy in Canada.
1981 $16.95

James Gillies

Where Business Fails. 1981 $9.95

Réjean Lachapelle &
Jacques Henripin

*The Demolinguistic Situation in Canada: Past
Trends and Future Prospects.* 1982 $24.95

OCCASIONAL PAPERS
W.E. Cundiff
(No. 1)

*Nodule Shock? Seabed Mining and the Future of the
Canadian Nickel Industry.* 1978 $3.00

IRPP/Brookings
(No. 2)

Conference on Canadian-U.S. Economic Relations.
1978 $3.00

Robert A. Russel
(No. 3)

The Electronic Briefcase: The Office of the Future.
1978 $3.00

C.C. Gotlieb
(No. 4)

*Computers in the Home: What They Can Do for
Us—And to Us.* 1978 $3.00

Raymond Breton &
Gail Grant Akian
(No. 5)

Urban Institutions and People of Indian Ancestry.
1978 $3.00

K.A. Hay
(No. 6)

*Friends or Acquaintances? Canada and Japan's
Other Trading Partners in the Early 1980s.*
1979 $3.00

Thomas H. Atkinson
(No. 7)

*Trends in Life Satisfaction Among Canadians,
1968–1977.* 1979 $3.00

Fred Thompson &
W.T. Stanbury
(No. 9)

*The Political Economy of Interest Groups in the
Legislative Process in Canada.* 1979 $3.00

Pierre Sormany
(No. 11)

*Les micro-esclaves : vers une bio-industrie
canadienne.* 1979 $3.00

Zavis P. Zeman &
David Hoffman, eds.
(No. 13)

*The Dynamics of the Technological Leadership of
the World.* 1980 $3.00

Russell Wilkins
(No. 13*a*)

Health Status in Canada, 1926–1976.
1980 $3.00

Russell Wilkins
(No. 13*b*)

L'état de santé au Canada, 1926–1976.
1980 $3.00

P. Pergler
(No. 14)

*The Automated Citizen: Social and Political Impact
of Interactive Broadcasting.* 1980 $4.95

Zavis P. Zeman
(No. 15)

Men with the Yen. 1980 $5.95

Donald G. Cartwright
(No. 16)

*Official Language Populations in Canada:
Patterns and Contacts.* 1980 $4.95

REPORT
Dhiru Patel

*Dealing With Interracial Conflict: Policy
Alternatives.* 1980 $5.95